MW01103614

With Our Boys

Honor Roll

Books in this series

With Our Boys
Honor Roll

With Our Boys
Our Sons

With Our Boys
Not Forgotten

With Our Boys

Honor Roll

Tammy M. Mullen

Kyle D. Mullen

Parma Hilton Historical Society
Parma, New York

Parma-Hilton Historical Society, Hilton, New York 14468

Copyright © 2018 Tammy M Mullen

All rights reserved. No part of this publication may be reproduced, distributed, or transmitted in any form or by any means, including photocopying, recording, or other electronic or mechanical methods, without the prior written permission of the publisher, except in the case of brief quotations embodied in critical reviews and certain other noncommercial uses permitted by copyright law. For permission requests, contact the publisher at the following e-mail address:

WithOurBoys@outlook.com

Published 2018
Printed in the United States of America

ISBN: 978-1-7326232-0-0 (paperback)
ISBN: 978-1-7326232-1-7 (e-book)

Library of Congress Control Number: 2018953286

Learn more at: www.withourboys.wordpress.com

On the cover: Town of Parma, New York. This image is Plate 6, showing the Town of Parma, New York, including hamlets of Parma Corners and Parma Center, taken from the 1902 Plat book of Monroe County, New York. Compiled from deed descriptions and plats finished by The Title and Guarantee Company of Rochester. Also from records and surveys by J.M. Lathrop & Company. J.M. Lathrop and Roger H. Pidgeon.

Everyone has a story–it just needs to be told.

UNITED STATES OF AMERICA
LIBERTY · INTERNATIONAL LAW
HONOR ROLL

ADAMS, HAROLD C.	FLEMMING, JOHN.	McCARTY, DR. FRED C.
ANDERSON, LESTER.	FLEMMING, SAMUEL.	MURRELL, EDGAR R.
BUSH, ELMER J.	FLEMMING, FRANK.	NEWCOMB, DOUGLAS A.
BUSH, WILLARD	HALL, MORLEY.	NEWCOMB, CARLYLE B.
BRIDGEMAN, JACK.	HISCOCK, GEORGE.	OVIATT, EDWIN.
BELL, HARRY.	HALL, FRED.	OVIATT, S. HAROLD.
BROWN, ROY L.	HALL, LYNN.	ODELL, HOMER C.
BROWN, COLONEL.	HOLMAN, AVERY.	PERRY, BURTON.
BAXTER, CLARENCE.	HOCHBRECKNER, GEO. N.	PAULSON,
BURRITT, EARL W.	HIGGS, EUGENE.	RANDALL, FRANK. GEORGE,
BIGGER, BENNETT, ANDREW G.	HISCOCK, LESTER.	RYDER, REV. WALTER S. QUINN,
GEORGE, W. BENNETT, LEWIS.	HISCOCK, FOSTER.	ROWLEY, GEORGE. GEORGE,
BAGLEY, LUCIUS.	HOVEY, ALLAN.	ROBINSON, CLARENCE.
COOPER, JOHN HARLAN.	HOVEY, WALTON.	SLEIGHT, ELTON B.
CLIFT, GEORGE.	INGRAHAM, HAROLD H.	SLEIGHT, VERNON A.
CLAPPER, WILLIAM IRA.	JAMISON, FRANK.	SIMON, ROSS DI.
COLLINS, CROOK, JOHN L.	KIRK, GEORGE.	SKINNER, HERMON.
LESTER, COLLINS, FRED.	KIRK, WILLIAM E. G.	SMITH, HENRY A.
CORBITT, MILES H.	KOSS, FRED.	SMITH, ARTHUR M.
CORBITT, RAYMOND.	KING, WILBUR	SWEETING, FLOYD, SOVIA,
CHURCH, KENNETH.	LEE, CHAMPNEY.	SMITH, KENNETH. THOMAS,
CHATTIN, VICTOR.	LEE, WILLARD J.	TURGON, FREDRICK. TURGON,
DAVENPORT, CLARENCE.	MERKEL, HARRY.	TURGON, WILLIAM V. ALFRED,
DUCOLON, EARL A.	MERKEL, RAYMOND.	TURGON, FRANK.
DONAHUE, DONALD.	MILLER, GEORGE.	WADSWORTH, ARTHUR G.
DEROLLER, RALPH.	MAGEE, JOHN.	WADSWORTH, ELMER.
DEAN, GEORGE H.	McCULLA, DR. FRANK.	WINTERS, WILLIS W.
FISHBAUGH, RAY A.	ABLE, FRANK C.	WELCH, F. L.
FISHBAUGH, GLENN.	TAYLOR WILLIAM.	WORDEN, HERMAN.
BARNEY, CECIL.	NICE, JAMES.	WILLIAMS, CHESTER.
HUNDLEY, JOHN A.	SLOCUM, DANIEL R.	WELLS, LYNDON H.
		McINTYRE, GERALD.

TOWN OF PARMA, NEW YORK STATE.
THE ABOVE MEN WERE IN THE U.S. ARMY OR NAVY
DURING THE WAR AGAINST GERMANY,
APRIL 6-1917 TO NOVEMBER 11-1918
FOR WORLD FREEDOM.
GOLD STARS INDICATE THOSE WHO DIED IN SERVICE.

Presented by the Town.

Dedicated to the men of the *Honor Roll* -
especially those who made the ultimate sacrifice.

CONTENTS

PREFACE

My involvement in this project was supposed to be minimal—research the World War I service records of ten men, all presumed to be from Parma, New York, whose names were extracted from a list of one hundred enshrined on a painting completed shortly after the war. In those ten names I uncovered stories of lives lived—amazing accomplishments and interesting experiences—that had either long been forgotten or never known. After meeting with the Town of Parma Historian, David Crumb, to discuss scope, context, and format of the researched material, I offered to consolidate the research from others like me and compile the short biographies of the one hundred names into one volume. As the information on the remaining ninety names trickled in, I quickly realized the research efforts and successes varied from person-to-person, name-to-name. Missing in those additional submissions were the stories and histories—the high points and heartbreaks I discovered in my ten names. I set out to discover more.

My initial goals were simple and straightforward: uncover their military service record, describe their "exploits" during the war, and provide a snippet of information on their personal history—births, marriages, deaths, and burials. My passion for genealogy, research, and pure curiosity drove me to continue delving into the details between the births and deaths of the additional men not originally assigned to me. I was on a journey and given an opportunity to put my skills to work. Traveling to the National Archives in Washington, DC; College Park, Maryland; and Saint Louis, Missouri; I had the unique opportunity to examine one-hundred-year-old documents housed in our nation's repositories, a gold-mine of our nation's history. In the end I met most of my goals as I learned the hieroglyphics on military service note cards did not provide the "exploits" I had expected, that we all have a muddy genealogy with some skeletons in the closet, and some people are truly ghosts—their stories and histories are just an apparition, never to be revealed.

Along my journey I learned about the history of my town, state, and nation. I discovered triumphs and tragedies, some of which still bring tears to my eyes. While I am not a historian, as a genealogist I find that research involves history and to understand a person's life requires researching the culture and mindset of the time. What decisions were made, what courses of action were chosen, how people lived, and the careers they chose were more often defined by needs and circumstances, not goals and desires.

Digging deeper doesn't necessarily mean you'll "strike it rich"—but you will have a bigger pile of… "stuff" to sort through. Searching various print and online repositories, I uncovered additional names with ties to the Hilton-Parma area. I learned the number of men and women from this small community, who answered the call and served their *nations* during World War I, went beyond the names on the *Honor Roll*. As we go to press with this book, I have at least one hundred more names to research and verify, above and beyond the names already researched for the *Honor Roll*, and I am sure there may be more I just haven't met yet.

Yes, "nations" is plural for a reason. I discovered that some of the men who served under the flag of the United States were not, in fact, citizens of the same nation, and a few of the local men served in or alongside the British, Canadian, or Italian armed forces instead of American units.

I also learned about "Gold Star Mothers and Widows," women who had lost sons and husbands during the war. Many would find closure as their loved ones were returned to the United States for interment in local or national cemeteries. There were a few, however, whose sons or husbands never returned and are buried in American cemeteries overseas. They were offered an opportunity–a pilgrimage–to see where their sons and husbands were buried and visit their graves. They have a separate story all to themselves that is equally important and must be told, too.

My "minimal involvement" turned into a labor of love, frustration, growth, and exploration…and the journey is just beginning. Everyone has a story…it just needs to be told.

Tammy M. Mullen
Hilton, New York
September 3, 2018

ACKNOWLEDGMENTS

This project would not have been possible without the help and support of several people and organizations. First and foremost is the generous support of the Parma Hilton Historical Society and the Historian's Office of both the Village of Hilton and the Town of Parma, New York. The access to artifacts, letters, photos, and family histories were invaluable in compiling this volume.

I must also acknowledge and thank my family for their support while researching, writing, and editing this first volume. "The Book" became another member of the family, one who frequently demanded all my attention. Sometimes it demanded their attention, too. Those were tasks they didn't sign up for but were willing participants.

I am eternally grateful.

INTRODUCTION

In 2016, as a prelude to the 100th Anniversary of the United States of America's entry into World War I, the Monroe County, New York, Historian, offered towns and villages a monetary grant to write about the members of their communities who served in the armed forces during "The Great War." Town of Parma and Village of Hilton Historian David Crumb approached the Parma Hilton Historical Society (PHHS) regarding the opportunity and the PHHS Board of Directors accepted the offer. The initial effort started with the list of names on a painting titled *Honor Roll*, which hangs in the Parma Museum on the Town of Parma campus. Painted by local artist B. Aylesworth Haines in 1919, the painting has, for many years, served as the definitive list of Parma's contribution to the Great War.

A closer examination of the painting revealed there are only ninety-nine names on the piece, not the "100 Valiant Men" as opined in other history tomes of the town and village–and includes several errors. This discovery led to more in-depth, follow-on research using online resources from the New York State Archives and the National Archives and Records Administration, accessed through Ancestry.com. It also incorporated the three-volume *World War Service Record of Rochester and Monroe County New York*, identifying at least one hundred additional individuals from the Hilton-Parma area who may have served in the armed forces during the war; these names are not included on the painting. During this additional research, another dozen and a half names were recorded for their contributions at home and abroad in a civilian or volunteer capacity.

There are nine men on the *Honor Roll* who were killed in action or died while in service during 1918; four are interred in American Military Cemeteries in both England and France. Researching the stories of these men revealed that two mothers of the men interred overseas participated in the "Gold Star Pilgrimage," a United States Government-funded passage for unwed widows and mothers to visit the graves of their husbands or sons. The remaining five soldiers were returned to the United States. Two are buried in Arlington National Cemetery, Virginia. The final three came "home" and are laid to rest in Parma Union Cemetery.

As additional names were discovered beyond the *Honor Roll*, and the scope, research, and collected material expanded, it was decided to partition the material into a series of three books. The name of the series, *With Our Boys*, was influenced from the heading of a weekly column in the *Hilton Record*, which reported the latest news and status of local men in the service. *With Our Boys–Honor Roll* (this book) focuses solely on the ninety-nine names found on the *Honor Roll* painting. *With Our Boys–Our Sons* describes the Gold Star Pilgrimage and the mothers' experiences on arranging passage, touring in Europe, and the voyage. *With Our Boys–*

Not Forgotten addresses the additional men and women who served in the Armed Forces, the American Red Cross, the Y.M.C.A., and on local boards and committees, who were not included on the *Honor Roll*. Their stories are equally important.

At the outset, the objective of this effort was to showcase the men listed on the painting, focusing on their military service first and family life second. Initial research focused solely on the military records available from online repositories. Draft registration cards, abstracts of World War I military service, and other muster rolls and lists were sourced using Ancestry.com's extensive repository of state and federal military records. In addition to online databases, the three-volume *World War Service Record Of Rochester and Monroe County New York*, compiled and edited by Edward R. Foreman, City of Rochester Historian, and published by the City of Rochester in 1924, proved extremely useful.

For information on their family–their genealogy–it was agreed that only data from government records, online repositories, and other published works would be cited. Genealogical research was conducted on each individual to determine their date and place of birth, who their parents were, and where they resided or how they were affiliated with the Hilton-Parma community. Personal recollections and stories passed down through the generations would not be used as primary sources but could be used as a starting point before accessing the sources. In all cases, attempts were made to obtain a photo of the individual either in uniform or in post-war civilian life. Using online newspaper repositories and other periodicals, every endeavor was made to gather additional information on the individuals–who they were, how they lived, their employment or occupation, and what organizations they belonged to. Finally, the extent of the genealogical profile was limited to the parents and spouses of the men enshrined on the painting. Family histories–both ancestors and descendants–were not included unless significant or relevant to the period surrounding the Great War or subsequent wars. The only exception: there are fourteen sets of brothers on the *Honor Roll* and their biographies are often intertwined.

The research process used for each man evolved and expanded as time progressed. New repositories were uncovered, search strategies were optimized, and new sources were utilized. Each of these techniques came from follow-on research and learning about the organization of the United States Armed Forces before, during, and after the war. Expanded use of open source and subscription-based internet repositories, containing archived local newspapers from across the United States, helped tell the stories of these men before and after the war. Lessons learned were applied to names already researched providing a more complete story for each person. While most of the basic military records and genealogical profiles were obtained from online sources, several cases required on-site review of records at the National Archives and Records Administration in Washington, DC; College Park, Maryland; and Saint Louis, Missouri. Phone calls, letters, request forms, and electronic mail were sent to clarify facts and verify stories.

This effort encompassed well over 8,000 hours of primary and general research through thousands of online source documents, microfilm rolls, and archival data. Each man on the painting received on average fifty to seventy-five hours of primary research; many receiving significant additional hours to complete the whole portrait or to verify and validate single-source assumptions. Whether they survived the war or died in service, each man received the full attention due them to properly tell their story.

1

CALLED TO SERVE

Europe was already embroiled in war when America joined the effort on April 6, 1917. Both men and women had opportunities to serve their country in different capacities. Some were already serving in the armed forces or active in the National Guard. There were various volunteer service organizations (Red Cross, Y.M.C.A., etc.) to support and a few opted to serve as volunteers with foreign militaries and service organizations. President Woodrow Wilson and Secretary of War Newton D. Baker selected United States Army General John J. Pershing to lead the American Expeditionary Forces; Pershing arrived in France on June 10, 1917.[1] Surveying the situation on the Western European battlefields, General Pershing cabled the War Department: "Plans contemplate sending over at least one million men by next May."[2] When the United States called for volunteers to join the war effort, the number that signed up fell grossly short of the government's expectations for a strong military force.

Throughout this volume different terms are used to identify how and when the men of Haines' *Honor Roll* came to serve in the military services. To assist the reader in understanding the scope of how the United States organized, trained, transported, and utilized those serving in the armed forces, the following sections offer a brief primer on common terms and military vernacular used throughout the biographies.

ORGANIZATION OF THE MILITARY

Army

In 1914, as the Great War is starting to take shape in Europe, the United States Army "comprised 98,000 men, of whom some 45,000 were stationed overseas. The regular army was backed up [by] the 27,000 troops in the National Guard."[3] When American entered the war in 1917, the strength of the United States Army "was about 200,000, 80,000 of whom served in National Guard units."[4] The National Defense Act of 1916 provided for a gradual expansion; however, it was evident that more would be needed to fight a war in France. "While many Americans rushed to recruiting stations and enlisted, the War Department recommended a draft to build what was called the National Army."[5]

The difference between the Regular Army and the National Army is probably best defined by General John J. Pershing in his book *My Experiences in the World War* (1931), Vol. 1, p. 130: "In the organization of our armies for the World War it was evident that if any considerable numbers were to be sent abroad, an additional force would be needed over and above the Regular Army and National Guard. The War Department therefore established what was called the National Army, to be composed principally of men who were to come into the service through the draft."[6]

> By Armistice Day, 11 November 1918, the Army had fielded 1 cavalry division, 1 provisional infantry division, and 62 infantry divisions. Of this total, 42 infantry divisions and the provisional division deployed to Europe, with one, the 8th Division, not arriving until after the fighting had ended. On the Western Front in France, 29 divisions (7 Regular Army, 11 National Guard, and 11 National Army) fought in combat. Of the others, 7 served as depot divisions, 2 of which were skeletonized, and 5 were stripped of their personnel for replacements in combat units, laborers in rear areas, or expeditionary forces in North Russia or Italy. The provisional black division was broken up, but its four infantry regiments saw combat. Starting from a limited mobilization base, this buildup, lasting eighteen months, was a remarkable achievement.[7]

To understand how and where the men of the *Honor Roll* served, it is useful to understand the breakout of Army infantry divisions during World War I. The 1st through 7th Divisions were considered Regular Army (RA) divisions; nearly all the officers and many of the non-commissioned officers (sergeants) were already on active duty–the divisions were brought up to full strength through men drafted into service. The 26th through 42d Divisions were formed from National Guard (NG) units brought together from multiple states, usually from the same region of the country. The 42d Division was the most notable, being "composed of National Guard troops from twenty-six States and the District of Columbia. Individual enlistments and later replacements brought into the organization representatives of practically every State in the Union, thus making this division a truly composite, all-American unit."[8] All of the National Guard units were federalized, sometimes referred to as "being enlisted into national service," and were supplemented by draftees. Some, like the Rochester-based 3d New York Infantry, had recently returned from the Mexican Border Campaign. The 76th through 83d Divisions, along with 88th through 93d Divisions, were formed as the National Army (NA). The core leadership of these units were drawn from active duty army personnel, but almost all of the enlisted men were drafted. Imbedded in these divisions were several different types of combat and support units, detailed later in this chapter.

The men on the *Honor Roll* served in all three categories: Regular Army, National Guard, and the National Army.

Army Air Service

During World War I nearly all aircraft and balloons were organized under the Army Air Service–or simply "Air Service"–which itself was a part of the Signal Corps. "By the time of the Armistice on November 11, 1918, there were 45 Air Service squadrons in Europe equipped with 740 airplanes. This number comprised 744 pilots, 457 observers, 23 aerial gunners, and sufficient support forces."[9]

In addition to the Army Air Service aircraft and personnel in Europe, there were also a significant number of bases and units in New York, Ohio, Illinois, Texas, and across the southeast United States. Perhaps the most unique units were the Provisional Squadrons in the Spruce Production Division of the Air Service. By the spring of 1917, the "Allies were in desperate need of flawless, lightweight, and strong lumber to build the aircraft needed to overcome the trench warfare stalemate."[10] Wood was needed in the production of airplanes and the civilian men working in the forests and mills were drafted into the war, hampering the harvesting and processing of wood.

Sitka spruce, available only in the coastal forests of Oregon, Washington, British Columbia, and Alaska, was the ideal material. Getting Sitka spruce trees out of the forests and into the airplane factories was not easy. The lumber industry wanted and tried to meet the increased demand without government assistance. By November of 1917, about 2 million feet of spruce was being produced per month, but the U.S. Government was requesting an increase to 10 million feet per month in order to meet the demands of the Allies and its own military for wood to build airplanes.[11]

The United States Army formed the Spruce Production Division and assigned men to the Pacific Northwest to work in the forests alongside civilians. Additional responsibilities of the Army soldiers were the building of roads and railroads allowing for accessibility to the spruce forests of the Pacific Coast and movement of the wood for processing. Spruce Squadrons were initially formed from the Air Service Signal Corps as "Provisional Squadrons," but were later renamed; all were demobilized after the war. Men of the *Honor Roll* served in Aero Squadrons overseas, as pilots and machinists in stateside squadrons, and with the Spruce Squadrons of the Pacific Northwest.

Navy and Marine Corps

The United States Navy also needed to build up to wartime strength. While considerable effort was made to build new ships, the Navy also had a need for personnel to man ships already held in reserve or used for coastal defense. Those that enlisted did so in the "regular" Navy, while others were part of the Naval Militia or enrolled in the Naval Reserve Force.

Up through the Civil War the Navy utilized merchant sailors and civilian volunteers to fill the additional manpower needed during wartime. Attempts to form a national reserve force failed at the start of the twentieth century and states formed their own naval militias. By 1914 there were over 7,500 sailors in twenty-two state militias,[12] New York being one of those states. The Naval Reserve Force was established in August 1916 and the Naval Militias were federalized as the National Naval Volunteers. In July 1918 the National Naval Volunteers were transferred to the Naval Reserve Force.[13] A point of historical note: the New York Naval Militia remained in force after 1918 and continued to support the state and federal service during times of war and peace. "Today, the New York Naval Militia is the only federally recognized Naval Militia with continuous, unbroken service dating back to the 1890s."[14]

When the United States entered the war in April 1917, the United States Marine Corps was comprised of "14,236 officers, warrant officers and enlisted men on active duty; between one-quarter and one-third of the force were on duty outside the continental United States or assigned to Navy ships."[15] By the end of the war the Marine Corps, to include reserves, had swelled to over 75,000 officers and enlisted men. In France, United States Marines were formed into the Fourth Infantry Brigade, one of the two infantry brigades of the United States' 2d Division.

Men of the *Honor Roll* served in the United States Navy, the Naval Reserve Force, the National Naval Volunteers/New York Naval Militia, and the United States Marine Corps.

SELECTIVE SERVICE–THE "DRAFT"

When America raised a call to arms with a need for over one million men, the response was met with 73,000 volunteers. [16] The Selective Service Act was passed by Congress on May 18, 1917, and the first of three draft registrations took place on June 5, 1917, requiring men between the ages of twenty-one and thirty-one–men born between June 6, 1886, and June 5, 1896–to register for selection by lottery to serve in the military.

Those men who turned twenty-one after the first registration—men born between June 6, 1896, and June 5, 1897—were required to complete the second registration on June 5, 1918. Eligible men who had not completed the first registration and were not already in the military were also required to register. A supplemental registration was held August 24, 1918, for men who had reached the age of twenty-one after June 5, 1918.

On August 31, 1918, the Selective Service Act was amended to include all men who were between the ages of eighteen and forty-five—men born between September 11, 1872, and September 12, 1900. The amended Act would greatly plus up the military's strength during the third and final registration on September 12, 1918.[17]

All registrations required the informant to provide their name, address, date and place of birth, place of employment, if they were responsible for a family member (mother, father, sibling, wife and/or child), and if they were requesting an exemption to the draft with the reasons for such to be stated on the card.

In the metropolitan Rochester, New York, area there were eight local draft boards in the city of Rochester (divided by Wards) and three in Monroe County. The Local Board for Monroe County Division No. 1 covered the towns of Greece, Parma, Hamlin, Clarkson, Chili, Ogden, and Riga; Division No. 2 covered the towns of Wheatland, Sweden, Gates, Henrietta, Rush, Mendon, and Brighton; and Division No. 3 covered the towns of Irondequoit, Penfield, Perinton, Pittsford, and Webster.

All boards were responsible for collecting registration cards for their area of jurisdiction. If a person was not available to register with their local board they could register at the closest board and the card would be forwarded. Provisions were established to allow for exemption from military service for very specific reasons. Those exemption considerations would include local, state, or federal officials; officers or enlisted men already serving in the armed forces; licensed pilots; clergy and students enrolled in theological school; someone convicted of treason or a felony; or someone who was either mentally or physically deficient, or both.

Exemptions could be claimed and approved if a registrant was the sole provider of income for dependent parents, siblings, spouse, or children where the lack of support would create a hardship. The hardship was defined as the absence of a provider's "mental or physical labor."[18] Additional sources of income, such as dividends as a result of stocks, bonds, or other investments, to include rent from real estate, would be an automatic rejection to an exemption claim because it was a source of income that could support a family.

Once complete, the local boards numbered the cards in sequence and were required to post the names and red ink serial number of each card. According to a War Department Provost Marshall Bulletin, published in 1917, the "red ink numbers are to be drawn by lot to determine the order in which registered persons are to be called by the various local boards."[19] Quotas were established for each state and board, from which the local board would "call upon persons whose cards are in its jurisdiction instructing them to present themselves for examination."[20] Boards would notify the registrant of the date they were to report for a medical examination.

Once drafted, a medical review board would evaluate each man's physical fitness based on a set of standards established by the Army. The physical requirements of the Army were changed throughout the year-and-a-half the draft was active. Strict height, weight, and fitness requirements were relaxed over subsequent drafts; men drafted later in the war were often not "acceptable" for frontline duty but could be utilized in support or non-combat rolls.[a]

---

[a] "By May 1918, more than 100,000 men declared unfit for overseas service had accumulated in training camps, taking up much needed space, and costing the Government a great deal of money. Such men later were placed in development battalions in which they were given instruction designed to fit them to do some kind of useful work

Registrants who passed their medical examination then had seven days to file a claim of exemption to their local board; those claiming exemption for industrial (held a particular skill or job needed in the war effort) or agricultural reasons were reviewed at the District Board. Specific instructions and procedures to file for exemption or discharge were posted via the bulletin, including criteria for explaining what decisions could be made at a local board. Once the dispositions of claims were settled, individuals would be notified when they had been selected for military service or formally exempted; however, a notice of selection was not necessarily an order into service—notices were sent when the Government was ready to receive the individual.

Men selected for the draft, who had passed the medical, physical and mental screenings, were inducted into the Army. In nearly all cases, men inducted were assigned to a National Army unit. It is important to understand that "drafted" was also used when describing service in the National Guard. Men from certain National Guard units were mustered in when the National Guard was drafted into the service of the United States under a Presidential Order effective August 5, 1917.[21]

Over 9.9 million men registered for the June 5, 1917, draft; another 900,000 completed registration cards the following year during the June 5, 1918, registration and supplemental registration of August 24, 1918; and over thirteen million men were registered during the September 12, 1918, iteration. While approximately twenty-four million men living in the United States completed draft registration cards (ninety-eight percent of the male population), only 2,810,296 were inducted.[22] Fifty-six men on the *Honor Roll* were inducted.

Slacker Lists

The War Department created rolls from Selective Service records known as "slacker lists"—men who were allegedly avoiding the draft. The War Department submitted these lists to newspapers across the United States to be published with the purpose of bringing attention to those who were not fulfilling their civic responsibility.

The slacker lists quickly became controversial, resulting in a movement against their publication. Several scenarios could land a man on the War Department's list to include not registering, enlisting in the military without notifying his local board, a name or address different from the draft registration, refusing to serve, or misidentification through clerical error.

An inordinate amount of time and resources were spent in the investigation of all men whose name made the lists to uncover the clerical errors from the true instances of avoidance or desertion, which could eventually lead to prosecution. Sometimes corrections and changes to the lists did not make the publication's deadline and the wrong information went to print.

The inaccuracies of the lists fueled public outcry. The accused were subject to ridicule, intimidation, and violence, including "slacker raids" against individuals, no matter whether they were furloughed, exempt, actively serving, or avoiding military service altogether.

Parma, New York, resident Miles Harold Corbitt was found on page four of the March 6, 1918, edition of the *Weekly Journal-Miner* (Prescott, AZ), misidentified and published on a "slacker" list. Closer examination of the paper shows Miles was already serving in the Navy and his location was the Puget Sound Navy Yard in Bremerton, Washington. [next page]

---

in the Army." Lerwill, *Personnel Replacement*, 188.

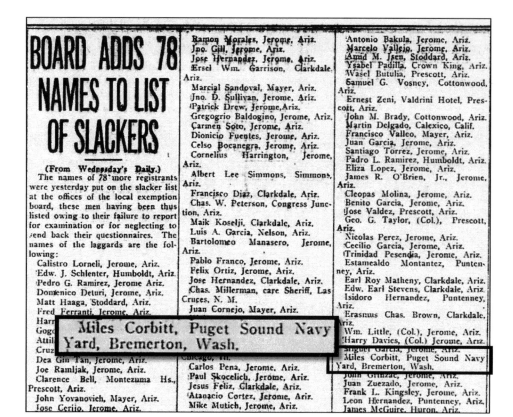

BOARD ADDS 78 NAMES TO LIST OF SLACKERS

(From Wednesday's Daily.)

The names of 78 more registrants were yesterday put on the slacker list at the offices of the local exemption board, these men having been thus listed owing to their failure to report for examination or for neglecting to send back their questionnaires. The names of the laggards are the following:

Calistro Lorneli, Jerome, Ariz.
Edw. J. Schlenter, Humboldt, Ariz.
Pedro G. Ramirez, Jerome Ariz.
Domenico Deturi, Jerome, Ariz.
Matt Haaga, Stoddard, Ariz.
Fred Ferranti, Jerome, Ariz.
Harr...
Gog...
Attil...
Cruz...
Dea Gin Tan, Jerome, Ariz.
Joe Ramljak, Jerome, Ariz.
Clarence Bell, Montezuma Hs., Prescott, Ariz.
John Yovanovich, Mayer, Ariz.
Jose Cerijo, Jerome, Ariz.

Ramon Morales, Jerome, Ariz.
Jno. Gill, Jerome, Ariz.
Jose Hernandez, Jerome, Ariz.
Ersel Wm. Garrison, Clarkdale, Ariz.
Marcial Sandoval, Mayer, Ariz.
Jno. D. Sullivan, Jerome, Ariz.
Patrick Drew, Jerome, Ariz.
Gregorio Baldogino, Jerome, Ariz.
Carmen Soto, Jerome, Ariz.
Dionicio Fuentes, Jerome, Ariz.
Celso Bocanegra, Jerome, Ariz.
Cornelius Harrington, Jerome, Ariz.
Albert Lee Simmons, Simmons, Ariz.
Francisco Diaz, Clarkdale, Ariz.
Chas. W. Peterson, Congress Junction, Ariz.
Maik Koselji, Clarkdale, Ariz.
Luis A. Garcia, Nelson, Ariz.
Bartolomeo Manasero, Jerome, Ariz.
Pablo Franco, Jerome, Ariz.
Felix Ortiz, Jerome, Ariz.
Jose Hernandez, Clarkdale, Ariz.
Chas. Millerman, care Sheriff, Las Cruces, N. M.
Juan Cornejo, Mayer, Ariz.

Carlos Pena, Jerome, Ariz.
Paul Skocelich, Jerome, Ariz.
Jesus Feliz, Clarkdale, Ariz.
Atanacio Cortez, Jerome, Ariz.
Mike Mutich, Jerome, Ariz.

Antonio Bakula, Jerome, Ariz.
Marcelo Vallejo, Jerome, Ariz.
Amd M. Isen, Stoddard, Ariz.
Ysabel Padilla, Crown King, Ariz.
Wasel Butulia, Prescott, Ariz.
Samuel G. Vosney, Cottonwood, Ariz.
Ernest Zeni, Valdrini Hotel, Prescott, Ariz.
John M. Brady, Cottonwood, Ariz.
Martin Delgado, Calexico, Calif.
Francisco Valleo, Mayer, Ariz.
Juan Garcia, Jerome, Ariz.
Santiago Torrez, Jerome, Ariz.
Padro L. Ramirez, Humboldt, Ariz.
Eliza Lopez, Jerome, Ariz.
James R. O'Brien, Jr., Jerome, Ariz.
Cleopas Molina, Jerome, Ariz.
Benito Garcia, Jerome, Ariz.
Jose Valdez, Prescott, Ariz.
Geo. G. Taylor, (Col.), Prescott, Ariz.
Nicolas Perez, Jerome, Ariz.
Cecilio Garcia, Jerome, Ariz.
Trinidad Pesendia, Jerome, Ariz.
Estamealdo Montantez, Puntenney, Ariz.
Earl Roy Matheny, Clarkdale, Ariz.
Edw. Earl Stevens, Clarkdale, Ariz.
Isidoro Hernandez, Puntenney, Ariz.
Erasmus Chas. Brown, Clarkdale, Ariz.
Wm. Little, (Col.), Jerome, Ariz.
Harry Davies, (Col.) Jerome, Ariz.
Miguel Garcia, Jerome, Ariz.
Miles Corbitt, Puget Sound Navy Yard, Bremerton, Wash.
John Gruzac, Jerome, Ariz.
Juan Zuezado, Jerome, Ariz.
Frank L. Kingsley, Jerome, Ariz.
Leon Hernandez, Puntenney, Ariz.
James McGuire, Huron, Ariz.

Miles Corbitt, Puget Sound Navy Yard, Bremerton, Wash.

One of the pitfalls of publishing a "slacker list" was the difficulty in day-to-day life identifying those who were exempt from service for legitimate reasons, or had received a furlough, versus those who chose to evade and ignore their civic responsibility. Some draft boards issued a registration certificate with an eagle embossed at the top. The certificate could be produced by the holder, if need be, to prove a registration took place on a specific date at a specified place.

If an exemption was granted the certificate holder had, in their possession, something to identify them as exempt. They would, however, have to produce their papers when queried as there wasn't a visible indication of status. Not too long after the start of the draft, "Exempt" pins were issued, to be worn on the lapel of any jacket making it easier to identify someone with an exempt status. So coveted were these pins that Argo Grindle of Kansas made a public plea on page one of the September 27, 1917 edition of the *Penalosa (KS) Times* when his overcoat with exemption pin on the lapel, were lost. [below]

LOST—Between Penalosa and Kingman, a brown coat seze 38, with Military exemption pin on lapel. Finder leave at W. A. Showalter's or notify Argo Grindle Penalosa Kansas.

UNITS & ROLES

Understanding the units or ships individuals were assigned to, and what role they performed, was just as challenging as understanding whether they were in the Regular Army versus the National Army, or the Navy versus the Naval Reserve Force. The following entries explain the purpose and roles of units or duties found throughout Chapter 2.

The American Expeditionary Force (AEF) was comprised of several echelons of command; the principal "maneuver" unit was the Division. On the Western Front the AEF was organized as three "armies:" First Army, Second Army, and Third Army. There were nine Army Corps assigned to the various armies at different periods of war and post-armistice occupation. Divisions were assigned to army corps as they rotated on and off the line. Each division, the primary combat unit, had two infantry brigades, each of them having two Infantry Regiments, and one artillery brigade with three artillery regiments. Divisions also included three machine gun battalions, a trench mortar battery, and an engineering regiment. Supporting the division were one each field signal battalion, train headquarters and military police, supply train, ammunition train, engineer train (usually associated with the aforementioned engineering regiment), and sanitary train. There were also field hospitals, each with an associated ambulance company, assigned to a division.

Some units were not assigned at the division level, rather they were utilized as a corps or numbered army asset. Two assets in this category were batteries of the Coast Artillery Corps and "heavy" guns from the field artillery. Because of their experience with handling large, fixed artillery pieces traditionally used in coastal defense, coast artillery units were sent to France to operate rail- and wagon-mounted artillery. These units would operate British and French artillery pieces for the duration of the war as American-built weapons would not make it to France before the armistice was signed. The coast artillery units also found themselves another unique niche role in France conducting anti-aircraft defense. Given their prowess in sighting artillery to moving targets, they were a good initial fit for a growing and vital role due to the expansion of combat aviation. Finally, certain field artillery regiments were held at the corps level. These units fired larger-sized howitzers that ranged several miles, lobbing shells down on top of enemy troops instead of the more direct fire of field artillery guns and canon. Throughout the biographies and in the letters home chapter that follows, you will note references to "heavy artillery," to "75s," and possibly "155s." Heavy Artillery are the larger, long-range howitzers recently mentioned. The numbers refer to the size of the artillery pieces in millimeters, measured as the diameter of the shell or barrel. Seventy-five millimeter were the most common and prevalent at the division level; one hundred fifty-five millimeter were less common, but deadlier.

Trains were not trains, at least as we may perceive them with a locomotives and rail cars. Sometimes it is easier to envision the trains of the World War akin to the wagon trains that moved Americans across the Great Plains and westward expansion. Likewise, rail, motorized and horse-drawn "trains" moved men, equipment and supplies from base areas near the ports in the rear to the front lines—and reverse.

Sanitary Trains were a sophisticated, and sometimes complicated, process of treating, triaging, transporting and attending to soldiers wounded in the field. Beginning with battalion aid stations and ending with evacuation hospitals, the sanitary train network of motorized and horse-drawn ambulances connecting aid stations, dressing stations, field hospitals, base hospitals, and evacuation hospitals provided rapid movement and continuous treatment of wounded soldiers. Each division had assigned a field hospital with four ambulance companies. Initial composition of field hospitals included three motorized ambulance companies and one horse-drawn ambulance company; horses were eventually phased out as roads and infrastructure improved. Once in rear areas, patients may have been moved by an actual train between base hospitals and evacuation hospitals or embarkation points for their trip home.

Similarly, the engineer, ammunition, and supply trains moved materials from rear staging areas to front line units. However, the expanded use of motorized transport with trucks and tractors created the need for motor transport groups and subordinate motor transport companies. These units were forerunners of today's modern transportation battalions and brigades, responsible for operation and maintenance of the vehicles used for moving the materials.

The Quartermaster Corps was responsible for acquisition, sustainment, and distribution of supplies such as food, water, uniforms, and certain aspects of transportation. Motorized vehicles, originally under the oversight of the Quartermaster Corps, were eventually moved to their own corps, the Motor Transport Corps. One element that remained with the Quartermaster Corps were horses. A remount squadron provided horses and, for a short period in France, veterinary services for the animals.

The other notable addition to the battlefield was above it. Used primarily as a means of observation, aircraft found their mark during the Great War not only in observation but also in ground attack, aerial bombardment, and in counter-air—destroying the enemy's air assets before they could bring harm on friendly forces. Aero squadrons, as described earlier, were organized within the Air Service as a part of the Signal Corps. Enlisted men assigned to aero squadrons served as mechanics, supply clerks, or ammunition loaders.

Building 100 Divisions

From the outset of America's involvement both the War Department in Washington, DC, and the AEF Commander, General Pershing, had one goal: build 100 American divisions. After the initial Regular Army and National Guard divisions were sent to France, the stateside units were busy "filling out" the remaining divisions of the National Army. "The calling of fillers for these units held first priority in [Army] General Staff thinking; the matter of loss replacements was regarded as secondary."[23] As men were inducted under the second and third drafts, they were usually sent to a "Depot Brigade." Depot brigades were responsible for in-processing the soldier: conducting a final medical examination, administering inoculations to prevent small pox and typhoid fever, providing uniforms and equipment, conducting training on the manual of arms and infantry drill, and then sending them on to their units.[24]

"The depot brigades in existence at the beginning of the war were capable of handling recruits and drafted men for the 20 contemplated Regular Army divisions, but they did not have the capacity to take care of the additional men needed for the National Guard and National Army divisions. The first draft levy, which was to bring the strength of the Armed Forces to 1,000,000 men, called for the induction of nearly 700,000. The actual number of men who could be inducted was limited by housing, clothing, and other supplies. Regular Army units occupying stations along the Mexican Border were moved to camps in the East and South late in the spring of 1917. Upon arrival at their new stations these units received men from the recruit depots and started to build up their ranks under the new Army organization."[25]

At the same time, National Guard units were being called to federal service. Many had just served on the Mexican Border, during which the National Guard had trained 110,000 men. These men formed the cadre for the National Guard build-up for World War I, being joined by another 200,000 who were recruited through enlistments. Due to inadequate facilities at their home stations, National Guard divisions organized and trained at sixteen temporary camps throughout the Southeast, lower Midwest, and Southwest in the United States. Letters home from the men of the *Honor Roll* reflect time in at least two of these camps: Camp Hancock, Georgia, and Camp Wadsworth, South Carolina.

Building up the National Army was an altogether different situation. "Permanent National Army cantonments were constructed in which the National Army divisions were organized and their training was completed. They were then moved out and replaced by new divisions. The National Army cantonments were authorized in May 1917, and construction was carried on while the National Guard tent camps were being established."[26]

> National Army cantonments were: Lewis, Wash.; Funston, Kans.; Custer, Mich.; Devens, Mass.; Dix, N. J.; Dodge, Iowa; Gordon, Ga.; Grant, Ill.; Jackson, S. C.; Lee, Va.; Meade, Md.; Pike, Ark.; Sherman, Ohio; Travis, Tex.; Taylor, Ky.; and Upton, N. Y. Each of the cantonments accommodated a division, but since a division contained only about 28,000 men and the capacity of each cantonment was 40,000 or more, there was room for camp-maintenance troops, newly drafted men, and regiments of auxiliary troops or replacement troops.
>
> The National Army cantonments were responsible for: (1) receiving all drafted men; (2) equipping, examining, and classifying all men received; (3) selecting and training specialists from the drafted men for the various organizations of the Army; (4) providing special treatment for drafted men unfit for combat but not eligible for discharge; (5) creating and maintaining the National Army divisions; (6) filling Regular Army and National Guard divisions to authorized strength; (7) organizing units or supplying selected personnel for corps and army troops, service of supply troops, and the various staffs and departments; and (8) training and forwarding replacement troops for all of these forces.[27]

Depot brigades were formed at both National Army and National Guard cantonment camps. As the war progressed, the utility of these brigades came under question as numbers swelled. "Depot brigades might have been satisfactory for training replacements for a military operation of less magnitude, but they were not adequate for the 30-division program and were entirely inadequate for the 80-division program." Training replacements for divisions already formed almost disappeared.

> By March 1918, men were accumulating in the depot brigades; they now contained more men than they could handle, with the result that a division of the work became necessary. All that the depots could accomplish was to receive draftees into the Army; separate the fit from the unfit, the literate from the illiterate; classify the men as to intelligence and vocational ability; put them in uniform and impart to them the rudiments of discipline; and, finally, group and entrain them for their units. There was little time for the training of replacements.

Specialized replacement training camps were organized, mostly in early 1918, to train recruits and draftees in certain skills and combat arms. Men from the *Honor Roll*, drafted later in 1917 and throughout 1918, could find themselves in one of these camps following induction at a depot brigade:[28]

> Infantry: Camps Lee, Va.; Gordon, Ga.; Pike, Ark.; MacArthur, Tex.; Grant, Ill.
> Machine Guns: Camp Hancock, Ga.
> Field Artillery: Camps Jackson, S. C.; Taylor, Ky.
> Quartermaster: Camp Joseph E. Johnston, Fla.
> Engineers: Camp Humphreys, Va.
> Medical Department: Fort Oglethorpe, Ga.; Fort Riley, Kan.
> Signal Corps: Camp Alfred Vail, N. J.
> Coast Artillery: Camp Abraham Eustis, Va.

As draftees kept pouring in, it became necessary to separate and categorize them earlier in the induction process. Citing the overcrowding issues above, the need to continue building the 100-division Army, and the call from Europe for replacements for those already lost in fielded divisions, Army planners on the Adjutant General's staff conceived the "automatic replacement draft." The automatic replacement draft set aside a specific number of inductees–at one point up to 20,000 men–to be automatically assigned as replacements for units fielded in Europe. While not a perfect solution–in fact, the field leaders in Europe protested the reduced quality of replacements–it did stem the bleeding of men from the remaining stateside divisions trying to form, allowing them to organize, build manpower, and train.

Once trained–or not–these replacements moved to ports of embarkation. While most went out of New York Harbor, several men of the *Honor Roll* departed from places like Brooklyn, New York; Hoboken, New Jersey; and Newport News, Virginia. Two camps were established to handle the movements through New York and New Jersey–Camp Merritt in Tenafly, New Jersey, and Camp Mills, located on Long Island, New York.[29]

Depot brigades and base units were also established in France for the reception, organization, and training of new arrivals. The only men from the *Honor Roll* that may have passed through these units were late arrivals to France or wounded passing through on their way home to America.

Building the Fleet

While not as daunting as building 100 divisions, the United States Navy, Naval Reserve Force, and National Naval Volunteers also faced a huge task in receiving, training, and processing new sailors. It is equally necessary to understand the process and terminology used in building the naval forces in World War I.

Men of the *Honor Roll* either enlisted in the United States Navy or enrolled in the United States Naval Reserve Force. Either way the primary path for most of these men started with the Recruiting Station in Buffalo, New York. In some instances, they were able to return home for a few days to a few weeks before reporting to their initial duty location. The Naval Training Station in Great Lakes, Illinois, north of Chicago near the shore of Lake Michigan, was the initial stop for the vast majority of the men on the *Honor Roll*. A few were sent to Naval Training Stations in Newport, Rhode Island, or Hampton Roads, Virginia.

With training behind them, most new sailors were sent to a Receiving Ship. A Receiving Ship was, in some ways, similar in function but smaller in scope as the Army's Depot Brigade–a place where new personnel reported in, received training, and were processed for their duty assignment. In larger naval station locations, the Receiving Ship might be several ships, rotating duty between receiving, training, and harbor or port patrols. Leaving the Receiving Ship, the sailor was usually destined for assignment to a permanent ship, air station, or other specific duty.

Name, Rank, and Specialty

Men from the *Honor Roll* served long enough that many received promotions or special ratings during their military service. Army personnel who entered during the first year of the war as privates were usually promoted to private first class during their service. Those serving overseas with noted distinction, especially in units with high casualty rates, often found themselves as corporals or sergeants. The Air Service officers entered as privates and were commissioned as second lieutenants after completing all their initial training.

A classification once common in the early twentieth century but now lost with modernization was "wagoner." These individuals were responsible for the care, grooming, and feeding of animals. They saw to the upkeep of vehicles and equipment used by wagon "teams." Wagoners were also responsible for the receiving and stowing of cargo, securing the loads of the wagon, hitching and unhitching animals, and keeping inventory of equipment.

Likewise, men serving in the Navy or Naval Reserve Force traditionally progressed during their time in uniform. Unique to the naval services, enlisted men are referred to by their "rate"– a combination of their rate (pay grade) and rating (occupational specialty). Where the army would refer to a recruit as being at the rank of Private, a new navy recruit is at the rate of Apprentice Seaman or Landsman. From there they moved up to Seaman Second Class and then full Seaman. Depending on their branch or duty, they may have been referred to by their rating: Machinists Mate, Ships Cook, Gunners Mate, Coxswain, Quartermaster, or Electrician, to name a few. Class suffixes on their rate indicated level of promotion whereby a First Class was more senior to a Third Class.

Getting There–and Back

Transporting a "million-man army" is no easy task. Not unlike the military services, the maritime forces were equally unprepared for the demands of transporting forces and supplies to and from Europe. Throughout the following biographies and letters from the men of the *Honor Roll*, all attempts were made to identify the ship the individual sailed on to and from Europe, even for the remains of the deceased. Volumes are written about the names and histories of the ships used. Some have long, storied pasts of military service while others were recategorized from civilian steamers and liners to troop transport. A few were even reflagged, having previously served under "enemy" flags before being captured or detained. Ship histories will not be told in these volumes; however, the following terms are defined to help the reader understand their category and nationality.

- USS–United States Ship. A commissioned ship of the United States Navy.
- USAT–United States Army Transport. A large troop or cargo transport ship operated by and under the authority of the United States Army.
- SS–Steam Ship. A commercial vessel powered by steam-driven propellers.
- HMS–His/Her Majesty's Ship. Commissioned vessels of the Royal Navy (UK).
- HMAT–His/Her Majesty's Australian Transport. Transport ships provided by the Australian military.
- MS–Motor Ship. A commercial vessel a ship propelled by an internal combustion engine, usually a diesel engine.
- RMS–Royal Mail Ship. Steam ships (liners, cargo, transport) that carry mail under contract to the British Royal Mail. The term was only to be used while contracted to carry mail. Whether they carried mail while transporting United States military personnel is not known.

LEXICON

By the Numbers

A brief note about unit letters and numbers, and how they are portrayed: Armies are referred to with ordinal numbers, spelled out–First Army. Corps are identified by Roman Numerals– II Corps (note this is a unit comprised of several divisions, not the United States Marine Corps). Divisions, brigades, regiments, squadrons and trains are also ordinal numbers, with a numeral–2d Division, 153d Depot Brigade, 108th Infantry, 68th Aero Squadron, 102d Sanitary Train. Note: during World War I the ordinal number convention for "second" and "third" dropped the letter before the "d"–2nd was 2d, 3rd was listed as 3d. Companies and batteries are either letters or numbers depending on their function–B Company, Ambulance Company 102, Battery D. Likewise, ranks and rates are more commonly seen in their shortened form of ordinal numbers but are fully spelled out in this series. An enlisted man is a Private First Class or Seaman Second Class, not a "Private 1st Class" or "Seaman 2nd Class." Similarly, an officer is a First Lieutenant not "1st Lieutenant" or "1st Lt."

Grammar and Language

A final note must be included about the content, specifically the difference between written text and text sourced from other books and newspapers. The *Chicago Manual of Style* (*CMOS*) 17th edition was used as a reference for style, grammar, punctuation, capitalization, and reference citations for the written text of this book. Text copied verbatim from reference materials cited in the Notes and Bibliography are in their native format and do not ascribe to *CMOS* style or guidelines, except for the citation. Letters, newspaper clippings, and other similar materials are presented as they appeared when published. Grammar and misspellings were not corrected and, except for two instances, derogatory terms were not omitted or sanitized (replaced by a more generic term). The term "Boche" or "Hun" is frequently used when referring to German troops and forces. Boche is a slang term, usually disparaging, used quite frequently in the vernacular of the early twentieth century to include newspapers and official military reports.

NOTES
Chapter 1–Called To Serve

1. Garamone, "Building the American military."

2. Garamone.

3. "The United States Army and the First World War," Causes and Events of WW1, First World War: Allied Forces, Spartacus Educational, accessed September 8, 2018, http://spartacus-educational.com/FWWusa.htm

4. Yockelson.

5. Garamone.

6. Yockelson.

7. Wilson, *Maneuver*, 73.

8. *Brief Histories of Divisions, U.S. Army 1917- 1918*, Historical Branch, War Plans Division, General Staff (1921), 55. http://handle.dtic.mil/100.2/ADA438001

9. U.S. Army, *Army in the World War*, vol. 15, 225.

10. Crosman, "Woods," 58.

11. Crosman, 58.

12. Braun, "Century."

13. Blazich, "World War 1."

14. "New York Naval Militia History," New York State Division of Military and Naval Affairs, last modified May 22, 2018, https://dmna.ny.gov/nynm/?id=history

15. McClellan, Edwin N., Major, USMC, *The United States Marine Corps in the World War* (Washington, DC: Historical Branch, G-3 Division, Headquarters, United States Marine Corps, 1920) Facsimile reprinted 1968, available online. https://www.marines.mil/Portals/59/Publications /The United States Marine Corps in the World War PCN 19000411300.pdf.

16 "World War I: Conscription Laws," Blogs, Library of Congress, last modified September 13, 2016, https://blogs.loc.gov/loc/2016/09/world-war-i-conscription-laws/

17. "About U.S., World War I Draft Registration Cards, 1917-1918," Ancestry, accessed September 15, 2018, https://search.ancestry.com/search/db.aspx?dbid=6482.

18. *Selective Service Regulations*, Form 999, Washington Government Printing Office, 1917

19. War Department, Provost Marshal General Office, *Bulletin of Information for Persons Registered* (Washington DC: Government Printing Office, 1917). Accessed from https://www.gjenvick.com/Military/WorldWarOne/TheDraft/SelectiveServiceSystem/1917 -BulletinOfInformationForPersonsRegistered.html

20. War Department, "Bulletin."

21. The Military Law of the Consolidated Laws of 1909 (nominally Chapter 41), as amended by Chapter 644 of the Laws of 1917, governed the New York National Guard during World War I. The New York National Guard was drafted into the service of the United States by presidential order effective August 5, 1917. http://www.archives.nysed.gov/common/archives/files /res_topics_mi_wwi.pdf

22. "Induction Statistics," About, History And Records, Selective Service System, accessed September 15, 2018, https://www.sss.gov/About/History-And-Records/Induction-Statistics

23. Lerwill, *Personnel Replacement*, 172.

24. Lerwill, 176-177.

25. Lerwill, 177.

26. Lerwill.

27. Lerwill, 178.

28. Lerwill, 185.

29. Lerwill, 187.

2
HONOR ROLL

This chapter contains the ninety-nine biographies of the names adorned on the *Honor Roll* painting by Parma, New York, resident and artist B. Aylesworth Haines. Completed in 1919, the *Honor Roll* was displayed in the State Bank of Hilton and later the American Legion Hiscock-Fishbaugh Post 788 home at 287 East Avenue in the Village of Hilton, before becoming a fixture in the Town of Parma Historian's collection. The Town of Parma presented the painting in honor of the men who served in the United States "Army or Navy during the War Against Germany" from April 1917 to November 1918. This honor roll of men was unofficially dubbed the "One Hundred Valiant Men" of Parma in Chapter 27 of Shirley Cox Husted's 1959 book *Pioneer Days of Hilton, Parma, and Ogden.*

As noted previously, the painting contains many errors. The names listed on the following pages are the legal, official names of the men honored. Spelling errors and incorrect given names were corrected and used as headings for everyone's biography. The most notable of these errors was Rosario De Simone, who was enshrined on the canvas as "Ross Di Simon."

Arranged alphabetically with military service data provided first, entries include how and when they joined the armed service, duty stations and units assigned, and travel information if they served overseas. Promotions, medals, decorations, and awards are noted if known; citations are included when and if they could be found. If they died in service, information about their burials and interments are included. Genealogies and life histories follow the military service data, concluding with dates of death and burial information if available.

REGISTRATION CARD

SERIAL NUMBER	2174		ORDER NUMBER	A 2213

1 _Frank John Abel_
  (First name)   (Middle name)   (Last name)

2 PERMANENT HOME ADDRESS:
3 _Churchill Pl Belmont Monroe Ky_
  (No.)   (Street or R. F. D. No.)   (City or town)   (County)   (State)

Age in Years	Date of Birth		
3 19	4 _Dec_	_2_	_1899_
	(Month.)	(Day.)	(Year.)

RACE

White	Negro	Oriental	Indian	
			Citizen	Noncitizen
5	6	7	8	9

U. S. CITIZEN			ALIEN	
Native Born	Naturalized	Citizen by Father's Naturalization Before Registrant's Majority	Declarant	Non-declarant
10	11	12	13	14

15
I. not a citizen of the U. S., of what nation are you a citizen or subject?

PRESENT OCCUPATION	EMPLOYER'S NAME
16 _Machinist_	17 _Eastman Kodak Co_

18 PLACE OF EMPLOYMENT OR BUSINESS:
State St Rochester Ky
  (No.)   (Street or R. F. D. No.)   (City or town)   (County)   (State)

NEAREST RELATIVE
19 Name _John Abel_
20 Address _No R.F.D Frankfort Monroe Ky_
  (No.)   (Street or R. F. D. No.)   (City or town)   (County)   (State)

I AFFIRM THAT I HAVE VERIFIED ABOVE ANSWERS AND THAT THEY ARE TRUE

P. M. G. O.
Form No. 1 (Red)   _Frank John Abel_
                      (Registrant's signature or mark)   (OVER)

FRANK JOHN ABEL
1899 – 1984

Frank passed initial examinations for entrance into the United States Marine Corps and enlisted on November 15, 1918, from the Recruiting Station in Buffalo, New York, at eighteen years old. He was sent to Company B, Marine Barracks, at Paris Island, South Carolina. On January 22, 1919, Frank qualified as a marksman and received his Army Rifle Marksmanship Badge on January 25, 1919. Frank was discharged "For the convenience of the Government" on March 24, 1919. His character was reported in the Muster Rolls for Company B as "EXCELLENT" per a letter dated February 21, 1919.

Frank John (Joseph, as listed on his marriage license) Abel was born December 21, 1899, in Parma, New York, to John and Catherine (Schidenhauer) Abel, who immigrated from Austria in 1891. Frank reported his place of employment as Eastman Kodak, where he worked as a machinist, on his World War I Draft Registration card. Anna Marie Schoeneman(n) and Frank married on September 18, 1923, and they made their home with Anna's parents in Rochester, New York. Upon his return from service in the U.S. Marine Corps, Frank continued his employment with Eastman Kodak Company and by 1930 was a foreman. In 1944 Frank celebrated twenty-five years of employment with Eastman Kodak and was one of 525 employees to receive recognition and a medal, presented by the company's president, during an anniversary dinner party located in the auditorium on State Street. In 1958 Frank was honored for his forty-years of employment in the Apparatus and Optical Division of Eastman Kodak, being inducted into the "Eastman Kodak Gold Card 40 Year Club." In the community Frank was a member of the Saint Margaret Mary's Men's Club, a social and service club. Frank passed away September 10, 1984, in Irondequoit, New York.

MANY PHYSICALLY FIT FOR MARINES

Names of Those Who Have Passed Examinations.

Yesterday was another busy day for the Marine Corps recruiters attached to the Rochester station. Many of those who took the preliminary examination on Tuesday were given the final physical examination yesterday, while as many more were put through the preliminary.

The following are the men examined on Tuesday and yesterday who have passed the final physical examination:

Philip C. Marshall, 18, 85 1-2 Reynolds street.
Maurice G. Le Roy, 19, 17 Grove place.
Walter W. Ruscher, 21, 9 Laser street.
John Foster, 22, 14 Saxton street.
Raymond G. Beckwith, 19, South Lima.
Charles W. Heffer, 20, Clifton, N. Y.
Rodney M. Hines, 19, 608 Frost avenue.
William R. Parsons, 36, 78 Plymouth avenue south.
Thomas L. Mattern, 19, 17 Depew street.
Isadore Delinsky, 18, 28 Baden street.
Frank J. Abel, 19, Spencerport.
Harold W. Ingraham, 20, Bristol.
Harold N. Jameson, 18, Phelps.
Gordon W. Martin, 20, 142 North Union street.
Frederick W. Norris, 20, 281 Wilkins street.
Raymond G. Voelk, 20, 14 Immel street.
Herbert B. Collins, 20, 283 Emerson street.
Patrick Milanetti, 19, 196 Brown street.
John T. McDonald, 35, 446 Flower City park.
John O. Ledermann, 18, 36 Rundell park.
Harold B. Louster, 18, Lyons.
Walter R. Lang, 22, South Lima.
Dalph M. Anderson, 20, 1080 South avenue.
John W. Farley, 18, 79 May street.
Arthur W. Herendeen, 20, East Rochester.
Walter D. Cameron, 22, 295 West avenue.
Bradford K. Southard, 20, Clifton Springs.
Edmund J. Wiesner, 20, 73 Sander street.
Louis A. Miller, 21, 52 Lorenzo street.
Edward F. Doyle, 19, 202 Keawood avenue.
Harry N. Philo, 18, 179 Field street.

Article from the *Democrat and Chronicle* (Rochester, NY).[1]

Form 1   REGISTRATION CARD /4/ | No. 28

1	Name in full _Harold_ (Given name) _Adams_ (Family name)	Age, in yrs. 21

2 Home address _Spencerport_ (No.) (Street) (City) _ny_ (State)

3 Date of birth _Dec_ (Month) _13_ (Day) _1895_ (Year)

4 Are you (1) a natural-born citizen, (2) a naturalized citizen, (3) an alien, (4) or have you declared your intention (specify which)? _Natural Born Citizen_

5 Where were you born? _Parma_ (Town) _ny_ (State) _Usa_ (Nation)

6 If not a citizen, of what country are you a citizen or subject?

7 What is your present trade, occupation, or office? _Farming_

8 By whom employed? _Chauncey Adams_
Where employed? _Parma Monroe Co ny_

9 Have you a father, mother, wife, child under 12, or a sister or brother under 12, solely dependent on you for support (specify which)? _No._

10 Married or single (which)? _Single_ Race (specify which)? _Caucasian_

11 What military service have you had? Rank _None_; branch
years _____; Nation or State

12 Do you claim exemption from draft (specify grounds)?

I affirm that I have verified above answers and that they are true.

Harold Adams
(Signature or mark)

If person is of African descent, tear off this corner

HAROLD CHAUNCEY ADAMS
1895 – 1966

Harold entered the United States Navy from the Recruiting Station in Buffalo, New York, on November 14, 1917, when he was twenty-one. He served at the Training Station in Newport, Rhode Island, from November 14, 1917, until December 7, 1917, with the rank of Apprentice Seaman. He was assigned to the USS *Oklahoma* on December 7, 1917, and remained there until February 28, 1918, as a Seaman Second Class; a rank he held for 257 days. Harold sustained an injury while in the naval service resulting in the loss of his leg, which was amputated above his knee. He was in the United States Naval Hospital at League Island in Pennsylvania from February 28, 1918, until his discharge on August 21, 1918. Harold was promoted to Seaman Third Class and designated a Gunner's Mate.

Harold C. Adams was born December 13, 1895, in Parma, New York, to Chauncey A. and Alice R. (Twentymon) Adams. Harold was employed by his father as a farm laborer when he enlisted at the age of twenty-one on June 5, 1917. He married Susan A. Coe of Parma on the 14th of January 1918 and the couple made their home in Rochester, New York. In 1930 Harold was working as an electrician for the Northeast Electric Company and the T.H. Green Company. By 1942 Harold was self-employed as an independent insurance agent, having started his own business, The Harold C. Adams Agency, located in Rochester. Harold was a member of many organizations including the Doris Council, Monroe Commandery, Hamilton Chapter, R.A.M., Elks Lodge, Flower City Lodge, Independent Order of Odd Fellows, Damascus Temple, Genesee Ark Rite, Frank L. Sines Lodge, and the Disabled American Veterans. Frank passed away on June 27, 1966, and is buried in Parma Corners Cemetery in Parma, New York.

Harold, above right, when he was assigned to the USS *Oklahoma*. He was home on a ten-day furlough following an accident and would return to the naval hospital.[2] The *Democrat and Chronicle* (Rochester, NY) included an advertisement, below, on page sixteen of the June 30, 1966, edition that The Harold C. Adams Insurance Agency would be closed in honor of Harold's death. His obituary, published the day prior, noted his success in the insurance business including a merger with the Wolfert Insurance Company.

Out of respect
to the memory
of
MR. HAROLD C. ADAMS
The Harold C. Adams Agency
191 Goodman Street South

WILL BE CLOSED
TODAY JUNE 30th

Form 1 REGISTRATION CARD No. 87

1. Name in full *Lester Curtis Anderson* Age, in yrs. 21
   (Given name) (Family name)

2. Home address _____ _____ *Wilton* *New York*
   (No.) (Street) (City) (State)

3. Date of birth *September 14 1896*
   (Month) (Day) (Year)

4. Are you (1) a natural-born citizen, (2) a naturalized citizen, (3) an alien, (4) or have you declared your intention (specify which)? *Natural-born*

5. Where were you born? *Parma New York U.S.A.*
   (Town) (State) (Nation)

6. If not a citizen, of what country are you a citizen or subject?

7. What is your present trade, occupation, or office? *28 Student*

8. By whom employed? _____
   Where employed? *Rochester University*

9. Have you a father, mother, wife, child under 12, or a sister or brother under 12, solely dependent on you for support (specify which)? *No*

10. Married or single (which)? *Single* Race (specify which)? *Caucasian*

11. What military service have you had? Rank *none* ; branch _____ ; years _____ ; Nation or State _____

12. Do you claim exemption from draft (specify grounds)? *No*

I affirm that I have verified above answers and that they are true.

L. C. Anderson
(Signature or mark)

If person is of African descent, tear off this corner

LESTER CURTIS ANDERSON
1895 – 1964

A twenty-two-year-old resident of Hilton, New York, Lester was inducted into the United States Army at Spencerport, New York, on September 26, 1917. He served in Company E, 303d Engineers, 78th Division, until his discharge.[3] He promoted to Private First Class on January 15, 1918, before sailing from Brooklyn, New York, on May 27, 1918, aboard the HMS *Kashmir*, arriving in England in June 1918. Lester was promoted to the rank of Corporal on August 10, 1918, while in France. Following the armistice, he embarked from Bordeaux, France, aboard the *Santa Anna* on May 24, 1919, arriving back in Brooklyn on June 6, 1919. He was honorably discharged on demobilization, June 12, 1919.

Born in Hilton on September 14, 1895, to Edward F. and Minnie A. (Curtis) Anderson, Lester attended Hilton schools and was treasurer of his class in 1911.[4]

Lester was admitted to the University of Rochester (NY) in 1916 and was expected to graduate with the Class of 1920, but his service during the war changed his timeline. During the seventieth annual commencement for the University of Rochester Class of 1920, Lester and several others received a War Certificate and were acknowledged in the *Seventy-First Annual Catalogue of The College of Arts and Science of The University of Rochester* for serving their country and not graduating with their expected class.[5]

PROF. LESTER C. ANDERSON
State Horticulturist in charge of Hudson valley fruit investigations. He promises interesting developments in fruit culture.

As a student at Cornell University, Lester–he was known by his classmates as Andy–was a member of the Cornell Chapter of Acacia and the Masonic Club. In 1922, Lester graduated with a bachelor of science degree in agriculture. Later that year, on November 18th, he married Lucie Helen Chapman in New York and started his first position with the Western New York Fruit Growers of Rochester. His passion for horticulture took him to Barrios, Guatemala, in 1924, on the vessel MS *La Playa* where he was a "Fruit Observer," researching the transportation of bananas from the tropics to New York City.[6]

He worked as a county agent in Seneca County, New York, before moving to the Hudson Valley where, in 1927, Lester was chosen to join the Cornell University faculty as an associate in research, responsible for fruit investigations in the university's laboratory. Andy was promoted from assistant professor on July 1, 1946, to associate professor of pomology (the science of growing fruit) at Cornell University.[7] On May 1, 1954, Professor Lester C. Anderson began his retirement.

He was a member of the Clio Lodge No. 779, Free & Accepted Masons of Hilton, a member of the Hudson Rotary Club, the American Legion Hudson Post 184 of Hudson, New York, president of the Columbia Golf and Country Club and a member of the New York State Horticultural Society.[8] Lester passed away on November 22, 1964, in Claverack, New York, and is buried in the cemetery of the Reformed Dutch Church of Claverack.

Cloudy Nights Won't Dim These Stars

LOOKING OVER THE NEW SERVICE FLAG *in front of the Greece Town Hall are Lucius Bagley, left, first man in Greece to enter the first World War; Gordon A. Howe, Town of Greece Supervisor, and Milton Carter, Greece Police Chief.*

Lucius Bagley enrolled in the United States Naval Volunteers before the call for draft registration. He is shown here, at left, displaying a banner at the Greece, New York, Town Hall with a new service flag (see Chapter 4) recognizing service personnel from the town of Greece in World War II.[9]

LUCIUS FRANK BAGLEY
1881 – 1953

At thirty-five-years-old, Lucius entered the National Naval Volunteers from the Recruiting Station in Rochester New York, on April 3, 1917. He was assigned to the Fourth Naval District Headquarters in Philadelphia, Pennsylvania, from April 6, 1917, through June 16, 1917. Following his first assignment at headquarters, he served aboard the USS *Wisconsin* and USS *Iowa*[b] as a Ship's Cook, First Class, until November 11, 1918. Lucius went on inactive duty on January 18, 1919, and was subsequently discharged on April 4, 1920. In the photo to the left, Lucius is seen in uniform in Hilton, New York. Standing left-to-right are Lucius, Miles Corbitt, and George Paulson.[10]

Lucius Frank Bagley was born to Henry J. and Ella A. (Moul) Bagley in North Greece, New York, on July 19, 1881. He worked alongside his parents on their farm and, around 1917, was scoutmaster for Troop 99 of the Boy Scouts of America in Hilton. In later life he worked as a building superintendent at the Greece Town Hall. Lucius was a life member of the Clio Lodge No. 779, Free & Accepted Masons of Hilton and a Deacon of the Hilton Baptist Church. He was active with the American Legion Hiscock-Fishbaugh Post 788, having held the positions of county committeeman and chaplain. Lucius died suddenly at the age of seventy-two on March 23, 1953, and is interred in Parma Union Cemetery in Parma, New York.

Town Cat Strays

If anybody's seen Fluffy, please direct her back to the Greece Town Hall immediately.

Fluffy is the Town Hall cat, who wandered—or was escorted—away from the premises last week and is missed by town officials and employees, particularly Lucius Bagley and John Raab, building superintendents to whom she belonged. The cat is a black angora.

Entry in the *Greece (NY) Press* (1943).[11]

---

[b] "[*Iowa*] was decommissioned at Philadelphia Navy Yard on 23 May 1914. At the outbreak of World War I, *Iowa* was placed in limited commission as a receiving ship on 23 April 1917. After serving as receiving ship at Philadelphia for six months, she was sent to Hampton Roads, Va., and remained there for the duration of hostilities, training men for other ships of the Fleet, and doing guard duty at the entrance to Chesapeake Bay. She was decommissioned for the final time on 31 March 1919."
(https://www.history.navy.mil/research/histories/ship-histories/danfs/i/iowa-ii.html)

Serial No. *45*   *20*   *X*   Registration No. *45*

1. Name in full *Elmer Cecil Barney*   Age, in yrs. *21*
   (Given name) (Family name)

2. Home address *Adams Basin N.Y.*
   (No.) (Street) (City or town) (State)

3. Date of birth *Oct* *5* *1896*
   (Month) (Day) (Year)

4. Where were you born? *Ogden* *N.Y.* *U.S.A.*
   (City or town) (State) (Nation)

5. I am
   1. A native of the United States.
   2. ~~A naturalized citizen.~~
   3. ~~An alien.~~
   4. ~~I have declared my intention.~~
   5. ~~A noncitizen or citizen Indian.~~
   (Strike out lines or words not applicable)

6. If not a citizen, of what Nation are you a citizen or subject? ——

7. Father's birthplace *Penfield* *N.Y.* *U.S.A.*
   (City or town) (State or province) (Nation)

8. Name of employer *N.Y. Central - Track dep't.*
   Place of employment *Adams Basin N.Y.*
   (No.) (Street) (City or town) (State)

9. Name of nearest relative *Mother - Lydia Barney*
   Address of nearest relative *Adams Basin N.Y.*
   (No.) (Street) (City or town) (State or Nation)

10. Race—White, ~~Negro, Indian or Oriental.~~
    (Strike out words not applicable)

I affirm that I have verified above answers and that they are true.

Elmer Cecil Barney
(Signature or Mark of Registrant.)

If person is of African descent, tear off this corner.

P. M. G. O.
Form 1 (blue)

REGISTRATION CARD.

24

ELMER CECIL BARNEY
1896 – 1981

Elmer was inducted into the United States Army at Spencerport, New York, at the age of twenty-one on August 25, 1918. He reported to the 157th Depot Brigade at Camp Gordon in Atlanta, Georgia, for initial training and was assigned to Company 5 of the October Automatic Replacement Draft on September 11, 1918. Elmer left New York City his for overseas duty on October 20, 1918, aboard the SS *Agapenor* and was assigned to 2d Battalion, 329th Infantry, 83d Division, on November 5, 1918. He transferred to Company C, 310th Infantry, 78th Division, on December 5, 1918, and finished his overseas tour. He returned to Hoboken, New Jersey, from Bordeaux, France, on May 16, 1919, aboard the USS *Julia Luckenbach*, arriving on May 29, 1919. Private Barney was discharged on June 6, 1919.

Elmer Cecil Barney was born to George S. and Lydia S. (Marks) Barney on October 5, 1896, in Ogden, New York. Cecil, as he was known, worked as a farm laborer and then for the New York Central Railroad Track Department before serving in the army. When he returned from service he found employment in Dewitt, New York, as a machinist in a machine shop. Cecil met his bride-to-be, Justine Edna Zenter, and the couple married in her home in Syracuse, New York, on September 27, 1920. Eventually, Elmer returned to Ogden with his family and supported them as a coal laborer. By 1930, according to the United States Federal Census, he was living in Solvay, New York, employed as a bench worker in the "typewriter works" industry. Elmer returned once more to Ogden, working as a gardener for W.B. Moore by 1940.

Elmer was a member of the American Legion Ferris-Goodridge Post 330 of Spencerport and held the position of post adjutant. He passed away August 19, 1981, in Adams Basin, New York, and is interred in Fairfield Cemetery in Spencerport, New York.

MONROE CO. MEN CALLED
Are Mobilized at Spencerport and Will Entrain To-night.

Spencerport, Aug. 25.—The following eleven young men from Monroe county District No. 1 have been called into service and reported at the Spencerport Masonic Temple at 3:30 o'clock this afternoon for mobilization. They will entrain from the Lehigh Valley station in Rochester at 7:40 o'clock to-morrow night for Camp Gordon, Atlanta, Ga.: John Emanuel Howard, Greece; Charles Wesley Crawford, Greece; Frank E. Defendorf, Greece; Bernard J. Quinn, Greece; Walter Crouter, Gloversville; Elmer Cecil Barney, Ogden; Norman Joseph Craft, Greece; Angelo Pallani, Greece; Herbert William Chrisley, Ogden; Clarence Lawrence Volkmar, Greece, and Damon Webster Chapman, Clarkson.

Thomas Bond of Riga will leave at the same time for Fort Slocum, N. Y.

LEGION SELECTS HEADS FOR YEAR

Bernard Riley has been elected commander of Ferris-Goodridge Post of American Legion in Spencerport.

Other officers are: First vice-commander, Martin Bracken; second vicecommander, Frank Sprong; adjutant, Cecil Barney; finance officer, Raymond L. Flagg; chaplain, the Rev. F. C. Rogers.

Delegates to convention, Russell Pinkley and Ralph Gravell; alternates, Harlow Stettner and Howard Amish. These officers will be publicly installed Wednesday, Oct. 3.

References to Elmer Cecil Barney in local newspapers.[12]

Form 1 *24* REGISTRATION CARD No. *10*

1. Name in full *Clarence S Baxter* Age in yrs. *21*
   (Given name) (Family name)

2. Home address *Cosman Terr Hilton N.Y.*
   (No.) (Street) (City) (State)

3. Date of birth *Oct* *6* *1895*
   (Month) (Day) (Year)

4. Are you (1) a natural-born citizen, (2) a naturalized citizen, (3) an alien, (4) or have you declared your intention (specify which)? *natural born citizen*

5. Where were you born? *Charlotte N.Y. U.S.*
   (Town) (State) (Nation)

6. If not a citizen, of what country are you a citizen or subject?

7. What is your present trade, occupation, or office? *Farm hand*

8. By whom employed? *Charlie Dunbar*
   Where employed? *Greece New York*

9. Have you a father, mother, wife, child under 12, or a sister or brother under 12, solely dependent on you for support (specify which)? *Mother and brother*

10. Married or single (which)? *Single* Race (specify which)? *Caucasian*

11. What military service have you had? Rank *none*; branch *none*;
    years _____; Nation or State _____

12. Do you claim exemption from draft (specify grounds)? *No*

I affirm that I have verified above answers and that they are true.

Clarence S. Baxter
(Signature or mark)

If person is of African descent, tear off this corner

26

★ CLARENCE S. BAXTER ★
1895 – 1918

Clarence Baxter was twenty-two when he was inducted into the United States Army on July 25, 1918, in Rochester, New York. He was initially assigned to Company 39 of the 153d Depot Brigade, but later transferred to Company H, 347th Infantry, 87th Division, on August 12, 1918, both at Camp Dix, New Jersey. He left for Europe on August 26, 1918, from New York City aboard the SS *Khiva*; the division's destination was a rest camp in England. On September 12, 1918, Baxter and other members of the 347th Infantry crossed the English Channel on the *Duchess of Argyll*, their embarkation and debarkation points marked "SECRET." Clarence died of lobar pneumonia in France on October 27, 1918. His remains were sent back to the United States from Saint-Nazaire, France, on October 1, 1920, aboard the USS *Pocahontas*, arriving in the port of Hoboken, New Jersey, on the 18th of October.

Clarence S. Baxter was born October 6, 1895, to Delbert C. and Della C. (Potter) Baxter in Charlotte, New York, and grew up in the towns of Howard and Kendall, New York. At the time of his draft registration on June 5, 1917, Clarence was living on Cosman Terrace in Hilton, New York, working as a farm hand for Charlie Dunbar in Greece, New York. A year after his draft registration and one month before his induction, Clarence married fifteen-year-old Benita B. Lockwood on June 26, 1918, in Fairport, New York.

After succumbing to pneumonia, Clarence was buried October 28, 1918, in a plot assigned to American soldiers in the French Cemetery Mehun-sur-Yevre located in Mehun, Cher, France. Clarence's wife requested his body returned to Rochester under the care of Genesee Valley Trust Company, the court-ordered guardian of her property. The trust company denied acceptance of responsibility for the body, asserting they had no authority in the matter. On November 12, 1920, after a new request by Benita, Clarence was interred in Arlington National Cemetery in Arlington, Virginia. Mrs. Benita L. Baxter was not able to attend the graveside service.[c] It is important to note that Clarence S. Baxter died while assigned to Company H, 347th Infantry Regiment, 87th Division, which is different from his headstone which reads 345th Infantry, 37th Division.

---

[c] Benita Lockwood was ordered by Monroe County Judge John B.M. Stephens to the New York Training School for Girls at Hudson, New York, shortly before she married Clarence Baxter, because of "improper guardianship." Clarence opted for $10,000 in war risk insurance before leaving for Europe. Benita inherited a share of Clarence's estate and the property was placed under the guardianship of the Genesee Valley Trust Company. She remained at the Hudson School until 1924.

Baxter,   Clarence S.   4,101,867
(Surname.)   (Christian name in full.)   (Army serial number.)

Pvt.   Co. H, 347 Inf.
                    (Rank and organization.)

State your relationship to the deceased...Wife

Do you desire the remains brought to the United States? ...Yes...
                                                              (Yes or no.)

}mains are brought to the United States, do you }...No...
wish them interred in a national cemetery?   }   (Yes or no.)

If you desire the remains interred at the home of the deceased, give full information below as to where they should be sent:

Genesee Valley Trust Co. Rochester, N.Y. ter., N.Y
(Name of person to receive remains.)   (Express office.)   (Telegraph office.)

21 Exchange St Rochester   New York
(Number and street.)   (City or town.)   (State.)

(Sign here) *Benita Lockwood Baxter*

N.Y. S Training School, Hudson New York
(Number and street or rural route.)   (City, town, or post office.)   (State.)

Read carefully the letter accompanying this card.   3—6713

Genesee Valley Trust Company

ROCHESTER, N.Y.

BOND DEPARTMENT
HERBERT C. HOWLETT
MANAGER

April 22nd, 1919.

The Adjutant General,
    War Department,
        Washington, D.C.

Dear Sir;

        We herewith return you circular letter of
March 21st, 1919, addressed to Mrs. Benitta Baxter
of this City, together with card, just received by
us.

        The Genesee Valley Trust Company has been
appointed guardian of the property of Benitta Lockwood Baxter, widow of Clarence S. Baxter, but we
are not the guardian of her person and so really
have no authority in the matter in question. Mrs.
Baxter is a minor at the age of sixteen years, at
present in the New York State Training School for
Girls at Hudson, N.Y. under commitment of the
county court of Monroe County, N.Y. Under the circumstances, we are uncertain as to whom your letter
should be forwarded and so we are returning it to
you.

        Yours truly,

DDS/B
eno   President.

Army records indicating Benita Lockwood Baxter's request for her husband's remains to be brought back from Europe to the United States, but not to be interred in a national cemetery (above). The Genesee Valley Trust Company acknowledged they were guardians of Benita's property, but denied authority as guardian of her "person."[13]

```
Civil
Beer-Fg
JAG 293.8                          2nd Ind.

War Department, J.A.G.O., May 9, 1919. -- To The Adjutant General.

        1.    Ref. AG 293.8 (Baxter, Clarence S.) May 6, 1919.    The
views of this office are desired in the matter of the disposition of
the remains of Private Clarence S. Baxter, who died overseas.    It
appears that a copy of the Circular Letter of The Adjutant General
sent out in such cases, addressed to Mrs. Benitta Baxter, Rochester,
New York, has been returned by the Genesee Valley Trust Company of
that city, with the statement that that company has been appointed
guardian of the property of Mrs. Baxter, but not of her person; that
Mrs. Baxter is a minor, sixteen years of age, and is at present in
the New York State Training School for girls at Hudson, New York,
under commitment of the county court of Monroe County, New York.

        2.    The facts stated above do not deprive the widow of this
soldier of her right to direct the disposition of his remains, and it
is recommended that she be requested to advise the Department of her
wishes in the matter.




                            E. A. KREGER    Esq.
                        Acting Judge Advocate General




      2 Inc.        24 REC'D BACK A G O, MAY 16 1949  MAY 19 19
```

After receiving a response from Genesee Valley Trust, the Army Adjutant General's office requested a review and opinion from the Judge Advocate General (legal office). The Judge Advocate General opined "the facts stated...do not deprive the widow of this soldier of her right to direct the disposition of his remains."[14] [above]

The Adjutant General's office replied to the Genesee Valley Trust company, requesting their assistance in obtaining disposition instructions from Mrs. Benita Baxter.

May 22, 1919.

Mr. Darrell D. Sully, President,
 Genesee Valley Trust Company,
  Rochester, New York.

Dear Sir:

Referring to your letter of April 22,1919, concerning the disposition of the remains of Private Clarence S. Baxter, I beg leave to advise you that the facts stated in your letter concerning the wife, Mrs. Benitta Baxter, and the appointment of your company as guardian of her property, do not deprive the widow of this soldier of her right to direct the disposition of his remains. It is requested, therefore, that she advise the Department of her wishes in the matter by filling out the inclosed card and returning it to this office in the inclosed envelope which requires no postage.

Very respectfully,

The Adjutant General
Per

W. V. Carter

3 incls.

MAY 23 1919
A. G. O.

One year later, in May 1920, the Army began the process of locating Clarence in France, making arrangements for disinterment, and returning him to the United States. A War Department telegram was sent to Benita at the Hudson School on October 30, 1920, informing her that the body of Private Clarence Baxter had arrived in New York City and requesting her confirmation that the body be shipped to Arlington National Cemetery. She replied via telegram on

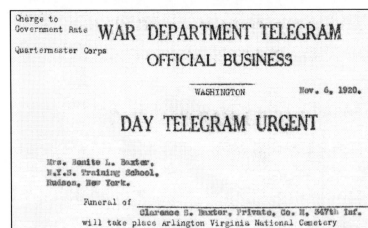

Charge to
Government Rate
Quartermaster Corps

WAR DEPARTMENT TELEGRAM
OFFICIAL BUSINESS

WASHINGTON   Nov. 6, 1920.

DAY TELEGRAM URGENT

Mrs. Benita L. Baxter,
N.Y.S. Training School,
Hudson, New York.

Funeral of _____
          Clarence S. Baxter, Private, Co. M, 347th Inf.
will take place Arlington Virginia National Cemetery
                                              on

Friday November 12, 1920, 2:30 P.M.
Travelers Aid Society Union Station Washington will give information and assistance concerning hotel accommodations and conveyance to Arlington.

                              ROGERS
                         Quartermaster General.

November 1, 1920. Mrs. Benita L. Baxter was invited by telegram to attend the funeral (burial) on November 12, 1920. [15] [above] The New York Training School for Girls at Hudson, holding guardianship over Benita, replied to the Quartermaster General's Office. They acknowledged receipt of the telegram and stated it was "impossible for her to attend."[16] [left]

STATE OF NEW YORK

NEW YORK STATE TRAINING SCHOOL FOR GIRLS

OFFICE OF THE SUPERINTENDENT

HORTENSE V. BRUCE, M. D.
SUPERINTENDENT

MANAGERS

ANNIE WINSOR ALLEN, PRESIDENT
MARY HINKLEY, VICE PRESIDENT
JOHN F. BRENNEN, TREASURER
HELEN ESSELSTYN, SECRETARY
LOUIS VAN HOESEN, M. D.
JOSEPH PERLMUTTER
MARK O'MEARA, M. D.

HUDSON, N. Y. _____ November 9, 1920

Rogers, Quartermaster General,
Cemeterial Branch,
Washington, D. C.

Dear Sir:-

        In the name of Mrs. Benita L. Baxter permit me to acknowledge receipt of your telegram advising her that the funeral of her husband, Clarence S. Baxter, Private, Co. M. 347 Infantry, will take place in the Arlington, Va. National Cemetery Friday, November 12th, at 2:30 P.M. Unfortunately it will be impossible for Mrs. Baxter to come to Washington for the service.

                    Very truly yours,

                    Hortense V. Bruce
LJC/B   Superintendent.

Form 1   H R   REGISTRATION CARD X 388 No. 13

1	Name in full *Harry* *Bell* (Given name) (Family name)	Age, in yrs. **27**

2 Home address   *Spencerport*   (Street)   (City)   *ny.*

3 Date of birth   *Sept*   *14*   *1889*   (Month)   (Day)   (Year)

4 Are you (1) a natural-born citizen, (2) a naturalized citizen, (3) an alien, (4) or have you declared your intention (specify which)?   *Naturalized citizen*

5 Where were you born?   *F Trenton*   *Canada*   (Town)   (State)   (Nation)

6 If not a citizen, of what country are you a citizen or subject?

7 What is your present trade, occupation, or office?   *Farmer*

8 By whom employed?   *Self*
   Where employed?   *Parma. Monroe Co ny*

9 Have you a father, mother, wife, child under 12, or a sister or brother under 12, solely dependent on you for support (specify which)?   *Mother*

10 Married or single (which)?   *Single*   Race (specify which)?   *Caucasian*

11 What military service have you had? Rank   *none*   ; branch
    years   ; Nation or State

12 Do you claim exemption from draft (specify grounds)?

I affirm that I have verified above answers and that they are true.

C A

Harry Bell

JOHN HENRY BELL
1889 – 1922

Inducted into the United States Army at Spencerport, New York, on September 26, 1917, Private John Bell, at the age of twenty-eight, was assigned to Battery D, 309th Field Artillery (Heavy), 78th Division. He transferred to Supply Company, 309th Field Artillery, on November 17, 1917, and was designated a Wagoner on December 14, 1917. Harry, as he was known, trained at Camp Dix in Wrightstown, New Jersey, and was sent overseas from Boston, Massachusetts, aboard the SS *Cardiganshire* on May 28, 1918. His obituary stated he was "gassed" during the war; however, it was unconfirmed in military records. Something did happen to Harry during the war, though exactly what is unknown. He was assigned to Convalescent Detachment No. 135, at Brest, France, where he departed for the United States on March 18, 1919, aboard the SS *Maui*. He is listed under the category "Mental Cases Class 'B'" on the ship's manifest. Harry arrived in Hoboken, New Jersey, on March 31, 1919, and was honorably discharged on July 9, 1919, with a Surgeon's Certificate of Disability, rated at ten percent.

John Henry Bell, known as Harry, was born in Trenton, Ontario, Canada, on September 14, 1889, to British-born father William B. and Canadian-born mother Catherine E. (Cross) Bell. As a family they immigrated to America when Harry was two years old. Harry was a fireman when he married Vera Charilla Quackenbush on June 20, 1911, and, by 1915, found employment with Eastman Kodak Company. When he signed his draft registration card on June 5, 1917, he was self-employed as a farmer and, interestingly, his marital status was recorded as single despite his marriage four years earlier. John Henry Bell died April 22, 1922, in the Iola Sanitorium in Rochester, New York, from tuberculosis as a "result of being gassed during the World War."[17] Military funeral services were held by the Parma Lodge, Independent Order of Odd Fellows, while the American Legion Ferris-Goodridge Post 330 of Spencerport, New York, provided the honorary firing squad, color bearers and color guard. Harry is buried in Parma Corners Cemetery in Parma, New York.

Parma, July 2.—Private Harry J. Bell, only son of Mrs. William Bell, has arrived safely overseas with the Supply Com-

HARRY J. BELL.

pany of the 309th Heavy Field Artillery. He left for Camp Dix last September.

Form 1	*1941*	REGISTRATION CARD	No. 2D

1 Name in full Andrew J. Bennett
(Given name)   (Family name)   Age, in yrs. **25**

2 Home address Lyndonville, N.Y.
(No.)   (Street)   (City)   (State)

3 Date of birth September 10 1892
(Month)   (Day)   (Year)

4 Are you (1) a natural-born citizen, (2) a naturalized citizen, (3) an alien, (4) or have you declared your intention (specify which)? Natural born

5 Where were you born? Town Yates, Orleans Co., N.Y.
(Town)   (State)   (Nation)

6 If not a citizen, of what country are you a citizen or subject?

7 What is your present trade, occupation, or office? Laboror

8 By whom employed? L.B.Resseguie
Where employed? Millers, N.Y.

9 Have you a father, mother, wife, child under 12, or a sister or brother under 12, solely dependent on you for support (specify which)? No

10 Married or single (which)? Single   Race (specify which)? Caucasian

11 What military service have you had? Rank None ; branch
years ; Nation or State

12 Do you claim exemption from draft (specify grounds)? Yes, physical disability

I affirm that I have verified above answers and that they are true.

Andrew J. Bennett
(Signature or mark)

If person is of African descent, tear off this corner.

34

ANDREW JACKSON BENNETT
1892 – 1950

Twenty-five-year-old Andrew registered for the draft on June 5, 1917. His *New York State Abstracts of World War I Military Service* card indicates Andrew was inducted through the draft at Albion, New York, on February 25, 1918.[18] Contradicting this record is an article in the *Democrat and Chronicle* (Rochester, NY) on February 26, 1918, which implies Andrew enlisted and was sent to Fort Leavenworth, Kansas, instead of Camp Devens, Massachusetts, with the other inductees. [below, right] It is plausible he enlisted and was sent to Fort Leavenworth based on his assignment to Battery A, 128th Field Artillery, 35th Division, where he remained until his completion of service.[d] The 35th Division was formed primarily from elements of Kansas and Missouri National Guard units. Andrew and the 128th Field Artillery left for overseas service on May 20, 1918, departing from New York, New York, aboard the British ship RMS *Saxonia*. While in Europe, Private Bennett was promoted to Private First Class on August 10, 1918. He returned to Boston, Massachusetts, on April 22, 1919, after departing Brest, France, on April 11, 1919, aboard the SS *Vedic*. Andrew was honorably discharged on May 1, 1919.

Andrew was born in Lyndonville, New York, on September 10, 1892, to Grant K. and Bertha (Kenyon) Bennett. After his mother's passing, the family moved to Spencerport, New York, in May 1913[19] and established themselves in the community. When Andrew registered for the draft in June 1917, he was employed in the poultry trade, working for Leon B. Resseguie in Millers, New York. Upon completion of his overseas assignment he was living in Washington, DC, and working for the government as a clerk. He returned to Orleans County and married Elizabeth Stella Keck on July 14, 1920, joining his brothers, Louis and Gordon, as partners in a meat market and grocery business in Spencerport, operating under the name "Bennett Brothers." The business was sold and renamed in 1927. Andrew continued to work as a meat cutter in Spencerport through 1940. When Andrew registered for the "Old Man's Draft" in 1942 he was

Men Go to Different Camps.

Albion, Feb. 25.—Orleans county's draft quota of twenty-two men left Albion this morning at 10 o'clock for Camp Devens. The men reported at the Court House here at 7:30, where Kenyon Brooks was placed in command and Leon Hawley designated as second in command.

County Clerk Harry D. Bartlett called the roll, to which all responded except Benjamin F. Jackson, of Medina, who is on his way here from Muskegon, Mich., and will be sent on upon his arrival in Albion. Edwin Brunetti, of Hulberton, was sent as alternate in place of Mr. Jackson.

The men left on a special train that also conveyed the draft contingents from Niagara and Monroe counties and is scheduled to reach Devens at 9:30 o'clock to-night. Among volunteers who were subject to draft and enlisted and were sent to Fort Leavenworth, Kansas, to-night were Harrison Higley, Reed Clapp, Keene Salisbury, Henry S. Jaworski and Jennings Van Stone, of Albion; Robert Jenny, of Shelby, and Andrew J. Bennett, of Lyndonville.

Charles Irwin, 19 years old, also left for Newport Naval Training Station to-day. Before leaving each man was given a sweater, helmet, muffler, two pair of woolen socks and a pair of wristlets by the Red Cross Chapter of Albion and a kit of sweets and smokes by the Patriotic Fund.

---

[d] To read more about the 35th Division, especially the failure of artillery leadership in the battle of the Meuse-Argonne in 1918, see Robert H. Ferrell's book *Collapse at Meuse-Argonne: The Failure of the Missouri-Kansas Division.* Excerpt on divisional artillery available at: http://www.worldwar1.com/dbc/ferrell2.htm

working at a small animal veterinary hospital in Rochester, New York, called Webber Brothers. Andrew passed away on June 18, 1950, and is buried in Creekside Cemetery in the village of Churchville, New York.

The following newspaper clippings reflect the significant impact the Bennet Brothers Market had on the Spencerport community.[20] [below and facing page]

To Open Spencerport Market.

Spencerport, Oct. 11.—The Bennett Brothers, who purchased the property on Union street, known as the old Merz Shoe Shop, from the Cole estate, have moved the building back and will start their new meat market building in a short time. It will be two stories and constructed of brick and cement blocks.

The meat market and grocery business, which has been conducted by the Bennett Brothers for the past few years has been sold to William Hallen Falls, and will be conducted under the name of Falls Brothers. The new firm has taken possession.

ARMICTICE CELEBRATION IN SPENCERPORT TO-DAY

Spencerport, Nov. 10.—The sixth annual Armistice Day dance will be given in the Masonic Temple by Ferris-Goodridge Post, American Legion, Tuesday evening.

There will be dancing from nine until one o'clock and will include old dances as well as modern dancing.

The Ladies Auxiliary of Ferris-Goodridge Post will hold a cooked food sale in Bennett Brothers market to-morrow afternoon beginning at 2:30 o'clock.

The Slayton class of the Congregational church will have a cooked food sale at Bennett Brothers' Market Friday afternoon, at 2:30 o'clock.

Form 1   194   REGISTRATION CARD   No. 44

1 Name in full _Louie Bennutt_ X   Age. o yrs. **27**
   (Given name)   (Family name)

2 Home address _Lyndonville Ny_
   (No.)   (Street)   (City)   (State)

3 Date of birth _March 9,   1890_
   (Month)   (Day)   (Year)

4 Are you (1) a natural-born citizen, (2) a naturalized citizen, (3) an alien (4) or have you declared your
   intention (specify which)? _Natural born_

5 Where were you born! _Town of Somerset, Niagara Co. N.Y., USA_
   (Town)   (State)   (Nation)

6 If not a citizen, of what country are you a citizen or subject?

7 What is your present trade, occupation, or office? _Locomotive Fireman_

8 By whom employed? _N.Y.C. R.R. Co._
   Where employed? _Buffalo_

9 Have you a father, mother, wife child under 12, or a sister or brother under 12, solely dependent on you for
   support? (specify which)? _No_

10 Married or single (which)? _Single_   Race (specify which)? _Caucasian_

11 What military service have you had? Rank _none_; branch
   years ____; Nation or State ____

12 Do you claim exemption from draft (specify grounds)? _No._

   I affirm that I have verified above answers and that they are true.

   Louie Bennutt
   (Signature or mark)

If persons of African descent, tear off this corner

LOUIE B. BENNETT
1890 – 1941

Louie was inducted at Albion, New York, at the age of twenty-eight on July 14, 1918. He was sent to the New York University Training Detachment at University Heights, New York, to participate in the Student Army Training Corps (SATC). A national program, New York University was one of 157 schools of higher education encompassing trade schools, colleges, and universities to participate in SATC. The total number would grow to 564 institutions, providing education and training in trades necessary to support the war. Louie completed his training on September 9, 1918, being one of 1,613 men who went through the program at New York University.

Louie was initially assigned to Casual Company, Tank Corps, located at Camp Colt[e] at the Gettysburg National Battlefield, Pennsylvania. Completing training, Private Third Class Bennett transferred to Motor Transport Corps, Mechanical Repair Unit 310, and sent overseas on October 27, 1918, embarking from Hoboken, New Jersey, aboard the USS *Leviathan*. Promoting to Private First Class on December 10, 1918, Louie would serve nine more months overseas until his return aboard the USS *Mount Vernon* with Group A, Section 2, Mechanical Repair Unit 310. He departed Brest, France, on September 10, 1919, and arrived back in Hoboken on September 18, 1919. Louie was honorably discharged four days after his return on September 22, 1919.

Born in Somerset, New York, on March 9, 1890, to Grant K. and Bertha (Kenyon) Bennett, Louie grew up in Orleans County and by the age of twenty was working as a store salesman in Lyndonville, New York. On his draft registration, at the age of twenty-seven, he listed his occupation as a locomotive fireman for the New York Central Railroad. After his discharge from service Louie returned to Yates County finding employment in a meat market. Louie experienced many changes in 1922–he married Helen Marie Knickerbocker, a teacher in Rochester, New York, on March 27th and the couple made their home in Spencerport, New York. Then Louie and his brothers, Gordon and Andrew, became business partners when they started their own grocery and meat market business named "Bennett Brothers Meat Market" in Spencerport. (see Andrew Bennett, preceding pages) Selling the business in 1927, Louie became a proprietor of the Spencerport Coal and Feed Corporation.[21] [below]

He was very active in his community as a member of the Parma Lodge, Independent Order of Odd Fellows; the Ogden Grange; American Legion Ferris-Goodridge Post 330; and Spencerport Congregational Church. Louie passed away on June 1, 1941, in Spencerport and is buried in Parma Corners Cemetery in Parma, New York.

> Spencerport Coal & Feed Corporation, Spencerport, has been incorporated with capital stock of 500 shares of preferred stock, par value $100, and 1,000 shares of common stock without par value. Among the incorporators are Clarence W. Barker, Louie Bennett and J. Thomas Osborne, all of Spencerport.

[e] Note of historical interest: Camp Colt was commanded by Captain Dwight D. Eisenhower during the time Louie was assigned there.

Name BIGGER- GEORGE WALTER		Service Number 111-84-51		
Enlisted XXXXXX Enrolled NAVY RECRUITING STATION BUFFALO N.Y. Date 5-14-18 260				
Age at Entrance 21 YRS	Rate SEAMAN 2 CLASS			UXXXX U.S.N.R.F,
Home Address XX B County XX		Town HILTON State NY.		
Served at	From	To	Served as	No. Days
NAVAL TRAINING STATION GREAT LAKES ILL.	6-7-18	7-29-18	SEAMAN 2 CLASS	181
NAVAL RIFLE RANGE AT CAMP LOGAN ILL.	7-29-18	8-18-18		
NAVAL RIFLE RANGE AT PEEKSKILL N.Y.	8-18-18	11-11-18		
Remarks:				
			SEAMAN	
Date Discharge 9-10-19 Place Inactive Duty USS MONGOLIA			Rating at Discharge	
Library Bureau 96-1533 -A				

George Bigger's *New York State Abstracts of World War I Military Service* card. George was too young to register for the first draft. He enrolled in the United States Naval Reserve Force before the second draft and did not have to complete a draft registration card.

GEORGE WALTER BIGGER
1897 – 1973

George, at the age of twenty-one, entered the United States Naval Reserve Force on May 14, 1918, in Buffalo, New York. Sent to Great Lakes, Illinois, he trained at the Naval Training Station from June 7, 1918, until July 29, 1918, and would further his training at the Naval Rifle Range at Camp Logan, Illinois, until August 18, 1918. George transferred to the Naval Rifle Range in Peekskill, New York, and remained there until November 11, 1918. George was placed on inactive duty when he was assigned to the USS *Mongolia* and was discharged as a Seaman Second Class on September 10, 1919.

George Walter Bigger was born to John A. and Louisa A. (Fields) Bigger on April 23, 1897, in New York, and grew up in the towns of Philadelphia (Jefferson County, New York) and Denmark (Lewis County, New York). He moved with his family to Hilton, New York, and in 1915 was employed as a building laborer. George and Naomi Emma Tripp were married on August 14, 1923, and made their home in Hilton. George supported his family in different occupations to include working as a clerk in a drugstore, a pharmaceutical salesman, a guard, and a farm laborer. He was a member of the Parma Union Cemetery Association. George died on March 14, 1973, and is buried in Parma Union Cemetery in Parma, New York.

Above is a photo of young George at an unknown age, extracted from a family photo with his eleven brothers and sisters.[22]

Below, George Bigger, second from left holding flag, is joined by John Murphy, Lucius Bagley, Miles Corbitt, and George Paulson (left to right) as they form up in the village of Hilton on what is presumed to be the August 2nd Town of Parma "Welcome Home" celebration for the war veterans in 1919.[23]

Army Form B. 2505.

DUPLICATE.

SHORT SERVICE.

(For the Duration of the War).

ATTESTATION OF

No. *23141* Name *Jack Bridgeman* Corps *Grenadier Guards*

Questions to be put to the Recruit before enlistment.

1. What is your name? — 1. *Jack Bridgeman*
2. What is your full Address? — 2. *Rosalyn, Mildenhall, Suffolk*
3. Are you a British Subject? — 3. *Yes*
4. What is your Age? — 4. *20* Years *5* Months.
5. What is your Trade or Calling? — 5. *Farmer assistant*
6. Are you Married? — 6. *No*
7. Have you ever served in any branch of His Majesty's Forces, naval or military, if so,* which? — 7. *Yes, 5th Batt. Suff. Regt.*
8. Are you willing to be vaccinated or re-vaccinated? — 8. *Yes*
9. Are you willing to be enlisted for General Service? — 9. *Yes*
10. Did you receive a Notice, and do you understand its meaning, and who gave it to you? — 10. *Yes* (Name) *A.G. Goodwin* (Corps)
11. Are you willing to serve upon the following conditions provided His Majesty should so long require your services? — 11. *Yes*

For the duration of the War, at the end of which you will be discharged with all convenient speed. If employed with Hospitals, depots of Mounted Units, and as Clerks, etc., you may be retained after the termination of hostilities until your services can be spared, but such retention shall in no case exceed six months.

I, *Jack Bridgeman*, do solemnly declare that the above answers made by me to the above questions are true, and that I am willing to fulfil the engagement made.

Jack Bridgeman SIGNATURE OF RECRUIT.
A.Goodwin Signature of Witness.

OATH TO BE TAKEN BY RECRUIT ON ATTESTATION.

I, *Jack Bridgeman* swear by Almighty God, that I will be faithful and bear true Allegiance to His Majesty King George the Fifth, His Heirs and Successors...

CERTIFICATE OF MAGISTRATE OR ATTESTING OFFICER.

on this *23* day of *February* 1915

Date *24-2-1915* Place *Bury St Ed*

AYLMER OCTAVIUS BRIDGEMAN
1894 – 1968

Jack served three months with the 5th Battalion, Suffolk Regiment, when he enlisted in the British Army at twenty-years-old on February 23, 1915, activating on February 25, 1915. He was reassigned to the 3rd Battalion, joining them "at the front" on May 19, 1916.[24] Jack was at Le Havre, France, on September 6, 1916, and can be found the following January in the Carpathian region of Eastern Europe (Austria, Czech Republic, Romania and Poland) before returning to England on the HMS *Saint George* in February 1917. Jack was transferred in December 1917 from the London Command Depot to Shoreham Army Camp, located on the southern coast of Great Britain. He transferred to the Grenadier Guards Division Base Depot on April 1, 1918, joining his Battalion in the field on April 6, 1918. He was wounded in action, having been shot in his right knee, on August 28, 1918. Jack was discharged on March 31, 1920.

Aylmer Octavius Bridgeman was born in Burwell, Cambridgeshire, England, in 1894 to Robert and Esther (Bell) Bridgeman; he was one of ten children. At sixteen, Jack, as he was called, was listed as a miller in a flour mill on the 1911 England Census.[25] He emigrated to the United States on March 12, 1912, sailing from Southampton, England, and arrived in New York, New York, on March 20, 1912, aboard the SS *Olympic* at the age of seventeen.[26]

Jack migrated to Hilton, New York, and found employment as a farm laborer for Fred Smith. Jack and his brother, Reginald Henry Bridgeman, returned to England via Montreal, Quebec, Canada, aboard the SS *Pretorian*, and arrived without incident in Glasgow, Scotland, on December 8, 1914. On February 23, 1915, Jack was living in Mildenhall, Suffolk, England, when he joined the British military service.

Jack's sister wrote to Wilfred Horex of Hilton and the letter was published in the *Hilton (NY) Record* in September 1918. Wilfred relayed that Jack had been shot on August 24, 1918. (Note: military records state he was shot on the 28th of August 1918.)[27]

Jack sailed across the Atlantic Ocean again, this time settling in Turtleford, Meadow Lake, Saskatchewan, Canada. He found work as a hotel keeper and met his future bride, Beatrice Margaret Francis. The pair were married on September 15, 1947, and by 1956 had moved to Vancouver, British Columbia, eventually settling in Victoria, British Columbia. Jack was working as a Commissionaire (security) at Rocky Point Park[28] for a few years until his passing on June 1, 1968, in Victoria, British Columbia, Canada.

Below, Jack and Beatrice on their wedding day [left] and Jack in Saskatchewan, Canada, enjoying the splendor of western Canada.[29] [right]

Form 1   1307   **REGISTRATION CARD**   No. _____   1434

		Age, in yrs.
1	Name in full _Colonel Loren Brown_ (Given name) (Family name)	23

2 Home address _____ Hilton RR2 NY_
(No.) (Street) (City) (State)

3 Date of birth _March_ _25_ _1894_
(Month) (Day) (Year)

4 Are you (1) a natural-born citizen, (2) a naturalized citizen, (3) an alien, (4) or have you declared your intention (specify which)? _natural born citizen_

5 Where were you born? _Parma,_ _N.Y._ _US_
(Town) (State) (Nation)

6 If not a citizen, of what country are you a citizen or subject? _____

7 What is your present trade, occupation, or office? _95 Supt of School Gardens_

8 By whom employed? _Board of Education_
Where employed? _Waverly NY_

9 Have you a father, mother, wife, child under 12, or a sister or brother under 12, solely dependent on you for support (specify which)? _no_

10 Married or single (which)? _single_   Race (specify which)? _Caucasian_

11 What military service have you had? Rank _____ ; branch _____
years _____ ; Nation or State _Scholastic, Cornell Un._

12 Do you claim exemption from draft (specify grounds)? _____

I affirm that I have verified above answers and that they are true.

Colonel Loren Brown
(Signature or mark)

44

COLONEL LOREN BROWN
1894 – 1981

Colonel Loren Brown was inducted into the United States Army on May 15,1918, as a twenty-four-year-old Private First Class and assigned to 2nd Company, 4th Officers' Training School at Camp Meade in Admiral, Maryland. [30] [below right] He transferred to Central Machine Gun Officers' Training School at Camp Hancock, Georgia, on June 17, 1918. Mustering out to accept a Commission on October 15, 1918, Colonel was discharged as a Second Lieutenant less than two months later on December 6, 1918, for the convenience of the government.

Colonel Brown was born to Loren H. and Annettie "Nettie" (Greenwell) Brown in Hilton, New York, on March 25, 1894. Not only was Colonel president of the Class of 1912 at Hilton High School, he was also the assistant editor of the 1911 *Hiltonian*, the school's annual publication (forerunner of today's yearbooks). Colonel was working as a superintendent of gardens for the Waverly, New York, school district at the time of his draft registration on June 2, 1917.[f]

A 1919 graduate of Cornell University, Colonel earned his degree in agriculture and was recognized in the university's 1919 yearbook, the *Cornellian*, for having served seven months in the United States Army as an infantryman. Janet Elizabeth Murphy married Colonel Brown on September 26, 1921, in Los Angeles, California, and the couple drove through Northern Mexico on their honeymoon. They made their first home in Los Angeles[31] but didn't stay on the West Coast for long. By 1924 they returned to New York where Colonel would become editor of the *New York Market News*.

Hilton, July 18.—Colonel L. Brown, son of Mr. and Mrs. Loren H. Brown, left Cornell College to enlist as a private at Camp Meade, Md. He has recently

COLONEL L. BROWN.
been transferred to Camp Hancock, Augusta, Ga., and is now a candidate in the Central Officers' Training School. Mr. Brown likes his work and enjoys army life.

Colonel was well respected as a representative of the United States Department of Agriculture,[32] his opinions and advice solicited. He attended events around New York State[33] and in October 1928 was a guest on the nationally-broadcasted radio show *National Farm and Home Hour*. Avid listeners heard his presentation titled "Do You Know Your Onions?"[34]

Colonel L. Brown, who writes exclusively for our Farm and Grove Section on Florida products, contributes a valuable series of news stories, among them the following:

Watermelon Market Hurt by Weather,
Florida Maintains its Lead in Fruits and Vegetables,
Late Florida Celery Prices Fairly High,
Florida Shipping Less to Chicago,
Egg Production shows sharp reduction,
Storage of Citrus More Successful This Season.

Mr. Brown's articles are of real practical value to Florida growers inasmuch as they tell what happens to the outstanding products of Florida farms after they reach the eastern markets.

Colonel L. Brown

---

[f] It is interesting to note the date his draft registration was signed (June 2, 1917) was actually three days ahead of the national registration date (June 5, 1917).

A newspaper article written by Colonel was prefaced with praise when published in the *Buffalo (NY) Evening News* on December 21, 1921, in which Colonel was cited as "a widely known market expert and writer on business topics." Colonel's articles on agricultural business markets were published in well-known Florida newspapers such as the *Orlando (FL) Sentinel*, the *Palm Beach Post* (West Palm Beach, FL), and the *News Press* (Fort Myers, FL)–an example on the preceding page.[35] His informational columns were published from coast-to-coast in the United States from the *Daily Press* (Newport News, VA), to the *Courier Journal* (Louisville, KY), the *Billings (MT) Gazette*, and the *Los Angeles Times*, to name a few. Below is an example from the *Orlando (FL) Evening Star*[36].

COLONEL L. BROWN

News and information concerning northern markets is of vital interest to farmers, growers and shippers. Through our Farm & Grove Section we endeavor to bring you each month a timely and interesting review furnished by our special representative in the Metropolitan District, Colonel L. Bown.

In this issue Colonel Brown tells us how the trade is reacting toward the movement to substitute the lug in place of the crate for Florida tomato shipments. There has been considerable said both for and against the plan and it is interesting to have this first hand, unbiased report of just how the trade feels in the matter.

Heretofore Colonel Brown has served Farm & Grove as a contributor, but we now take pleasure in announcing that arrangements have just been completed whereby this capable and experienced agricultural journalist becomes a member of Farm & Grove staff and hereafter he will supply us with complete and comprehensive reports, not of the Metropolitan District alone but as they relate to all of the larger eastern markets, and in addition will contribute feature articles occasionally that will be of intense interest and value to Farm & Grove readers.

Colonel Brown enjoys a wide acquaintance in eastern marketing circles and is recognized as an outstanding authority on subjects relating to conditions in the fruit and vegetable trade from a marketing standpoint. We feel confident his addition to Farm & Grove staff will provide our readers with much of genuine interest and value during the coming year.

* * * *

Though retired, Colonel continued to work his pen, offering his opinions by writing letters to the editor, which were printed in the *Journal News* (White Plains, NY). He was an active philatelist and spoke at numerous meetings on the preservation of stamp collections. Colonel was the Mount Vernon Stamp Club president, secretary, and treasurer in Mount Vernon, New York. Colonel died on May 18, 1981, in Cambridge, New York, at the age of eighty-seven.

The recovery ladder

By COLONEL L. BROWN

VIEWPOINT

At this point we are fighting inflation first and recession second. Once inflation is controlled, or at least reduced, danger of depression diminishes greatly. They cannot both be fought successfully at the same time. When the auto manufacturers and other big companies started dumping their employes in the streets, the natural reaction of everyone was to cut spending to the bone, and conditions have to change so that normal buying can be resumed.

During 1973 and 1974 there was a big overproduction of manufactured goods and a tremendous stockpiling of raw materials. With prices rising steadily, this seemed the logical thing to do, but instead was feeding the fires of inflation.

IN PARTIAL defense of the auto makers, it should be said that they lost control of their business, and engineering decisions were made in Washington, not in Detroit. This increased the cost of cars without noticeable effect in controlling pollution. Their mistake was in thinking that people would buy f r e e l y at inflated prices.

The oversized stockpiles of autos, other manufactured goods, basic raw materials and many kinds of f o o d s will have to go through the wringer before conditions can improve. Consumer debt will have to be reduced.

Once prices have been adjusted downward, and consumer debt reduced, normal buying will start again. If all government bodies reduced expenditures by 10 per cent, it would give more money to pay for useful goods and services.

WE HAVE two kinds of welfare recipients today. First, there are the poor,

the sick, the old and the unemployed who are unable to support themselves. Second, there is the army of political drones and bureaucrats who are handsomely paid but perform no services. Great savings could be made by discharging them and putting them on regular welfare.

Here are some other things that I think might help to right the economy:

● Make the New York subway pay its way. Everybody else in the United States pays his own transportation costs.

● Tax alcoholic beverages, cigarettes and even soft drinks ahead of gasoline for raising revenues. Gasoline and heating oil are prime necessities and should not be taxed more than another five cents per gallon. Take a hard look at tax-exempt real estate. We have some free riders.

● Dump the Interstate Commerce Commission, the Environmental Protection Agency and the Federal Trade Commission and reduce some of the other alphabets. The chief work of the ICC has been to bankrupt our once-great railroad system.

● Make every effort to d e v e l o p energy by every means possible. This means oil, gas, coal, shale oil, nuclear power, water power and solar power. This will take longer and be more expensive than many believe.

● Use care in tampering with oil production. Eliminating our oil depletion is a sure way to eliminate jobs. Rationing is organized foolishness. Counterfeiters already have a supply of coupons. In World War II, ra-

tioning was poorly-organized foolishness.

● Keep up the strength of our armed forces, but we had better double-check to see if we are getting what we are paying for. Some other nations are producing better and cheaper weapons than we are.

I am in favor of spending money for purposes that will create jobs and improve the country at the same time. I favor release of the $2 billion fund for road work. Somehow or other we need to raise substantial sums for maintenance of dwellings, apartment houses, colleges, public buildings and the like.

Above all else, we need to aid public utilities in whatever way we can. It is popular among some segments of the population to rave and froth at the mouth about the public utilities. I am certainly not saying they are perfect but I would rather see them operating normally than to be sitting in the dark, cold and hungry.

We can afford to spend money for useful things but not for make work. During the 1930s we had "workers" painting the walls of post offices. I once had some of these "workers" coming to me to gather statistics on cabbage.

Since neither the President nor the Congress has any t h i n g resembling a workable program, it is possible that our salvation lies in their talking and talking and doing nothing. Samson slew the Philistines with the jawbone of an ass. It may be that inflation and recession will both be slain by the jawbones of asses.

The writer lives in Valley Cottage.

This opinion (left), written by Brown in 1975, was printed in the *Journal News* (White Plains, New York) and illustrates the breadth and depth of his economic thinking, as several issues are in today's (2018) news.[37]

Below, articles about the Mount Vernon Stamp Club, published in the *Daily Argus* (White Plains, New York) while Colonel Brown was the club president.[38][39]

MEMBERS TALK AT STAMP CLUB

Four Philatelists Address Fellow Collectors—Views On Hobby Discussed

Home talent night was observed last evening by the Mount Vernon Stamp Club at a meeting in the Young Men's Christian Association. Four members gave their viewpoints on stamp collecting and illustrated talks with exhibitions taken from their collections.

Lithuania was the subject chosen by Alex Steponaitis, the first speaker. He showed stamps from this European country starting with the first issues and concluding with the current series. He also showed air mail varieties, and some specimens printed in New York to finance an ill-fated trans-oceanic flight to Lithuania.

Colonel L. Brown chose United States plate numbers as his subject. He illustrated this with two volumes from his collection. The first one contained plate number blocks of the National Park series including color variations and the second volume included other 20th century commemorative blocks.

POTATO STAMPS—From Washington comes the report that the potato stamps will not be available for collectors. The sale of these stamps is at present limited to certain sections of southern states where the potato crop is now being harvested.

Colonel L. Brown sends the information that these stamps can be obtained at some post offices in Texas.

Form 1

REGISTRATION CARD

No. 41

1. Name in full Roy L. Brown
(Given name) (Family name)
Age, in yrs. 22

2. Home address Spencerport N.Y.
(Street) (City)

3. Date of birth April 19th 1895
(Month) (Day) (Year)

4. Are you (1) a natural-born citizen, (2) a naturalized citizen, (3) an alien, (4) or have you declared your intention (specify which)? Natural Born Citizen

5. Where were you born? Rochester N.Y. U.S.A.
(Town) (State) (Nation)

6. If not a citizen, of what country are you a citizen or subject?

7. What is your present trade, occupation, or office? I Farming

8. By whom employed? Self
Where employed? Parma

9. Have you a father, mother, wife, child under 12, or a sister or brother under 12, solely dependent on you for support (specify which)? None

10. Married or single (which)? Single Race (specify which)? Caucasian

11. What military service have you had? Rank None ; branch
years ; Nation or State

12. Do you claim exemption from draft (specify grounds)? None

C A
87

I affirm that I have verified above answers and that they are true.

Roy L. Brown.
(Signature or mark)

If person is of African descent tear off this corner

48

ROY LESLIE BROWN
1895 – 1957

Roy was inducted into the United States Army at Spencerport, New York, on September 26, 1917, at the age of twenty-two. Assigned to Battery D, 2d Battalion, 309th Field Artillery, 78th Division, Private Brown received his training at Camp Dix in Wrightstown, New Jersey. On May 21, 1918, Roy was promoted to Corporal and five days later, on May 26, 1918, embarked aboard the SS *Arawa* from Boston, Massachusetts, to France. He participated in the military actions at Saint-Mihiel, Meuse-Argonne, and Grandpré, as well as the Preny Raid. Corporal Brown departed Marseille, France, on April 26, 1919, aboard the SS *Infanta Isabel* and arrived in Hoboken, New Jersey, on May 10, 1919, and was discharged on the 17th of May 1919.

Born to Charles H. and Nellie M. (De Jonge) Brown on April 19, 1895, Roy Leslie Brown

Young Lodge Leader

ROY L. BROWN
. . . *Noble Grand-elect*

worked alongside his parents as a clothing cutter for Michaels Stern & Company, a tailor shop located in Rochester, New York, prior to entering the war. After returning from service in the United States Army, Roy was a clothing salesman for the National Clothing Company. Mildred Arlie Thurston exchanged vows with Roy on June 19, 1920, in Rochester but the couple later divorced.

Roy married Minna B. Willer on July 22, 1939, and the couple made their home on East Ridge Road in Irondequoit, New York. Roy was very active in his community and held various positions in the many civic organizations he belonged to. He was elected Vice Grand Monarch of the Kheder Khan Sanctorium in 1935.[40] [right] As a member of Frankfort Lodge of the Independent Order of Odd Fellows he was elected Noble Grand in 1936.[41] [left] In addition, Roy was a member of the Ancient Mystic Order of Samaritans, a social and charitable sect within the Odd Fellows. He also belonged to the United Commercial Travelers.

Roy belonged to Voiture 111 of the 40 & 8[g] and the 309th Field Artillery Association. Within the Veterans of Foreign Wars, he belonged to the 309th Field Artillery Post, serving as trustee, service officer, and was on the board of directors in 1935. In 1939 he was commander of the American Legion William W. Doud Post 98. Roy passed away November 25, 1957, and is buried in Mount Hope Cemetery in Rochester, New York.

Double Ceremony For Rochester And Central

Frankfort Lodge of Odd Fellows will convene Wednesday at 8 p. m. for routine business, and at 9 the new officers for the next six months will be publicly installed by D. D. G. M. William J. Beckler and staff of District 3.

Noble Grand elect Roy L. Brown is one of the younger members of Frankfort Lodge, having joined only a few years ago, has risen rapidly in fraternal circles and is also vice grand monarch of Kheder Khan Sanctorium, AMOS.

---

[g] To learn more about the Forty and Eight visit http://www.fortyandeight.org

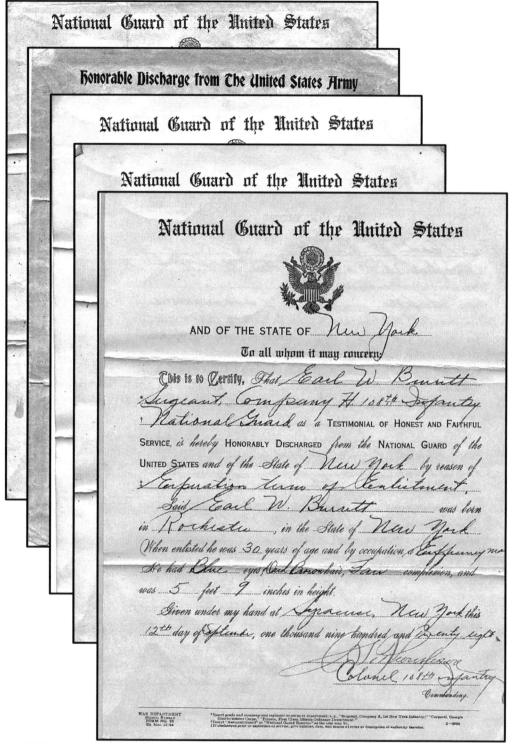

Earl W. Burritt was already a member of the New York National Guard when the United States entered World War I. He continued his service in the New York National Guard through re-enlistments until his honorable discharge on September 12, 1928.[42]

EARL WALTER BURRITT
1897 – 1960

Earl, through continuous re-enlistments, served in the New York National Guard between 1916 and 1928. His first enlistment began at the age of nineteen on November 28, 1916, in Rochester, New York. Private Burritt was assigned to Machine Gun Company, 3d Infantry, New York National Guard, later designated as Machine Gun Company, 108th Infantry, 27th Division, when drafted into federal service. His photo from the regimental history book is shown at right.[43] Earl trained with the rest of the 27th Division at Camp Wadsworth in Spartanburg, South Carolina, before heading to Europe. He left for overseas duty from Newport News, Virginia, on May 10, 1918, aboard the passenger steamer *Kursk*, arriving in

Brest, France, around May 23, 1918. While overseas he served in both France and Belgium, participating in many actions including the Hindenburg Line, La Selle River, Vierstraat Ridge, Jonc-de-Mer Ridge, Dickebusch Lake, and the Saint Maurice River. Earl returned home on the RMS *Mauretania*, departing from Brest, France, on March 6, 1919, en route to Camp Merritt in New Jersey; he was discharged on March 31, 1919. Earl's remaining enlistments in the New York National Guard were all with Company H, 108th Infantry, where his machine gun skills were recognized.[44] [below] He was honorably discharged from the National Guard on the 12th of September 1928.

Company H to Defend Pistol Championship

Company H, 108th Infantry, New York National Guard here, is practising for the regimental pistol match in Syracuse next month. The company has won the trophy for the last three years and expects to repeat again this year.

Sergeant Earl W. Burritt, 2183 Main Street East, of Company H recently received $25. prize for the highest machine gun score in the 108th Regiment while at Camp Smith.

The company has had one re-enlistment since its return from camp, Gilbert V. H. Delph, 9 Fuller Place, having signed up for another "hitch."

Born as Earl Walter Hanley on November 22, 1897, in Rochester, he was adopted and raised by Frank M. and Mary Elmina "Mina" (Welch) Burritt of Parma, New York.[45] Growing up, he worked on the family's fruit farm until his enlistment five months prior to the United States entering World War I. Earl found employment after the war as an office supply salesman before marrying Margaret Cummings on October 14, 1925, in Luzerne, Pennsylvania. The couple settled in Rochester, where Earl worked as a street car conductor. Eventually they took up residence in Pittsford, New York, and Earl worked for the United States Postal Service in a custodial position.

Earl was a member of Rochester Chapter 15, Disabled Veterans of the World War, receiving his disability because he was gassed on the Hindenburg Line during the war. In 1934, Earl and the disabled veterans group filed a suit against the City of Rochester's administration, claiming they were not allowing the Municipal Civil Service Commission to establish a new, eligible list for Civil Service laborer positions. (see article[46], next page) "After hearing argument of Louis I. Bunis, attorney for Burritt, and Corporation Counsel Charles B. Forsyth, who is opposing the move of Burritt, …[Supreme Court Justice Benn] Kenyon reserved decision, although implying he would grant an alternative writ of mandamus to permit hearing of the issues."[47] The attorney for Burritt and the disabled veterans claimed the City of Rochester had not produced a new list of civil service labor positions since 1932, further asserting the "rights of veterans have been cast aside for political purposes by the Democratic administration."[48] Forsyth contended that Earl had incorrectly registered on the 1932 list, consequently the job for which he registered was not available. He further "averred the lists were suspended since 1932 because the Federal and State governments asserted, that the positions he sought had been filled through [Temporary Emergency Relief Administration] and the [Public Works Administration] took over administration of relief and laborer jobs were filled through those agencies."[49]

LABORER SUIT REVOLVES ON ELIGIBLE LIST

Referee to Hear Claim Disabled Veteran Sidetracked

Issues of fact in the action of Earl W. Burritt, 538 Cedarwood Terrace, to compel city officials and the Municipal Civil Service Commission to appoint him to a laborer job for which he registered are to be heard by a referee, through ruling of Supreme Court Justice Benn Kenyon.

After hearing argument of Louis I. Bunis, attorney for Burritt, and Corporation Counsel Charles B. Forsyth, who is opposing the move of Burritt, a member of Rochester Chapter 15, Disabled War Veterans of the World War, Justice Kenyon reserved decision, although implying he would grant an alternative writ of mandamus to permit hearing of the issues.

The Court told the attorneys for both sides the case might be submitted to former Justice Nathaniel Foote, official referee, or if he is not available, that another referee could be agreed upon.

Bunis said the mandamus suit is the battle of the disabled veterans to force the city administration to establish a new eligible list for Civil Service laborer positions. No new lists have been made since 1932, he said, the old list having been continued since, with suspension of registration. Bunis asserted rights of veterans have been cast aside for political purposes by the Democratic administration.

Bunis said that Burritt, a mechanic, registered for a job as motor flusher operator in March, 1932, and in 1933 submitted his name for the list as qualified for 19 positions. Since Apr. 9, 1934, ten men have been given jobs as motor flusher operators, he asserted.

Deputy Corporation Counsel Forsyth contended Burritt was improperly registered on the 1932 list. He argued no vacancies existed for the job for which he registered. Forsyth denied the rules governing eligible lists were changed for political reasons. He averred the lists were suspended since 1932 because the Federal and State governments through TERA and PWA took over administration of relief and laborer jobs were filled through those agencies.

New Laborers' List Asked by Veteran

Civil Service Action Put Off Until January 7

Hearing in the mandamus action brought by Earl W. Burritt, 538 Cedarwood Terrace, to compel city officials to establish a new eligible list for Civil Service laborer positions, was adjourned yesterday by Supreme Court Justice Marsh N. Taylor to Jan. 7.

Burritt is a member of Rochester Chapter 15, Disabled Veterans of the World War, and he brought the action through Louis I. Bunis, attorney for the disabled veterans, asserting the present city administration has not allowed the Municipal Civil Service Commission to establish a list since 1932.

The hearing was deferred because Deputy Corporation Counsel Charles B. Forsyth was engaged in trial term.

Former City Judge Named Suit Referee

Will Hear Arguments of Veteran for Job

Former City Judge Raymond E. Westbury has been appointed referee to hear issues of fact in the Supreme Court suit of Earl W. Burritt, 538 Cedarwood Terrace, to force city officials to give him a laborer job in the public works department.

The appointment, made known yesterday, was by Justice Benn Kenyon, who Jan. 8 heard argument of Louis I. Bunis, attorney for Burritt, and Deputy Corporation Counsel Charles B. Forsyth, representing the city manager, commissioner of public works and Municipal Civil Service Commission.

Bunis said the mandamus suit is the battle of disabled veterans of the World War to compel the city officials to establish a new eligible list for Civil Service laborer positions.

In Rochester, Earl participated in many civic organizations such as the American Legion Burton-Miller Post 238, Veterans of Foreign Wars James H. Lundgren Post 8949, the 27th Division Association, and Machine Gun Company, 108th Infantry, 27th Division association, having been elected president of the latter. Earl passed away on December 19, 1960, and is buried in the veterans section of Riverside Cemetery in Rochester, New York.

Facing page, left article, from the December 1934 *Democrat and Chronicle* (Rochester, NY); [50] facing page, right article, from the January 1935 *Democrat and Chronicle*;[51] article at left from the March 1935 *Democrat and Chronicle*. [52]

The *Hilton (NY) Record* reported that Frank Burritt was travelling to New York City to watch the 27th Division's Victory Parade in March 1919.[53] [below]

—Frank Burritt left last Friday for New York to witness the Victory Parade of the 27th Division of which his son, Earl Burritt, is a member.

Form 17_

REGISTRATION CARD | No. 333

1 Name in full _Elmer J. Bush_   Age, in yrs. **32**
(Given name)   (Family name)

2 Home address _44 Parkway, Roch._
(No.)   (Street)   (City)   (State)

3 Date of birth _Sept 30th 1894_
(Month)   (Day)   (Year)

4 Are you (1) a natural-born citizen, (2) a naturalized citizen, (3) an alien, (4) or have you declared your intention (specify which)? _Natural Born_

5 Where were you born? _Hilton   N. Y._
(Town)   (State)   (Nation)

6 If not a citizen, of what country are you a citizen or subject? _U. S._

7 What is your present trade, occupation, or office? _Sheet Metal Worker_

8 By whom employed? _Yawman Erby Co_
Where employed? _St. Paul St._

9 Have you a father, mother, wife, child under 12, or a sister or brother under 12, solely dependent on you for support (specify which)? _No_

10 Married or single (which)? _Single_   Race (specify which)? _White_

11 What military service have you had? Rank _No_ ; branch _No_ ;
years _No_ ; Nation or State _No_

12 Do you claim exemption from draft (specify grounds)? _No._

I affirm that I have verified above answers and that they are true.

Elmer J. Bush.
(Signature of boat.)

If person is of African descent, tear off this corner

54

ELMER J. BUSH
1894 – 1969

Elmer enlisted in the United States Army at the age of twenty-two in Rochester, New York. He was sent to Fort Slocum, New York, as a Private on August 1, 1917, before heading to the 68th Aero Squadron, Signal Corps, located at Kelly Field, Texas. He transferred into the 3d Aero Squadron, at the same base, on August 25, 1917. While his *New York State Abstracts of World War I Military Service* card does not reflect a change in unit or station, his brother's obituary (see Willard Edward Bush) confirms he moved with the 3d Aero Squadron to Post Field, Fort Sill, Oklahoma. The 3d Aero Squadron was re-designated Squadron A, as one of the many flying school detachments across the United States. He was promoted to Private First Class on December 1, 1917, then Corporal on March 1, 1918. Elmer was designated a "Chauffeur"[h] on January 9, 1919, prior to his discharge on March 8, 1919.

Vincent and Malinda (French) Bush welcomed their son, Elmer J. Bush, on September 30, 1894. Elmer grew up helping his parents on the family farm and was employed as a sheet metal worker at Yawman and Erbe Manufacturing Company before entering the army. After his discharge from the military, Elmer found employment in the clothing industry–first as a tailor, then as a cutter with Fashion Park, Inc. Elmer married Lois Gilhooly on May 6, 1926, in Rochester. He was a member of the Amalgamated Clothing Workers of America, Local No. 205. Elmer Bush passed away on August 19, 1969, and is interred at Holy Sepulchre Cemetery in Rochester, New York.

> **The following men were officially accepted yesterday:**
>
> ### ARMY.
>
> Harold P. B____om, 22, No. 162 Caroline street, aviatio____ Signal Corps.
>
> Carl L. North, 20, No. 49 Shelter street, aviation, Signal Corps.
>
> Walter P. Leschander, 22, No. 18 Kislingbury street, a____ation, Signal Corps.
>
> Elmer J. Bush, No. 44 Parkway, aviation, Signal Corps.

The *Democrat and Chronicle* (Rochester, NY) listed Elmer as officially accepted for military service on page thirteen of the July 31, 1917, edition.

---

[h] Chauffeur was more a designation than rank, indicating "any soldier, not a member of the Motor Transport Corps, who's primary job was to operate motor vehicles to include winch and gas trucks."
http://www.usmilitariaforum.com/forums/index.php?/topic/71495-need-some-help-on-this-wwi-rank/

3281
225.

REGISTRATION CARD | No. 30

1. Name in full *Willard Edward Bush* Age, in yrs. 28
   (Given name) (Family name)

2. Home address *92 Parkway* *Rochester* *N.Y.*
   (No.) (Street) (City) (State)

3. Date of birth *April* *21* *1889*
   (Month) (Day) (Year)

4. Are you (1) a natural-born citizen, (2) a naturalized citizen, (3) an alien, (4) or have you declared your intention (specify which)? *Natural Born*

5. Where were you born? *Fitton* *New York* *U.S.A.*
   (Town) (State) (Nation)

6. If not a citizen, of what country are you a citizen or subject? *U.S.A.*

7. What is your present trade, occupation, or office? *optical worker* 22

8. By whom employed? *Bausch & Lomb Co.*
   Where employed? *85 Paul St*

9. Have you a father, mother, wife, child under 12, or a sister or brother under 12, solely dependent on you for support (specify which)? *No*

10. Married or single (which)? *Single* Race (specify which)? *white*

11. What military service have you had? Rank *No* ; branch _____
    years _____ ; Nation or State _____

12. Do you claim exemption from draft (specify grounds)? *No*

I affirm that I have verified above answers and that they are true.

Willard E Bush
(Signature or mark)

If person is of African descent, tear off this corner.

★ WILLARD EDWARD BUSH ★
1889 – 1918

At twenty-nine-years-old Willard joined the United States Marine Corps on June 3, 1918, in Rochester, New York. Records indicate he was not inducted into service, instead enlisting at Parris Island, South Carolina, on June 13, 1918, and was assigned to Company V, Marine Barracks. On July 19, 1918, he was transferred to Company Z. On the evening of August 7, 1918, while at the Marine Barracks, Parris Island, South Carolina, Willard Edward Bush died of a "gunshot wound to the brain." At the end of an investigation, the incident was ruled a suicide. Official records indicate Willard's character would have been listed as "Fair" had he been discharged. Furthermore, official records and muster rolls suggest Willard would not have advanced with the rest of his company, many of whom were headed to the Overseas Depot, Marine Barracks, Quantico, Virginia. The Overseas Depot facilitated replacements to Marine Corps units serving in France.

Willard Edward Bush was born in Hilton, New York, on April 21, 1889, to Vincent and Malinda (French) Bush. Growing up in Hilton, Willard worked as a farm laborer and apprentice machinist before moving to Rochester, where he found employment as an optical worker at Bausch and Lomb Company on Saint Paul Street. Willard was buried on August 12, 1918, in Parma Union Cemetery in Parma, New York.

Willard Bush.

Hilton, Aug. 14.—The funeral of Willard Bush, son of Mr. and Mrs. Vincent Bush, was held this afternoon at the home on the West town line at 2 o'clock. He enlisted in the service June 7, 1918, and was in camp at Paris Island, where he died. He was 29 years of age and the first Hilton boy to give his life in the service. Besides the parents the survivors are one sister, of Hilton; one brother, of Rochester, and one brother in the service, Elmer Bush, in camp in Oklahoma. A military service was held at the burial at Parma Union cemetery.

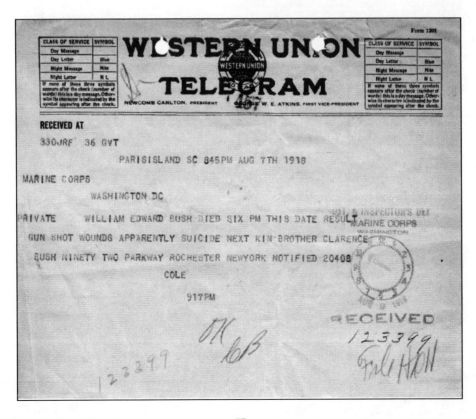

WESTERN UNION TELEGRAM

NEWCOMB CARLTON, PRESIDENT — W. E. ATKINS, FIRST VICE-PRESIDENT

Form 1201

RECEIVED AT

330JRF 36 GVT

PARISISLAND SC 845PM AUG 7TH 1918

MARINE CORPS

WASHINGTON DC

PRIVATE   WILLIAM EDWARD BUSH DIED SIX PM THIS DATE RESULT

GUN SHOT WOUNDS APPARENTLY SUICIDE NEXT KIN BROTHER CLARENCE

BUSH NINETY TWO PARKWAY ROCHESTER NEWYORK NOTIFIED 20408

COLE

917PM

RECEIVED

N. M. C. 321; A & I.

File No. 123399

UNITED STATES MARINE CORPS

I, Willard Edward Bush, born April 21, 1889

in Hilton, in the State of New York

desiring to enlist in the UNITED STATES MARINE CORPS for the duration of war do declare that I have neither wife nor child; that I am at least eighteen years of age; that I know of nothing wrong with my health or body that the doctor did not find when he examined me; that I am of good habits and character; that no judge or jury has ever found me guilty of a crime; that I have never deserted from the United States Army, Navy, Marine Corps, Coast Guard, or Revenue-Cutter Service, or been dishonorably discharged therefrom, or received a bad-conduct discharge therefrom; that I am by present occupation a Apprentice Machinist; and that I am a citizen of the United States.

I agree to accept from the United States such bounty, pay, rations, and clothing as are or may be established by law, and if discharged by sentence of general court-martial I agree to surrender my uniforms in exchange for civilian clothing.

Given at Rochester, N.Y., this 3rd. day of June, 1918

†WITNESS:

Charles S. Hayden   Willard Edward Bush
                                          (Signature of applicant, in full.)

Sergeant, U.S.M.C.   Provisions of selective draft

Forms rectg. 45 & 46 complied with   regulations complied with
                    DATE AND NATURE OF ANY WAIVER.

None.

Accepted, June 3, 1918, at Rochester, N.Y.

and transferred, June 7th, 1918, to M.B. Port Royal, S.C.

I, Willard Edward BUSH, DO HEREBY ACKNOWLEDGE to have voluntarily enlisted as a **PRIVATE** in the UNITED STATES MARINE CORPS, for * duration of war, unless sooner discharged by proper authority. And I do solemnly swear (or affirm) that I will bear true faith and allegiance to the United States of America; that I will serve them honestly and faithfully against all their enemies whomsoever; and that I will obey the orders of the President of the United States, and the orders of the officers appointed over me, according to the Rules and Articles for the Government of the Army, Navy, and Marine Corps of the United States. And I do further swear (or affirm) that all statements made by me, as now given in this record, are correct.

Willard Edward Bush
(Signature of recruit, in full.)

Subscribed and duly sworn to before me at MB Paris Island, S.C. this thirteenth day of June, A. D. 1918., and I CERTIFY that I minutely inspected the above-named man previous to his enlistment, and that he was entirely sober when enlisted; that, to the best of my judgment and belief, he fulfills all legal requirements; that, after fully informing him of the nature of the service he is to perform, I have enlisted him into the service of the United States under this contract of enlistment as duly qualified to perform the duties of an able-bodied marine, and in doing so have strictly observed the Regulations which govern the recruiting service; also that the prior service as shown on the reverse side has been verified by me personally from the man's discharge certificates, and that I am satisfied that his status as to citizenship is ‡ US

Major, U. S. M. C., Recruiting Officer.

Name and address of person to be notified in case of emergency, giving degree of relationship; if friend, so state:
Clarence Bush, 92 Park Way., Rochester, N.Y.   Brother.
(Name.)   (Address, including name of street and number of house.)   (Relationship.)

* Insert "duration of war," "term of four years," etc., as appropriate.
† To be signed by the officer or noncommissioned officer accepting the applicant on probation.
‡ Native born, use initials U. S.; naturalized, N. U. S.; alien, intention declared, A. D. I.

Front page of Willard Edward Bush's enlistment papers.[54]

January 31, 1921.

My dear Mr. Bush;

        I am directed by the Major General Commandant to forward to you herewith Victory Medal with ribbon, to which you are entitled as next of kin of the late Private Willard B. Bush, Marine Barracks, Parris Island, S.C.

        It is hoped that this insignia which is awarded you as the brother and next of kin of the late Private Bush, reaches you in good order, and I know that you will ever cherish its possession in precious memory of your dear brother, who died while in the service of his country.

        Will you please sign and return the enclosed receipt card, using the accompanying envelope, which requires no postage.

                Very sincerely,

                H. LAY,
            Lieutenant Colonel,
        Asst. Adjutant & Inspector.

Enclosures 3.

Mr. Clarence Bush,
92 Parkway,
Rochester, New York.

Willard's family applied for death benefits but were ineligible for compensation due to his serving less than sixty days. The Marine Corps forwarded a World War Victory Medal to Willard's brother, Clarence, who was listed as the next-of-kin. Additional records in the National Archives and Records Administration burial case files indicate his mother continued to seek compensation; all requests were denied.[55]

Serial No. ___ X___   **5 5**   Registration No. **147**

1 | Name in full   *Victor Chattin*   Age, in yrs. **21**
      (Given name)   (Family name)

2 | Home address   *27   Ranier. Rochester N.Y.*
      (No.)   (City or town)

3 | Date of birth   *July*   *23*   *1896*
      (Month)   (Day)   (Year)

4 | Where were you born?   *Hilton N.Y.*   *U.S.*
      (City or town)   (State)   (Nation)

5 | I am
1. A native of the United States.
2. A naturalized citizen.
3. An alien.
4. I have declared my intention.
5. A noncitizen citizen Indian.
(Strike out lines or words not applicable)

6 | If not a citizen, of what Nation are you a citizen or subject?

7 | Father's birthplace   *Hilton   N.Y.*   *U.S.*
      (City or town)   (State or province)   (Nation)

8 | Name of employer   *Eastman Kodak Co.*
Place of employment   *Kodak Park. -*
      (No.)   (City)   (County)   (State)

9 | Name of nearest relative   *Irene Chattin (Wife)*
Address of nearest relative   *27 Ranier St Rochester N.Y.*
      (No.)   (Street)   (City or town)   (State or Nation)

10 | Race—White, Negro, Indian, or Oriental.
(Strike out words not applicable)

I affirm that I have verified above answers and that they are true.

Victor Chattin

P. M. G. O.   (Signature or Mark of Registrant.)
Form 1 (blue)

REGISTRATION CARD.   3—5729

If person is of African descent, tear off this corner.

VICTOR WILLIAM CHATTIN
1896 – Unknown

Victor was inducted into the United States Army at Rochester, New York, on September 3, 1918, as a twenty-two-year-old Private. He was assigned to the 156th Depot Brigade and was discharged on December 2, 1918, due to the conclusion of the war.

Born in Hilton, New York, on July 23, 1896, to Chauncey and Mary (Cosman) Chattin, Victor was working as a farm laborer when he married Irene Bills on February 20, 1918, in a ceremony in Monroe County, New York. By 1920, Victor and Irene were both employed by Eastman Kodak Company's film division.

While married to Irene, Victor married Elvera Kruspe in a ceremony in Cuyahoga, Ohio, on December 26, 1922. Irene filed for divorce in which a judge's decision was "reserved" in the divorce action in 1923.[56] A final divorce decree was granted to Irene in January of 1924. On June 30, 1924, Victor and Elvera married again, this time in Summit County, Ohio; the couple would later divorce. Victor worked as a railroad conductor in Cleveland, Ohio, in 1930.

Victor exchanged marriage vows with Myrtle Hahn on December 23, 1935, in Ripley, Chautauqua County, New York. When he registered for the "Old Man Draft" in 1942 he was supporting his wife, Myrtle through his employment with the Bailey Company, a department store chain, in Cleveland, Ohio. The last know whereabouts of Victor and his wife, name unknown, was from the *Hilton (NY) Record*, published on July 30, 1953, which reported them living in Detroit, Michigan.

No further information could be found about Victor W. Chattin, including his date or place of death.

Victor's *Abstracts of World War I Military Service* card, from the New York State Archives.[57]

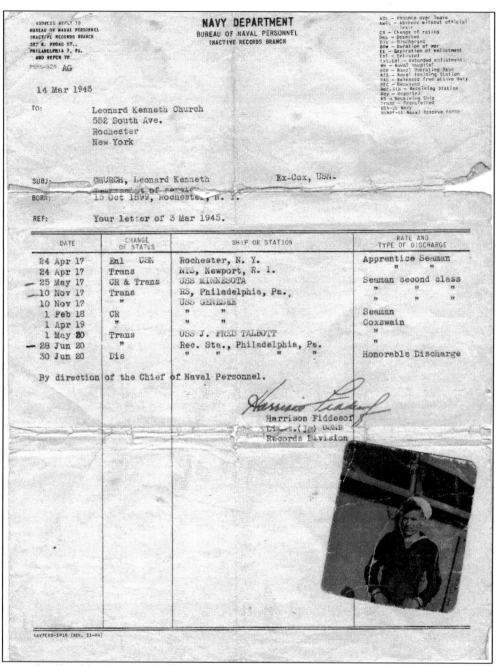

NAVY DEPARTMENT
BUREAU OF NAVAL PERSONNEL
INACTIVE RECORDS BRANCH

Leonard enlisted in the Navy before he was eligible—or required—to fill out a draft registration card. This summary of World War I service was provided by the Bureau of Naval Personnel in March 1945, at his request.[58]

LEONARD KENNETH CHURCH
1899 – 1976

Identified on the *Honor Roll* as Kenneth, but known as Casey, he enlisted at seventeen years old in the United States Navy in Rochester, New York, on April 24, 1917, as an Apprentice Seaman. He was sent to the Naval Training Station in Newport, Rhode Island, and remained there until May 25, 1917, when he changed rate to Seaman Second Class and was transferred to the USS *Minnesota*. On November 10, 1917, at the Receiving Station in Philadelphia, Pennsylvania, he was transferred to the USS *Genesee*. He changed rate to full Seaman on February 1, 1918, then to Coxswain on April 1, 1919. In January of 1920, records indicate the USS *Genesee* was in the Italian Province of Spalato, Dalmatia. Casey transferred to the USS *J. Fred Talbott* on May 1, 1920, before returning to the Receiving Station in Philadelphia, Pennsylvania, on June 28, 1920, where he was honorably discharged from active service on June 30, 1920.

Leonard Kenneth Church was born on October 16, 1899, to William D. and Florence Mary (Barlow) Church in New York. At the age of fourteen Casey was living with the Pisher family at their home on Ridge Road, near the hamlet of Parma Corners, in the town of Parma, New York.

Casey was married twice–his first marriage was to Genevieve A. Johnson and his second marriage to Marjorie M. Forgue was on July 23, 1938. Casey and Marjorie raised their family in Rochester where he worked in general construction as a carpenter and as an auto mechanic. Leonard Kenneth Church passed away on April 29, 1976, in Rochester, New York, and is buried in Riverside Cemetery.

Form 1   **1249**   REGISTRATION CARD   *1453*   No. *42*

1   Name in full   *William J Clapper*   Age, in yrs. *21*

2   Home address   *Hilton*   *N Y*

3   Date of birth   *October*   *26*   *1896*

4   Are you (1) a natural-born citizen, (2) a naturalized citizen, (3) an alien, (4) or have you declared your intention (specify which)?   *Natural Born*

5   Where were you born?   *Parma*   *N Y*   *USA*

6   If not a citizen, of what country are you a citizen or subject?

7   What is your present trade, occupation, or office?   *Farming*

8   By whom employed?   *Father*   Where employed?   *Parma*

9   Have you a father, mother, wife, child under 12, or a sister or brother under 12, solely dependent on you for support (specify which)?   *None*

10   Married or single (which)?   *Single*   Race (specify which)?

11   What military service have you had? Rank   *None*   ; branch   ; years   ; Nation or State

12   Do you claim exemption from draft (specify grounds)?

I affirm that I have verified above answers and that they are true.

William J Clapper
(Signature or mark)

If person is of African descent, tear off this corner.   *1453*

WILLIAM IRA CLAPPER
1895 – 1964

William Ira Clapper, at age twenty-two, was inducted into the United States Army in Rochester, New York, on March 4, 1918. Private Clapper was assigned to the 16th Provisional Squadron, Air Service, Signal Corps, in the Pacific Northwest. The 16th, later designated the 82d Spruce Squadron, was in the Yaquina Bay District, Spruce Production Division, in western Oregon. He remained in this area supporting the wood harvesting effort, needed for aircraft production, until his honorable discharge on January 13, 1919.

William Ira Clapper was born on October 26, 1895, in Hilton, New York, to Philo B. and Mary E. (Berridge) Clapper. Known as Ira, he grew up working on the family farm in Hilton alongside his father. Prior to entering military service Ira was working for the Railway Signal Company of Rochester. He married Nettie Smith on August 16, 1920, and they made their home on East Avenue in Hilton, where Ira would live and farm for the remainder of his days. Newspaper advertisements were frequently found in the *Democrat and Chronicle* (Rochester, NY) and the *Hilton (NY) Record* seeking qualified help to work on the farm or for the sale of farm equipment or supplies. William Ira Clapper passed away on October 20, 1964, and is buried in Parma Union Cemetery in Parma, New York.

350 Pupils Aid Hilton Area Harvest

Hilton—Approximately 350 junior and senior high school pupils are helping the farmers in the Hilton area to harvest their fruit. The first week of school, the pupils were dismissed at 3:15, but the demand for labor was so great that Principal C. W. Luffman has called school at 8:45 this week and dismissed the pupils at 12:30.

A great percent of the older boys work at night. They work until dark and then go into the barns to sort and pack the fruit.

The younger girls are picking lima beans for Ira Clapper who says that he will have work for them until a heavy frost comes. Others are picking tomatoes, peaches, apples, and prunes.

The demand for help is so great that the youngsters cannot begin to harvest the entire crop in this area. The farmers here have sent out an SOS to those men who work at night in the city, to ministers, to women who are not already employed in the canning factory, and to school teachers. Of the last named, all the men on the faculty are working afternoons and evenings and a majority of the women teachers are picking apples.

St. Paul's Lutheran Church Buys Farm

Impressive and exciting plans for the future are revealed in the announcement of the purchase of the 85 acre farm on East Avenue, owned by Frank Rose of Uniontown, Pennsylvania and farmed by Ira Clapper.

St. Paul's Lutheran Church has completed purchase of the cite for building expansion and development. The Rev. Theodore Kohlmeier, in speaking of the transactions, states that present plans call for the construction of a 2 or 3-room educational unit and to that end, consultations with architects from the firm of Benedict Ade of Rochester are underway.

It is expected that Mr. Clapper will continue on as tenant of the farm, utilizing the land not involved in the building program.

Hilton was going strong as a fruit-growing community in September 1941 when the call went out for additional harvest help. As the article from the *Times-Union* (Rochester, NY) describes (upper right), students and teachers from the local school cut classes to pick, sort, and process the harvest.[59]

In February 1960, Ira's days of farming would begin to subside as the family farm on East Avenue in the village of Hilton was sold to Saint Paul's Lutheran Church.[60] Ira slowly reduced the size and scope of his farm over the next few years. A barn located behind the church, slated for demolition, was struck by lightning on July 30, 1962.[61]

Form 1   *1680*   **REGISTRATION CARD**   No. *10*

1 Name in full   *George Clift*   Age, in yrs. *28*
(Given name)   (Family name)

2 Home address   *Kendall Orleans Co New York*
(No.) (Street) (City) (State)

3 Date of birth   *June 30 1888*
(Month) (Day) (Year)

4 Are you (1) a natural-born citizen, (2) a naturalized citizen, (3) an alien, (4) or have you declared your intention (specify which)? *Declarant*

5 Where were you born? *Esher England British*
(Town) (State) (Nation)

6 If not a citizen, of what country are you a citizen or subject? *British*

7 What is your present trade, occupation, or office? *Clerk*

8 By whom employed? *Ray J. Mulford*
Where employed? *Kendall N.Y.*

9 Have you a father, mother, wife, child under 12, or a sister or brother under 12, solely dependent on you for support (specify which)? *No one*

10 Married or single (which)? *Married*   Race (specify which)? *Caucasian*

11 What military service have you had? Rank *None*; branch _____
years _____; Nation or State _____

12 Do you claim exemption from draft (specify grounds)? *No*

I affirm that I have verified above answers and that they are true.

George Clift
(Signature or mark)

If person is of African descent, tear off this corner

66

GEORGE CLIFT
1888 – 1971

At the age of twenty-nine, George was inducted into the United States Army from Orleans County, New York, on June 27, 1918, and reported to Company G, 348th Infantry, 87th Division, at Camp Dix, New Jersey—where he was granted United States citizenship.[62] His *New York State Abstracts of World War I Military Service* card states he transferred to Company 27, 7th Battalion, 153d Depot Brigade, on August 10, 1918. The card shows him transferring, again, on November 6, 1918, to Company 47, 12th Training Battalion, 153d Depot Brigade. The card is unclear on his assignment or station from November 19, 1918, until his discharge on January 6, 1919.[63] A small note in the *Hilton (NY) Record* published on January 9, 1919, noted he recently received an honorable discharge while "doing duty in Hospital No 31 at Carlyle, Pa."[64]

> —George Clift of this village, who has been in Uncle Sams Army, doing duty in Hospital No 31 at Carlyle, Pa., has received an honorable discharge and returned here to join his wife, and baby which was born since he has been gone.

George Clift was born in Esher, Surrey, England, on June 30, 1888, to parents John and Elizabeth Jane (Fowler) Clift. In 1911 George was employed as a footman in Pangbourne, Berkshire, England, before emigrating to the United States aboard the RMS *Franconia*, arriving in Boston, Massachusetts, on October 10, 1911. In 1915 George was working as a farm laborer in Kendall, New York.

He married Florence Baxter in Hilton, New York, on January 4, 1917, and the couple made their home in Hilton where George found work in a factory as a "sawyer." George would later find work in a button factory and as a janitor at Hilton High School.[65]

George was active in the American Legion Hiscock-Fishbaugh Post 788 where he was selected as a delegate to the Monroe County American Legion convention in 1935 and was elected post commander in 1937. He was also a member of Hilton Lodge 940 of the Independent Order of Odd Fellows.[66] George Clift was a resident of Hilton until his death on April 29, 1971, and is buried in Parma Union Cemetery in Parma, New York.

George Clift Heads American Legion Post

George Clift has been elected commander of Hiscock-Fishbaugh Post, American Legion. Other officers of the Post are vice-commander, Charles Merritt, Rochester; adjutant, George Paulson; treasurer, Henry A. Smith; chaplain, J. Harlan Cooper; sergeant-at-arms, William Kirk; finance officer, Albert Mehle.

Hilton has invited the County Convention to meet next summer in this village, but the decision as to whether it will come to Hilton or Honeoye Falls is left to the discretion of the County Executive Committee.

The following members of the local Post attended the county convention which met Saturday in Greece Memorial Hall; Herman Worden, A. L. Kirchgessner, Albert Mehle, Charles Merritt, William Kirk, George Paulson.

* * *

Golfers are developing a sixth sense — a mathematical one—in blind bogy tournaments. A Mr. George Clift entered the blind bogie at Westridge, calmly picked a 25 handicap, then shot a 101 and net 76 — which was just right.

Serial No. *31* *106* X Registration No. *31*

1. Name in full *Fred William Collins*
   (Given name) (Family name) Age, in yrs. *21*

2. Home address *Clarkson N.Y.*
   (No.) (street) (City or town) (State)

3. Date of birth *Apr.* *23* *1897*
   (Month) (Day) (Year)

4. Where were you born? *Clarkson N.Y. U.S.A.*
   (City or town) (State) (Nation)

5. I am { 1. A native of the United States.
   2. A naturalized citizen.
   3. An alien.
   4. I have declared my intention.
   5. A noncitizen or citizen Indian.
   (Strike out lines or words not applicable)

6. If not a citizen, of what Nation are you a citizen or subject?

7. Father's birthplace *Parma N.Y. U.S.A.*
   (City or town) (State or province) (Nation)

8. Name of employer *(Farm work)*
   Place of employment *Around Clarkson N.Y.*
   (No.) (Street) (City or town) (State)

9. Name of nearest relative *(Father) Theodore Collins*
   Address of nearest relative *Clarkson, N.Y.*
   (No.) (Street) (City or town) (State or Nation)

10. Race—White, Negro, Indian, or Oriental
    (Strike out words not applicable)

I affirm that I have verified above answers and that they are true.

Fred William Collins
(Signature or Mark of Registrant.)

If person is of African descent, tear off this corner.

P. M. G. O.
Form 1 (blue)

REGISTRATION CARD.   3—5759

FREDERICK WILLIAM COLLINS
1897 – 1947

Fred served in both World War I and World War II. Inducted into the United States Army as a Private at twenty-one years of age at Spencerport, New York, on September 3, 1918, Fred was part of the Field Artillery Replacement Draft. He was sent to Camp Jackson, located in Columbia, South Carolina, where he transferred to the 19th Battery of the October Automatic Replacement Draft, on October 7, 1918. He was sent overseas, departing Newport News, Virginia, on October 28, 1918, aboard the SS *Powhatan*. Records are inconclusive, but suggest Private Collins remained at a base depot in France, never being assigned to a field unit.[67] He was assigned to Bordeaux Casual Company 82 when he returned on the USS *Pastores*, departing Bordeaux, France, on April 21, 1919, and was discharged on May 17, 1919.

> —Fred Collins, son of Mr. and Mrs. Theodore Collins, arrived home last Monday from Camp Upton, at which place he had been for 15 days after arriving from overseas. He left Camp Jackson for France and arrived there about the time the armistice was signed, so did not engage in any battles.

Collins enlisted in the United States Army on April 29, 1942, entering at the rank of Private, and was assigned to Camp Campbell, Kentucky, where he remained until his honorable discharge on September 17, 1943. The American Legion Hiscock-Fishbaugh Post 788 sent a copy of the *Hilton (NY) Record* to Fred in 1942 while he was on active duty. Fred wrote to the editor of the *Hilton Record* to offer his appreciation on hearing news from around town. Corporal Collins informed Mr. Cooper his elbow was broken, and he was anticipating a five-week stay in the New Cantonment Hospital at Fort Knox, Kentucky, having already been in-residence for three weeks.[68]

One Dead, Train Hits Hamlin Truck

One Critically Hurt

George W. King, 62, of Redman Road, Hamlin, was killed at the Redman Road crossing of the Rome-Watertown railroad Tuesday, when the truck he was driving was demolished. Riding with him and in dangerous condition in Brockport Hospital is Fred Collins, also of Hamlin, who suffered a fractured pelvis, cuts and bruises. He was pulled out of the wreckage after being carried 500 feet. According to deputies King was killed when he was thrown clear of his truck.

The engineer claims that he blew a warning whistle but King failed to heed it. The crossing is unguarded.

Mr. King is survived by his wife, Ora Collins King; two brothers, Wilbur King of Brockport and Harry King of Hamlin; a sister, Mrs. Sarah Fox, and several nieces and nephews. Funeral services will be conducted Friday at 2 p.m. in the King home. Burial will be in Parma Union Cemetery.

Frederick William Collins was born to Theodore W. and Oranna Christina (Pier) on April 23, 1897, in Clarkson, New York. Growing up in the farming community of Clarkson, Fred found work in the local area as a farm laborer, storage laborer, and worked for the state highway department. Fred passed away in his home on Brooks Avenue in Hilton on March 13, 1947, and is buried in Parma Union Cemetery in Parma, New York.

Collins was critically injured when the truck he was riding in, driven by his brother-in-law, failed to yield to a train on the Rome, Watertown, and Ogdensburg Railroad ("Hojack" Line) in Hamlin, New York, on October 9, 1945. George King, husband to Fred Collins' sister, Ora, was killed in the crash.[69] [left]

Form 1 1284 **REGISTRATION CARD** 350 77

1	Name in full _Lester Collans_ (Given name) (Family name)	Age, in yrs. 27

2 | Home address: _Walker_ (No.) (Street) _N Y_ (City) (State)

3 | Date of birth _January 11 1890_ (Month) (Day) (Year)

4 | Are you (1) a natural-born citizen, (2) a naturalized citizen, (3) an alien, (4) or have you declared your intention (specify which)? _natural Born_

5 | Where were you born? _Parma_ (Town) _N Y_ (State) _usa_ (Nation)

6 | If not a citizen, of what country are you a citizen or subject? ....

7 | What is your present trade, occupation, or office? _Farming_

8 | By whom employed? _Henry White_
Where employed? _Hamlin_

9 | Have you a father, mother, wife, child under 12, or a sister or brother under 12, solely dependent on you for support (specify which)? _Mother_

10 | Married or single (which)? _Single_ Race (specify which)? _White_

11 | What military service have you had? Rank ....; branch ....;
years ....; Nation or State ....

12 | Do you claim exemption from draft (specify grounds)? ....

C A

I affirm that I have verified above answers and that they are true.

Lester Collins
(Signature of mark.)

If person is of African descent, tear off this corner

70

LESTER D. COLLINS
1890 – 1927

Twenty-seven-year-old Lester was inducted into the United States Army from Spencerport, New York, on September 26, 1917, at the rank of Private. He was assigned to Company I, Military Police, 303d Train Headquarters and Military Police, 78th Division, at Camp Dix in Wrightstown, New Jersey. He transferred to Company A, 325th Infantry, 82d Division, on November 11, 1917, and was promoted to Corporal on December 11, 1917. He was sent overseas with Company H, 325th Infantry, from Camp Upton, New York, on April 25, 1918, aboard the SS *Khyber*, which departed from New York, New York. Lester's regiment participated the Saint-Mihiel Operation, September 12-16, 1918, and the Meuse-Argonne Operation, October 6-31, 1918.[70] He returned from France aboard the USS *Pastores*, embarking from Bordeaux, France, on January 31, 1919. He arrived in the United States on February 15, 1919, and was discharged on March 10, 1919.

Lester D. Collins was born on January 11, 1890, to Alonzo L. and Flora (Pier) Collins. He was working in Hamlin, New York, as a farm laborer for Henry White when he registered for the draft on June 5th, 1917. He returned to his work on the farm after his discharge from military service. On July 17, 1927, at the age of thirty-seven, Lester was killed in an automobile accident on West Town Line Road in Hilton and is buried in Parma Union Cemetery in Parma, New York.[71]

Goes to Jail After Leaving Hospital

Martin Balliet, of Parma, was arrested for manslaughter, second degree, yesterday when he was released from St. Mary's Hospital, where he had been confined since July 17th with injuries received in an automobile accident.

He was taken to the Monroe County Jail, where he will be kept pending an investigation by the Grand Jury of charges that his negligence was responsible for the death of Lester Collins, of Curtis road, Parma, who was killed instantly in the July 17th accident. According to authorities, Balliet was driving his car in the Parma town line road when it crashed into a machine parked in front of the home of Fred Marlowe. Collins was riding with Balliet.

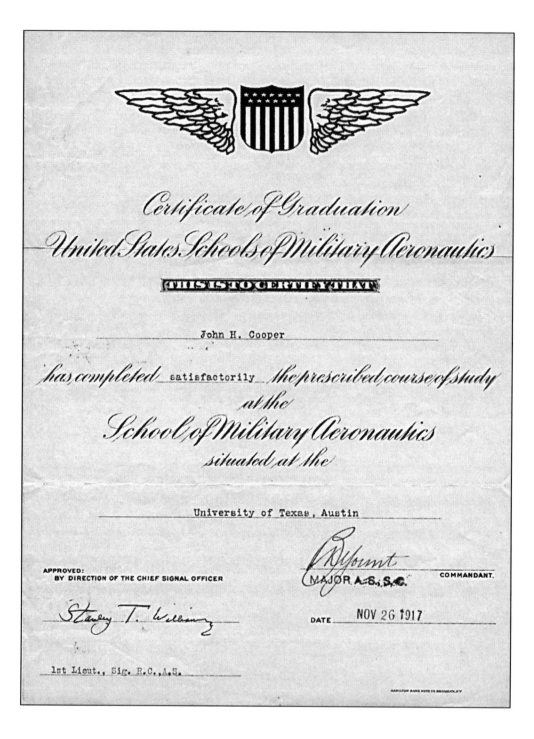

Certificate of Graduation

United States Schools of Military Aeronautics

THIS IS TO CERTIFY THAT

John H. Cooper

has completed satisfactorily the prescribed course of study

at the

School of Military Aeronautics

situated at the

University of Texas, Austin

APPROVED:
BY DIRECTION OF THE CHIEF SIGNAL OFFICER

MAJOR A.S., S.C.   COMMANDANT.

DATE   NOV 26 1917

1st Lieut., Sig. R.C., A.S.

JOHN HARLAN COOPER
1892 – 1978

Harlan enlisted in the United States Army Signal Corps on April 24, 1917, at Columbus Barracks, Columbus, Ohio, at the age of twenty-four. He was sent to Kelly Field, near San Antonio, Texas, assigned to the 24th Aero Squadron, and felt right at home when he discovered cans of Peck & Pratt apples.[72] [left] On August 28,

—J. Harlan Cooper who is still in the aero squadron at Kelly Field near San Antonia, Texas, writes that he recently saw some cans of apples there from Peck & Pratt's factory in this village.

1917, he transferred to the 84th Aero Squadron and began ground school at the School of Military Aeronautics, located at the University of Austin, Texas. He promoted to Private First Class on September 3, 1917, and completed the course on November 26, 1917. He was discharged on January 27, 1918, to accept his commission as a Second Lieutenant and remained at Kelly Field for the duration of the war. [below left][73][right][74] In a telegram received by his family, dated May 28, 1918, Lieutenant Cooper was reported injured in an airplane accident, suffering a fracture of his right clavicle, a possible shoulder dislocation, and a laceration over his left eye with minor bruises. He was admitted to the hospital at Kelly Field where his injuries were considered not serious with the expectation he would be released the first week of June in 1918. He was discharged from the Regular Army on March 13, 1919, and transferred to the Officer's Reserve Corps. He was appointed a First Lieutenant of the Aviation Section of the Signal Corps, on flying status, one month later on April 18, 1919.[75] When he resigned his commission from the Officer Reserve Corps is unknown. What is known is that Lieutenant Cooper and his flying buddies traveled to California in the spring of 1919[right][76] where they homesteaded land–this from a letter postmarked from Long Beach, California.[77]

—Lieutenant John Harlan Cooper after having been in the air service at Camp Kelley, San Antonia, Texas, the past two years, has received his honorable discharge and a telegram was received from him by his father John E. Cooper on Tuesday morning dated at Long Beach, California.

John Harlan Cooper was born in Middleport, New York, on December 3, 1892, and his parents, John E. and Sarah Mae (Rose) Cooper moved the family to Hilton, New York, in 1897. Known as Harlan, he attended Hilton High School but graduated from East High School in Rochester, New York, in the spring of 1911, having participated in his school's Glee Club and the class baseball team.[78] An undergraduate student at Purdue University for electrical engineering[79] from 1911[80] until 1914, he was a member of Sigma Phi Epsilon fraternity[81] and the Civil Engineering Society,[82] but left Purdue without

earning a degree.[83] The 1915 New York State Census recorded Harlan living at home with his parents and sister, employed as a telephone lineman.[84] A September 1916 edition of the *Hilton (NY) Record* reported that Harlan had been "employed by the General Railway Signal Co. of Rochester for several months...left for Chicago, to report to the branch office there, and will assist in installing one of their signal systems at a junction of three railroads near that city. He expects to be absent several months."[85]

After the war he returned to Hilton and by 1921 was an assistant to the district manager of both the Rochester Gas & Electric Company and Hilton Telephone Company. Harlan married Luella Maude Cross on June 7, 1924, and they made their home in Hilton where he continued to immerse himself in his community through fraternal and civic organizations.

He was master of Clio Lodge No. 779, Free & Accepted Masons, in 1930 and later became district deputy grand master of the First Monroe District Masons in 1939. A member of the American Legion Hiscock-Fishbaugh Post 788 of Hilton, Harlan also served as post commander.

Hilton Baptists Pledge $30,000

Pledges for funds to remodel the 65-year-old Hilton Baptist Church have reached $30,000, J. Harlan Cooper, chairman of the building fund, said yesterday. Twenty-five teams, working to achieve the $50,-000 goal, will continue canvassing church members throughout this week, Cooper said.

Teams headed by Ralph Palmer and Burton Hendershot have raised the greatest totals so far, Cooper announced. At a victory dinner at the church at 8 p. m. Friday, it is expected the full amount will be subscribed.

Harlan was on the Board of Education for the Hilton School District in 1932 and took part in a decision to reduce salaries for a district with 400 pupils and eighteen teachers.[86] In the same year he became chairman of the depositors committee, which was responsible for the reopening of the State Bank of Hilton. The bank had closed its doors on December 16, 1931, to protect its assets and six months later, on June 18, 1932, reopened for business to the community.[87]

In 1933 Harlan became a district manager for the Rochester Gas & Electric Company and in 1935 manager of the Hilton Telephone Company, becoming president of the latter in 1936. On the civic front Harlan was chairman of the building fund at the Hilton Baptist Church and, in 1937, elected to the position of chairman of the board of trustees. He sang in the church's choir for many years and spearheaded a fundraising campaign in 1949, allowing the church to remodel the sanctuary in 1952.[88] [above]

A successful fundraiser and manager, he used his skills for several years as Parma's chairman for both the American Red Cross and Community Chest campaigns and was recognized in the *Democrat and Chronicle* (Rochester, NY) for exceeding the goal, meeting 150 percent of Parma's Community Chest quota in 1953.[89]

Harlan was president of the Brockport Club of Kiwanis International in 1951, and elected lieutenant governor of the Genesee Kiwanis Division in 1954.

He retired from Rochester Gas & Electric in 1957 and moved with his wife to Clearwater, Florida, where Harlan continued his civic involvements. He was a member of Saint Paul's United Methodist Church in Largo, Florida; the Egypt Temple Shrine in Tampa, Florida; was president of the High-12 International Club of Clearwater in 1967 (an organization of Master Masons that support Masonic causes with emphasis on patriotic events and youth); and was commander of the Green Acres Barracks, World War I Veterans No. 3359, in Clearwater.[90]

For twenty-one years Harlan and his wife traveled between Clearwater and Hilton, visiting friends and relatives—events that were highlighted in the *Hilton Record* throughout the years. Thirteen days before his passing he received his sixty-year pin and certificate at East Gate Lodge in Florida for his continuous membership with the Masons. John Harlan Cooper passed away on May 28, 1978, in Clearwater; he is buried in Serenity Gardens Memorial Park, in Largo, Florida.

Hilton Phone Staff Headed by Cooper

Hilton Telephone Company elected these officers and directors: President, J. Harlan Cooper; vice-president, G. Y. Webster; secretary, Corrine K. Blair; treasurer, Joseph Ingham; directors, Joseph Ingham, Edward Shutts, Fred Peck, Corrine K. Blair, A. G. Klock, Mrs. J. E. Cooper, J. H. Cooper, Eugene Collamey and George Y. Webster.

Davison Named Chief Of Hilton Phone Firm

Donald F. Davison of Spencerport, president and manager of the Ogden Telephone Company, will assume the duties of president and manager of the Hilton Telephone Company on June 1, when the resignation of J. Harlan Cooper, present manager, becomes effective.

Cooper is district manager of the Rochester Gas & Electric Corporation. The RG&E will open an office in the building owned by O. A. Green, formerly the Fraser block, with an entrance on Hovey Street.

J. Harlan Cooper had a long run at the Hilton Telephone Company from his start in the early 1920s. He was elected president of the firm in January 1936.[91] [above left]

On June 1, 1945, Harlan resigned as president of the telephone company, devoting his full attention to his role as district manager for Rochester Gas & Electric Company.[92] [above right]

Harlan's flying buddy, Wallace B. Harwood of Brownsville, Texas, brought his family to Hilton to visit the Coopers in 1934. The photo at right was printed in the June 2, 1934, *Times-Union* (Rochester, NY).[93]

Buddies of War Days Reunited

Two men who defied death daily testing Army planes at Kelly Field, Tex., during the World War and then dared fortune homesteading in California are having a reunion this weekend in Hilton, after a 15-year separation. Wallace B. Harwood of Brownesville, Tex., and family arrived yesterday to be the guests of Mr. and Mrs. J. Harlan Cooper of Hilton. The picture shows Mr. Cooper (left) now manager of the Hilton Telephone Company, manager of the Hilton Record and district manager of the Rochester Gas & Electric Corporation, with Mr. Harwood in their training days at Kelly Field.

Form 1	REGISTRATION CARD	No.

1. Name in full _Raymond C. Corbit_ (Given name) (Family name) — Age, in yrs. **29**

2. Home address _Barnard_ (No.) (Street) (City) _N.Y._ (State)

3. Date of birth _August_ (Month) _31st_ (Day) _1888_ (Year)

4. Are you (1) a natural-born citizen, (2) a naturalized citizen, (3) an alien, (4) or have you declared your intention (specify which)? _Natural born_

5. Where were you born? _West Greece_ (Town) _N.Y._ (State) _U.S.A._ (Nation)

6. If not a citizen, of what country are you a citizen or subject?

7. What is your present trade, occupation, or office? _Book Keeper_

8. By whom employed? _Shafer Bros._ Where employed? _Rochester_

9. Have you a father, mother, wife, child under 12, or a sister or brother under 12, solely dependent on you for support (specify which)? _None_

10. Married or single (which)? _Single_ Race (specify which)? _Caucasian_

11. What military service have you had? Rank _None_; branch _____ years _____; Nation or State _____

12. Do you claim exemption from draft (specify grounds)? _None_

I affirm that I have verified above answers and that they are true.

Raymond C. Corbit.
(Signature or mark)

If person is of African descent, tear off this corner.

RAYMOND CHARLES CORBIT
1887-1944

On November 21, 1917, thirty-year-old Raymond was inducted into the United States Army at Spencerport, New York, and assigned to the 153d Depot Brigade. He transferred to Company F, 7th Infantry, 3d Division, on December 14, 1917, promoting to Corporal on January 14, 1918, and Sergeant on March 1, 1919.

Raymond left Hoboken, New Jersey, on April 6, 1918, aboard the SS *America* bound for Europe and while overseas was recognized for his meritorious service.[94] [below] He attended Army Candidate School starting October 2, 1918, and was assigned to the 331st Infantry, 83d Division, on November 6, 1918. He transferred to the 54th Guard Company, Army Service Corps, on November 22, 1918. Raymond embarked from Bordeaux, France, on July 5, 1919, on the SS *Floridian* and arrived in Brooklyn, New York on July 15, 1919. Raymond was discharged on July 23, 1919.

HEADQUARTERS 3RD DIVISION AMERICAN EXPEDITIONARY FORCES

8. July 1919.

GENERAL ORDERS,
No. 22.

The Commanding General desires to record in General Orders the valor and devotion to duty of these officers and men of the 3rd Division. Their individual deeds, summed up, have created the glorious record enjoyed by the Marne Division, from those unforgetable days at Château-Thierry, in the defense of Paris, to the Victory Drive which began on the banks of the Marne and continued relentlessly until its brilliant conclusion in the Argonne before Sedan:

Corbett, Raymond, Corporal, 541730, Company "F", 7th Infantry. On July 15th, 16th and 17th, 1918, at Fossoy, by his untiring and unselfish devotion to his work and by repeatedly risking his life under shell fire, was able to organize and maintain, unbroken, a liaison system by runners, between seventeen different organizations, hastily sent to positions for the defense of the right flank of the 7th Infantry attacked by the enemy.

Raymond Charles Corbit was born on August 31, 1887, in Greece, New York, to James and Mary L. (Pitcher) Corbit. Five years after leaving military service R.C., as he was known, married Lillian Pfahl on November 8, 1924, in Greece and earned a living as a bookkeeper for Schafer Brothers. He continued in their employ promoting from a salesman, to sales manager, and eventually president of the organization.

A resident of the town of Parma, New York, for fifty-three years,[95] R.C. was active in his community, serving on the Planning Board in addition to being on the committee that determined the town's zoning laws. He was on the New York State Selective Service Draft Board 559 of Monroe County during World War II.[96] He was a member and post commander of the American Legion Ferris-Goodridge Post 330 in Spencerport and vice commander of the Monroe County American Legion. Raymond passed away on September 23, 1944, and is buried in Parma Corners Cemetery in Parma, New York.

Ferris-Goodridge Post, under Corbit's charge, assumed duties of decorating graves when the Grand Army of the Republic (G.A.R.) Post had only one surviving member remaining.[97] [right]

One G. A. R. Man

Spencerport, May 29—Plans have been completed by Ferris-Goodridge Post, American Legion, with Raymond Corbit, commander, for the observance of Memorial Day. In accordance with the custom of past years, delegations from Ferris-Goodridge Post will decorate the graves in the Spencerport cemeteries and those in the surrounding vicinity. For years this task was in charge of the members of John H. Martindale Post, G. A. R., but there is now but one surviving member of the organization, Sigmund Stettner of Ogden, who is 87 years of age and because of failing health will not be able to participate in the Memorial Day exercises. In Masonic Temple the exercises of the day will take place.

New Administration Takes Charge of Legion Work

Officers of Monroe County American Legion inducted into office last night, from left, R. Leighton Gridley, adjutant; Dr. Joseph G. Spoto, vicecommander; Stalham S. Baker, commander; Raymond Corbit, vicecommander; George K. Beach, treasurer.

Corbit was inducted as Monroe County American Legion Vice Commander in July 1932.[98]

Draft Board 559 Asked to Resign

State Selective Service dissatisfaction with progress in reclassifying 3-A registrants led to a demand from the state for resignations of all members of Draft Board 559, one resigned member revealed last night.

Four of the members resigned, with the fifth, Herbert W. Bramley of Brockport, the chairman, refusing to take the step, it was said. Two of the resignations have been accepted, the former member said.

Resigned are George B. Draper of Spencerport, retired deputy city corporation counsel, and Thomas Toal, a farmer of Greece.

2 Still on Board

Other members, who Draper said submitted resignations at the same time he and Toal did, are Paul Hanks, Brockport, and Raymond C. Corbit, 4702 Ridge Rd. W., Greece, who still are on the Board.

GEORGE B. DRAPER   **THOMAS TOAL**

According to Draper, Maj. Richard Quaintance of Syracuse, upstate occupational adviser for the state Selective Service, demanded resignation of the entire board Mar. 8, about a week after he complained to them about progress in reclassifying the 3-A cases. The 3-A calssification, providing deferment on the basis of dependency claims, was abolished in February.

Bramley said last night he refused to resign, but he referred all other questions to Major Quaintance.

Haste Asked in Talk

Draper declared the board had in early March between 800 and 1,000 cases to reclassify. Major Quaintance came to the board and asked if the work could not be completed in 10 days, Draper said, and the board agreed "to do the best it could."

"He came back a week later and put the resignations in front of us," Draper declared.

Draper denied that any questions other than the progress of reclassification were involved in the matter. He said the board acted in complete harmony in its decisions.

"We did nothing more than was permitted by the regulations and did, in the opinion of the board, what was proper in deferring men," Draper said. "We used our judgment in determining whether a man was more useful in civilian life than in the Army."

All 3-As Reclassified

Since the question arose, Draper said, all the 3-A cases in the board have been reclassified.

Toal, who is 79, said he received notification of the acceptance of his resignation Mar. 25. He said he had asked to be relieved of his duties. Draper, who is 75, said acceptance of his resignation was received about the same time.

It was reported last night that Rolland Reitz of Big Ridge Road, a farmer, and Omer Langford, an oculist of Stone Road, Greece, had been appointed to Board 559 to replace the resigned pair.

Board 559, with headquarters in Town Hall, Greece, covers the towns of Greece, Sweden, Parma, Hamlin, Ogden and Clarkson. Bramley, Draper and Toal are original members of the board, and Hanks and Corbit were added late last year because of pressure of work in the large territory.

Raymond Corbit was a member of World War II Draft Board 559 in April 1944, with responsibility for the towns of Clarkson, Greece, Hamlin, Ogden, Parma, and Sweden. The board was asked to resign amid complaints from the State of New York for their delay in processing requests for deferment on the basis of dependency. The classification category 3-A had been abolished in February 1944.

Form 1 568

REGISTRATION CARD No. 1336

1 Name in full _Miles 3059 Corbitt_
   (Given name) (Family name)

Age, in yrs. _25_

2 Home address _Jerome, Ariz_
   (No.) (Street) (City) (State)

3 Date of birth _July 19 1892_
   (Month) (Day) (Year)

4 Are you (1) a natural-born citizen, (2) a naturalized citizen, (3) an alien, (4) or have you declared your intention (specify which)? _natural born citizen_

5 Where were you born? _Charlott New York._
   (Town) (State) (Nation)

6 If not a citizen, of what country are you a citizen or subject?

7 What is your present trade, occupation, or office? _carpenter 29_

8 By whom employed? _Gilmore, Switters, Chesney._
   Where employed? _Jerome_

9 Have you a father, mother, wife, child under 12, or a sister or brother under 12, solely dependent on you for support (specify which)? _No._

10 Married or single (which)? _Single_ Race (specify which)? _Caucasian_

11 What military service have you had? Rank _no_ ; branch _—_ ;
    years _—_ ; Nation or State _—_ ;

12 Do you claim exemption from draft (specify grounds)? _No._

I affirm that I have verified above answers and that they are true.

Miles Corbitt
(Signature or mark)

If person is of African descent, tear off this corner

80

MILES HAROLD CORBITT
1891(1892) – 1963

Miles was either twenty-five or twenty-six years old when he enrolled in the Naval Reserve Force at Puget Sound, Washington, on March 6, 1918, serving aboard the Receiving Ship in Philadelphia, Pennsylvania, until April 6, 1918. He was assigned to the Naval Air Station in Pauillac, France, until April 28, 1918, at which time he moved to Paimboeuf Naval Air Station in Paimboeuf, France, where he served until November 11, 1918. He was placed on inactive duty as a Carpenter's Mate, First Class, on December 21, 1918. [below][100]

Miles Harold Corbitt was born in Charlotte, New York, to Robert C. and Lucille (Baxter) Corbitt on July 19th of either 1891 or 1892. The birth year listed on the many primary and secondary source records is inconsistent, including documents Miles signed. His World War I draft registration indicates 1892 but his World War II draft registration indicates 1891.[101] Even though his headstone lists 1891, his true birth

> —Miles Corbitt, who has just returned from eight months service in France in naval aviation is the guest of his cousin C. O. Crook and family. He is a son of the late Robert Corbitt, who at one time resided in Hilton.

year remains unconfirmed. Living in Yavapai, Arizona, in 1917, he was working for Gilmore, Schwitters, and Chesney, a contracting firm located in Jerome, Arizona, that performed trestle, culvert, and concrete work for the Arizona Central Railway Company (a subsidiary of the Santa Fe Railway).

In 1920, after leaving naval service, Miles lived in Great Falls, Montana, where he worked as a carpenter. Having honed his skills, he returned to New York, continuing his work as a carpenter in Spencerport, New York. He married Alice Gertrude Cosgrove on the 18th of November 1925. Eventually, Miles left the carpenter and building trade for the employ of Bausch and Lomb in Rochester, New York. Miles died on September 6, 1963, and is buried in Fairfield Cemetery in Spencerport, New York.

Miles Corbit, front right, is seen with John Murphy, George Bigger, Lucius Bagley, and George Paulson, left to right, as they form up in the village of Hilton on what is presumed to be the August 2nd Town of Parma "Welcome Home" celebration for the war veterans in 1919.[102]

Serial No. *38*　　*77*　X　Registration No. *38*

1　Name in full　*John Leo Crook*　Age, in yrs. *21*
　　(Given name)　　　　(Family name)

2　Home address　*Hilton　N. Y.*
　　(No.)　(Street)　(City or town)　(State)

3　Date of birth　*Nov.　13　1896*
　　(Month)　(Day)　(Year)

4　Where were you born?　*Hilton　N. Y.　U. S. A.*
　　(City or town)　(State)　(Nation)

5　I am { 1. A native of the United States.
　　2. A naturalized citizen.
　　3. An alien.
　　4. I have declared my intention.
　　5. A noncitizen or citizen Indian.
　　(Strike out lines or words not applicable)

6　If not a citizen, of what Nation are you a citizen or subject?

7　Father's birthplace　*Hilton　N. Y.　U. S. A.*
　　(City or town)　(State or province)　(Nation)

8　Name of employer　*Work for self　clothing merch.*
　Place of employment　*Hilton　N. Y.*
　　(No.)　(Street)　(City or town)　(State)

9　Name of nearest relative　*Mother　Mrs. Bessie Crook*
　Address of nearest relative　*Hilton　N. Y.*
　　(No.)　(Street)　(City or town)　(State or Nation)

10　Race— White, negro, oriental, Indian, noncitizen, citizen.
　　(Strike out words not applicable)

I affirm that I have verified above answers and that they are true.

John Leo Crook
(Signature or Mark of Registrant.)

If person is of African descent, tear off this corner.

P. M. G. O.
Form 1 (blue)

REGISTRATION CARD.　5—5739

JOHN LEO CROOK
1896 – 1963

John was twenty-one-years-old when inducted into the United States Army from Rochester, New York, on September 3, 1918, and assigned to Battery B, 1st Regiment, Field Artillery Replacement Depot, Camp Jackson, South Carolina. He remained with the depot until December 10, 1918, when he transferred to Battery D, 60th Field Artillery, promoting to Private First Class on January 18, 1919. John continued his assignment with the 60th Field Artillery until his discharge on February 12, 1919.

John Leo Crook was born on November 13, 1896, to Chauncey O. and Bessie (Flood) Crook, in Hilton, New York. John worked as an insurance agent for over thirty years and was concurrently active in politics. A Parma Republican committeeman, John was elected to the positions of councilman, justice of the peace and supervisor in the town of Parma.

While supervisor, John served on the Monroe County Board of Supervisors as chairman of the Public Health and Sanitation Committee, was a member of the Highway, Ways and Means, Salaries and Personnel, Parks and Recreation and Erroneous Assessments committees.[103]

Hilton

New officers of Hiscock-Fishbaugh Post, American Legion, were installed in office last week by Ray Corbett, commander of Spencerport Post. New officers and committees are: Commander, John L. Crook; vicepresident, Warner K. Heffron; adjutant, Harlan Cooper; treasurer, Henry A. Smith; financial secretary, Alton V. Sleight; chaplain, William Kirk; county committee, A. V. Sleight Herman Worden, Bert Perry; finance committee, Merton Thompson, George Clift, A. J. Wadsworth; membership committee, Herman Worden, Frank Randall, Henry A. Smith; welfare, George Paulson, William A. Kirchgessner, Frank Randall; service officer, George Bigger; sergeant-at-arms, Dewey DeHey; color bearers, William Langwager and John Morehouse; color guards, William Pilon and Frank Turgoa.

John married Ruth W. (nee Blair) Johnson on January 1, 1960, and the couple made their home in Hilton. He was very involved in his community and local civic organizations as both a member and past master of the Clio Lodge No. 779, Free & Accepted Masons, a past commander of the American Legion Hiscock-Fishbaugh Post 788 [left][104] and was a member of Hilton Baptist Church. John passed away suddenly on October 4, 1963, and is interred at Parma Union Cemetery in Parma, New York.

PROCLAMATION

JOHN L. CROOK

WHEREAS, the first town meeting in Parma was held in 1809, and

WHEREAS, the Sesqui-Centennial Committee of the Town of Parma devoted much time and energy to the organization of an appropriate celebration of this historic and auspicious occasion by recreating this, and other events of that momentous occasion by recreating this, and other events of that momentous year, with persons closey resembling our esteemed ancestors,

THEREFORE, the Supervisor of the Town of Parma, John L. Crook and the said Sesqui-Centennial Committee of the Town of Parma do hereby

PROCLAIM, that on Saturday, July 25, 1959, between the hours of 1 and 6 p. m., a Centennial holiday be declared for the Town of Parma with appropriate action taken by the residents of Parma to celebrate this auspicious occasion.

(Signed) John L. Crook
Supervisor, Town of Parma

John Crook was supervisor when the town of Parma celebrated its 150th (Sesquicentennial) Anniversary in July 1959. Saturday, July 25th, was a "Centennial Holiday" in the town with a parade through the village of Hilton and a community celebration.[105] [above]

As supervisor, John Crook was a respected member of the Monroe County Board of Supervisors. With his sudden passing in October 1963, the board issued a resolution recognizing his service to his community.[106] [facing page]

JOHN L. CROOK

November 13, 1896 - October 4, 1963

By Sup. Tofany—

Intro. No. 413

RESOLUTION NO. 351 OF 1963

Expressing Regret of the Board of Supervisors in the Passing of John L. Crook, Late Supervisor of the Town of Parma.

Once again we are called upon to pay tribute to the memory of one of our late colleagues, John L. Crook, Supervisor of the Town of Parma.

John's untimely death was a distinct shock to all of us who knew him so well. He was so vital such a short time ago it seems inconceivable that he is gone.

John, an affable soft-spoken gentleman of the old school, served his community with honor and distinction in business, fraternal and governmental endeavors. We will miss him greatly.

Now, Therefore, to record our esteem for our late colleague, be it

Resolved, That we, the members of the Board of Supervisors of the County of Monroe, do hereby express our deep sympathy and regret in the death of Supervisor John L. Crook, and be it

Further Resolved, That the Clerk of this Board is hereby instructed to forward a copy of this Resolution to the bereaved family, and to set aside a page in the minutes of the Board for this Memorial.

This Memorial Resolution was unanimously adopted, each Supervisor rising in his place.

Form 1 1048   **REGISTRATION CARD** 687 No. 39

		Age, in yrs.
1	Name in full *Clarence Trowbridge Davenport* (Given name) (Family name)	25

2 Home address (No.) (Street) *Lowville* (City) *NY* (State)

3 Date of birth *December* (Month) *29* (Day) *1892* (Year)

4 Are you (1) a natural-born citizen, (2) a naturalized citizen, (3) an alien, (4) or have you declared your intention (specify which)? *Natural Born*

5 Where were you born? *Hornell* (Town) *New York* (State) *USA* (Nation)

6 If not a citizen, of what country are you a citizen or subject? ....

7 What is your present trade, occupation, or office? *Farming*

8 By whom employed? *Clark Davenport.* Where employed? *Lowville*

9 Have you a father, mother, wife, child under 12, or a sister or brother under 12, solely dependent on you for support (specify which)? *none*

10 Married or single (which)? *single* Race (specify which)? *Caucasian*

11 What military service have you had? Rank *none*; branch ....
years ....; Nation or State ....

12 Do you claim exemption from draft (specify grounds)? ....

I affirm that I have verified above answers and that they are true.

X *Clarence Trowbridge Davenport*
(Signature or mark)

If person is of African descent, tear off this corner

CLARENCE TROWBRIDGE DAVENPORT
1892 (1893) – 1965

Clarence entered the service at either twenty-four or twenty-five years of age from Lowville, New York, on February 22, 1918. He was inducted into the United States Army as a Private and assigned to the 151st Depot Brigade at Camp Devens, Massachusetts, until April 18, 1918. He transferred to Camp Upton, New York, joining Battery B, 305th (light) Field Artillery, 77th Division, and was sent

> —Clarence Davenport who resided in this village for about two years has been transferred from Camp Devens to Camp Upton and has written friends hear that he expects to be sent to France in a few days.

overseas on April 26, 1918, embarking from Hoboken, New Jersey, aboard the SS *Northern Pacific*. The division participated in the Oise-Aisne Offensive from August 18th until September 16th, 1918, moving to another sector to participate in the Meuse-Argonne Offensive from September 26th until November 11th, 1918. Clarence returned to the United States aboard USS *Agamemnon* from Brest, France, departing April 21, 1919, and arriving in Hoboken, New Jersey, on April 29, 1919. He was honorably discharged on May 10, 1919.

> —Word has been received here this week of the safe arrival of Clarence Davenport, formerly of this village, in France. He reports a pleasant voyage.

Born to Addison Clark and Ella (Wallace) Davenport in Hornell, New York, on December 29th in either 1892 or 1893, Clarence Trowbridge Davenport grew up in Lowville but later moved to Hilton, New York. His birth year is inconclusive as primary and secondary source records list both dates. Around May 1916 he began working as a night operator and trouble man for Hilton Telephone Company as well as Hilton Power and Light Company. A year later he returned home to Lowville to assist his father as a laborer on his family's dairy farm.[107]

After the war, Clarence worked briefly for the predecessor to Niagara Mohawk Power Company before going into business for himself. Collaborating with a partner, sometime around 1924, they formed Magee & Davenport Radio and Accessories store, opening for business on the "front part of the main floor of the Wright block."[108] They offered radios, parts, supplies, and repair services. As electricians, they provided estimates on wiring a new home or performing repair work on a house, barn, or cottage.

Known as Pete, he married Alma Herrick Cooper of Hilton on June 29, 1935, and the couple made their home on South Avenue. He earned a living working for Rochester Gas & Electric Company and Hilton Telephone Company. Clarence held an amateur ham radio license operating under the call sign W2YJK[109] and was one of five men who founded the Hilton Amateur Radio Association in 1947. He retired in 1959, after twenty-five years of service with Rochester Gas & Electric Company, having worked as a lineman, trouble shooter, and utility serviceman.[110] While retired he planned to operate a business out of his home repairing televisions and radios.

Clarence was active with the American Legion Hiscock-Fishbaugh Post 788 and was elected post commander in 1930. Clarence died June 15, 1965, and is buried in Parma Union Cemetery in Parma, New York.

Five Radio Amateurs Take Federal Exams

Five members of the Hilton Amateur Radio Association took Federal examinations Thursday, March 11, at the Federal Building in Buffalo. Accompanied by Paul Rood, the men are as follows: Millard Rowley, LaVergne Stothard, Clarence Davenport, Howard Cox and Kenneth Herbstsommer.

These examinations were necessary so that transmitting licenses might be procured, but it will be at least 30 days before the results will be known.

A meeting of the Association was held Monday evening at the home of Paul Rood. A motion was made and carried not to accept any new members until all present members have been licensed.

[Left] Clarence and four others from the Hilton Amateur Radio Association traveled to Buffalo for their radio licensing exams in March 1948.[111]

[Below and below left] Magee & Davenport Radio and Accessories Store frequently advertised in the *Hilton (NY) Record.*[112][113]

RADIOS

2 Tube Radiola with head phones and tubes, reduced to . $25.00
Crosley, 2 and 3 Tubes, at $18.50 and $30.00
Freshman, complete, for only . . $115.00

Electrical Wiring and Supplies

Magee & Davenport
WRIGHT BLOCK
Phone 22-F-3
HILTON, N. Y.

Why Not Have Your House Wired Now?

Let us estimate your job.

We also do repair work.

Magee & Davenport
HILTON, N. Y.

Clarence Davenport's retirement was big news at the time, earning him recognition in the *Democrat and Chronicle* (Rochester, NY) [below][114] and the *Hilton (NY) Record* [left][115]

3 from RG&E To Retire Today

Three men who have helped maintain the power lines, buildings and equipment of Rochester Gas & Electric Corp. will retire Jan. 1.

Clarence T. Davenport for nearly 25 years has been a lineman, trouble shooter and utility serviceman in the Hilton area. Davenport, who lives in Hilton, recently was feted by co-workers.

Clarence Davenport Feted At Retirement

A retirement party for Clarence "Pete" Davenport was held Tuesday night at the Plante-ation Pines to honor Mr. Davenport for his many years of service to the Rochester Gas & Electric Corporation.

"Pete" worked for the company's local predecessor, the Hilton Power & Light Company, before World War I, and also for Niagara Mohawk before going into business for himself. He became an R.G.&E. employee 24 years ago.

About 65 attended the dinner in his honor, at which he was presented with a spinning rod and reel for use in his future "job."

Although officially retired, "Pete" plans to do radio and TV repair work at his home.

Form 1   1301   **REGISTRATION CARD**   1228   No. 94

		Age, in yrs.
1	Name in full *Rosario De Simone* (Given name) (Family name)	25

2 Home address _____ (No.) _____ (Street) _____ *Hilton* (City) _____ *N.Y.* (State)

3 Date of birth _____ *October* (Month) _____ *2* (Day) _____ *1891* (Year)

4 Are you (1) a natural-born citizen, (2) a naturalized citizen, (3) an alien, (4) or have you declared your intention (specify which)?   *Declared intention*

5 Where were you born?   *Montella* (Town) _____ (State) _____ *Italy*

6 If not a citizen, of what country are you a citizen or subject?   *Italy*

7 What is your present trade, occupation, or office?   *Laborer 38*

8 By whom employed?   *N.Y.C.R.R.*   Where employed?   *Hilton*

9 Have you a father, mother, wife, child under 12, or a sister or brother under 12, solely dependent on you for support (specify which)?   *no*

10 Married or single (which)?   *no*   Race (specify which)?   *White*

11 What military service have you had? Rank _____ *no* _____ ; branch _____ ; years _____ ; Nation or State _____

12 Do you claim exemption from draft (specify grounds)?   *no*

I affirm that I have verified above answers and that they are true.

Rosario De Simone
(Signature of Person)

1228   If person is of African descent, tear off this corner

ROSARIO DE SIMONE
1891 – 1972

Rosario entered the United States Army at age twenty-six by induction at Camp Crane in Pennsylvania on April 24, 1918. He was assigned to Battalion 16, Section 602, of the United States Army Ambulance Service. He left the United States on June 13, 1918, from Jersey City, New Jersey, sailing across the Atlantic Ocean on the SS *Giuseppe Verde*, a steamship sponsored by the Italian government. He served overseas with the American Expeditionary Forces, alongside the Italian Army, until August 22, 1918. Rosario transferred to the Motor Repair Shop Detachment of the Ambulance Service where he remained until his discharge. He returned to the United States aboard the vessel *Duca Degli Abruzzi*, departing from Genoa, Italy, on April 7, 1919, and arriving in New York City on April 23, 1919. Rosario was honorably discharged from active service on April 26, 1919.

> —A letter from Henry Smith received here announced that John Magee and Rossario Di-simone both of this village, had left Camp Crane and they will shortly be heard from across seas.

Rosario De Simone was born in the Italian town of Montella, in the province of Avellino, region of Campania, on October 2, 1891, to parents Alessandro (Alejandro) and Pico De Simone. He immigrated to the United States aboard the *Tomaso Di Savoia*, arriving in New York harbor on June 21, 1909.

He was immediately detained at Ellis Island while a telegram was sent to the person sponsoring him in the United States, requesting ticket money so he could continue to his destination. While waiting, Rosario was provided breakfast, lunch, and dinner for two days.[i]

Rosario found employment in Orleans County in 1910, working as a laborer for the railroad. On his June 5, 1917, draft registration card he listed his address as Hilton, New York, and was employed by New York Central Railroad. On the card he also declared his intention to become a naturalized United States citizen. Almost a year later, while he was serving on active duty in Pennsylvania, two Army officers attested to his "excellent service and good conduct" and his petition to become a naturalized citizen of the United States was declared on the May 23, 1918.

In 1949, Rosario's name appears in a newspaper advertisement by Philadelphia Electric Company recognizing his twenty-five years of service with the company. This information puts him in the metropolitan Philadelphia, Pennsylvania, area around 1924. Rosario remained with Philadelphia Electric until his retirement. Never having married, Rosario passed away in Wilmington, Delaware, on December 2, 1972, and is interred at Cathedral Cemetery in Wilmington, Delaware.

---

[i] It was a requirement for all immigrants arriving at Ellis Island to have follow-on travel arrangements completed before entry. Any administrative costs related to their delay in admittance to the United States generated a monthly bill to the steamship company transporting the immigrants. The company was ultimately responsible for the expenses associated with detaining the immigrant(s) they transported to the United States.

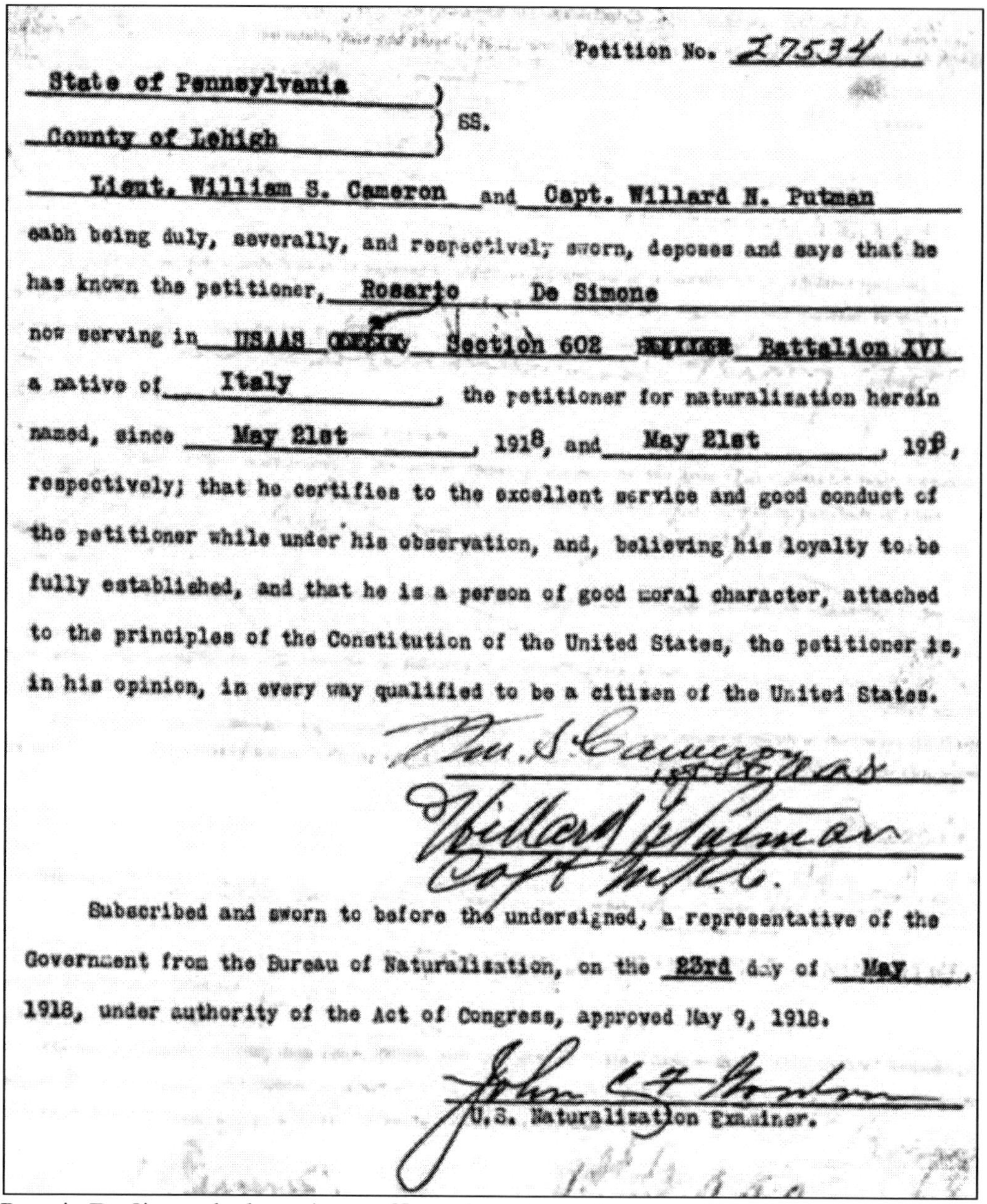

Petition No. 27534

State of Pennsylvania)
) SS.
County of Lehigh   )

_____Lieut. William S. Cameron_____ and __Capt. Willard N. Putman__
each being duly, severally, and respectively sworn, deposes and says that he
has known the petitioner, _____Rosario_____ De Simone_____
now serving in____USAAS_____ Section 602 _____ Battalion XVI
a native of_____Italy_____, the petitioner for naturalization herein
named, since _____May 21st_____, 1918, and____May 21st____, 198,
respectively; that he certifies to the excellent service and good conduct of
the petitioner while under his observation, and, believing his loyalty to be
fully established, and that he is a person of good moral character, attached
to the principles of the Constitution of the United States, the petitioner is,
in his opinion, in every way qualified to be a citizen of the United States.

_____

_____

      Subscribed and sworn to before the undersigned, a representative of the
Government from the Bureau of Naturalization, on the __23rd__ day of __May__,
1918, under authority of the Act of Congress, approved May 9, 1918.

_____
U.S. Naturalization Examiner.

Rosario De Simone had two Army officers from Camp Crane certify to his "excellent service and good conduct," having only known him for two days.[116]

92

Philadelphia Electric Company annually recognized their employees with over twenty-five years of service through a full-page advertisement in the *Pottstown (PA) Mercury*. Rosario De Simone first appears in the 1949 roster; the last time his name appears is 1967. It is estimated Rosario was employed with Philadelphia Electric for about forty-three years and whether he returned to Hilton after his service in World War I is unknown.

Form 1   1215   **REGISTRATION CARD**   217   No. 6

1 Name in full _George H Dean_
   (Given name)   (Family name)   Age, in yrs. _21_

2 Home address ___ (No.) (Street) _Hilton_ _New York_
                                        (City)   (State)

3 Date of birth _March_ _30_ _1896_
              (Month)   (Day)   (Year)

4 Are you (1) a natural-born citizen, (2) a naturalized citizen, (3) an alien, (4) or have you declared your intention (specify which)? _Natural-born_

5 Where were you born? _Sweden_ _New York_ _U.S._
                        (Town)   (State)   (Nation)

6 If not a citizen, of what country are you a citizen or subject? ___

7 What is your present trade, occupation, or office? _Painter 30_

8 By whom employed? _Elmer Bigler_
   Where employed? _Parma Monroe Co New York_

9 Have you a father, mother, wife, child under 12, or a sister or brother under 12, solely dependent on you for support (specify which)? _No_

10 Married or single (which)? _Single_   Race (specify which)? _Caucasian_

11 What military service have you had? Rank _None_ ; branch ___ ;
   years ___ ; Nation or State ___

12 Do you claim exemption from draft (specify grounds)? ___

    I affirm that I have verified above answers and that they are true.

                          George H Dean

94

GEORGE HENRY DEAN
1896 – 1932

George was inducted at Spencerport, New York, on February 24, 1918, as a twenty-one-year-old Private and designated to the United States Army Quartermaster Corps. He transferred to Company A, 5th Supply Train, Quartermaster Corps, 5th Division, on May 25, 1918. George was promoted to Private First Class on May 8, 1919, before going overseas from Hoboken, New Jersey, on June 10, 1918, aboard the USS *Mount Vernon*. He arrived at Brest, France, on June 19, 1918, and participated in the battles of Saint-Mihiel and the Argonne. He departed Brest, France, on July 13, 1919, aboard the USS *Agamemnon* and arrived back in Hoboken on July 21, 1919. He was discharged from Camp Upton, located on Long Island, New York, on July 26, 1919.

George Henry Dean was born in Sweden, New York, to Canadian parents John J. and Sarah Jane (Kenyon) Dean on March 30, 1896. George worked as a painter, employed by Elmer Bigelow, at the time of his draft registration on June 5, 1917–an occupation he would return to after his discharge from military service. His marriage license reported his occupation as decorator.

He married Gertrude F. Hahn on November 25, 1920, and by 1925 the family moved to Niagara Falls, George finding work as a time keeper. George and the family returned to Rochester, New York, by 1930, where George worked as a clerk in the manufacturing division at Kodak Park for Eastman Kodak Company.

George was a charter member of the American Legion Hiscock-Fishbaugh Post 788 before transferring his membership to the Genesee Valley Post. He was a member of the Veterans of Foreign Wars and the Improved Order of Red Men (America's Oldest Fraternal Organization promoting patriotism). George died on August 4, 1932, at the Soldiers and Sailors Hospital in Bath, New York, and was afforded military burial rites by the Veterans of Foreign Wars.[117] George is buried in Parma Union Cemetery in Parma, New York.

George (front row, second from left) forms up in the village of Hilton with fellow Army veterans on what is presumed to be the August 2nd Town of Parma "Welcome Home" celebration for the war veterans in 1919.[118]

Form 1   **861**   **REGISTRATION CARD** *1220*   No. *225*

1. Name in full   *Ralph De Roller*   Age, in yrs. *29*
    (Given name)   (Family name)

2. Home address   *33*   *Lyndhurst*   *Rochester*
    (No.)   (Street)   (City)   (State)

3. Date of birth   *July*   *13*   *1888*
    (Month)   (Day)   (Year)

4. Are you (1) a natural-born citizen, (2) a naturalized citizen, (3) an alien, (4) or have you declared your intention (specify which)?   *Natural born*

5. Where were you born?   *Rochester NY*
    (Town)   (State)   (Nation)

6. If not a citizen, of what country are you a citizen or subject?

7. What is your present trade, occupation, or office?   *Wholesale Plumbing*

8. By whom employed?   *Hunting Co*
    Where employed?   *127 Railroad St*

9. Have you a father, mother, wife, child under 12, or a sister or brother under 12, solely dependent on you for support (specify which)?   *No.*

10. Married or single (which)?   *Single*   Race (specify which)?   *Caucasian*

11. What military service have you had? Rank ———— ; branch ————
    years ———— ; Nation or State ————

12. Do you claim exemption from draft (specify grounds)?   *No*

I affirm that I have verified above answers and that they are true.

Ralph De Roller
(Signature or mark)

If person is of African descent, tear off this corner

96

RALPH HENRY DeROLLER
1888 – 1971

Ralph was inducted into the United States Army at the age of twenty-nine from Rochester, New York, on February 8, 1918, at the rank of Private. He spent the duration of his assignment at Fort Hancock in Sandy Hook, New Jersey, with 5th Company of the United States Army's Coast Artillery Corps. He was discharged on December 11, 1918.

Ralph Henry DeRoller was born in Rochester on July 13, 1888, to Amon and Catherine (Gaeb) DeRoller. He grew up in Parma, New York, working on the family farm. At the time of his draft registration in 1917, Ralph was working in the plumbing trade. He would continue this occupation after his return from military duties, attaining the position of foreman. He married Anna M. Maguire in Rochester on September 6, 1922, and the couple made their home in Irondequoit, New York, before settling in Brighton, New York. Ralph passed away on November 22, 1971, and is buried in Holy Sepulchre Cemetery in Rochester, New York.

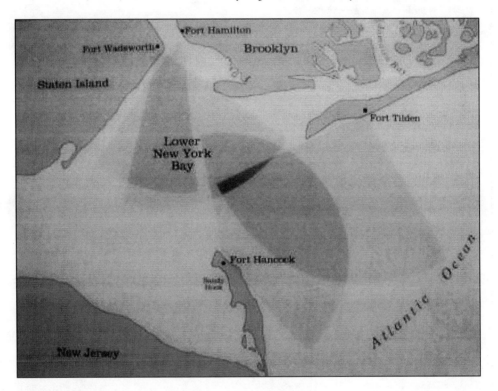

This graphic highlights the coastal defense sites around the entrance to the New Jersey and New York harbor areas. It shows the importance of Fort Hancock at Sandy Hook, New Jersey, and the role a coast artillery company, like the one Ralph belonged to, played in defending vital sea ports.[119]

Form 1   9? | REGISTRATION CARD 808 | No. **115**

1. Name in full ..... *Donald Donoghue* | Age, in yrs. **25**
   (Given name)   (Family name)

2. Home address *104 South ave.* *Rochester* *N.Y.*
   (No.)   (Street)   (City)   (State)

3. Date of birth ..... *June* *14* *1892*
   (Month)   (Day)   (Year)

4. Are you (1) a natural-born citizen, (2) a naturalized citizen, (3) an alien, (4) or have you declared your intention (specify which)? *Natural - born*

5. Where were you born? *Rochester* *N.Y.* *U.S.A.*
   (Town)   (State)   (Nation)

6. If not a citizen, of what country are you a citizen or subject? ....

7. What is your present trade, occupation, or office? *Hotel Clerk* 2?

8. By whom employed? *Osborn House*
   Where employed? *South ave. Roch. N.Y.*

9. Have you a father, mother, wife, child under 12, or a sister or brother under 12, solely dependent on you for support (specify which)? *None*

10. Married or single (which)? *Single* Race (specify which) *Caucasian*

11. What military service have you had? Rank ....; branch ....;
    years ....; Nation or State ....

12. Do you claim exemption from draft (specify grounds)? *No*

I affirm that I have verified above answers and that they are true.

Donald Donoghue
(Signature or mark)

If person is of African descent, tear off this corner.   C

98

DONALD MCDONALD DONOGHUE
1893 (1892) – 1966

Donald entered service with the United States Army in Rochester, New York, being inducted on April 3, 1918, at the age of twenty-four; he was sent to the 153d Depot Brigade, Camp Dix, New Jersey. Private Donoghue was assigned to Company B, 307th Machine Gun Battalion, 78th Division, on April 22, 1918. He continued training with the 78th Division at Camp Dix in Wrightstown, New Jersey, before leaving on May 19, 1918, aboard the USS *Nestor*, embarking from Brooklyn, New York.

Donald participated in military actions while in Saint-Mihiel and Meuse-Argonne, France. He was designated a Cook on April 1, 1919, and departed shortly after from Marseille, France, aboard the SS *Infanta Isabel*, docking in Hoboken, New Jersey, on May 10, 1919. He was discharged on May 16, 1919.[120] [above]

> —Donald Donoghue has been discharged from Co. B. 307th Machine Gun Co., and is at the home of his parents at Parma Corners.

Donald McDonald Donoghue was born to Charles H. and Adelaide M. (Yellowlee) Donoghue in New York on June 14th of either 1892 or 1893. His federal and state census rolls, as well as the Social Security Death Index, all suggest a birth year of 1893–a date he attested to on his World War II draft registration card when he signed it. However, his World War I draft registration card, with Donald's signature and dated June 5, 1917, reports his birth year as 1892. Donald married Florence Anna Marie Schuyler in a ceremony on April 2, 1921, in Rochester. After twenty-eight years of marriage, Florence passed away in 1949. Donald married Ruth (Wahl) DeBack on May 24, 1952, making their home together in Irondequoit, New York.

Donald was one of 459 Eastman Kodak Company employees honored on November 16, 1944, at an anniversary dinner recognizing employees with twenty-five years of service with the company.[121] Honorees were awarded a medal with the image of George Eastman on one side and the recipient's name on the other, personally presented by the company's president. In 1959, Donald was once again recognized for his loyalty and service with Eastman Kodak, this time for forty years of employment.[122] [left]

Donald received a citation by the Junior Chamber of Commerce traffic courtesy spotters during their Traffic Courtesy Week in April of 1952, for his road safety skills.[123] He was a member of the American Legion Irondequoit Post 134. Donald passed away on March 27, 1966, and is buried in Irondequoit Cemetery in Irondequoit, New York.

Serial No. 21   Registration No. 229

1 | Name in full ... Earle A. Ducolon .... | Age, in yrs.
(Given name)   (Family name) | 21

2 | Home address Y. M. C. A Box 517 Rochester N. Y.
(No.) (Street) (City or town) (State)

3 | Date of birth February 2 1897
(Month) (Day) (Year)

4 | Where were you born? Buffalo N. Y. U. S. A
(City or town) (State) (Nation)

5 | I am {
1. A native of the United States.
2. A naturalized citizen.
3. An alien.
4. I have declared my intention.
5. A noncitizen noncitizen Indian.
(Strike out lines or words not applicable)

6 | If not a citizen, of what Nation are you a citizen or subject? ....

7 | Father's birthplace N. Greece Monroe Co. N. Y. U. S.
(City or town) (State or province) (Nation)

8 | Name of employer E. W. Snow & Co.
Place of employment 29 N Water St. Rochester N. Y.
(No.) (Street) (City or town) (State)

9 | Name of nearest relative Charles E Ducolon (father)
Address of nearest relative R. F. D. Hilton N. Y.
(No.) (Street) (City or town) (State or nation)

10 | Race— White, Negro, Indian, or Colored.
(Strike out words not applicable)

I affirm that I have verified above answers and that they are true.

Earle A. Ducolon

P. M. G. O.
Form 1 (blue)   (Signature or Mark of Registrant.)

If person is of African descent, tear off this corner.

REGISTRATION CARD.   3—5739

EARLE ADKINS DuCOLON
1897 – 1978

Earle was inducted into the United States Army at Rochester, New York, on August 8, 1918, as a twenty-one-year-old Private and was assigned to Company 1, later Company A, of the 12th Ammunition Train, 12th Division. The 12th Division was organized at Camp Devens, Massachusetts, on July 9, 1918, however the 12th Field Artillery Brigade and 12th Ammunition Train were organized at Camp McClellan, Alabama. Whether Earle was sent to Camp Devens or to Camp McClellan is unknown. Only advance elements of the division sailed from New York City on October 27, 1918, arriving in Europe on November 8th. The signing of the armistice suspended all further oversea movements, keeping Earle in the United States for the duration of his enlistment.[124] Earle was promoted to Private First Class on January 15, 1919, and was discharged on February 13, 1919.

Earle Adkins DuColon was born to Charles E. and Lillian Mary (Adkins) DuColon on February 2, 1897, in Buffalo, New York. By 1910, Earle's family had purchased their own farm in Parma, New York. By the age of twenty, in 1917, Earle was working for the Rochester-based E. W. Snow & Company, an electrical supply firm.

After the war he returned to live with his family in Parma; Earle found employment as a general carpenter. He married Leona B. Wilder on October 30, 1937, making their home in Parma. Earle supported his new bride as a self-employed farmer on Wilder Road.

Earle was a member of the Clio Lodge No. 779, Free & Accepted Masons, attaining the position of worshipful master,[125] and was a member of Hilton Baptist Church. Earle passed away on March 19, 1978, and is buried in Parma Union Cemetery in Parma, New York.

Thirteen in Hilton Class.

Hilton, Feb. 5.—The senior class of the Hilton High School, numbering thirteen, has just organized with the following officers: President, John Crook; vice-president, Pearl Smith; secretary, Agnes Conroy; treasurer, Lockey Madden; class historian, Willard Lee; class poet, Alta Haight; class prophet, Barbara Fraser. The other members of the class are Altha Wood, Wilma Defendorf, Ruth Anderson, Jennie Hubble, Alice Chamberlain, Earle Ducolon. Some time this month the class will present a play entitled "Diamonds and Hearts."

Earle was a member of Hilton High School Class of 1915, along with fellow *Honor Roll* members John L. Crook and Willard J. Lee.[126]

Glenn W. Fishbaugh's *Abstracts of National Guard Service in World War I* card from the New York Adjutant General's Office.[127] Glenn mustered in to his National Guard unit and was already in active military service in June 1917 and therefore would not have completed a draft registration card.

★ GLENN WAY FISHBAUGH ★
1895 – 1918

Glenn entered the New York National Guard at twenty years old from Rochester, New York, on June 19, 1916. He was sent to Camp Whitman in Green Haven, New York, and then to Texas with the unit to participate in the Mexican Punitive Campaign, protecting United States citizens along the United States-Mexico border. He mustered out October 5, 1916.

Still assigned to Company H of the 3d Infantry Regiment, New York National Guard, Glenn mustered back in for World War I service on April 17, 1917. His regiment was renamed the 108th Infantry Regiment, 27th Division, and trained at Camp Wadsworth in Spartanburg, South Carolina; Glenn promoted to Corporal on June 24, 1917. He was promoted to Sergeant on January 8, 1918, and together with his brother, Ray, left Newport News, Virginia, for overseas duty aboard the USS *President Grant* on May 17, 1918. He participated in the battle of Le Catelet, Hindenburg Line, near Bony, Aisne, France, and was wounded in action while on the Hindenburg Line on September 29, 1918.

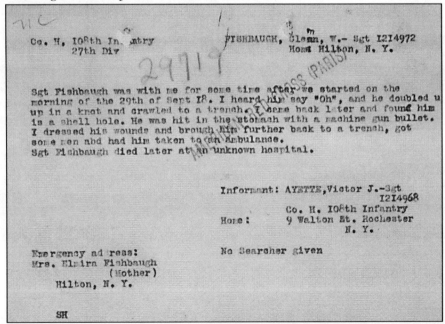

Sergeant Victor Ayette provided an eye-witness account of how Glenn was wounded.[128]

Glenn was cited in Special Order 86, 27th Division, in 1919 for "courage, determination and marked qualities of leadership in effectively commanding a platoon under heavy fire during the battle of the Hindenburg Line, east of Ronssoy, France, September 29, 1918."[129]

Sergeant Glenn W. Fishbaugh died in a field hospital from his wounds on October 5, 1918, and was initially buried in British Military Cemetery, Doingt Communal Cemetery Extension, in Somme, France.[130] Upon the request of the family to return his remains to the United States, Glenn was disinterred on January 20, 1921. Sergeant Glenn Fishbaugh arrived home aboard the USAT *Cambria* on April 7, 1921, and was interred on April 14, 1921, in Arlington National Cemetery, Virginia.

Born to Henry and Elmira (Way) Fishbaugh in Avoca, New York, on December 3, 1895, Glenn, his mother, and two siblings moved to Hamlin, New York, after the loss of Glenn's father–the result of a workplace accident at the Avoca Wheel Factory in 1899. Myra, as she was known, supported the family as a dressmaker, living with her brother and father in Hamlin, New York. By 1915, Glenn and his brother, Ray, were living in Rochester's 12th Ward, working as a stenographer and bookkeeper, respectively.

Parma's American Legion Post 788, organized on November 30, 1919, and chartered August 1, 1920, with seventeen World War I veterans,[131] was named the Hiscock-Fishbaugh Post to honor two of Parma's own who were killed in action–Glenn W. Fishbaugh being one and Lester P. Hiscock the other.

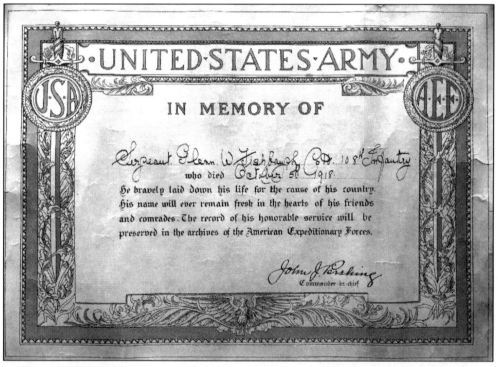

Certificate given to the Fishbaugh family following Glenn's death.[132]

WAR DEPARTMENT
Q. M. C. Form No. 14
Revised Oct. 6, 1928

Interment in the _____ ARLINGTON, VA. _____ National Cemetery

To—The Quartermaster General, Washington, D. C.

NAME	RANK	COMPANY	REGIMENT OR VESSEL			DIVISION, IF WORLD WAR SOLDIER
			Number	State	Arm	
FISHBAUGH, GLENN N.Y. 1214972	SGT.	H	108th		INF.	27th Div. World War

DATE OF DEATH			DATE OF INTERMENT			GRAVE MARK		REMARKS Date of discharge and number of Pension Certificate, Disinterments, etc.
Month	Day	Year	Month	Day	Year	Section	Grave No.	
Oct. in France	5	1918	April	14	1921	White Europe	1592	Orig.Bur. Grave #1, Row A, Plot 3, #721 British Military Cemetery, Doingt, Somme, France.
								C.R. April 1921

Shipping point for headstones _____

(See Instructions on Reverse Side)

Superintendent.

3—2550

sem

Above, the War Department form used by the Quartermaster Corps to record Glenn's burial in Arlington National Cemetery;[133] a photograph of his headstone below.[134] At right, a formal portrait of Private Fishbaugh shortly after he joined the New York National Guard in 1916.[135]

Ray Fishbaugh's *Abstracts of National Guard Service in World War I* card from the New York Adjutant General's Office.[136] Ray mustered in to his National Guard unit and was already in active military service when the June 5, 1917, draft registration was called. He would not have completed a draft registration card.

RAYMOND ALTON FISHBAUGH
1891 – 1982

Raymond, at twenty-four-years-old, enlisted in the New York National Guard on June 12, 1916, in Rochester, New York, joining Company H, 3d New York Infantry Regiment, as a Private. His first assignment was in support of the Mexican Punitive Campaign protecting United States citizens along the United States-Mexico border. He mustered out on October 5, 1916, and promoted to Corporal on February 27, 1917. [right][137]

Ray mustered in for World War I service on April 17, 1917, with the same unit–re-designated the 108th Infantry Regiment, 27th Division–and trained at Camp Wadsworth, South Carolina. On May 17, 1918, Ray departed Newport News, Virginia, with his brother Glenn, aboard the USS *President Grant*. [below][138]

Ray was selected to attend Army Candidates School in France on September 7, 1918. Two months later, on November 6, 1918, he transferred to the 54th Guard Company of the Army Service Corps. While overseas Corporal Fishbaugh participated in the Battles of the Hindenburg Line near Bony, France, and three campaigns in Belgium–East Poperinghe Line, Vierstraat Ridge and Dickebusch Sector. He returned to the United States on July 13, 1919, aboard the SS *Housatonic*, having departed from Bordeaux, France, on July 1, 1919. Ray was honorably discharged on July 18, 1919.

Born in Avoca, New York, to Henry and Elmira (Way) Fishbaugh on October 31, 1891, Raymond Alton Fishbaugh grew up in Hamlin, New York, with his mother and siblings after the death of his father in a workplace accident in 1899. As a young man he found employment in Hamlin as a farm laborer. By the time he entered Army service in 1916, he was living in Rochester and working as a bookkeeper,[139] a profession he would return to after the war. Ray and Julia Erma Ungerland were united in marriage on September 11, 1920, in Rochester and the couple shared forty-two years together until Julia's passing in 1962.

Ray married Fanny Susan (nee Klock) Orth on June 10, 1967,[140] and they shared ten years together before Fanny passed away. Ray was active in the Parent Teacher Association for Lexington School No. 34 in Rochester, assisting in fundraisers and acting as treasurer for the organization.[141] Ray died on March 10, 1982, and is buried in Blossom Cemetery, also known as Clarkson Union Cemetery, in Hamlin, New York.

Hilton, July 4.—Corporal Ray Fishbaugh, of Company H, 108th Infantry, has arrived safely overseas and writes his mother, Mrs. Myra Fishbaugh, that he and his brother are both well, and not to worry. He says the weather is fine, warm days and cool nights; that the country is beautiful and very productive; the fields are separated by hedges, while the buildings are of stone and very picturesque. He enlisted for

CORPORAL RAY FISHBAUGH.

service and was sent to Camp Wadsworth, S. C., August 11, 1917. He was also in the service on the Mexican border. The motto of his company is: "To Berlin or bust."

Form 1 1242 REGISTRATION CARD 832 No. 35

1 Name in full _Frank L Flemming_ Age, in yrs. **26**
(Given name) (Family name)

2 Home address _15 Grove Place Rochester N.Y._
(No.) (Street) (City) (State)

3 Date of birth _October 16 1890_
(Month) (Day) (Year)

4 Are you (1) a natural-born citizen, (2) a naturalized citizen, (3) an alien, (4) or have you declared your intention (specify which)? _Natural born_

5 Where were you born? _Hamlin New york U.S._
(Town) (State) (Nation)

6 If not a citizen, of what country are you a citizen or subject? _____

7 What is your present trade, occupation, or office? _Automobile Mechanic_

8 By whom employed? _15 George Bangs_
Where employed? _Rochester Monroe Co New york_

9 Have you a father, mother, wife, child under 12, or a sister or brother under 12, solely dependent on you for support (specify which)? _No._

10 Married or single (which)? _Single_ Race (specify which)? _Caucasian_

11 What military service have you had? Rank _None_ ; branch _____
years _____ ; Nation or State _____

12 Do you claim exemption from draft (specify grounds)? _____

I affirm that I have verified above answers and that they are true.

Frank L Flemming
(signature or mark)

832 C
2

If person is of African descent, tear off this corner

FRANK LOUIS FLEMMING
1890 – 1968

Twenty-eight-year-old Frank enrolled in the United States Naval Reserve Force at the Buffalo, New York, Recruiting Station on May 23, 1918.[142] [below] He received his training at the Naval Training Station, Great Lakes, Illinois, from June 12, 1918, until November 11, 1918, promoting through the rates of Landsman, Machinist's Mate Aviation, and Machinist's Mate Second Class Aviation. Never having served overseas, Frank was discharged on January 15, 1919.

> —Frank Flemming was here Saturday and Sunday. He went to Buffalo Monday, to join the aviation section of the U. S. Navy in the gasolene engine department.

In Hamlin, New York, Frank Louis Flemming was born to Charles and Emma (Pencylean) Flemming on October 16, 1890. At the time of his World War I draft registration he was working as an automobile mechanic in Rochester, New York. The 10th of May 1921 was a special day for Frank and Iola Sophia Hoxie when they exchanged wedding vows in Rochester. The newlyweds made their home in Frank's hometown of Hamlin.

Frank was talented and applied his skills to many fields in Rochester between 1915 and 1925, working as an automobile mechanic, engineer, millwright in a candy factory, shipping clerk, and carpenter. Taking those skills west, Frank moved his family to Buffalo, New York, where he supported them as a stationary engineer at a laundry facility, an engineer at the Culliton Ice Cream Company, and a stationary engineer at the Gerhard Lang Brewery. Frank was a member of the Germania Lodge No. 722, Free & Accepted Masons, of Rochester.

In 1948, Frank and his family lived in San Diego, California, but returned to Buffalo where he was chief engineer of Deaconess Hospital. In 1966, Frank was enjoying his retirement with Iola, back in San Diego. On November 3, 1968, Frank passed away in Florissant, Missouri, and is buried in Garland Cemetery in Clarkson, New York.

form 1 *1907* **REGISTRATION CARD** | No. *17*

1 Name in full *John Henry Fleming*   Age, in yts. *28*
(Given name) (Family name)

2 Home address *R. F. D.* *Sodus* *N. Y.*
(No.) (Street) (City) (State)

3 Date of birth *Mar* *8* *1889*
(Month) (Day) (Year)

4 Are you (1) a natural-born citizen, (2) a naturalized citizen, (3) an alien, (4) or have you declared your intention (specify which)? *Nat. Born Citizen*

5 Where were you born? *Hamlin* *N. Y.* *U. S. A.*
(Town) (State) (Nation)

6 If not a citizen, of what country are you a citizen or subject?

7 What is your present trade, occupation, or office? *Farm Laborer*

8 By whom employed? *H. C. Allen*
Where employed? *Sodus N. Y.*

9 Have you a father, mother, wife, child under 12, or a sister or brother under 12, solely dependent on you for support (specify which)? *No*

10 Married or single (which)? *Single* Race (specify which)? *Caucasian*

11 What military service have you had? Rank _____; branch _____
years _____; Nation or State _____

12 Do you claim exemption from draft (specify grounds)? *No*

705   I affirm that I have verified above answers and that they are true.

C A *John Henry Fleming*
(Signature or mark)

If person is of African descent, tear off this corner.

JOHN HENRY FLEMMING
1889 – 1971

John Flemming was twenty-nine when he was inducted into the United States Army from Lyons, New York, on April 3, 1918. As a Private, he was assigned to Headquarters Company, 309th Infantry, 78th Division, for the duration of his enlistment. He embarked from Brooklyn, New York, on May 20, 1918, aboard the vessel SS *Morvada* to serve in Europe. He returned to the United States on May 16, 1919, from Bordeaux, France, aboard the HMS *Lancaster*, arriving on May 31, 1919. John was honorably discharged on June 7, 1919.

John Henry Flemming was born to Charles and Emma (Pencylean) Flemming in Hamlin, New York, on March 8, 1889. John was twenty-eight when he registered for the draft and was working on the F.C. Allen farm in Sodus, New York. He married Anna W. (nee Lawvey) Slater on January 13, 1928, and they made their home on Latta Road in Greece, New York.

He worked for Eastman Kodak manufacturing as a maintenance mechanic at Kodak Park and was honored in 1963 for his twenty-five years of service to the company.[143] Known as the "Mayor" of North Greece,[144] John moved to his daughter's home in Hamlin from the family home on Latta Road. He would spend the remainder of his days in the Cupola Nursing Home in Brockport, New York. On June 4, 1971, John passed away and was interred in Falls Cemetery in Greece, New York.

N. Greece 'Mayor' Feted At Party

The "Mayor" of North Greece, John H. Flemming, received a royal send-off on December 7 when 55 North Greece neighbors gave him a "going-away" party prior to his moving to Hamlin to make his home with his step-daughter, Mrs. Luther Kelso and Mr. Kelso of West Fork Road. He will journey to Florida in January, using the new luggage presented him at the party which was held in the North Greece Fire Hall.

John H. Flemming

Mr. Flemming's brothers, Frank and Albert of Rochester, William of Bailey Road and George of Hilton were all at the party. His sister, Mrs. Benjamin Unterborn of Parma-Clarkson Town Line Road was unable to attend because of ill health.

Mr. Flemming, who was employed at Eastman Kodak, had lived in the family home at 3587 Latta Road for over 25 years.

North Greece Fire District Elects Commissioner

Taxpayers of the North Greece Fire District turned out on December 6 to vote on a fire commissioner for the community. Seen here marking his ballot is Charles Ahrns as John O'Tier deposits his slip while John Flemming looks on.
PRESS Photo

The "Mayor" of North Greece, seated at right, helped the North Greece Fire District with their annual election on December 6, 1938. [above][145]

John Flemming was honored [left][146] by his North Greece neighbors before moving to live with family in Hamlin.

Form 1   **1247**   REGISTRATION CARD   1419   No. **40**

1 Name in full   *Samuel W. Flemming*   Age, in yrs. **29**
   (First name)   (Family name)

2 Home address   *Hilton   N.Y.*
   (No.)   (Street)   (City)   (State)

3 Date of birth   *May   18   1894*
   (Month)   (Day)   (Year)

4 Are you (1) a natural-born citizen, (2) a naturalized citizen, (3) an alien, (4) or have you declared your
   intention (specify which)?   *natural born*

5 Where were you born?   *Hamlin   N.Y.   U.S.A.*
   (Town)   (State)   (Nation)

6 If not a citizen, of what country are you a citizen or subject?

7 What is your present trade, occupation, or office?   *30 Laborer*

8 By whom employed?
   Where employed?   *Parma*

9 Have you a father, mother, wife, child under 12, or a sister or brother under 12, solely dependent on you for
   support (specify which)?   *none*

10 Married or single (which)?   *Single*   Race (specify which)?   *White*

11 What military service have you had? Rank   *none*   ; branch   ;
   years   ; Nation or State

12 Do you claim exemption from draft (specify grounds)?   *Rheumatism*

I affirm that I have verified above answers and that they are true.

Samuel W Fleming
(Signature or mark)

If person is of African descent, tear off this corner. 1419

112

SAMUEL WILLIAM FLEMMING
1894 – 1922

Samuel, at age twenty-three, was inducted into the United States Army from Rochester, New York, on February 24, 1918, at the rank of Private. He was assigned to the 30th Company, 8th Training Battalion, 151st Depot Brigade, at Camp Devens, Massachusetts. He was discharged on March 29, 1918, with a Surgeon's Certificate of Disability.[147][148]

> —Samuel Fleming, who was a-
> mong the boys that went Camp
> Devens, Mass., from the place,
> returned home last week having
> received an honorable ischarge
> because of physical disab

> Twenty-five Years Ago—1918
> Hilton's quota for the Third Liberty
> Loan was $49,100.
> Samuel Flemming returned from
> Camp Devens, Mass., having received
> an honorable discharge because of
> physical disability.

   Samuel William Flemming was born to Charles and Emma (Pencylean) Flemming on May 18, 1894, in Hamlin, New York. He was employed as a farm laborer in Parma, New York, when he registered for the draft. Samuel married Georgia G. DeFrain on November 26, 1919, just three years before he passed away on December 4, 1922. Samuel is buried in Parma Union Cemetery in Parma, New York.

From the Albert R. Stone Negative Collection, Rochester Museum & Science Center, Rochester, N.Y.

> Samuel Fleming is taking treatment
> at Iola Sanitarium. Sam's friends
> here hope to see him improved in
> health in a short time.

> Mrs. B. J. Unterborn of Clarkson
> visited her brother, Samuel Fleming,
> at Iola Sanitarium last Sunday, and
> was accompanied by Mrs. William
> Hueser, also of the town of Clarkson,
> and Mrs. Clifford Zarpentin of Spen-
> cerport.

Samuel Flemming was a patient of the Iola Sanitarium in Rochester in October 1921. [left][149] All hopes for a speedy recovery were short lived; Samuel passed away a year later. [above][150]

Form 1   2043   **REGISTRATION CARD** 576 | No. 50

1 Name in full ___ Fred C. Hall | Age, in yrs. 26
(Given name) (Family name)

2 Home address ___ 42 ___ Elizabeth ___ Roch ___ N.Y.
(No.) (Street) (City) (State)

3 Date of birth ___ June ___ 26 ___ 1890
(Month) (Day) (Year)

4 Are you (1) a natural-born citizen, (2) a naturalized citizen, (3) an alien, (4) or have you declared your intention (specify which)? ___ U.S.A.

5 Where were you born? ___ Parma ___ N.Y. ___ U.S.A.
(Town) (State) (Nation)

6 If not a citizen, of what country are you a citizen or subject? ___

7 What is your present trade, occupation, or office? ___ Meat Cutter 12

8 By whom employed? ___ J. W. Ellis
Where employed? ___ 285 W Main St

9 Have you a father, mother, wife, child under 12, or a sister or brother under 12, solely dependent on you for support (specify which)? ___ Wife

10 Married or single (which)? ___ Married ___ Race (specify which)? ___ Caucasian

11 What military service have you had? Rank ___ ; branch ___ ;
years ___ ; Nation or State ___

12 Do you claim exemption from draft (specify grounds)? ___ No

I affirm that I have verified above answers and that they are true.

Fred C Hall
(signature or mark)

If person is of African descent, tear off this corner

114

FRED C. HALL
1890 – 1936

Fred was inducted into the United States Army from Rochester, New York, on December 16, 1917, as a twenty-seven-year-old Private. He was assigned to Battery D, 57th Artillery, Coast Artillery Corps, and trained at Fort Hancock in New Jersey. He was promoted to Corporal on April 10, 1918, and embarked from New York City aboard the SS *Ryndam* for overseas duties as a Cook on May 10, 1918. [right][151] He was assigned to Battery B, 43d Artillery, Coast Artillery Corps, First Army, on July 26, 1918, transferring once again to Headquarters, 1st Battalion, 43d Artillery, Coast Artillery Corps, First Army, on August 10, 1918. Being assigned to a First Army heavy artillery unit, Fred was involved in the Saint-Mihiel operations in late August to mid-September of 1918, and the Meuse-Argonne offensive of October and November 1918.[152] (see article, next page) He returned home on the USS *Zeelandia*, departing from Saint-Nazaire, France, on December 9, 1918, arriving in Newport News, Virginia, on December 21, 1918. He was discharged January 10, 1919.

—M. J. Hall has received word of the safe arrival of his son Fred over seas, and that his other son, Lynn, expects to come home next Saturday on a furlough previous to his leaving for France, about the 15th. He is nearly well from his fall from a horse, which happened several weeks ago.

Fred C. Hall was born in June 26, 1890, to Mervin J. (known as M. J.) and Sarah Jennie (Calcutt) Hall in Parma, New York. Fred grew up in Parma and in 1914 was secretary of the Fire Council. He found work as a meat cutter for J.W. Ellis on Main Street in Hilton.

Harriett C. Robb, a resident of Greece, New York, and Fred were married in Cuyahoga County, Ohio, on September 8, 1915. The couple made their home in Parma, New York. Fred applied for an exemption from military service when he registered for the June 5, 1917, draft claiming a dependent wife. The exemption claim was initially denied by the division board and then reversed on appeal to the district board. [right][153] However, the case was reopened, and the decision revoked when it was discovered Harriett was employed.[154]

—Last Tuesday's Rochester Union and Advertiser contained the following: "Fred C. Hall, 269 Tremont street, denied exemption by Division 3 on plea of dependent wife; ruling reversed by District Board and exemption granted; case reopened and discovery of employment of wife and exemption revoked." Mr. Hall is a son of M. J. Hall of this village.

He expanded his role in the meat market and grocery business when, in 1921, he became a business partner alongside his father, M. J. Hall, who owned the Hilton Market and Grocery. By 1930, Fred was living in Hornell, New York, when he met and married Lulu Hattie Bell (nee Miller) Griffin on November 14, 1932. They moved to Tonawanda, New York, and Fred supported his family working as a clerk. Fred passed away in Tonawanda, New York, on April 20, 1936, and is interred in Pine Hill Cemetery in Buffalo, New York.

Sixty-five Rochester Men Who Were in Hot Fighting Expect to Return to Home City in a Body

"Sixty-five Rochester men arrived at Camp Eustis, Virginia, from St. Nazarre, France to-day," writes Sergeant Samuel Rosenberg, of Battery B, Forty-third Artillery, in a letter to the Democrat and Chronicle, under date of December 26th. The men expect to be discharged within ten days and return home in a body. Sergeant Rosenberg's letter follows:

"Every one of these soldiers has seen hard fighting at the front and the service record of each man shows that he has been in the offensives of St. Mihiel, Argonne, Meuse and Verdun. The fighting boys from overseas had many tales to tell of the battle field and in every corner of the camp they were surrounded by groups of soldiers who lost their chance of going over by the sudden ending of the war.

"Battery B was one of the artillery units that used the eight-inch railroad guns that are mounted on flat cars and did such wnoderful work in backing up the infantry in the American drives. The entire battery was cited for bravery for remaining at the guns under a heavy shell fire from the enemy.

"The men told of their hardships while at the front. There were times when the men did not remove a stitch of clothes for nearly three weeks, and in some of their positions water had to be carried nearly five miles.

"The boys left Rochester with the draft contingent that went to Fort Hancock on December 17, 1917. After a few months' training they were sent to France. They all wear the war service chevron for six months' foreign service and a few of them also wear wound stripes, most of them being wounded by shrapnel from the enemy's guns."

Following is a list of the Rochester men in the battery:

Sergeants Samuel Rosenberg and Charles R. Trentman.
Engineer Russell Haggith.
Fireman Fred A. Schlink.
Corporals Guilford Porter, Thomas Rankin and George H. Hotchkins.
Mechanic Winnie D. Wheeler.
Cooks Joseph A. Sykes, James A. Sidman and Fred C. Hall.
Bugler Joseph Rivers.
Privates, first class, Clifton O. Dasson, George W. Jones, Harry H. Kester, George Lay, William Pearson, Paul D. Sweeney, Ulrich F. Froicke.
Privates – Angelo Amore, Vincent C. Bailey, Clarence J. Alway, Philip Bova, Job Croston, Robert G. Crouch. Pasquale Danielle Guiseppangelo DePetris, Robert D. Emery, William A. Geers, Stanley E. Geerer, John C. Graham, Walter J. Hanifin, Jacob C. Hoffman, Edmund T. Howard, Claude V. F. Kampke, Edwin Kane, Ernest Kauffman, Leo C. Knapp, Walter Kolesnick, August J. Kronk, Michael J. Larkin, Harry S. Lauch, Louis Longo, John J. Mungenast, Albert McCabe, William J. McHale, Daniel J. McMahon, Anthony Norwich, Joseph Patulski, Hyman Pekarsky, William J. Plicker, Loreto Ranalet, Max L. Robson, Frank J. Schunski, Irving R. Smith, Garson Trott, Edward J. Weaver, George D. Wilder, Arthur C. Wulle, James N. Yates, Louis E. Zimmerman. Joseph Rothstein and Harry Wolin.

This December 29, 1918, article in the *Democrat and Chronicle* (Rochester, NY) describes the exploits of Battery B, 43d Coast Artillery, in France and the conditions they faced. Fred Hall's name is found in the right column, identified as a Cook, near the top of the list of men from Rochester in the battery. The unit had just returned to Virginia when this article was written.[155]

AMERICAN LEGION

The Hiscock-Fishbaugh Post Formed Here. Officers Named

American Legion

The Hiscock-Fishbaugh Post Formed Here, Officers Named

Sunday afternoon a meeting was held in the First Baptist Church parlors fort the purpose of forming a Post of the American Legion in the Town of Parma.

Seventeen ex-service men were present and, all being in favor of forming a Post, signed an application for a charter.

The Post is to be named after two well known to the community and who gave their lives in the Worlds War, for the sake of Humanity. These two heroes who we all mourn are Lester Hiscock and Glenn Fishbaugh. The Post will be called, "The Hiscock-Fishbaugh Post."

The following officers were elected, Lucius Bagley, County Committeeman; Fred C. Hall, Chairman; J. L. Crook, Secretary; Henry A. Smith, Treasurer.

Members of the Post and those who should be members will be notified when the next meeting will be held, which probably wont be before the charter is received.

Herman Worden, Frank Randall and Champney Lee were appointed a committee to secure a suitable meeting place.

suitable meeting place.

Returning to Hilton after his discharge from Fort Eustis, Virginia, in January 1919, Fred didn't waste time uniting his fellow veterans. Seventeen World War I veterans met at the First Baptist Church to form an American Legion Post in the town of Parma on Sunday, November 30, 1919. Fred was elected Chairman, a title he only held until the temporary charter for the American Legion Hiscock-Fishbaugh Post 788 was granted on January 1, 1920, at which time he became the "Commander."[156] The permanent charter was granted on August 1, 1920.[157] (The December 4, 1919, article from the *Hilton Record* is retyped for easier reading. The archival image saved to microfilm is poor in quality.)

Fred Hall is pictured with his first wife, Harriet C. Robb, in an undated family photo.[158] [above] Fred and Harriet parted ways sometime between 1920 and 1925. Fred is listed on the 1925 New York State Census as single and living with his parents.

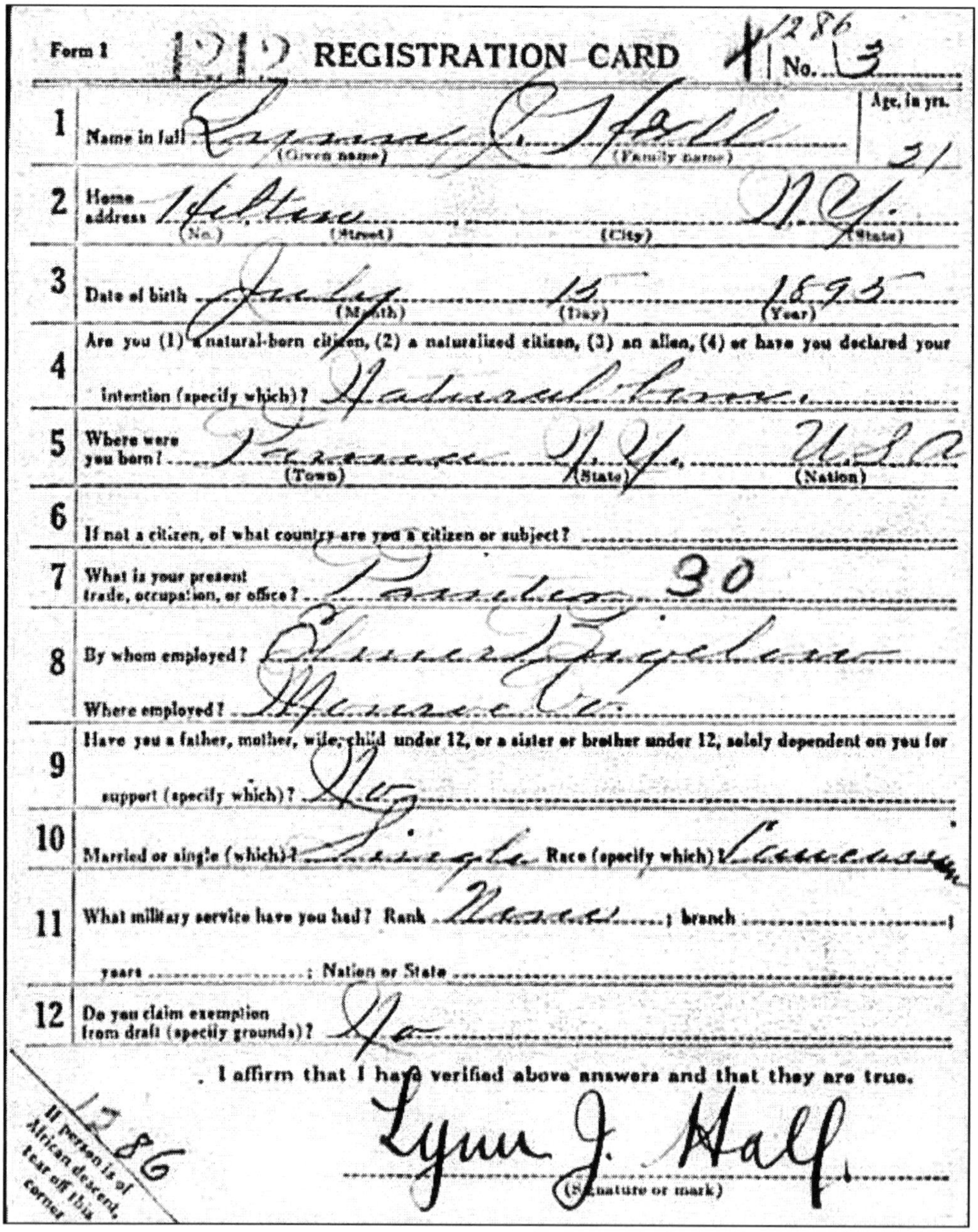

LYNN JAMES HALL
1895 – 1947

Lynn entered the United States Army through induction at Spencerport, New York, on February 24, 1918, as a twenty-two-year-old Private. By July 21, 1918, Lynn had been promoted twice, first to Corporal, then Sergeant. He mustered out on June 5, 1919, to accept an appointment as an army field clerk.[j] He was stationed at Camp Devens in Ayer, Massachusetts, for the duration of his enlistment and was discharged August 21, 1919.

Lynn James Hall was born on July 15, 1895, to Mervin J. (known as M. J.) and Sarah Jennie (Calcutt) Hall in Parma, New York. He attended Rochester Business Institute in 1911 and worked as a painter for Elmer Bigelow between 1915 and 1918. In 1920 he was living in the Rochester, New York, working as a salesman in a shoe store.

He married Mildred F. Henderson on August 7, 1920, and they made their home in Rochester where Lynn worked in two professions—painting and retail grocery. Lynn filed bankruptcy, owing to creditors such as Rochester Packing Company and the H. J. Heinz Company;[159] the bankruptcy decision was finalized in 1926. He remained active in the grocery business as shown in this May 1932 photo from the *Times-Union* (Rochester, NY).[160] [right]

Like Vegetables Fresh?

Lynn J. Hall, manager of Uncle Sam Store 33, which was opened Saturday at 984 Monroe Avenue, is explaining the advantages of the fountain of youth to one of his first customers, Miss Janet Osterman, 962 Monroe Avenue. The fountain of youth is a vapor spray hydrator and cooling system, the latest device for keeping green vegetables in prime condition. The Uncle Sam Company is now employing 100 people, the largest number in 12 years. H. J. Arent is president of the company and J. M. Solomon, secretary.

At the time of his World War II draft registration in 1942, he listed his place of employment as C.P. Ward Inc., a Rochester-based general construction contractor. By 1944 Lynn owned and operated John's Market,[161] a grocery store located on Chili Avenue in Rochester. He posted regular advertisements in the wanted section of the *Democrat and Chronicle* (Rochester, NY) looking for help.

He was a member of the Painter Union Local 150,[162] the Retail Food Merchants Association, the Rochester Leiderkranz Club (a choral society), and the 19th Ward Republican Club. Lynn died on August 7, 1947, and is interred in Mount Hope Cemetery in Rochester, New York.

---

[j] At that time, an army field clerk was an appointed position based on prior performance and merit. An enlisted man would need to request a discharge from their enlistment to accept the appointment, like Air Service pilots and other commissioned officers.

The following hospital order will show the routine of the hospital at this period:

BASE HOSPITAL NO. 19

ROCHESTER, NEW YORK

February 18, 1918.

HOSPITAL ORDER
NUMBER 32.

The following list of calls is published, effective this date:

Reveille, First Call	6.00 A.M.
Assembly	6.10 A.M.
Setting Up Exercise (10 minutes)	6.20 A.M.
Mess Call	6:30 A.M.
Fatigue Call	7.00 A.M.
Reveille and Setting Up Exercises will be dispensed with on Sundays and Holidays.	
Drill, First Call	7:20 A.M.
Assembly	7:30 A.M.
School Call	9:00 A.M.
Officers Call	10:00 A.M.
Sick Call	10:05 A.M.
Recall from School	11:55 A.M.
Mess	12:00 Noon
Guard Mount, First Call	12:20 P.M.
Assembly	12:30 P.M.
Fatigue and School Call	1:00 P.M.
Recall from Fatigue and School	4:00 P.M.
Retreat, First Call	4:20 P.M.
Assembly	4:30 P.M.
Mess Call	5:00 P.M.
Tattoo	9:00 P.M.
Call to Quarters	10:45 P.M.
Taps	11:00 P.M.
Sunday Church Call	9:00 A.M.
Saturday Inspection, First Call	9:20 A.M.
Assembly	9:30 A.M.

Beginning this date, all members of this Detachment will be required to be in their quarters, unless on pass, not later than 11:30 P.M.

By Order of the Commanding Officer:

HARRY A. SADDEN,
Captain, M. R. C.,
Adjutant.

[14]

Morley Hall was too young to register for any of the drafts; he enlisted with Base Hospital No. 19 in Rochester, New York. This is the hospital's daily schedule, prior to heading to France.[163]

MORLEY CLIFTON HALL
1899 – 1969

Morley enlisted in the United States Army Enlisted Reserve Corps at the age of nineteen on February 21, 1918, in Rochester, New York, and joined Base Hospital No. 19 in Rochester. [right][164] He traveled overseas aboard the RMS *Baltic*, departing from New York City on June 4, 1918, and was stationed in Vichy, Allier, Auvergne, in central France.[165]

Private Hall became Private First Class Hall when he was promoted on September 15, 1918. He returned aboard the USS *Freedom*, embarking from Saint-Nazaire, France, on April 13, 1919, arriving in the United States on April 28, 1919, and was discharged on May 7, 1919.

Morley Clifton Hall was born to Robert and Mary Ida (Heard) Hall on February 2, 1899, in

Enlisted Thursday

Morely C. Hall the nineteen year old son of Mr. and Mrs. Robert Hall of Burritt street, went to Rochester last Thursday and enlisted in the Base Hospital unit which expects shortly to leave for France. He was needed on the farm, but although out of draft age felt it his duty to go and so enlisted. May he be of much use and return safe again to his parents and friends.

Oshawa, Ontario, Canada. He immigrated with his parents and siblings to the United States in 1906, the family settling in Parma, New York. Morley was vice president of the Class of 1916 at Hilton High School [bottom left][166] as well as a delegate representing Hilton at the 1916 New York State Fair. [bottom right][167]

On December 27, 1922, Morley exchanged vows with Jean E. Foss and the couple made their home in Rochester before moving to Parma by 1930. Morley was deported to Canada and would spend the rest of his life a Canadian citizen;[k] he occasionally returned to visit his parents at their home in Hilton. He passed away in 1969 in Brantford, Brant County Municipality, Ontario, Canada, and is buried in Mount Hope Cemetery in Rochester, New York.

The Senior Class of Hilton High School was organized with the following officers: President, Carlyle Newcomb; vice-president, Morley Hall; secretary, Jennie Pickett; treasurer, Ida Thurston. Other members of the class were William Lear, Leona Chattin, Elizabeth Holman and Genevieve Luce.

—Every county in the state is entitled to send one young man from among the farming community to attend the State Fair at Syracuse. Morley Hall, son of Robert Hall of the Burritt street, this town, was chosen to represent this county and he left for there last Friday and will remain throughout the fair. The young men are staying in camps.

---

[k] Naturalization records were not found to indicate Morley Hall applied for naturalization or became a citizen of the United States.

FIRST OFFENDERS PUT ON PROBATION

Four Admitting Guilt Get Suspended Sentences.

Morley C. Hall, 25 years old, of Spencerport, who admitted forgery and attempted forgery, was given a suspended sentence of from two to four years in Auburn prison.

Two indictments, one charging attempted forgery and the other forgery, second degree, were returned against Morley C. Hall, 25 years old, of Spencerport. The first accuses him of forging the name of Cecil McMahon to a $60 check and presenting it for payment at the State Bank of Commerce at Brockport on June 2d. The second accuses him of obtaining $70 by means of a check forged with the name of W. M. Bender from the Lincoln-Alliance Bank on July 3d.

Morley Hall was indicted on forgery and attempted forgery charges in 1924. According to the *Democrat and Chronicle* (Rochester, NY) he received a suspended sentence in the Auburn, New York, prison. [168] [above] Morley Hall found himself in trouble, again, when he allegedly forged multiple checks and was arraigned in 1925. He admitted to violating the terms of his probation and was sentenced from two to four years at Auburn prison. [169] [below]

ADDITIONAL FORGED CHECKS ARE CHARGED TO PRISONER, ALLEGED MASTER 'PENMAN'

Following the arrest of Morley C. Hall, of No. 104 Fulton avenue, and arraignment yesterday morning in City Court on a charge of forgery, second degree, for the alleged signing of the name of his landlord, Howard M. Stone, to a check for $39, additional alleged bad checks, attributed to his skillful penmanship, have been pouring into police headquarters.

Hall pleaded not guilty to the charge and was held in $5,000 bail for a hearing on June 19th. Almost a year ago he was convicted of a similar charge in County Court and paroled after the sentence was suspended.

Eight bank clerks are said to have identified Hall as the casher of a number of alleged bad checks, four of which were produced by the Union Trust Company. The investigation was begun at their instigation.

Hall steadfastly denies the forgeries, despite the statement of Detectives Sharpe and Popp, who said he was a clever imitator of signatures and believed he was one of the cleverest forgers operating in this city for years.

BAD CHECK CHARGE ENDS MAN'S FREEDOM

Admitting violation of the terms of his probation, Morley C. Hall, 25 years old, yesterday was sent to Auburn prison to serve a sentence of from two to four years imposed on July 22d, 1924, when he pleaded guilty to an indictment for forgery, second degree. Hall admitted he recently forged the name of W. D. Bender, of Lyell avenue, to a $70 check. The district-attorney's office claimed Hall was responsible for several other forgeries.

Morley C. Hall, of No. 104 Fulton avenue, waived examination when arraigned on charges of forgery, second degree, and was held for the action of the Grand Jury.

Hall has been held in jail since his arrest last week by Detectives Sharpe and Popp for the alleged forgery of the name of Howard Stone, his landlord, to a check for $121. He also is accused of other forgeries.

WILL DEPORT PARMA MAN

Morley Hall's Habeas Corpus Plea Refused by Judge Hazel.

Morley Hall, 28 years old, Parma, N. Y. will be deported at once by the Immigration department following refusal of Federal Judge Hazel to issue a habeas corpus on his application heard in Federal court Wednesday morning. He is charged with having committed a crime involving moral turpitude within five years after his entrance into this country. Hall, who served with the American army in France for a year, has lived in this country since coming here with his parents from Canada 22 years ago. He is married to an American girl and has one child.

He was charged with forgery, second degree, pleaded guilty in 1924, and served a sentence of two and a half years in Auburn. In 1921 he returned from Canada, where he had spent a week on his wedding trip. He sought the writ of habeas corpus Wednesday on the claim that his entry should be figured from 1905, when he originally came here, and that the trip of one week in Canada should not be considered a re-entry

4th Deportation Faced by Veteran

Morley C. Hall, 37, Hilton, today faces his fourth deportation to Canada. He pleaded guilty to entering the country illegally before Federal Judge Harlan W. Rippey yesterday, was given a suspended term in Monroe County Penitentiary, placed on probation and ordered turned over to immigration authorities.

Immigration Inspector Henry W. Fogarty said Hall, who is stated to have served 11 months overseas with Base Hospital, 19, would be deported this morning.

Morley Hall of Brantford, Ontario, was a guest of his parents, Mr. and Mrs. Robert Hall on Saturday.

Between 1927 and 1936 Morley was charged, arraigned, and sentenced multiple times for forgery and parole violations. In 1936 he was facing his fourth deportation to Canada and could only visit family and friends in Hilton on the weekends as the lower right clip from the *Hilton (NY) Record* in 1955 reports.[170]

	REGISTRATION CARD	No. 69

Form 1   1206

1 Name in full *Eugene E. Higgs*   Age, in yrs. **22**
(First name) (Family name)

2 Home address ___ (No.) (Street) *Hilton* (City) *New York* (State)

3 Date of birth *November 6* (Month) (Day) *1894* (Year)

4 Are you (1) a natural-born citizen, (2) a naturalized citizen, (3) an alien, (4) or have you declared your intention (specify which)? *Natural born*

5 Where were you born? *Rhinebeck* (Town) *New York* (State) *U.S.A.* (Nation)

6 If not a citizen, of what country are you a citizen or subject?

7 What is your present trade, occupation, or office *30 Section Hand*

8 By whom employed? *New York Central R.R.*
Where employed? *Parma Monroe Co New York*

9 Have you a father, mother, wife, child under 12, or a sister or brother under 12, solely dependent on you for support (specify which)? *No*

10 Married or single (which)? *Single*   Race (specify which)? *Caucasian*

11 What military service have you had? Rank *None*; branch ___;
years ___; Nation or State ___

12 Do you claim exemption from draft (specify grounds)? *No*

I affirm that I have verified above answers and that they are true.

Eugene E. Higgs
(Signature or mark)

If person is of African descent, tear off this corner.

EUGENE F. HIGGS
1894 – 1924

Twenty-three-year-old Eugene was inducted into the United States Army at Rochester, New York, on April 28, 1918, at the rank of Private. He was assigned to Company 11, 3d Training Battalion, 153d Depot Brigade, at Camp Dix, New Jersey. He transferred to Company K, 311th Infantry, 78th Division, on May 8, 1918, upon completion of training.

He departed from Brooklyn, New York, for his overseas assignment on May 20, 1918, on the SS *Vestris*, arriving in England the first week of June 1918. After a brief stay in rest camps, the division infantry sailed for Calais, France, moved by train to the Lumbres Training Area, and affiliated with the British 34th Division. Eugene was promoted to Private First Class on August 1, 1918, designated a Mechanic on August 12, 1918, and promoted to Sergeant on August 23, 1918. Sergeant Higgs participated in the Saint-Mihiel Operation September 12-16, 1918. On October 25, 1918, while the division was advancing its line into the Bois de Bourgogne, Eugene was wounded. The extent of his wounds unknown, it is presumed that Eugene remained in a hospital or convalescent status until he began his return journey to the United States on October 17, 1919. He departed from Brest, France, aboard the USAT *Edellyn*, the manifest listing his group as the Brest Sanitary Special Company #5284, and arrived in Hoboken, New Jersey, on October 29, 1919. On the 1920 United States Federal Census he is listed as a patient in the United States Army General Hospital No. 31, which was in Carlisle Barracks, west of Harrisburg, Pennsylvania. Eugene was honorably discharged on February 2, 1920.

Eugene F. Higgs was born in Rhinebeck, New York, on November 6, 1894, to Francis (Frank) J. and Grace (Traver) Higgs. He grew up moving west across New York, living in Madison, Oswego, and Cayuga Counties before settling in Ogden, New York. He worked at a few jobs before entering the service to include a laborer on his family's farm, painter, section hand for the New York Central Railroad and, in 1917, was employed by Hilton High School as "labor on school grounds."[171]

Eugene's middle name–Frank–or corresponding initial "F" are found in the United States Army Transport Service Passenger Lists,[172] the 1905 United States Federal Census and his headstone. The signature he provides on his World War I Draft Registration card shows an "E" for middle name or initial.

Eugene passed away on May 25, 1924, at his parents' Brockport home and is buried in Lakeview Cemetery in Brockport, New York.

> —Eugene Higgs, who recently returned from France, was in this village this week visiting friends. His father, Frank Higgs and family are now residing at Seneca Falls.

The April 22, 1920, edition of the *Hilton (NY) Record* announced Eugene's return to Hilton for a visit following his discharge from the hospital and army.[173]

Form 1
719

168.   REGISTRATION CARD   No. *179*

1 Name in full *Foster Hitchcock*   Age, in yrs. *26*
(Given name)   (Family name)

2 Home address *245 Mill St*
(No.)   (Street)   (City)   (State)

3 Date of birth *Feb 24 - 1891*
(Month)   (Day)   (Year)

4 Are you (1) a natural-born citizen, (2) a naturalized citizen, (3) an alien, (4) or have you declared your intention (specify which)? *natural born*

5 Where were you born? *Hilton   Monroe County N.Y.*
(Town)   (State)   (Nation)

6 If not a citizen, of what country are you a citizen or subject?

7 What is your present trade, occupation, or office? *Teamster*   30

8 By whom employed? *Geo Bautell*
Where employed? *Lake Ave*

9 Have you a father, mother, wife, child under 12, or a sister or brother under 12, solely dependent on you for support (specify which)? *Wife*

10 Married or single (which)? *Married* Race (specify which)? *White*

11 What military service have you had? Rank *no*; branch
years ; Nation or State

12 Do you claim exemption from draft (specify grounds)? *no*

I affirm that I have verified above answers and that they are true.

Foster Hitchcock
(Signature or mark)

If person is of African descent, tear off this corner

126

FOSTER FRANK HISCOCK
1891 – 1952

Foster enlisted in the United States Army on November 2, 1910, and was assigned as a Trumpeter to Troop C, 11th Cavalry. He was discharged on October 29, 1913, from Fort Bayard in New Mexico on a Surgeon's Certificate of Disability; his character was listed as "Excellent," his service as "Honest and Faithful."[174] At the age of twenty-six, he was inducted into the United States Army on December 16, 1917, at Rochester, New York. He was assigned to Battery F, 57th Artillery, Coast Artillery Corps, probably at Fort Hancock, New Jersey, for most of his one year and seven-month enlistment. [right, top][175] His mother thought he had been sent to France[176] when, in fact, he had been in quarantine (reason unknown) and unable to write home.[177] [right, middle] He was discharged on August 11, 1919, probably from Camp Merritt, Bergen County, New Jersey. [right, bottom][178]

Foster Frank Hiscock was born to James Duane and Jennie M. (Wheeler) Hiscock on February 24, 1891, in Parma, New York. He married Anna Dietrick of Hamlin, New York, on October 1, 1911. After the war he was living in Manhattan, New York, where he worked as a chauffeur, clerk, and a truckman for a construction company when he married Mary Dooley on October 18, 1919. Required to fill out the World War II draft registration card at the age of fifty-one, he was living in Bronx, New York, employed as a clerk. Foster died August 1, 1952, and is buried in Parma Union Cemetery in Parma, New York.

—Foster Hiscock of Fort Hancock, N. J., was home from Friday night to Saturday night on a furlough.

—Mr. and Mrs. Duane Hiscock have not heard from their eldest son Foster for quite a while and expect that is now in Fran[ce]. The other son Lester was here [a] week but was called back to Camp Upton and it is expected that [he] also is now on his way to France.

—Mrs. Duane Hiscock requests to state that Foster has not gone [to] France as was thought but was [in] quarantine, so could not write [ho]me. Also that Lester was accompanied to Rochester on his [w]ay back to camp by his uncle.

—Foster Hiscock returned last week from the U. S. service and is visiting his parents, Mr. and Mrs. Duane Hiscock. He has been stationed at Camp Merritt.

Truck Driver Arrested After Accident

Charged with driving while intoxicated, Fred Huff, 31, of 12 Hilton, was arrested after a large truck he was driving collided with another machine in Clinton Avenue North near Lillian Place last night.

Foster Hiscock, 44, also of Hilton, Huff's helper, was arrested on an intoxication charge. Both were taken into custody by Policeman Michael Callahan of the Franklin Street Station.

Driver of the other car was Conrad Kreuzer of 740 St. Paul Street. His wife, Louise, and their 4-year-old daughter, Margaret, suffered shock, and were treated by a physician.

Foster Hiscock was involved in a motor vehicle accident in Rochester according to this November 3rd, 1934, article in the *Democrat and Chronicle* (Rochester, NY).[179] [left] The evening edition of the *Times-Union* (Rochester, NY), same date, reported that Foster "pleaded guilty to a charge of public intoxication and was given a suspended sentence."[180]

Serial No. 75   121   X   Registration No. 75

1   Name in full   *George E. Hiscock*
       (Given name)   (Family name)   Age, in yrs. *21*

2   Home address   *186 Pullman Ave. Rochester. N.Y.*
      (No.)   (street)   (City or town)   (State)

3   Date of birth   *May 9 1897*
      (Month)   (Day)   (Year)

4   Where were you born?   *Rush N.Y. U.S.A.*
      (City or town)   (State)   (Nation)

5   I am { 1. A native of the United States.
         2. A naturalized citizen.
         3. An alien.
         4. I have declared my intention.
         5. A noncitizen or citizen Indian.
      (Strike out lines or words not applicable)

6   If not a citizen, of what Nation are you a citizen or subject?

7   Father's birthplace   *Penn. U.S.A.*
      (City or town)   (State or province)   (Nation)

8   Name of employer   *Eastman Kodak Co.,*
    Place of employment   *Kodak Pk. Rochester N.Y.*
      (No.)   (Street)   (City or town)   (State)

9   Name of nearest relative   *(Father) Jesse S. Hiscock*
    Address of nearest relative   *Hilton N.Y.*
      (No.)   (Street)   (City or town)   (State or Nation)

10   Race—White, Negro, Indian, or Oriental.
     (Strike out words not applicable)

I affirm that I have verified above answers and that they are true.

George E. Hiscock
         (Signature or Mark of Registrant.)

If person is of African descent, tear off this corner.

P. M. G. O.
Form 1 (blue)

REGISTRATION CARD.   3—0738

GEORGE E. HISCOCK
1897 – 1972

Twenty-one-year-old George was inducted into the United States Army at Rochester, New York, on July 17, 1918, at the rank of Private and assigned to the 14th Company, Coast Defense of Southern New York, Coast Artillery Corps, organized at Fort Hamilton, New York.[181] He was discharged on December 17, 1918.

George was born in Rush, New York, on May 9, 1897, to Jesse and Mary (Harradine) Hiscock and by the turn of the century the family was living in Greece, New York. Farm work was plentiful and George found work as a farm laborer before trading that work for a position with Eastman Kodak Company at Kodak Park in Rochester prior to entering military service.

He married Gertrude Kanous on August 10, 1920, and the couple made their home in Spencerport, New York, where George worked as a carpenter to support his family. He was an active member of many civic organizations including Parma Lodge, Independent Order of Odd Fellows, where he was the recording secretary in 1931.[182] He was active in the Red Jacket Council of the Boy Scouts[183] [right] and appointed to head training for the North District in 1939,[184] [below] and led the training committee in 1940.[185] [lower right]

George was a member of the American Legion Ferris-Goodridge Post 330 in Spencerport and in 1938 was elected a delegate from the post to the Monroe County convention held in Hilton the same year.[186] George Hiscock passed away on March 26, 1972, and is interred in Parma Union Cemetery in Parma, New York.

Red Jacket's Wooden Anniversary

Plans for the "Wooden Anniversary" of Red Jacket council were officially approved at the Executive Board meeting held Thursday, at Rochester. Schuyler Arnold, president, announced the following chairmen of committees: Charles Burnett, Parma Corners, program and arrangements; George Hiscock, Spencerport, exhibits; Elmore Turner, Gates, souvenir folder; Walter Parker, Henrietta, attendance.

North Star District will be host to the meeting of the Council at the banquet held on the evening of March 23, Grange hall, Spencerport. Scoutmasters of the North Star district will meet March 4th to complete plans for the scouting exhibit. It will cover displays on cubbing, scouting, senior scouting, and special features.

Red Jacket council was organized in Spencerport in 1934, and received its first charter from the National council March 17, 1934. A speaker of national note will feature the evening. Eagle citations, Beaver awards, and special recognition will be given to scouters who have contributed to the success of the scouting program over a period of years.

Leaders Appointed In North District

The following appointments have been announced by Dr. John B. Whitelaw, chairman of the North District, Red Jacket Council, Boy Scouts:

District commissioner, Ellery Burnett; recording secretary, E. Crippen; advancement, Charles Kenyon; camping and activities, Dr. Milton C. Cummings; health and safety, Clayton Goodridge; finance, John White; training, George Hiscock, and member-at-large, Fred B. Huff.

Five Training Courses on the introduction to Scouting are being conducted by the training committee of Red Jacket Council, of which George Hiscock of Spencerport is chairman. This committee will meet March 11 at the new Scout office in Rochester to lay plans for the second part of the course. Sessions during the past few weeks were held in the following locations: Swan Library, Albion troop headquarters, Spencerport; Grange Hall, Greece; Town Hall, Rush; and Legion Hall, Fairport. The training committee consists of the following men: George Hiscock, Spencerport; Elliott Smith, Penfield; George Rich, West Henrietta; Marion F. Westfall, Gates; Francis Goodwin, Albion; and Edward Besley, North Chili. Certificates for the training course will be presented at the annual Council meeting on March 21.

A. R. Gilman of Pomona Drive, Greece, is field commissioner of training for Red Jacket Council.

Form 1   1257   REGISTRATION CARD X40 No. 50

1 Name in full Lester P Hiscock   Age, in yrs. 21
      (Given name)   (Family name)

2 Home address _____ Hilton, New York
      (No.)   (Street)   (City)   (State)

3 Date of birth June   26   1896
      (Month)   (Day)   (Year)

4 Are you (1) a natural-born citizen, (2) a naturalized citizen, (3) an alien, (4) or have you declared your intention (specify which)? Natural born

5 Where were you born? Parma   New York   U.S.A.
      (Town)   (State)   (Nation)

6 If not a citizen, of what country are you a citizen or subject?

7 What is your present trade, occupation, or office? Labor on Farm

8 By whom employed? Myron Roberts
   Where employed? Hamlin Monroe Co New York

9 Have you a father, mother, wife, child under 12, or a sister or brother under 12, solely dependent on you for support (specify which)? No

10 Married or single (which)? Single   Race (specify which)? Caucasian

11 What military service have you had? Rank None ; branch _____
    years _____ ; Nation or State _____

12 Do you claim exemption from draft (specify grounds)? _____

I affirm that I have verified above answers and that they are true.

C A   Lester P Hiscock
      (Signature or mark)

If person is of African descent, tear off this corner.

★ LESTER PETER HISCOCK ★
1896 – 1918

Lester, at age twenty-one, was inducted into the United States Army at Spencerport, New York, on September 26, 1917. At the rank of Private, he was assigned to Battery D, 309th Field Artillery, 78th Division, at Camp Dix, New Jersey. Lester was caught in the shuffle of men to fill out stateside divisions and, on November 13, 1917, was transferred to Company A, 325th Infantry, 82d Division, at Camp Gordon, Georgia. The division moved via Camps Mills and Upton to embarkation ports in the northeast on April 10, 1918; Lester departed New York City on April 25, 1918, aboard the SS *Khyber*.

Once in France, the division trained with the British 66th Division, during which time Lester was promoted to Private First Class on May 19, 1918. After participating in the Saint-Mihiel Operation in mid-September, the 82d Division participated in the Meuse-Argonne Operation beginning October 6, 1918; Lester was wounded on October 14, 1918. Military records show two dates of death for Lester–either the 16th or 17th of October–though no discrepancy has been found on the date of his burial which was the 17th of October 1918. He was buried in an "American Battle Area Cemetery" located in the Commune of Les Islettes, Meuse, France.

Lester was disinterred on June 2, 1918, and buried in Meuse-Argonne American Military Cemetery located east of the village of Romagne-sous-Montfaucon in Meuse, France. On July 13, 1921, he was disinterred again, at the request of his family, and returned home to Hilton, New York, departing Antwerp, Belgium aboard the USAT *Wheaton* and arriving in Hoboken, New Jersey, on August 6, 1921. Lester arrived in Parma, New York, on September 15, 1921, and was buried on September 18, 1921, in Parma Union Cemetery in Parma, New York.

Born in Hilton, New York, to James Duane and Jennie M. (Wheeler) Hiscock on June 26, 1896, Lester Peter Hiscock grew up in Hilton and worked as a general laborer at a local warehouse. American Legion Post 788, organized on November 30, 1919, by seventeen World War I veterans, was named the Hiscock-Fishbaugh Post 788 in honor of Lester P. Hiscock and Glenn W. Fishbaugh, both of whom were killed in action on the battlefields of France.

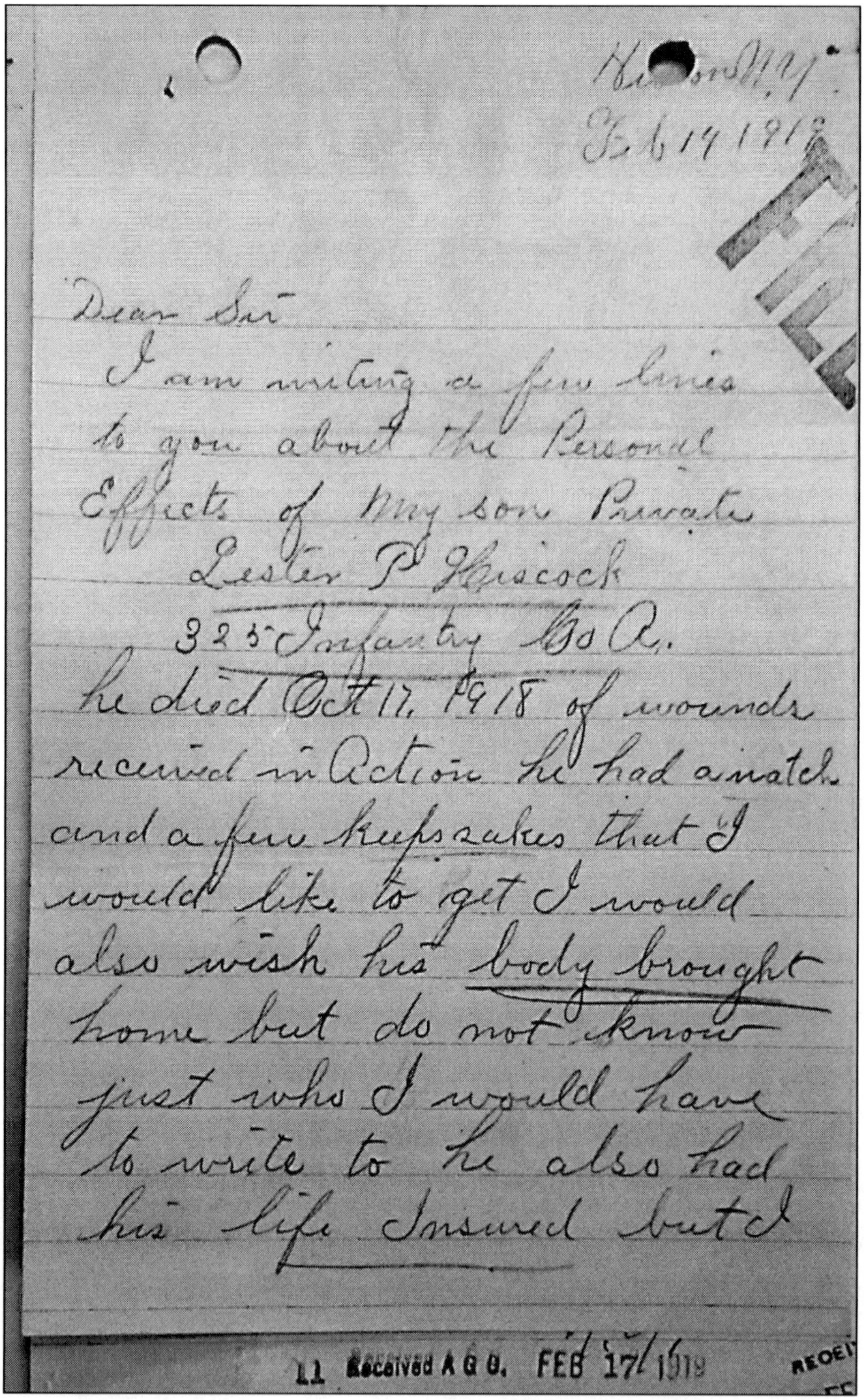

Hudson N.Y.
Feb 17 1919

Dear Sir
I am writing a few lines
to you about the Personal
Effects of my son Private
Lester P Hiscock
325 Infantry Co A.
he died Oct 17, 1918 of wounds
received in Action he had a watch
and a few keepsakes that I
would like to get I would
also wish his body brought
home but do not know
just who I would have
to write to he also had
his life Insured but I

11 Received A.G.O. FEB 17/1919 RECEI

do not hear any thing about that it seem as if it is time I received some notice and I have tried thru the Red Cross to find out where he was wounded and how long he was in the Hospital but I have not heard a word If you could help me any I would be very thankful

Yours.

Mrs Jennie Hiscock
Hilton
Monroe Co.
N.Y.

L1 Received A G O. FEB 17 1919

Lester's mother, Mrs. Jennie Hiscock, wrote to the War Department in February 1919 seeking information on where he was wounded, what happened to his personal effects, who to write to about his insurance, and to also express her wish to have "his body brought home." [187] [above and facing page]

293.8 Hiscock, Lester P.
(Misc. Div.) DDR:EBB

February 18, 1919.

Mrs. Jennie Hiscock,
Monroe Co.,
Hilton, N. Y.

Dear Madam:-

The inclosed Memorandum is sent to you in response to your letter of February 14th, relative to the
return of the body of your son, Private Lester P. Hiscock.

With reference to his personal effects, you
should communicate with the Effects Bureau, Port of Embarkation, Hoboken, N. J., and with the Director, Bureau of
War Risk Insurance, Washington, D.C., concerning his insurance. For further information in regard to his death, you
should write to the Commanding Officer, Company A, 325th
Infantry, American Expeditionary Forces, as this office is
not advised in these matters.

It is desired to express to you the deep sympathy
of the Department on account of the loss of your son, and to
commend you for the sacrifice you have made for the cause of
Democracy.

Very sincerely yours,

J. O. Assears
Adjutant General.

1 Incl.

The Adjutant General's office replied to Jennie Hiscock
with few answers other than a list of offices for her to
contact. [above] [188]

The one artifact that was returned and is now in the files
of the National Archives and Records Administration in
Saint Louis, Missouri, was one of Private First Class Lester
P. Hiscock's identification tags. [right] [189]

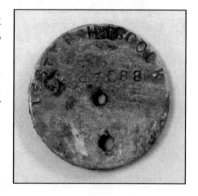

Hilton N.Y.
Jan 19, 1920

Dear Sir
I thought I would write a few lines to you to find out if I could what the Government was agoing to do about bringing to Bodies of the Soldiers boys home I can not tell by the papers for one time they say they are and the next time it says they are not *my son* he is layed in the Argonne by a town name Les Islettes we would like to have his body if we could Pledre Write and let me know if you can Yours.

Duane Hiscock
Hilton Monroe Co

WAR HERO BURIED

American Legion Honors the Late Lester Hiscock at Services with Full Military Honors

The body of Lester Hiscock, son of Mr. and Mrs. Duane Hiscock, arrived in Hilton from France last Thursday morning. Lester was a member of Co. A., 325th Infantry, 82nd Division. He entered the service Sept. 27th, 1917, arriving in France in the spring of 1918, after training in Camp Dix and Camp Gordon. After several engagements he was wounded at Fleville near the Argonne Forest, on the 14th of October, 1918, and died three days later. He leaves, besides his parents, one brother, Foster of New York City.

The funeral service was held Sunday afternoon and was probably the largest funeral ever held in Hilton. It was a complete military service, in charge of the Hiscock-Fishbaugh Post, American Legion. After a brief service at the house, the body was carried by the military bearers, escorted by the guard of honor, and followed by the members of the Post and the mourners to the Baptist Church. The chaplain of the day was the pastor, Rev. A. T. Mercer, who gave the address, paying tribute to the great service of the heroic dead. Interment took place in the Parma Union Cemetery, with a final salute by the military squad, and "taps" sounded by the bugler.

In the words of General Pershing, "He bravely laid down his life for the cause of his country. His name will ever remain fresh in the hearts of his friends and comrades."

Lester's father also inquired of the War Department, a year after his wife's request, as to what the government was doing about bringing the bodies of the fallen soldiers home. [above] [190]

A year and a half later, on Sunday, September 18, 1921, Lester Hiscock was finally "home" when he was laid to rest with full honors following a memorial service at the Baptist Church. [right][191]

Name HOCHBRUECKNER - GEORGE NICHOLAS			Service Number 173-12-29 2|6	
Enlisted at NAVY RECRUITING STATION BUFFALO N.Y.				
XXXXX		Date 1-7-18		
Age at Entrance 18 YRS. 10 MO. Rate APPRENTICE SEAMAN				U.S.N. XXXX.XXF.
Home Address 217 BRONSON AVENUE		Town ROCHESTER		
K County		State N.Y.		
Served at	From	To	Served as	No. Days
HOME-AWAITING ORDERS	1-7-18	2-18-18	APPRENTICE SEAMAN	72
NAVAL TRAINING STATION				
NEWPORT R.I.	2-18-18	3-20-18	SEAMAN SECOND CLASS	226
USS MARTHA WASHINGTON	3-20-18	11-11-18	SEAMAN	10
Remarks:				
Date Discharge 2-12-19 RECEIVING SHIP AT				
Place XXXXXXXX PELHAM BAY PARK N.Y.			Rating at Discharge SEAMAN	
Library Bureau 26-1533 -4				

George Hochbrueckner's *New York State Abstracts of World War I Military Service* card from the New York State Archives. George was too young to register for the draft when he enlisted in the United States Navy and did not have to complete a draft registration card.[192]

GEORGE NICHOLAS HOCHBRUECKNER
1899 – 1963

George enlisted in the United States Navy at the age of eighteen at the Recruiting Station in Buffalo, New York, on January 7, 1918. From February 18, 1918, until March 20, 1918, George received his training at the Naval Training Station in Newport, Rhode Island. He was assigned to the USS *Martha Washington*, transferring off the ship on November 11, 1918. He progressed through the ranks from an Apprentice Seaman to Seaman Second Class before his discharge as a Seaman on February 12, 1919.

George Nicholas Hochbrueckner was born in March of 1899 to John J. and Louise (Brueck) Hochbrueckner. In 1905, his mother, a dressmaker, was a patient at the Rochester State Hospital for the insane in Rochester, New York, and in May of 1908 his father John, a tailor, passed away. Now on their own, George, age fifteen, and his brother, Edward, were living as lodgers on Ridge Road in Parma, New York, and attending Spencerport schools. As a freshman, George was treasurer of the Class of 1914. After his discharge from the navy he returned to Parma and found employment as an auto mechanic.

George married Ruth Eddy of Albion, New York, on November 6, 1929, and together they made their home in the hamlet of Parma Corners, New York. [right][193]

Hochbrueckner—Eddy

Miss Ruth Eddy of Albion and George Hochbrueckner of Parma Corners were married on Wednesday evening at the home of the officiating clergyman, the Rev. A. F. Groesbeck.

Mr. and Mrs. Hochbrueckner will reside in Parma Corners.

In the mid-1930's George served his community as a fire commissioner for the Ogden-Parma Fire District. [below][194] By 1940 he was working for the Town of Parma as a tax collector [left][195] while his wife worked as a telephone operator. George died in the Batavia Veterans Hospital on April 28, 1963, and is interred in Mount Albion Cemetery in Albion, New York.

Party Raidings Noted in Report For Primaries

Continued from Page Eleven

Ogden Democrats nominated Carbos Wolfram for supervisor and Fred Roach for peace justice by a writein. Wolfram, present peace justice, was selected for supervisor after the death of Supervisor Joseph E. Morgan. In Parma, write-ins in the Democratic primary resulted in the nomination of William MacDermand, Democrat, Robert Stuart and George Hochbrueckner, Republicans, for town clerk, peace justice and collector.

Riga Democrats by a writein nominated Willis deBerger, a Democrat, for highways' superintendent. In Wheatland, where no assessor candidate was designated by the town Democratic nomination, Clarence Armstrong, Democrat, was nominated in a writein.

HEADS FIRE DISTRICT

George Hochbrueckner has been re-elected commissioner of the Ogden-Parma Fire District, it was announced last night. Others chosen for the board were Morton Pisher, Hugh J. Coyle, Michael Ryan and William Niblock. Frank M. Harroun was named district treasurer.

	Holman, Avery H		395,842		White	2½
	(Surname)	(Christian name)	(Army serial number)		(Race: White or colored)	
Residence:		Hilton	Monroe		NEW YORK	
	(Street and house number)	(Town or city)	(County)		(State)	

*Enlisted in
†Born in
Organizations:

RA at Ft Slocum NY —   June 30/18
Pittsburg Pa   —   18 1/12 yrs
Camp Humphreys Engrs Tng Rgt to Sept 12/19; Co C 545 En
Engrs to disch

Grades:

Sgt Sept 1/18   —   —

Engagements:

—   —

Wounds or other injuries received in action: None.
‡Served overseas: Sept 22/18 to June 27/19
§Hon. disch.
Was reported   July 3/19   Re-enlistment
                                    per cent disabled on date of discharge, in view of occupation.
Remarks: 0
                                    —

Form No. 724-2½ A.G.O.   *Insert "R. A.", "N. G.", "E. R. C.", "N. A.", as case may be, followed by place and
March 12, 1920.   date of enlistment.   †Give place of birth and date of birth, or age at enlistment.
                        ‡Give dates of departure from and arrival in the United States.   §Give date and cause.

Avery Holman's *New York State Abstracts of World War I Military Service* card. from the New York State Archives. Avery was too young to register for the draft when he enlisted in the United States Army and did not have to complete a draft registration card.[196]

AVERY H. HOLMAN
1900 –1969

Avery enlisted in the Regular Army at eighteen-years-old on June 30, 1918, at Fort Slocum, New York. [below, right][197] After initial in-processing and training at Fort Slocum, Private Holman transferred to Camp Humphreys (now Fort Belvoir) in Accotink, Virginia, to attend replacement training school for the Corps of Engineers. He was promoted to Sergeant on September 1, 1918, and was assigned to Company C, 545th Engineers, on September 12, 1918.

> Mrs. Adeline Holman is visiting her son, Sergeant Avery H. Holman, in Washington, D. C.

> —Avery Holman of this village, son of Mrs. Adaline Holman, went to Rochester last Friday and enlisted in the U. S. Engineering Corp. He returned here that night, but on Saturday he left Rochester for Fort Slocumb, Long Island. His mother got a letter from him on Tuesday from that place.

After a visit with his mother in Washington, DC, [above][198] he left to serve overseas on September 23, 1918, embarking at Hoboken, New Jersey, aboard the USS *Rijndam*. While in France, Avery participated in the Meuse-Argonne campaign. He returned from Saint-Nazaire, France, on June 14, 1919, arriving in Brooklyn, New York, aboard the USS *Tiger* on the 27th of June 1919. Avery was discharged on July 3, 1919, and re-enlisted for another three years.

Avery H. Holman was born in Pittsburgh, Pennsylvania, on May 28, 1900, to Dr. Samuel and Adaline (Thomas) Holman. By 1905, the family had moved to Parma, New York, but after the death of Avery's father in 1910, Adaline moved the family to Rochester, New York, to support them as a dressmaker.

Avery moved to Tonawanda, New York, between 1923 and 1925, and worked as a carpenter. He met his future bride, Marie Antoinette Mendonsa, in Buffalo and exchanged wedding vows on the 9th of July 1926. The couple lived in Rochester, then moved to East Aurora, New York.[199] [below, right] Avery worked in construction to support his family. He was a member of the Knights of Pythias, Aurora Grata Lodge 39, while in Rochester and was chancellor commander in 1930. [below, left][200] Avery died in April of 1969 in East Aurora, New York.

Knights of Pythias

Avery Holman will be installed as the new chancellor commander at the next meeting of Aurora Grata Lodge 39, Knights of Pythias, following his election at the annual meeting of the lodge. The installation will be put on by the district deputy grand chancellor, Garson Grossman.

M. D. O'Loughlin was re-elected keeper of records and seals of the order for another year. He has occupied that office for the last 30 years.

Knights of Pythias

F. S. Sullivan, vice-chancellor of Aurora Grata Lodge 39, Knights of Pythias, will assume the chair of chancellor commander at the lodge's meeting in Hiokatoo Hall, Reynolds Arcade, tomorrow evening. Avery Holman, previous chancellor commander, has moved to East Aurora. Names of candidates for the rank of Page will be balloted on tomorrow night also, preparatory to putting on the degree at the next convention.

Hovey Justus Allan   White   2½

| (Surname) | (Christian name) | (Army serial number) | (Race: White or colored) |

Residence: xx   New York   NEW YORK

| (Street and house number) | (Town or city) | (County) | (State) |

* Enlisted in   NG New York N Y May 9/16   —

† Born in   Hilton N Y   —

Organizations: Co I 71 Regt NY NG to disch   —

See 105 Inf

Grades: Pvt   —

Engagements: xx   —

* Wounds or other injuries received in action: None.

‡ Served overseas: no   —

§ Hon. disch.   Nov 26/17 To accept commission   —

Was reported   xx   per cent disabled on date of discharge, in view of occupation.

Remarks:

Form No. 724-2½ A.G.O.   *Insert "R. A.", "N. G.", "E. R. C.", "N A.", as case may be, followed by place and
March 12, 1920.   date of enlistment.   † Give place of birth and date of birth, or age at enlistment.
‡ Give dates of departure from and arrival in the United States.   § Give date and cause.

Hovey Justus Allan   OFFICER—ORC   White

| (Surname) | (Christian name) |

Residence   xx   New York   NEW YORK

| (Street and house number) | (Town or city) | (County) | (State) |

* Born in   Hilton N Y July 4, 1891   —

† Called into active service as   1st Lt Inf Nov 27/17 fr NG   ‡ Training Camp.

Promotions: none   —

Organizations and staff assignments: 610 Sq to--; 1 Tng Bn to disch   —

Principal stations: Leon Springs Tex; Kelly Fld Tex;
Coronado Calif; Rockwell Fld Calif   —

Engagements: xx   —

* Wounds received in action: None.

§ Served overseas   no   —

|| Hon. disch.   Jan 4/19   for convenience of the Government, services no longer required.

Was reported   0   per cent disabled on date of discharge, in view of occupation.

Remarks: Enl serv   —

Form No. 84c–1   * Give place and date.   † Insert (a) grade; (b) arm or staff corps or department; (c) date;
A.G.O.   (d) source, civil life (CL), RA, NG, ORC, NA; and (e) designation of training camp attended, if
Mar. 17, 1921.   any.   ‡ Strike out if he did not attend a training camp.   § Give dates of departure from and return
to the United States. || Give date.   3—8091

Justus Allan Hovey's *New York State Abstracts of World War I Military Service* cards. Allan enlisted in the New York National Guard a year before the war and mustered in before the United States declared war. Being on active duty, he was not required to complete a draft registration card. Following training at the Plattsburg Training Camp he was discharged from the New York National Guard (top card) to accept a commission in the Officer Reserve Corps (bottom card).[201]

JUSTUS ALLAN HOVEY
1891 – 1984

Enlisting in the New York National Guard in New York City at the age of twenty-four on May 9, 1916, Private Hovey mustered in on June 26, 1916, with Company I, 71st Infantry. The 71st entrained for Mexican Border service on June 27, 1916, arriving on July 2nd.[202] Private Hovey was appointed Private First Class on August 28, 1916, before the unit returned to New York City on September 6, 1916;[203] he mustered out on October 6th. He mustered back in on March 30, 1917, with the same unit. He was allowed to visit family in Hilton, New York, in June 1917. [right][204] His National Guard records are confusing and contradictory at this point.

He was listed as furloughed from August 5th until September 5, 1917, yet placed on detached service at the Plattsburg Training Camp (NY) starting August 26, 1917. Next, he is listed as transferring to Company I, 105th Infantry, on October 25, 1917, only to be transferred back to Company I, 71st Infantry, on November 24, 1917. One fact not in dispute: Justus Allan Hovey was at the Plattsburg Training Camp, for reserve officer training, in October and November 1917. Private Hovey was discharged on November 26, 1917, to accept a commission.

—J. Allan Hovey of the New York State Militia, who has been doing guard duty for several weeks, will arrive here on Friday afternoon of this week to visit his parents, Mr. and Mrs. V. A. Hovey, until Saturday afternoon, when he will go back to New York City to join his company. He expects shortly to be sent to Georgia or on to France.

First Lieutenant Hovey was called into service on November 27, 1917, and sent to Leon Springs, Texas, in December of 1917. He was assigned to the Air Service on January 1, 1918, and appointed officer-in-command of the 610th Aero Squadron (Supply) at Kelly Field in San Antonio, Texas. [right][205] Transferring to Rockwell Field, in San Diego, California, on February 19th of 1918, he accepted an appointment as assistant adjutant of the post. He honed his skills as a student pilot and was appointed officer-in-command of Squadron M at Rockwell Field. He was discharged January 2, 1919, and returned home to Hilton. [left][206]

—Lieutenant Allan Hovey of this place is now at Kelly Field, San Antonio, Texas, along with John Harlan Cooper and Kenneth Smith, also of this village. The young men enjoy being together.

—Lieutenant Allen Hovey, who has been stationed at Rockwell Field, San Diego, California, together with Mrs. Hovey, arrived in Hilton a few days ago. Mrs. Hovey has since left to accept a position as teacher of music and drawing in the High School at Franklinville, N. Y. Mr. Hovey is undecided just what he will do. Their many friends were glad to see them again.

Born July 4, 1891, to Van Allen and Caroline "Carrie" Augusta (Higley) Hovey in Hilton, Allan, as he was called, attended his freshman year at the University of Rochester, completing his education at Harvard, starting his sophomore year at the university. He graduated in 1912 with notable classmates John Russel Sibley (Sibley, Lindsay & Curr Co.) of Rochester, New York, and Joseph Patrick Kennedy Sr. of Massachusetts.

His engagement to Lois Eugenia Clark was announced in 1918, while he was stationed at Kelly Field in San Antonio, Texas. They were married on May 1, 1918, but divorced on February 5, 1932. Allan later married Jane Katherine Telford on May 16, 1936, in New Jersey.

Ad Club Men to Attend Comedy of 'Adam and Eva'

A delegation of Rochester Ad Club men will attend the performance of "Adam and Eva" to-night in the assembly hall of the Baptist Temple, in recognition of the Rochester stage debut of J. Allan Hovey, one of the editors of the Bumblebee.

J. Allan Hovey debuted on the Rochester theater stage in a performance of *Adam and Eva* in 1927, which was attended by his peers from the Ad Club. [left][207]

Allan worked as a publisher and editor for multiple advertising and print agencies in New York and Pennsylvania. He was a member of the Rochester Ad Club and an editor for its weekly publication, *Bumblebee*. While working for the advertising agency Stewart, Hanford & Froham in Rochester, Allan was recognized and awarded for his submission to a slogan contest for *Grand Hotel*, a radio program which aired on radio station WHAM. [right][208]

Rochesterian Wins Slogan Test Award

J. Allan Hovey, of the advertising agency of Stewart, Hanford & Froham Inc., yesterday received a check for $100 for his entry in a slogan contest conducted in conjunction with the "Grand Hotel" program broadcast over Station WHAM.

Mr. Hovey also won one of the major prizes in a recent contest conducted by the "Bawl Street Journal," the annual humorous publication of New York Stock Exchange members.

Allan shared his talents with many advertising firms, companies, and publications: Addison Vars Inc. advertising agency and the advertising service department of printing firm John P, Smith Co., both of Rochester; the circulation and promotion department of Nast Publications in New York City; the advertising department of B. F. Goodrich Co. in Akron, Ohio; assistant advertising manager at F. E. Davis Fish Co. in Gloucester, Massachusetts; and Gray & Rogers, The Buckley Organization, Geare-Marston, Lamb & Keen, and Rohrabaugh & Gibson—all of which were located in Philadelphia, Pennsylvania.

He was a member of both the Poor Richard Club of Philadelphia, Pennsylvania, and the Lion's Club of West Bucks County, Pennsylvania. Justus Allan passed away on September 4, 1984, at the age of ninety-three, while living in the Bethany Retirement Home in Horseheads, New York.

JUSTUS ALLAN HOVEY

Allan appeared in the *Harvard College Class of 1912 Twenty-Fifth Anniversary Report*, his graduation photo on the left; the image on the right was submitted for printing in 1937.[209]

Justus Allan Hovey submitted this undated photo of himself in his flying uniform to the New York *World War I Veterans' Service Data and Photographs* project.[210] For more information on the project, see "Letters of Homer Chauncey Odell" on page 326 in Chapter 3.

A New Slogan Is Evolved

"Three members of the publicity committee for the Y.M.C.A. membership drive, Oct. 17 to 23, drawing up the slogan to be used in the campaign. Willis G. Broadbrooks (center) is publicity chairman; Melvin M. Schwartz (left) of the "Y" staff and J. Allan Hovey are members of the committee."[211]

REGISTRATION CARD

SERIAL NUMBER	673		ORDER NUMBER	a 1390

1 *Walton Hovey*

   (First name)   (Middle name)   (Last name)

2 PERMANENT HOME ADDRESS.

Hilton   *Mo*   *NY*

(No.) (Street or R. F. D. No.) (City or town) (County) (State)

Age in Years	Date of Birth		
3 33	4 *Feb*	*18*	*1885*
	(Month.)	(Day.)	(Year.)

RACE

White	Negro	Oriental	Indian	
			Citizen	Noncitizen
5 X	6	7	8	9

U. S. CITIZEN			ALIEN	
Native Born	Naturalized	Citizen by Father's Naturalization Before Registrant's Majority	Declarant	Non-declarant
10 ✓	11	12	13	14

15 If not a citizen of the U. S., of what nation are you a citizen or subject?

PRESENT OCCUPATION	EMPLOYER'S NAME
16 *Labor*	17 *V. A. Hovey*

18 PLACE OF EMPLOYMENT OR BUSINESS:

Hilton   *Mo*   *NY*

(No.) (Street or R. F. D. No.) (City or town) (County) (State)

NEAREST RELATIVE	Name	19 *V. A. Hovey*
	Address	20 *Hilton* *Mo* *NY*

   (No.) (Street or R. F. D. No.) (City or town) (County) (State)

I AFFIRM THAT I HAVE VERIFIED ABOVE ANSWERS AND THAT THEY ARE TRUE

P. M. G. O.
Form No. 1 (Red)

Walton Hovey

(Registrant's signature or mark)

(OVER)

144

WALTON HIGLEY HOVEY
1885 – 1964

Dr. Walton Hovey, 1st Lieutenant 2nd Ambulance Co., left yesterday, the 20th, for Fort Benjamin Harrison, Indianapolis, Ind., for 3 months special training at the Medical Officers training camp. Lieutenant Hovey will take with him 2 non-commissioned officers and several nurses. In September he will join his command for service in France. The Lieutenant states that horse drawn ambulances are to be discarded and replaced with modern motor ambulances, and that this change will prove beneficial to certain of our local boys who have recently been enlisted with his command.—Hilton Record.

Walton H. Hovey, age thirty-two, enlisted in the New York National Guard May 14, 1917, and mustered in with the 2d Ambulance Company in Buffalo, New York, as a First Lieutenant on June 22, 1917. He was sent to the Medical Department Training Camp at Fort Benjamin Harrison, outside Indianapolis, Indiana, and remained there until November 1917. When the New York National Guard was drafted into federal service on August 5, 1917, his unit was re-designated, and he was assigned to Ambulance Company 106, 102d Sanitary Train, 27th Division. Walton was listed as sick for extended periods at Fort Ontario, Oswego, New York, and at Camp

—The 2nd Ambulance Company of Rochester, of which Dr. Walton Hovey of this village is lieutenant and Frank Randall a member, has received orders to be prepared to move to a southern concentration camp by Saturday of this week. It is not known just what camp they will be sent to but it is expected that it will be at Asheville, N. C.

Wadsworth, South Carolina, until he was honorably discharged with a Surgeon's Certificate of Disability from Camp Wadsworth on April 4, 1918.

Walton was born in Kent, New York, to Van Allen and Caroline "Carrie" Augusta (Higley) Hovey on February 18, 1885. Walton graduated Hilton High School in 1903 and attended the University of Buffalo Medical College, graduating in 1907.[212] He was named senior house surgeon of the Homeopathic Hospital in Rochester, New York.[213] In 1911, Walton took residence in Poughkeepsie, New York, and was an assistant physician employed with the Hudson River State Hospital[214] before taking temporary charge of a hospital in Sodus, New York.[215]

After working in Sodus, Walton immersed himself in both his hometown and the community of Fairport, New York. At left he is shown (seated) with eleven of his cohorts, known as the "Old Barbershop Gang," in this undated photo, reproduced in a January 25, 1968, edition of the *Hilton (NY) Record*.

The Old Barbershop Gang. (Left to Right) Merle Seavey, Leon Doud, Henry Smith, Herbert Verney, Guy Albiker, Peter Wheeler, William Lais, Orin Curtis, Philo Clapper, Chas. Ainsworth, Andrew Albiker. Walton Hovey, seated)

Dr. Hovey opened a medical office in the Clark Building in the village of Fairport on November 12, 1914. One month later he moved to 84 South Main Street in the village, renting rooms for both his office and his residence. In the spring of 1916 he closed his Fairport practice and opened a medical office in the home of his parents on Hovey Street in Hilton, New York. He married Esther Walbeck of Fairport in her parent's home on August 8, 1916.

DR. WALTON HOVEY
HILTON, N. Y.

Office and Residence: Hovey St.

Hours 1-3, 7-8.   Phone 40r2

WALTON HOVEY, M. D.
Office and Residence
84 South Main Street

Office Hours:
Until 9 A. M.
1 to 8 and 7 to 8 P. M.   Both Phones

A member of two communities, he was a well-known physician, mentioned frequently in the local newspapers for taking care of the townspeople of Fairport, and was a member of the Fairport Chamber of Commerce.[216] Walton was scheduled to address the Hilton Mother's Club during their monthly meeting in January 1917, but was unable to attend. [right] His topic for that meeting was read by his sister, Luella, on "Children's Diseases and their Treatment."[217] After his discharge from the army, he was a charter member of American Legion Hiscock-Fishbaugh Post 788 in Hilton, helping organize and establish the post in 1920.[218]

Walton, having been discharged from military service on a certificate of disability, sought in-residence medical treatment for drug

—The Hilton Mother's Club will hold its regular meeting, Tuesday afternoon, Jan. 30th, at 3.30 p. m., in the High School building. Members and others please note the change of day from Monday to Tuesday. That will be the clubs meeting day hereafter, as it seems most convenient. The meeting will be addressed by Dr. Walton Hovey. His topic will be "Children's Diseases and their Treatment." Everyone is invited. The meeting will be free to all who are interested.

addiction ("narcoticism"), back pain ("myalgia lumbar"), chronic arthritis, and an inner ear infection (otitis media) at National Homes for Disabled Volunteer Soldiers from July 1927 until sometime in 1930 or later. Walton was admitted to homes in Hampton, Virginia; Dayton, Ohio; and Bath, New York. [219] Completing those treatments, Walton moved to Bath, New York, where in 1932 he was working as a physician and held the position of secretary to the adjutant at the Veterans Home by a civil service appointment.[220]

Doctor At CGW Joins Med Group

Dr. Walton Hovey of Corning Glass Works was elected to membership in the Steuben County Medical Society at the Spring luncheon meeting held today at the Baron Steuben Hotel.

Walton was working in Steuben County, New York, for Corning Glass Works in 1943 when he was elected to the Steuben County Medical Society during their spring luncheon at the Baron Steuben Hospital.[221] Walton continued to serve as a physician until his retirement. In 1957 he moved from Bath to the Bay Pines Veterans Domiciliary in Florida, where he lived for seven years and attended the Baptist Church. Walton passed away in the Bay Pines Veterans Hospital in Bay Pines, Pinellas, Florida, on February 13, 1964.

The Hoveys Of Hovey Street—In this portrait, taken about 1897, Van Allen was 47; the mother, Carrie, 37; Walton, 12, Allan, 6, Luella, 3. Allan comments: "I don't remember sitting for this picture, though I obviously must have. This was the year that I learned to swim in the swimming hole in the creek back of the Newcomb home on West Avenue between the two churches. It was also the year of my first blood sucker, which scared me a lot more than its ability to harm anyone warranted." Carrie died August 5, 1959, in Scranton, Pennsylvania, at the age of 99. Van Allen passed away in Hilton, June 8, 1922.[222]

Nine Ambulance Men Go to Camp for Officers

Captain Charles O. Boswell, commander of the Second Ambulance Company, has been ordered to send some officers and men to the Medical Department Training Camp, Fort Benjamin Harrison, Indiana. He has designated Lieutenants Alfred F. Cassebeer and Walton Hovey, Acting Sergeants Fowle and Nixon and First Class Privates Brown, Blank, Gale, Zimmerman and Fitch to this duty. The detail will report at the camp next Wednesday and take a three months' course.

Dr. Clarence C. Nesbit, of Holley, has been commissioned as first lieutenant of the ambulance unit to fill the place left vacant by Dr. Willis Linn, who resigned to accept a captaincy in the New York State Constabulary. Captain R. D. Richman has resigned so that the work of rounding the company into shape will fall on the shoulders of Captain Boswell and Lieutenant Nesbit in the next three months. The men who go to Fort Benjamin Harrison will rejoin their command at the completion of the course.

The Ambulance Company had its last drill for two weeks at the Armory last evening. Captain Boswell has put in the required number of drills and has allowed the men a vacation of two weeks. The company is at full war strength of 150 men.

Dr. Walton Hovey was one of nine men from the 2nd Ambulance Company, New York National Guard, sent to Fort Benjamin Harrison, Indiana, in June 1917.[223]

Form 1 *1210*   REGISTRATION CARD *1153* No. *1*

1 Name in full *John G. Hundley*   Age, in yrs. *21*
   (Given name) (Family name)

2 Home address *Hinge* *Hilton* *New York*
   (No.) (Street) (City) (State)

3 Date of birth *December* *22* *1896*
   (Month) (Day) (Year)

4 Are you (1) a natural-born citizen, (2) a naturalized citizen, (3) an alien, (4) or have you declared your
   intention (specify which)? *Natural born*

5 Where were you born? *Kingston* *Mich.* *U.S.G.*
   (Town) (State) (Nation)

6 If not a citizen, of what country are you a citizen or subject? *U.S.G.*

7 What is your present trade, occupation, or office? *Cook* *29*

8 By whom employed? *Blessed Lunch*
   Where employed? *Detroit, Mich.*

9 Have you a father, mother, wife, child under 12, or a sister or brother under 12, solely dependent on you for
   support (specify which)? *No.*

10 Married or single (which)? *Single* Race (specify which)? *Caucasian*

11 What military service have you had? Rank *None* ; branch
   years ; Nation or State

12 Do you claim exemption from draft (specify grounds)? *No.*

I affirm that I have verified above answers and that they are true.

1153

John G. Hundley
(Signature or mark)

JOHN ALBERT HUNDLEY
1894-1954

John enlisted in the United States Army at Camp Syracuse, New York, on July 27, 1917, at the age of twenty-two and rank of Private. He was assigned to Company D, 49th Infantry, at Camp Merritt, New Jersey, before transferring to Company D, 23d Infantry, 3d Brigade, 2d Division, on August 17, 1917. He left on September 7, 1917, sailing from Hoboken, New Jersey, on the USS *Huron* and arrived at Saint-Nazaire, France, on September 20, 1917. A combination of United States Marine Corps and United States Army units, the 2d Division spent the remainder of 1917 and first half of 1918 organizing and training their forces in partnership with various French Army units. On June 1st of 1918 the division moved to the front with three French divisions, participating in the Aisne Operation, and remained engaged throughout the month and into July. One particularly dangerous engagement began in the late evening of June 23rd, in retaliation for an attack by the Marines earlier in the day. Just before midnight and continuing until the early morning, German forces launched well over 3,000 shells of mustard gas against the 5th Marine, 9th Infantry, and 23d Infantry sectors causing more than 500 casualties, nearly 200 in the 23d Infantry. The 23d Infantry commander sent a dire message to the brigade commander: "Urgently request replacements."[224] On July 1st the 3d Brigade, which included John Hundley's 23d Infantry, began an assault on the village of Vaux while participating in the Belleau Wood campaign. Again, retaliation was fierce and was noted in a captured German report: "From 12:00 to 2:00 a.m. yellow cross drenching bombardments were carried out on Bois des Clerembauts, Thiolet, and the adjoining farms."[225] The 23d Infantry commander passed word to his companies: "Keep masks on all night if necessary, dispose your troops to avoid results." Throughout the night almost 12,000 rounds of high explosive, as well as poison gas, were dropped in the sector; in the morning of July 3rd almost 300 men were reported wounded. John Hundley was wounded near Bois des Clerembauts, France, on July 2, 1918.

The September 21, 1918, issues of the Buffalo (NY) *Evening News*, Chicago *Daily Tribune*, Geneva (NY) *Daily Times*, Plattsburgh (NY) *Daily Press*, and the Schenectady (NY) *Gazette* all reported John A. Hundley of Hilton, New York, having died of disease, which wasn't the case. [right][226]

Died of Disease.
Private Charles Murray, Albany.
Private John A. Hundley, Hilton.
Private Valentine N. Kessell, Brooklyn.
Private August Sadowsky, New Brighton
Mechanic Lawrence J. Rizzo, Brooklyn.

He was listed on a ship's manifest to return to the United States in April of 1919, but alternatively transferred to a base hospital. His travel arrangements finally set, he returned home aboard the USS *Missouri* departing from Brest, France, on July 14, 1919. John was awarded the Purple Heart and discharged on August 4, 1919. He re-enlisted and continued to serve until his honorable discharge at the rank of Cook on July 20, 1921.

John Albert Hundley was born to George F. and Mamie (Elliott) Hundley in Kingston, Tuscola, Michigan, on December 22, 1894. He moved with his family to Hilton around 1903 and settled on Heinz Street; his father was employed as a farm laborer. John listed his address on his World War I draft registration card as Hilton but was working in Detroit, Michigan, as a cook for the organization Blessed Lunch.

Following his return to the United States and re-enlistment in the army, John found himself stationed at Columbus Barracks, Ohio, where he met and married Mary L. Welch, known as Lela M., on August 11, 1920, in Franklin, Ohio. Lela remained in the couple's home in Cass City, Michigan, in 1926, during her husband's stay in the United States National Home for Disabled Volunteer Soldiers, located in Dayton, Ohio. John and his wife settled in Chicago,

Illinois, returning to visit his family in Hilton on occasion. While a patient in the Hines Veterans Hospital in Hines, Illinois, John passed away unexpectedly on October 11, 1954. John Hundley was interred in Parma Union Cemetery in Parma, New York, where military services were performed by the American Legion Hiscock-Fishbaugh Post 788.

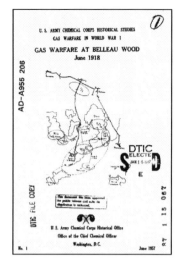

A United States Army Chemical Corps study of gas warfare in the summer of 1918, in the Belleau Wood region of France, described the dangerous situations faced by John Hundley and the 23d Infantry.

Below, excerpts from reports of the 24th of June 1918, leading up to the attacks that wounded John.

The seriousness of the gas bombardment was not at first recognized. At 11:30 a.m. on the 24th, a company commander of the 23rd Infantry said of his gas cases: "Casualties were...men...observed without masks just after the second gas attack this morning; they are therefore marked not in line of duty."[142] Not until a report of at least a hundred gas cases was made on the afternoon of the 24th was the serious nature of the attack known. At 7:40 p.m. that evening, 162 cases had been reported and Col. Malone sent the following message to Brig. Gen. Lewis at Domptin:

Troops were moved to avoid the effects of gas and masks were worn in some cases for 8 hours and on the average for about 4 hours. Due to the shortage of officers with the troops masks were in some cases prematurely removed especially by the troops recently arrived. Mustard only appeared to have been used. The forward line is now lightly held and the troops are as much disposed as safety will permit. Urgently request replacements.[143]

A message from a machine gun company of the 23rd Infantry said: "After the gas attacks last night and this morning I have not enough men to man my guns and hold the positions."[144]

The Report of Operations on the 24th listed 104 wounded and gassed from the 9th and 23rd Infantry and 13 from the 7th Infantry. The Journal of Operations later that day corrected the figures to 152 gas casualties in the 9th Infantry, 162 in the 23rd, and 25 in the 5th MG Battalion. The 5th MG Gas Officer subsequently reported 1 officer and 42 men gassed as a result of taking their masks off after four hours, then sleeping in the gassed area.

The narrative below describes the bombardment and gas attack on the night of July 2, 1918, against the 23d Infantry and the area where John Hundley was reported being wounded.

"Towards 10:00 p.m." on 2 July a French artillery unit seems to have fired "about 30 gas shells medium caliber on the ravine south of Bonne."[161] Shortly after 11:00 p.m., 'the enemy artillery retaliated for Vaux and Bonne with almost 5,000 mixed HE and gas shells along the new 2nd Division front, other gas on the Bois de la Marette and Clerembauts, and on other sensitive points as far west as La Cense Ferme and Triangle Ferme. The Germans reported: "From 12:00 to 2:00 a.m. yellow cross drenching bombardments were carried out on Bois des Clerembauts, Thiolet, and the adjoining farms."[162]

With the first gas shells, Malone of the 23rd Infantry called his companies: "Keep masks on all night if necessary, dispose your troops to avoid results. Be careful of repetition of attack later in the morning. Get disinfecting squads on the job at day break (FM to E-1, 11:45 p.m., 2 Jul, Records 5)." All through the night of 2-3 July, the German batteries continued their intense fire, throwing almost 12,000 rounds of HE, in addition to the gas, into the divisional sector, with the heaviest fire along the new front. At 6:00 a.m., 3 July, 294 men were reported wounded.[163]

—It was reported that John Hundley, son of Mr. and Mrs. George Hundley of this village, was killed in France the 21st day of September. Such is not the case however as Mrs. Hundley has received a letter from him dated Oct. 10th in which he says he is well and happy.

Information from "over there" was not swift and often in error. John Hundley was certainly not "killed in France the 21st day of September" in 1918. Since he was wounded in battle on July 2nd it was more likely he was convalescing in a hospital in late September.[227]

	REGISTRATION CARD	Age, in yrs.
Form 1		

1 Name in full *Harold Holder Ingraham* — Age 21
(Given name) (Family name)

2 Home address *Milton, N.Y.*
(No.) (Street) (City) (State)

3 Date of birth *February 7 1896*
(Month) (Day) (Year)

4 Are you (1) a natural-born citizen, (2) a naturalized citizen, (3) an alien, (4) or have you declared your intention (specify which)? *Natural-born*

5 Where were you born? *Rochester N.Y. U.S.A.*
(Town) (State) (Nation)

6 If not a citizen, of what country are you a citizen or subject?

7 What is your present trade, occupation, or office? *Farm Laborer*

8 By whom employed? *George Anderson*
Where employed? *Parma (or Milton)*

9 Have you a father, mother, wife, child under 12, or a sister or brother under 12, solely dependent on you for support (specify which)? *No*

10 Married or single (which)? *Single* Race (specify which)? *Caucasian*

11 What military service have you had? Rank *None* ; branch
years ; Nation or State

12 Do you claim exemption from draft (specify grounds)? *No*

I affirm that I have verified above answers and that they are true.

C A

Harold H. Ingraham
(Signature of person)

If person is of African descent, tear off this corner

HAROLD HOLDEN INGRAHAM
1896 – 1972

Harold was inducted into the United States Army at Spencerport, New York, on September 26, 1917, as a twenty-one-year-old Private. He was initially assigned to Battery D, 309th Field Artillery, 78th Division, at Camp Dix, New Jersey. On November 13, 1917, he transferred to Camp Gordon, Georgia, and joined Machine Gun Company, 328th Infantry, 82d Division–the same infantry regiment as Sergeant Alvin C. York, one of the most decorated United States Army soldiers of World War I. Harold went overseas with the division on May 1, 1918, departing from Boston, Massachusetts, aboard the RMS *Grampian*. Promoting to Private First Class on May 15, 1918, Harold returned home a year later aboard the SS *Ohioan* from the port of Bordeaux, France, on May 10, 1919, and arrived in the United States on May 22, 1919. He received an honorable discharge on May 29, 1919.

Harold Holden Ingraham was born to George and Grace Amelia (Holden) Ingraham on February 9, 1896, in Rochester, New York. By 1910, Harold and his family were living in Hilton, New York. As a teenager Harold found work on George Anderson's farm. He was president of the Epworth League, an organization for young adults within the Methodist Church, prior to entering the United States Army.

Within a month of his discharge from military service he married Leona Draffin on June 5, 1919, and they made their home Clarkson, New York. They moved to Orchard Hills Farm in Fairport, New York, but were forced to leave when the farm was foreclosed on and sold at public auction June 11, 1936. Returning to Parma, New York, Harold resumed farming and would occasionally advertise in the *Hilton (NY) Record* and the *Democrat and Chronicle* (Rochester, NY) listing different animals for sale such as puppies, horses, and ponies; he once placed an advertisement for the sale of his farm. [below][228]

Harold's wife, Leona, passed away in 1960 and Harold remarried in 1961 to Julia Kincaid, the widow of his brother, Paul. Together the pair made a life with each other, which included pacer horse racing. Harold was the owner of two horses that competed in pacer races in New York State. Ease Up's Hal competed at the Allegany County Fair in 1960, coming in second in the first heat. The couple's second pacer horse, Mr. Steele, raced in 1962 and had a strong year in 1963, winning a total of nine races by September 1967. [below left][229]

FOR SALE—My farm on Hill Rd. Phone 70-F-6. Harold H. Ingraham, 369 Hill Road.

Harold was very involved in his community and wore many hats as a fire commissioner, Hilton school board member, and was elected to a four-year term as Parma's tax assessor in 1962. He was a charter and life member of the American Legion Hiscock-Fishbaugh Post 788 of Hilton and a member of the Parma Grange. Harold passed away on January 21, 1972, and is buried in Parma Union Cemetery in Parma, New York.

Mr. Steele Wins Batavia Pace for 9th First This Year

BATAVIA—Owned by Mr. and Mrs. Harold H. Ingraham of Hilton, Mr. Steele is having a good year as a 4-year-old after a poor season last year.

Form I   2886   **REGISTRATION CARD** 565 | No. 52

1 Name in full _Frank Jamieson_   Age, in yrs.
   (Given name)   (Family name)   25

2 Home address _74_ _Elba_, _Rochester_, _NY_
          (No.)   (Street)   (City)   (State)

3 Date of birth _Sept_ _13_ _1891_
          (Month)   (Day)   (Year)

4 Are you (1) a natural-born citizen, (2) a naturalized citizen, (3) an alien, (4) or have you declared your
   intention (specify which)? _natural born_

5 Where were you born? _Erie_, _Pa_, _USA_
          (Town)   (State)   (Nation)

6 If not a citizen, of what country are you a citizen or subject? _____

7 What is your present trade, occupation, or office? _Tinsmith_

8 By whom employed? _Foster & Friend_
   Where employed? _119 Exchange St_

9 Have you a father, mother, wife, child under 12, or a sister or brother under 12, solely dependent on you for
   support (specify which)? _No_

10 Married or single (which)? _Single_   Race (specify which)? _Caucasian_

11 What military service have you had? Rank _____ ; branch _____ ;
   years _____ ; Nation or State   _None_

12 Do you claim exemption from draft (specify grounds)? _No_

I affirm that I have verified above answers and that they are true.

Frank Jamieson
(Signature or mark)

If person is of African descent, tear off this corner

154

FRANK JAMIESON
1891 – 1966

Frank was inducted on December 16, 1917, into the United States Army and at twenty-six served with Battery B, 57th Artillery, of the Coast Artillery Corps until discharge. Initially assigned to Camp Hancock, New York, he embarked from New York City on May 10, 1918,

> Private Frank Jamieson has arrived overseas with the Fifty-seventh Artillery, C. A. C. He left Rochester on December 17, 1917. He is the son of Mr. and Mrs. G. G. Jamieson.

sailing to France aboard the USS *Ryndam*. As a First and Second Army asset, Frank's battery of artillery would have participated in most of the major campaigns and battles in the latter half of 1918. He returned to the United States less than a year later, departing from Brest, France, aboard the USS *Huntington* on the 2nd of January 1919. Frank was discharged January 18, 1919, four days after his return from France.

Frank Jamieson was born on September 13, 1891, to George G. and Margaret (Strachan) Jamieson in Erie, Pennsylvania; by 1900 the family was living in Rochester, New York. Frank grew up in the 19th Ward and Rochester would be the future home of Frank and his bride, Emma Regina Nuessle; the couple married on June 26, 1919. Frank first worked as a tinsmith for a furnace company before joining Eastman Kodak Company. He remained employed with Kodak for twenty-eight years as a sheet metal worker.

Frank was a member of the Frank L. Simes Lodge No. 990, Free & Accepted Masons, of Rochester. Frank and Emma moved to Florida in 1958. Frank passed away on November 5, 1966, in the Saint Petersburg Hospital in Saint Petersburg, Florida. Frank was interred in Mount Hope Cemetery on November 9, 1966, in Rochester, New York.

Frank Jamieson, back row far right, is pictured with other officers of Monroe District No.4 of the Independent Order of Odd Fellows.[230]

Form 1   **REGISTRATION CARD** 3 89 | No. **23**

1 Name in full _Wilbur F King_
(Given name)   (Family name)   Age, in yrs. **21**

2 Home address _____ _Wilton_ _N.Y_
(No.) (Street) (City) (State)

3 Date of birth _September 5 1896_
(Month) (Day) (Year)

4 Are you (1) a natural-born citizen, (2) a naturalized citizen, (3) an alien, (4) or have you declared your intention (specify which)? _Natural-born_

5 Where were you born? _Hamlin_ _N.Y_ _U.S.A._
(Town) (State) (Nation)

6 If not a citizen, of what country are you a citizen or subject?

7 What is your present trade, occupation, or office? _Laborer in Factory_ **30**

8 By whom employed? _Multicroft Co._
Where employed? _Wilton N.Y_

9 Have you a father, mother, wife, child under 12, or a sister or brother under 12, solely dependent on you for support (specify which)? _Father + Mother_

10 Married or single (which)? _Single_ Race (specify which)? _Caucasian_

11 What military service have you had? Rank _None_; branch _____
years _____; Nation or State _____

12 Do you claim exemption from draft (specify grounds)? _____

I affirm that I have verified above answers and that they are true.

Wilbur F King
(Signature or mark)

WILBUR F. KING
1895 – 1965

Twenty-one-year-old Wilbur enlisted in the Regular Army at Camp Syracuse, New York, on August 3, 1917, as a Private; he was assigned to Company E, 50th Infantry. He transferred to Company E, 23d Infantry, 3d Brigade, 2d Division, on August 16, 1917, and left for his overseas assignment aboard the USS *Huron* on September 7, 1917. Wilbur likely faced the same intense artillery shelling and gas attacks that John Hundley experienced, being in the same infantry regiment. (see page 149) Wilbur was listed as "slightly wounded" on July 20, 1918. As the need for replacement artillery officers and non-commissioned officers grew, Wilbur was selected to attend the Saumur Artillery School in France in October 1918. The armistice on November 11, 1918, likely cut short his training but not before he earned a promotion to Private First Class on November 21, 1918. He returned to the United States with Casual Company 164 aboard the USS *Mexican*, departing from Saint-Nazaire, France, on February 20, 1919. They arrived in Hoboken, New Jersey, on the 7th of March 1919; Wilbur was discharged on March 13, 1919.

Wilbur F. King was born in Hamlin, New York, to Francis and Silvia (King) King on September 15, 1895. Growing up in Hamlin, he worked on the family farm until he enlisted in the United States Army. He married Iva Wright on February 24, 1921, in Rochester, New York, and the couple made their home in Brockport, New York, where Wilbur, like his father, took up farming to support his family. Wilbur was a member of the Disabled American Veterans. He passed away on May 3, 1965, and is interred in Fairfield Cemetery in Spencerport, New York.

```
WOUNDED   (Degree Undetermined)
          Lieutenants
Albert G. Jefferson, Oak Park, Ill.
Charles J. Jones, Dallas, Tex.
Lawrence T. Wyly, Duluth, Minn.
Orin F. Torbron, Gainesville, Tex.
Bugler Huntington S. Parish, Oneonta,
   N. Y.
          Privates
George P. Flanagan, Rochester, N. Y.
Albert J. Gagern, Buffalo, N. Y.
Frank A. Matt, Amsterdam, N. Y.
Willard Roberts, Clyde, N. Y.
Wilbur King, Hilton, N. Y.
```

News of Wilbur being wounded was covered in the local papers and by at least two papers from outside the metropolitan Rochester area including this entry from Plattsburg, New York.[231]

George Kirk returned to England on November 17, 1915. Whether he intended to return to the United States is unclear. The far-right columns on the manifest were used to record "Country of Intended Future Permanent Residence." George's entry has a tick mark under England, yet it also indicates a superscript "US" like many other passengers.

GEORGE SAMUEL KIRK
1892 – 1978

A military service record for George S. Kirk was not located for his biography. Research of United States military records, a review of online digital British military records, and direct genealogical inquiries, to include newspapers, could not produce actionable nor verifiable information. The ship manifest on the preceding page is the last known trans-Atlantic record of his travels–this one going west to east.

George Samuel Kirk was born in Acle, Norfolk, England, on April 30, 1892, to James John and Emily Elizabeth (Watts) Kirk. George was six years old when his mother passed away. By the age of eight he was living with his Aunt and Uncle, Hannah M. and Samuel J. Watts, on their farm in Upton with Fishley in Norfolk, England. He remained with them until March 28, 1912, when George emigrated to the United States.

George departed Liverpool, England, arriving in the port of New York on April 6, 1912, aboard the White Star Line SS *Baltic*. Between this date and December 9, 1914, George went back to England. When he returned to the United States in December 1914, he entered through Buffalo, New York, and declared his intent to return to his residence in Hilton, New York. In 1915 he is a lodger with Milton S. and Bessie B. Smith on Lake Road[1] earning wages as a farm laborer.[232] In April 1915, George was a charter member of the Hilton Lodge No. 940, Independent Order of Odd Fellows.[233] [right]

On November 17, 1915, he returned to England once more on the RMS *Cameronia*, arriving in Liverpool, England. According to the ship's manifest George listed his "country of intended future permanent residence" as England.[234]

George married Nellie M. Sargent in Mutford, Suffolk, England, in the first quarter of 1928. In the 1939 England Census, the last census taken before the outbreak of World War II, George and Nellie are living in Suffolk, England, with George working as a general farm laborer. George passed away in Great Yarmouth, Norfolk, England, in 1978.

Hilton Lodge of Odd Fellows Instituted in 1915

Hilton Lodge, No. 940, Independent Order of Odd Fellows, was instituted on April 9, 1915, with a membership of fifty-one, and since that time many new members have joined this organization and many have transferred to other lodges, and many are deceased. Of the original fifty-one members, there are only six still belonging to this lodge, as follows: P. D. D. G. M. William Kerrison, P. G. Merle D. Amidon, P. G. William Wheeler, P. G. J. Walter Way, Henry A. Smith and Edgard Merle Seavey.

The charter members were Charles V. Babcock, Wayne T. Wolfrom, Wm. A. MacDermand, William O. Richardson, George S. Kirk, Guy W. Albiker, John A. Billings, Frank Coleman, Paul M. Hoeppner, Otis Ely, John Lacey, Merle D. Amidon, Adelbert L. Root, Herbert S. Wolfrom, and Raymond A. Warren.

The lodge held its meeting first in the Masonic Hall for nearly two years, then moving to the Simmons Block over Cornish Market, later moving to the M. J. Hall Block and finally to the building which they now own and occupy on Railroad Street.

---

[1] Lake Road is referring to the current day NYS Route 259, known as Lake Avenue in the village of Hilton or North Avenue in the town of Parma.

Form 1   REGISTRATION CARD   No. *8 0*

1   Name in full *William E. G. Kirk*   Age, in yrs. *23*
     (Given name)   (Family name)

2   Home address *Hilton*   *Hamlin*   *N.Y.*
     (No.)   (Street)   (City)   (State)

3   Date of birth *Dec.*   *4*   *1894*
     (Month)   (Day)   (Year)

4   Are you (1) a natural-born citizen, (2) a naturalized citizen, (3) an alien, (4) or have you declared your intention (specify which)? *Declared intention*

5   Where were you born? *Upton*   *Norfolk*   *England*
     (Town)   (State)   (Nation)

6   If not a citizen, of what country are you a citizen or subject? *England*

7   What is your present trade, occupation, or office? *Farm laborer*

8   By whom employed? *Geo. Frase*
     Where employed? *Parma*

9   Have you a father, mother, wife, child under 12, or a sister or brother under 12, solely dependent on you for support (specify which)? *No*

10   Married or single (which)? *Single*   Race (specify which)? *Caucasian*

11   What military service have you had? Rank *No* ; branch
     years   ; Nation or State

12   Do you claim exemption from draft (specify grounds)? *No*

I affirm that I have verified above answers and that they are true.

A William E. G. Kirk
     (Signature or mark)

If person is of African descent, tear off this corner.

62

160

WILLIAM EWART G. KIRK
1894 – 1975

Inducted into the United States Army at twenty-three-years-old at Spencerport, New York, on October 31, 1917, Private Kirk was assigned to Battery D, 309th Field Artillery. On January 17, 1918, he transferred to 442d Company, Engineer Motor Transport Service. William departed for overseas duty on March 6, 1918, from Hoboken, New Jersey, aboard the USS *Tenadores*. He listed his father, James John Kirk, who was stationed at Walpole Marsh, Wisbech Camp, England, as his next-of-kin on the manifest. Private William E.G. Kirk was promoted to Private First Class on April 21, 1918. On November 30, 1918, William was assigned to Motor Transport Company 684 and promoted to Corporal on the 16th of December 1918. William was discharged on August 7, 1919; records of his return to the United States on a military transport were not located.

William was born to James John and Emily Elizabeth (Watts) Kirk on December 4, 1893, in Upton, Norfolk, England. At the age of nineteen he emigrated to the United States, arriving in 1913, and as reported in the 1915 New York State Census, he is living with and working for the Weigart family on their Hill Road farm in Parma, New York. After his discharge from the army in August 1919, it is supposed he found passage from France to England, instead of returning to America. One month later he married Alice Hunter on September 13, 1919, in Christ Church in Southwark, Surrey, England. Together the newlyweds moved to America, sailing from Southampton, England, aboard the SS *Lapland*, arriving in New York City on November 3, 1919. On the ship's manifest, William reported becoming a naturalized citizen in December 1916 in Rochester, New York; his address in the United States was listed as "Frisby Hill, Hilton, N.Y."[235]

The newlyweds established their first home in Parma with William working as a farmer in Greece, New York. They owned a home on Frisbee Hill Road and William became a poultry dealer, known for raising and selling sex-linked pullets.[m] [below][236][237]

When he filled out his World War II draft card he listed his employer as the Board of Education in Hilton, New York. William was involved in his community, allowing a group of 4-H boys taking an electrical course to assist in the installation of a burglar alarm in his home; was co-chairman of the dinner committee for the Hilton Men's Club; and was a member of the Clio Lodge No. 779, Free & Accepted Masons.

William held several positions within the American Legion Hiscock Fishbaugh Post 788. He was elected commander of the post in 1926, appointed to the post's welfare committee in 1932, and in 1944 served as vice commander. William died on August 9, 1975, and is buried in Parma Union Cemetery in Parma, New York.

FOR SALE—Halbertas this week; Crawfords following week. Phone 92F5. William Kirk, Frisbee Hill Road.

Expects to Broadcast From New York City

An egg with a dark green yolk produced by hens owned by William Kirk of Frisbee Hill Road may be seen in the window of the Red & White store. This will prove to skeptics that "Bill" really is telling the truth about the colored yolks.

William Kirk of Frisbee Hill Road has obtained permission of the feed company, whose feed mixture produces various colored egg yolks, to broadcast over the radio on the "We the People" program. Mr. Kirk was to have spoken on this (Thursday) evening but was unable to obtain permission in time. However another date will no doubt be given him, probably December 9 or 16.

---

[m] "Sex-linked" pullets refer to cross-bred chickens whose color at hatching is differentiated by its sex and a pullet being a hen less than one year old.

Hilton Legionnaires 'Save' Ill Farmer's Cherry Crop

Members of Hiscock-Fishbaugh Post, American Legion, yesterday traded their blue uniforms for coveralls and "invaded" the cherry orchards of William E. Kirk in Hilton.

The more than 60 Hilton Legionnaires moved in on the cherry orchards at 7:30 a. m. and before noon had cleared the area of the entire crops. Armed with ladders, baskets and buckets, the contingent, led by Commander Fred Clift stripped the trees with the speed of an advancing American armored column.

The agricultural onslaught was prompted by the illness of Kirk, who is in Highland Hospital recovering from a recent operation. The cherries might have rotted on the trees had not Charles B. Tubb talked the Legion members into action.

They began arriving at the Frisbee Hill Road farm in pairs about 7 a. m. Then later comers brought their children and all turned their efforts to the trees weighted down with cherries.

Some picked, some gathered up the buckets and dumped them into market baskets and some crated the yield and stacked it in the barn. Mrs. Kirk and her two daughters, Mrs. Fern Murphy and Miss Helene Kirk were busy preparing sandwiches and coffee for the workers.

Busiest on the whole farm was Kirk's little spaniel, Prince. The dog hastened to meet every newcomer, wagged his tail, sniffed and then trotted away obviously disappointed. He wanted to see his master.

Members of Hiscock-Fishbaugh Post 788 were truly a "legion" when they arrived en masse to harvest William Kirk's cherry crop in July 1946. As reported in this July 22nd article in the *Democrat and Chronicle*, Kirk was recuperating in Highland Hospital (Rochester, NY) following surgery and his friends were concerned the whole crop might be lost.[238]

Facing page: everyone was part of the effort.

ROCHESTER, N. Y., MONDAY, JULY 22, 1946

THEY PREPARED MEALS . . . **WHILE PALS LIKE THIS PICKED . . . TO SAVE HIS CROP**

Hilton Legionaires turned out yesterday to pick the cherry crop of a veteran incapacitated by an operation and confined to the hospital. At left, his daughter, Helene Kirk, and Mrs. William E. Kirk prepare lunch for the 60 pickers; center, Fred Clift, post commander, busy in a tree; right, Nurse Helene Jacobs at Highland Hospital shows Kirk a basket of his crop, which was maturing so rapidly that it would spoil in few days.

Form 1   1707   REGISTRATION CARD   No. 22

1   Name in full _Frederick Earnest Koss_   Age, in yrs. 22
      (Given name)   (Family name)

2   Home address _Kendall_ _Orleans Co_ _New York_
      (No.)   (Street)   (City)   (State)

3   Date of birth _June_ _1st_ _1895_
      (Month)   (Day)   (Year)

4   Are you (1) a natural-born citizen, (2) a naturalized citizen, (3) an alien, (4) or have you declared your intention (specify which)? _Natural born_

5   Where were you born? _Parma_ _New York_ _U.S.A_
      (Town)   (State)   (Nation)

6   If not a citizen, of what country are you a citizen or subject? _____

7   What is your present trade, occupation, or office? _Telegraph operator_

8   By whom employed? _N.Y.C. R.R._
      Where employed? _Kendall N.Y._

9   Have you a father, mother, wife, child under 12, or a sister or brother under 12, solely dependent on you for support (specify which)? _No_

10 Married or single (which)? _Single_   Race (specify which)? _Caucasian_

11 What military service have you had? Rank _none_ ; branch _____
      years _____ ; Nation or State _____

12 Do you claim exemption from draft (specify grounds)? _No_

I affirm that I have verified above answers and that they are true.

Frederick Earnest Koss
(Signature or mark)

If person is of African descent, tear off this corner

164

FREDERICK EARNEST KOSS
1895 – 1941

Frederick was inducted into the United States Army at age twenty-two at Albion, New York, on April 3, 1918. He was assigned to Machine Gun Company, 309th Infantry, 78th Division, at Camp Dix, New Jersey. On May 15, 1918, he transferred to the 153d Depot Brigade at Camp Dix but did not sail to France with the 78th Division. He was reassigned to Company C, 32d Battalion, United States Guards[n] on October 25, 1918, where he remained until his discharge on December 31, 1918.

Frederick Earnest Koss was born to Charles F. and Augusta E. (Oehlbeck) Koss in Parma, New York, on June 1, 1895. Fred started working at a young age, performing various jobs to include well digging in May 1915.[239] [right] Growing up, Fred worked in a retail grocery store and was a farm laborer before securing a job with New York Central Railroad as a telegraph operator in Kendall, New York.

MISCELLANEOUS

WELL DIGGING—We wish to give notice to the public that we are prepared to dig wells for anyone who may wish same. Terms reasonable.

Roy Huffer,
Fred Koss,
John Riley.

Returning home after his service to his country, Fred worked on farms before returning to the railroad as a telegraph operator. He married Lucy E. Bigger on November 3, 1921, and the couple made their first home in Hilton, New York. Fred served as temporary station agent in Walker, New York, before moving with Lucy to Carlton, New York, where he was employed as an agent, then station agent. In 1932 he transferred to Kent, New York, to work as a station agent.

CARLTON

R. R. Employees Changed
Fred Koss has been transferred to Kent as station agent and Mr. Carlin of Lyndonville is taking his place here.

Fred, along with his brother-in-law, William, opened the K & B Tea Room in the summer of 1934 on the Coloney Farm, located on Ridge Road in Gaines, New York. He helped William grow and operate the restaurant, which became quite popular. With the end of Prohibition, the business partners applied for a liquor license. After a year-and-a-half of business success, tragedy struck in November 1935 when the restaurant was destroyed by a fire which broke out in the kitchen; an overheated stove was presumed to be the source. The local fire department had been called but was unsuccessful in stopping the fire through water and chemical sources.

Fred died suddenly in Carlton on February 15, 1941, and is buried in Parma Union Cemetery, Parma, New York.

NOTICE
Notice is hereby given that license B-5585 has been issued to the undersigned to sell beer at retail in a restaurant under section 132a of the Alcoholic Beverage Control Law on the Ridge Road in town of Gaines, county of Orleans, on premises for consumption.
Fred Koss and William Bigger.
6t2   Carlton, N. Y.

Making Improvements at K & B Tea Room
Extensive improvements in the way of enclosing and enlarging the dining room are being made at the K & B Tea Room located on the Ridge between Childs and Gaines. This eating place which was taken over this summer by Fred Koss and Bigger has proven very popular. Large crowds have been attending their Wednesday night fish frys. Last night they featured a tenderloin steak supper.

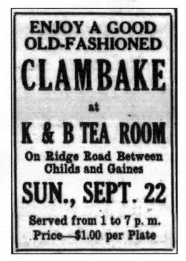

ENJOY A GOOD OLD-FASHIONED **CLAMBAKE** at **K & B TEA ROOM** On Ridge Road Between Childs and Gaines **SUN., SEPT. 22** Served from 1 to 7 p. m. Price—$1.00 per Plate

---

[n] The United States Guards were used to preserve and protect major utilities in the United States, essential to the war effort, and also to enforce the President's proclamation pertaining to alien enemies.

Champney Lee's *New York State Abstracts of World War I Military Service* card from the New York State Archives. Champney was too young to register for the June 1918 draft when he enrolled in the United States Naval Reserve Force. He was not required to complete a draft registration card.

GERALD CHAMPNEY LEE
1898 – 1951

Twenty-year-old Champney enrolled in the United States Naval Reserve Force at the Recruiting Station in Buffalo, New York, on July 15, 1918. He trained at the Naval Training Station, Great Lakes, Illinois, as a Landsman Machinist's Mate in Aviation until November 11, 1918. He was placed on inactive duty on December 30, 1918, from the Naval Training Station but re-enrolled in the service and was discharged on September 30, 1921.

Fifty-five Years Ago—1913
The following boys were sworn in as members of Lookout Mountain Patrol, Boy Scouts: Albert Wood, Court Lee, Carlyle Newcomb, Champney Lee, Willard Lee, Fenton Coakly, Harry Daily, Richard Clapper, Fred Turgon, Kenneth Smith, and Arthur True. Rev. Harry Greensmith was Scoutmaster.

Gerald Champney Lee was born on March 7, 1898, to George H. and Grace (Tucker) Lee in Morton, New York. Champney, a young entrepreneur at thirteen years old, placed an ad announcing his purchase of a popcorn business and the subsequent availability of "fresh buttered popcorn on Saturday nights."[240] An active youth, Champney was sworn in as a member of the Lookout Mountain Patrol No. 2 in Monroe County[241] [left] and as a high school student he was secretary of the rifle club for boys. Champney graduated from Hilton High School (Hilton, NY) in 1917.

After returning home from military service he went into business with his brother and two friends, starting the Miller-Lee Motors, Inc. dealership in Rochester, New York.[242] Miller-Lee Motors handled sales, parts, and service of Overland and Willys-Knight automobiles. [left][243]

On November 11, 1926, Champney married Linda Schwing and the couple established their home in Pittsford, New York. With Champney as vice president, Miller-Lee Motors closed its doors in 1928, but he continued working in the automobile profession until 1942. He went to work for Gleason Works, in Rochester, as a highly skilled mechanic in 1943.[244]

Champney bred Doberman Pinschers. He was considered an outstanding authority of the breed and served as a twelve-year member on the board of directors for the Genesee Valley Kennel Club.[245] In 1944,

Dog's Life Saved As Marine Corps Accepts Him

Rochester — (AP) — A 4-year-old doberman pinscher condemned to die for having bitten a child, was reprieved Friday when the Marine Corps accepted him for service.

Peace Justice Sidney K. Backus of Webster, before whom Max was tried June 13, had ruled the dog must die unless accepted by one of the armed services.

Max's charges appeared slim, when it was discovered Canine Corps enlistments had been halted, but G. Champney Lee of Pittsford, Genesee Kennel Club member, received notice Friday Max would be allowed to fill one of two vacancies at the Marine base at New River, N. C.

Champney's expertise with Doberman Pinschers helped secure a position in the United States Marine Corps for "Max," a dog who was ordered to be euthanized by Webster, New York, Justice Sidney Backus.[246] [right]

In 1945, Champney was elected commander of the American Legion Sargent Force Post 1228. He passed away on January 25, 1951, and is buried in Mount Hope Cemetery in Rochester, New York.

Name	LEE WILLARD JUDD				Service Number	180-92-78	

Enlisted:
Enrolled at RECRUITING STATION BUFFALO N.Y. Date 7-15-18

Age at Entrance 21 YRS 1 MO. Rate LANDSMAN MACHINIST MATE AVIATION XXX U.S.N.R.F.

Home Address — Town HILTON

County MONROE State N.Y.

M	Served at	From	To	Served as	No. Days
	NAVAL TRAINING STATION GREAT LAKES ILL.	7-16-18	11-11-18	LANDSMAN MACHINIST MATE AVIATION	119

Remarks:

Date Discharge XXXX 1-11-19 NAVAL TRAINING STATION   -LANDSMAN MACHINIST MATE
Place Inactive Duty GREAT LAKES ILL.   Rating at Discharge AVIATION

Library Bureau 20-1522

Willard Lee's *New York State Abstracts of World War I Military Service* card. Willard was too young to register for the first draft. He enrolled in the United States Naval Reserve Force one month after the second draft and did not have to complete a registration card.

WILLARD JUDD LEE
1898 – 1959

After enrolling in the Naval Reserve Force at the Recruiting Station in Buffalo, New York, on July 15, 1918,[247] twenty-year-old Willard transferred to the Naval Training Station in Great Lakes, Illinois. Like fellow veteran Champney Lee (no relation), he trained as a Landsman Machinist's Mate in Aviation. Willard completed training on November 11, 1918, and placed on inactive duty on January 11, 1919.

—Willard Lee and Champney Lee were at Buffalo last week and enlisted in the aviation section of the navy. Court Lee went also but was not accepted, owing to physical disability. It is not known as yet just how soon the boys will be called.

Willard Judd Lee was born in June of 1898 to Nicholas and Carrie K. (Judd) Lee of Churchville, New York; by 1910 the family owned a farm in Parma, New York. In 1913, Willard took a sworn oath as a member of the Lookout Mountain Patrol No. 2 in Hilton, New York, an organization which was the precursor to the Boy Scouts.[248]

Willard graduated from Hilton High School in 1915 and attended the University of Rochester between 1915 and 1917. Upon completion of his naval training and service in 1919, he enrolled at Hahnemann Medical College in Philadelphia, Pennsylvania, graduating in 1923 with a medical degree. He worked as a physician and house officer of the Fifth Avenue Hospital in Hempstead, New York.[249]

In 1923 he moved to Garden City, Long Island, New York, where he met Olive Evelyn Dutton.[250] [below] The couple exchanged vows in Manhasset, New York, on July 12, 1930.[251] Willard worked as a physician in a private practice in the New York City area. He passed away in Garden City, New York, on May 11, 1959, and is buried in Parma Union Cemetery in Parma, New York

Long Island Society

Miss Olive Evelyn Dutton's Engagement Announced To Dr. Willard Judd Lee

Mr. and Mrs. Louis Dutton of Plandome, L. I., announced at a tea yesterday the engagement of their daughter, Miss Olive Evelyn Dutton, to Dr. Willard Judd Lee of Garden City, L. I., son of Mrs. Nicholas Lee of Rochester, N. Y., and the late Mr. Lee.

Miss Dutton was graduated from Bradford Academy, Bradford, Mass., in 1926. Dr. Lee attended the University of Rochester at Rochester and was graduated from the Hahnemann Medical School in Philadelphia in 1923.

No date has been set for the wedding.

Form 1 1213 REGISTRATION CARD X 618 No. 4

1. Name in full *John Henry Magee* | Age, in yrs. *24*
(Given name) (Family name)

2. Home address *Hilton, N.Y.*
(No.) (Street) (City)

3. Date of birth *August 9, 1892*
(Month) (Day) (Year)

4. Are you (1) a natural-born citizen, (2) a naturalized citizen, (3) an alien, (4) or have you declared your intention (specify which)? *declaration of Intention*

5. Where were you born? *Little York Ontario Canada*
(Town) (State) (Nation)

6. If not a citizen, of what country are you a citizen or subject? *Canada*

7. What is your present trade, occupation, or office? *Student 26*

8. By whom employed? *Y.M.C.A. College*
Where employed? *Springfield Mass.*

9. Have you a father, mother, wife, child under 12, or a sister or brother under 12, solely dependent on you for support (specify which)? *Mother*

10. Married or single (which)? *Single* Race (specify which)? *White*

11. What military service have you had? Rank *none* ; branch
years ; Nation or State

12. Do you claim exemption from draft (specify grounds)? *Mother dependent*

I affirm that I have verified above answers and that they are true.

John H. Magee
(Signature of Registrant)

If person is of African descent, tear off this corner

JOHN HENRY MAGEE
1892 – 1994

John was inducted into the United States Army from Monroe County, New York, on April 20, 1918, as a twenty-five-year-old Private. He was assigned to the Medical Department at Camp Crane in Allentown, Pennsylvania, where the United States Army's Ambulance Service (USAAS) housed their training camp. Section 601 was made up mostly of men from Battle Creek, Michigan; John was assigned to this unit on May 16, 1918.[252] While at Camp Crane he petitioned to become a United States citizen on May 23, 1918.[253] Promoting on June 1, 1918, Private First Class Magee came home on furlough before sailing overseas with Section 601 aboard the SS *Giuseppe Verdi*, departing Jersey City, New Jersey, on June 13, 1918. Section 601 landed at Genoa, Italy, on June 27th and the unit proceeded over the Alps to France, supporting Italian Army units. True to his promise, Magee sent many letters to *Hilton (NY) Record* editor John E. Cooper. [above and Chapter 3][254]

> —The many friends of John Magee, who has been serving "Uncle Sam" in Italy for a number of months, were glad to have him return to town last Saturday evening. "Jack" had the opportunity to see a lot of the best places in Italy but prefers the "States." Ross the Italian who left here for Italy with John also returned on the same boat but has not as yet showed up in Hilton.

John transferred to Section 565 of the USAAS, supporting the Italian Army in France, instead of moving north with Section 601 to support American units.[255] Returning stateside from Genoa, Italy, on April 7, 1919, aboard the SS *Duca Degli Abruzzi*, John arrived in New York City on April 23, 1919. He was sent to Camp Dix, New Jersey, where he was discharged two days later on April 25, 1919.

Frequently referred to as Jack, John Henry Magee was born in Little York, Toronto, Canada, on August 9, 1892, to James and Martha (Gentle) Magee. The family immigrated to the United States on July 7, 1894. After the death of his father, some time before 1900, John and his family moved to Hilton, New York, where he and his siblings were raised by their mother. John graduated from Hilton High School in 1912 and attended college in Springfield, Massachusetts, at the Young Men's Christian Association (Y.M.C.A.) training school. He joined the staff at Hilton High School in August of 1917 as "physical instructor"[256] and returned to this position after the war.[257] [right][258]

Isabelle C. Nash of Rochester, New York, and John were married in Hilton on June 18, 1927, and made their home in Rochester. John worked as an auto repair mechanic and, by 1942, was working for Eastman Kodak Company at Kodak Park. At the age of 101, John passed away on February 6, 1994, in Sarasota, Florida. Following a graveside memorial service, John was buried in Ridge Chapel Cemetery in Williamson, New York.

> The Athletic Association of the Hilton High School has just re-organized under its new Constitution. The Constitution provides a new method of government for the Association which promises to be very satisfactory. The officers are all taken from a Board of Managers which consists of the President of the Board of Education, the Principal of the School, the boys of the Senior Class and the Managers of the Athletic Teams. The Board has full control over all business of the Association and all transactions must receive its approval before they can be carried on.
>
> The Board of Managers met for the election of officers on Friday, Feb. 2. The following were elected: President, James Pease; Vice-President, John H. Magee; Secretary, Floyd S. Lear; Treasurer, Colonel L. Brown; Manager, Base Ball Team 1912, Homer C. Odell; Reporter, James L. Pease.
>
> The President appointed a committee consisting of Messrs. John H. Magee and Homer C. Odell to find out whether we could rent the storage of Smith & Willenbrock as a gymnasium for the remaining part of the term. The Association has under way a play which will be given sometime in March. The proceeds will be used to help the Base Ball team next season.

Form 1   REGISTRATION CARD   No. *29.*

1   Name in full   *Harry W. Markel*   Age, in yrs. *22*
    (Given name)   (Family name)

2   Home address   *Spencerport*   *NY*
    (No.)   (Street)   (City)   (State)

3   Date of birth   *Dec*   *30*   *1894*
    (Month)   (Day)   (Year)

4   Are you (1) a natural-born citizen, (2) a naturalized citizen, (3) an alien, (4) or have you declared your intention (specify which)?   *Natural Born*

5   Where were you born?   *Dorloo*   *N.Y.*   *USA*
    (Town)   (State)   (Nation)

6   If not a citizen, of what country are you a citizen or subject?

7   What is your present trade, occupation, or office?   *Farming*

8   By whom employed?   *William Green*
    Where employed?   *Parma Monroe Co NY*

9   Have you a father, mother, wife, child under 12, or a sister or brother under 12, solely dependent on you for support (specify which)?   *No.*

10   Married or single (which)?   *Single*   Race (specify which)?   *Caucasian*

11   What military service have you had? Rank   *none*   ; branch
    years   ; Nation or State

12   Do you claim exemption from draft (specify grounds)?   *No.*

I affirm that I have verified above answers and that they are true.

If person is of African descent, tear off this corner

Harry W Markle
(Signature or mark)

172

HARRY WILFRED MARKEL
1894 – 1977

Harry was inducted into the United States Army on April 28, 1918, at twenty-three years old. He was assigned to Company K, 311th Infantry, 78th Division, at Camp Dix, New Jersey. His unit sailed for England on the 20th of May 1918 aboard SS *Vestris*, departing from Brooklyn, New York. After a brief stay in rest camps in England, the division infantry sailed to Calais, France, in early June. Private Markel was promoted to Private First Class on August 1, 1918. He returned home from Bordeaux, France, aboard the SS *Mexican* on May 10, 1919, and arrived in Hoboken, New Jersey, on May 22, 1919. He was discharged May 30, 1919.

Harry Wilfred Markel was born in Dorloo, New York, on December 30, 1894, to Judson E. and Lillian May (Kinns) Markel. He grew up in the farming communities of Schoharie and Otsego counties of New York. When the 1910 Federal Census was taken, Harry was not living with his family, who had moved to Troy, New York. Census records indicate he may have been living with the Allen family in the town of Roseboom,° New York, as a hired farm laborer. The entire family had moved to Ogden, New York, and Harry was working as a farm laborer for William Green in Parma, New York, according to his 1917 draft registration card.

When he returned from his military service, Harry and Daisy Hoyt of Hilton, New York, exchanged vows on December 23, 1922. The newlyweds made their home in Ogden and Harry supported his family working on the street railway with his brother, Ray.

By 1930, Harry was a truck driver hauling lumber and returned home each evening to the village of Spencerport, New York. Harry moved his family east to the town of Wolcott, located in Wayne County, New York, and purchased his own farm. In the early 1940s he opened a restaurant called the "Markel Restaurant" in Red Creek, New York. He purchased the adjoining barbershop business in 1959, with the intent to convert it into habitable space allowing him to live next to his business. [below][259]

He was a member of the American Legion Peterson-Hall Post 436 and held the elected positions of post chaplain and, in 1952, adjutant. In 1961, after retiring from the restaurant business, Harry and Daisy moved from Red Creek to Zephyrhills, Florida, where he passed away on September 8, 1977.

RED CREEK, Sept. 1 — Mr. and Mrs. Harry Markel of Red Creek have purchased Robert Talcott's barbershop, which adjoins the Markel restaurant in the Red Creek business section. The Markels plan to use the building as living quarters.

° The town of Roseboom is on the western border of Otsego County, adjacent to the town of Seward in Schoharie County, where the hamlet of Dorloo is located.

Serial No. _____ ✓ 157 Registration No. 138

1	Name in full *Ray Frederick Markel* (Given name) (Family name)	Age, in yrs. 21

2 Home address *105 South Union St Rochester N.Y.* (No.) (Street) (City or town) (State)

3 Date of birth *March 20 1897* (Month) (Day) (Year)

4 Where were you born? *Seward N.Y. U.S.A.* (City or town) (State) (Nation)

5 I am {
1. A native of the United States.
2. A naturalized citizen.
3. An alien.
4. I have declared my intention.
5. A noncitizen or citizen Indian.
(Strike out lines or words not applicable)

6 If not a citizen, of what Nation are you a citizen or subject? _____

7 Father's birthplace *Horseheads N.Y. U.S.A.* (City or town) (State or province) (Nation)

8 Name of employer *American Express Co.*
Place of employment *N.Y.C. Bldg. Central Av. Rochester* (No.) (Street) (City or town) (State)

9 Name of nearest relative *Mrs. Lillian Markel mother*
Address of nearest relative *Spencerport N.Y. U.S.A.* (No.) (Street) (City or town) (State or Nation)

10 Race—White, Negro, Indian, or Oriental— (Strike out words not applicable)

I affirm that I have verified above answers and that they are true.

Ray Fredrick Markel

If person is of African descent, tear off this corner.

P. M. G. O. Form 1 (blue)

(Signature or Mark of Registrant.)

REGISTRATION CARD. 3—6730

174

RAYMOND FREDERICK MARKEL
1897 – 1966

Raymond was inducted into the United States Army on September 3, 1918, at age twenty-one, and sent to Camp Jackson in Columbia, South Carolina, assigned to the 156th Depot Brigade. Never having served overseas, Ray spent the duration of his service with the 156th until his discharge on January 2, 1919.

Born in Dorloo, New York, on March 20, 1897, to Judson E. and Lillian May (Kinns) Markel, Raymond Frederick Markel grew up in the farming communities of Schoharie, Otsego, and Rensselaer counties before moving with his parents and siblings to Ogden, New York.

After serving in the military, Ray returned to Rochester, New York, and found employment alongside his brother, Harry, working as a laborer on a street railway. He married Jennie M. Auten on August 6, 1924, in Rochester. Ray worked to support his family as a machinist for a shoe manufacturing company in 1930 and, after moving to Greece, New York, started working for Bausch and Lomb as a lens grinder.

Jennie and Ray celebrated their twenty-fifth wedding anniversary in 1949 with announcements in both the newspaper and on Rochester radio station WHEC.[260] Ray was a member of the American Legion Ira Jacobson Post 474 and was an alternate delegate to the county committee in 1940. Ray passed away on October 28, 1966, and is buried in Riverside Cemetery in Rochester, New York.

A Family Dinner: One Potato!

Busy digging up potatoes on his Fairhaven farm this week, Harry Markel uncovered the top of one, pulled lustily, and the potatoes kept on coming and coming. Altogether, the monstrosity amounted to a 9-in-1 potato. He presented it to his brother, Ray of Wedgewood Park, in Greece, pictured showing the whole nine

In 1936, Ray's picture was in the October 22nd edition of the *Democrat and Chronicle* (Rochester, NY), showing off the rather unusual potato his brother Harry dug up from his farm and presented to him. [left][261]

175

Form 1   2315   REGISTRATION CARD   1750 | No. 74

1 Name in full   Fredrick Eugene McCartg   Age, in yrs. 4
   (Given name)   (Family name)

2 Home address   Main   Wellsville N Y
   (No.)   (Street)   (City)   (State)

3 Date of birth   April   20   1893
   (Month)   (Day)   (Year)

4 Are you (1) a natu. born citizen, (2) a naturalized citizen, (3) an alien, (4) or have you declared your
   intention (specify which)?   1 Yes

5 Where were you born?   Hilton   N Y   USA
   (Town)   (State)   (Nation)

6 If not a citizen, of what country are you a citizen or subject?

7 What is your present trade, occupation, or office?   Physician & Surgeon

8 By whom employed?   Practicing
   Where employed?   Wellsville N Y.

9 Have you a father, mother, wife, child under 12, or a sister or brother under 12, solely dependent on you for
   support (specify which)?   wife

10 Married or single (which)?   married   Race (specify which)?   Caucasian

11 What military service have you had? Rank _____ branch _____
   years _____ ; Nation or State _____

12 Do you claim exemption from draft (specify grounds)? _____

I affirm that I have verified above answers and that they are true.

1750   Fredrick Eugene McCartg
                    (Signature or mark)

If persons of African descent tear off this corner.

FREDERICK EUGENE McCARTY
1893 – 1942

Frederick McCarty was accepted into the United States Army Officer Reserve Corps as a twenty-four-year-old First Lieutenant medical officer on February 8, 1918. He reported to Camp Greenleaf at Fort Oglethorpe, Georgia, for medical training on April 1, 1918. [left][262] At the conclusion of training he was sent to Camp Mills on Long Island, New York, as part

CHUMS IN MEDICAL SERVICE

Hilton Officers Who Have Been Reared Together, Serve Together.

Hilton, March 29.—Lieutenant Fred McCarthy and Lieutenant Frank Mc-Culla were in town this week visiting their parents before going to Camp Greenleaf, Fort Oglethorpe, Ga., where they will receive their training. Both boys were graduated from the Hilton High School in the class of 1911, and from the Buffalo Medical School in 1915. Lieutenant McCarthy was practicing at Wellsville, and Lieutenant McCulla at Frewsburg. They were graduated from two schools together, enlisted in Buffalo together on January 24th, were called to service at nearly the same time, and both are stationed at Camp Greenleaf.

of the Camp Greenleaf Replacement Draft, assigned to Company No. 7. He departed New York City on June 8, 1918, aboard the HMS *Aquitania*, arriving in Liverpool, England, on June 15th. From there he traveled to Southampton, England, for deployment to France where it is presumed he reported to the 32d Division.

Lieutenant McCarty's *New York State Abstracts of World War I Military Service* card initially recorded that he was "severely" wounded on August 11, 1918, at Champagne, France; information on the card was partially erased and the entry changed to "slightly" wounded on August 14, 1918. Two newspapers also addressed McCarty's wounds: the *Morning Express* (Buffalo, NY) in October 1918[263] and a brief mention in the *Hilton (NY) Record* in April 1919.[264] The latter entry reported that McCarty "lost an eye an[d] narrowly escaped losing the other from gas poison."[265] No other military records or newspaper sources mention McCarty being wounded during the war. If he had been wounded, he likely would have returned to the United States sometime in the latter half of 1919 as part of a casual company or convalescent unit. Instead, he returned home with the 121st Field Artillery, 32d Division, sailing from Brest, France, aboard the USS *Georgia* on April 30, 1919, and arrived in Boston, Massachusetts, on May 12, 1919. Frederick was honorably discharged from Camp Devens, Massachusetts, on May 16, 1919, and placed on the reserve officers list.

Frederick Eugene "Mac" McCarty was born in Parma, New York, on the 20th of April 1893, to Enos and Lois (Baxter) McCarty. He was raised in Parma, graduating from Hilton High School in 1911. He attended the University of Buffalo (NY) Medical School, graduating in 1915 along with his fellow Hilton classmate Francis John McCulla. He served his internship at Buffalo's General Hospital.

Cornelia Hoefner, of Buffalo, married Mac on August 23, 1916, and the couple moved to Wellsville, New York, where Mac became president of the Allegany County Medical Society and a member of the New York State Medical Society.

In 1920 Mac was offered an appointment as Captain in the United States Army Reserve but he declined. His medical practice flourishing, he pursued the establishment of a hospital in the Wellsville area. He immersed himself in his community, becoming an active member of many civic organizations: Wellsville Lodge No. 1495 Benevolent and Protective Order of Elks, where he served as exalted ruler; the Brookland Club, a hunting, fishing, and shooting club; Hornell Lodge of Elks; a charter member of the Wellsville Lodge of Moose; assisted in the organization of the Veterans of Foreign Wars Frank B. Church Post; helped form the American Legion Morrison-Hayes Post 702; and was the first commander of the Allegany County American Legion.

Mac had an interest in politics and in 1936 was named an alternate delegate for the Forty-Third Congressional District to the Democratic National Convention. Two years later Mac withdrew his request for nomination, while it was still under consideration, as the candidate to represent the Forty-Third Congressional District of New York in the House of Representatives.

Mac was elected to a two-year term as town supervisor of Wellsville in 1939 and was re-elected in 1941. Mac never finished his second term, passing away on January 10, 1942. He is buried in Parma Union Cemetery, in Parma, New York.

—Dr. Frank McCulla arrived in this village last Saturday and is the guest of his parents, Mr. and Mrs. Fred McCulla, on East Avenue. Dr. Frank did fine service in France and Germany and had many thrilling experiences and narrow escapes from death, one in particular when a shell killed the driver of an ambulance in which he was riding with wounded soldiers. We understand that his classmate in the Medical College, also a former town of Parma boy, Dr. McCarty, lost an eye an narrowly escaped losing the other from gas poison.

Wounded severely—Lieutenant Howard L. McCall, No. 331 Hawley street, Rochester; Lieutenant Frederick E. McCarty, No. 1009 Michigan avenue, Buffalo; privates Howard H. Beebe,

Reports of McCarty being wounded in France vary from source to source. At left, the *Hilton (NY) Record* reported he lost an eye in April 1919.[266] Above, the *Illustrated Buffalo Express* reported him as "wounded severely" in their weekly column "On the Field of Honor" in October 1918.[267]

Fred McCarty was also very active in local politics. The *Evening Observer* (Dunkirk, NY) announced his candidacy in August 1938 for the Forty-Third Congressional District.[268] [right]

JAMESTOWN DEMOCRATS TO SUPPORT McCARTY

Jamestown. Aug. 5—The Democratic city committee will support the candidacy of Dr. Frederick E. McCarty of Wellsville for the nomination to representative from the 43rd ongressional district, according to announcement made here Thursday. He is expected to oppose the Republican incumbent, Daniel A. Reed of Dunkirk.

Dr. Frederick McCarty Is Named Alternate

WELLSVILLE — Dr. Frederick E. McCarty of Wellsville, chairman of the Allegany County Democratic Committee, Saturday was named alternate delegate for the 43rd Congressional District to the Democratic National Convention in Philadelphia this June.

Active in the Allegheny Democratic Committee, Fred was designated an alternate to the national convention in 1936.[269] [left]

Below, excerpts from the *Daily Reporter* (Wellsville, NY) obituary for Mac reflect the love and respect his community held for him.[270]

Prominent Surgeon Had Wide Circle of Friends — Active In Civic, Fraternal Life

"'Mac' is dead!"

Up and down Main Street, over telephone and telegraph wires, from farm to farm and house to house this was the word which spread throughout Wellsville and vicinity Saturday afternoon following the death at 4:45 o'clock of Dr. Frederick Eugene McCarty in Jones Memorial hospital after a long illness.

Those three words—better than a volume—told the story of the death of surgeon, fraternal leader, political leader and the man. It was a story which hundreds of loyal friends and admirers had long expected, but even in their expectation it came as a shock. To most people it was not just the loss of Dr. McCarty, Supervisor McCarty or Brother McCarty. Hundreds had lost a friend. They had lost "Mac."

It was only about 49 years ago on April 20, 1893, in a farm home near Hilton, N.Y., that "Mac" was born, a son of Enos and Lois Baxter McCarty. In all probability, on some April day when his parents' thoughts were of the farm, the crops and the Spring, this baby boy was expected to become another son of the soil. But Fate decided otherwise.

Raised On Farm

"Mac" did grow up on the farm, did his share of the chores and went to school. An apt student, the elementary grades were easily hurdled and then came Hilton high school. Some time during those four years, the farm boy learned two great loves and ambitions—to be a major league baseball catcher and a surgeon. To the good fortune of his fellow men he never realized the first ambition—but in the latter he succeeded through study and a pair of hands destined to become known in medical circles for their great skill and sureness. He traded the catcher's mitt for the scalpel, the chest protector for the surgical gown and instead of hoping for three strikes to put men out, he went into the game when two strikes were often already called and with his surgical skill kept men in the game of life.

From Hilton high school, where he was graduated in 1911, "Mac" went to the University of Buffalo Medical School. Ahead were four years of hard work, study and research. Standing beside him were determined parents who no longer saw a son of the soil in their boy. Those four years were not easy for the boy from the farm who wanted to be a surgeon.

After the war "Mac" returned to Wellsville and resumed his practice. He was an older man, he had seen much in those war torn battlefields of France but he had also gained experience for those skillful hands, as day after day he worked in hospitals seeking to save the lives of men.

It was at this period that "Mac" really started to become a part of Wellsville and to carve for himself a place in the hearts of hundreds of citizens.

Wellsville needed a hospital. Then came the munificent gift and the establishment of Jones Memorial Hospital. "Mac" took a keen interest in the establishment of the hospital and was always a loyal supporter of the institution which today serves Wellsville and a large surrounding territory.

The young surgeon continued to ly and sought to add to his skill. He became the first surgeon here to perform a successful Caesarian and the first to perform goitre operations. The Hippocratic Oath was his Bible and his professional life was devoted to the service of his fellow men.

He was active in the work of, and past president of the Allegany County Medical Society. He was a member of the New York State Medical Society.

Briefly, that is a picture of Dr. F. E. McCarty.

But in hundreds of homes today are told other stories of "Mac"—the doctor. They are private stories of the big, cheerful man who went into those homes when sickness came. The man who made professional calls, talked to Mother about her cooking, talked to Dad about the current sports season, politics or the farm; talked to the kids about their play and made a friend of the family pets. That is the man who could always find time to give his skill, under any condition, and gain from life the pleasure which he loved and found among the people.

That was "Mac" the friend of man. There is sadness today in many other circles outside the homes of Wellsville.

Active In Clubs

The fraternal and patriotic orders of Wellsville have lost a real friend. In more than one clubhouse yesterday, groups gathered to recall

In 1939 he accepted his party's candidacy for supervisor of Wellsville township. His friends had not forgotten, and when the votes were counted "Mac" had been elected to the office by a large majority.

Then came the fall of 1941. "Mac" was a sick man but he wanted to hold his office. He was again nominated by the Democrats and again his friends rallied to the cause. "Mac" lay in his hospital bed that cold November day but his friends went to the polls by the hundreds and that night a sick man learned that he was still the people's choice.

His health, however, continued to fail and he was never to live to meet again with his friends on the Board of Supervisors in Belmont. His interest, however, never weakened and at every meeting of the board there came either telephoned or written word from "Mac." He was still the supervisor.

His politics, however, were played in the election field and not in official activities. It must be said that always his first thought was for Wellsville and Allegany county—for the best interests of his people and his community.

That is the "Mac" who loved Wellsville, her people and her wide interests.

Today "Mac" is dead. A brilliant career is ended and a community mourns. Wellsville joins his family in their hour of grief.

REGISTRATION CARD

Form 1   **REGISTRATION CARD** 1 22 No. 87

1	Name in full *Francis John McCulla*	Age, in yrs. **23**
2	Home address *Frewsburg N.Y.* (No.) (Street) (City) (State)	
3	Date of birth *August 21st 1893* (Month) (Day) (Year)	
4	Are you (1) a natural-born citizen, (2) a naturalized citizen, (3) an alien, (4) or have you declared your intention (specify which)? *Natural born citizen*	
5	Where were you born? *Carlton N.Y. U.S.A.* (Town) (State) (Nation)	
6	If not a citizen, of what country are you a citizen or subject?	
7	What is your present trade, occupation, or office? *Physician* **28**	
8	By whom employed? *Self* Where employed? *Frewsburg N.Y.*	
9	Have you a father, mother, wife, child under 12, or a sister or brother under 12, solely dependent on you for support (specify which)? *No*	
10	Married or single (which) *Single* Race (specify which) *Caucasian*	
11	What military service have you had? Rank *None* ; branch ; years ; Nation or State	
12	Do you claim exemption from draft (specify grounds)? *No*	

I affirm that I have verified above answers and that they are true.

Francis John McCulla
(Signature or mark)

If person is of African descent, tear off this corner.

FRANCIS JOHN McCULLA
1893 – 1967

At twenty-four-years-old, Francis John McCulla was called into active service from the Officer Reserve Corps as a First Lieutenant in the United States Army Medical Corps on April 8, 1918; he reported to Camp Greenleaf at Fort Oglethorpe, Georgia, for medical training. At the end of training he was sent to Camp Mills on Long Island, New York, as part of the Camp Greenleaf Replacement Draft, assigned to Company No. 8. He departed New York City on June 8, 1918, aboard the HMS *Aquitania*, arriving in Liverpool, England, on June 15th. From there he traveled to Southampton, England, for deployment to France where he joined Ambulance Company 127, part of the 107th Sanitary Train, 32d Division. It's possible that he transferred to the medical detachment of the 324th Field Artillery, 83d Division, at some point while serving in France as indicated on his *New York State Abstracts of World War I Military Service* card. What is certain is that Lieutenant McCulla did not return from overseas duty with either Ambulance Company 127, 107th Sanitary Train, or the 324th Field Artillery. He returned from France as a casual officer aboard the SS *America* under the classification "For Orders," departing from Brest, France, on March 28, 1919, and arriving in Boston, Massachusetts, on April 5, 1919. He was sent to Camp Devens, Massachusetts, where he was discharged on April 11, 1919.

Francis John McCulla was born on August 21, 1893, in Carlton, New York, to Frederick and Bridget McCulla. He grew up in Parma, New York, where the family was farming their own land by 1900. Known as Frank, he was president of the Hilton High School Class of 1911. Together with his Hilton classmate, Frederick Eugene McCarty, he entered the University of Buffalo (NY) Medical School, graduating in 1915.

Upon his return from the war, Frank married Bessie Mae Caughell of East Hamburg, New York, on May 23, 1919; the couple made their first home in Frewsburg, New York. Frank's first post-war position was with Buffalo General Hospital and later he purchased an existing medical practice in Jamestown, New York.

Sometime in the 1930s or 1940s, Frank began an association with the United States Maritime Commission, working as a ship's surgeon on trans-Atlantic voyages. In September of 1947, Frank was working as a doctor in the Lake City Veterans Hospital located in Lake City, Florida.[271] Francis John McCulla passed away in August 1967 and is buried in Holy Cross Cemetery in Jamestown, Chautauqua, New York.

Frank wrote to his parents from France and his mother shared the news with the *Hilton (NY) Record*. The article on the left from July 1918,[272] the article on the right from August 1918.[273]

—Mrs. Frank McCulla of this village, has received a letter from her son, Lieutenant F. J. McCulla of the U. S. Medical Reserve Corp. now in France, in which he states that he is feeling fine and is near enough to the fighting line so that he can hear the big guns.

—Mr. and Mrs. Frank McCulla of this village about two weeks ago received a letter from their son, Dr. Frank McCulla, who is now in France. Among other things he said that he had seen German prisoners being brought in who were only 14 years of age and that even German women were made to fight, being chained to the big guns so they could not get away, and so found when our troops advanced.

McIntyre,	Gerald D	381,150	White	1½
(Surname)	(Christian name)	(Army serial number)	(Race: White or colored)	

Residence:_____ Spencerport_____ NEW YORK
(Street and house number)   (Town or city)   (County)   (State)

* Enlisted in N A Ft Slocum N Y   May 23/18

† Born in Spencerport N Y   19 1/12 yrs

Organizations:

Q M C Rct Dep Ft Slocum N Y to June 1/18; Q M C Camp Johnston Fla to July 25/18; F Rmt Sq 322 to Disch

Grades:

Pvt 1 cl Nov 1/18

Engagements:

Wounds or other injuries received in action: None.

‡ Served overseas: Sept 8/18 to Nov 9/19

§ Hon. disch. Nov 11/19 on demobilization

Was reported   per cent disabled on date of discharge, in view of occupation.

Remarks: 0

Form No. 724-1½, A. G. O.   *Insert "R. A.", "N. G.", "E. R. C.", "N A.", as case may be, followed by place and
March 12, 1920.   date of enlistment.   † Give place of birth and date of birth, or age at enlistment.
3—7683   ‡ Give dates of departure from and arrival in the United States. § Give date.

Gerald McIntyre's *New York State Abstracts of World War I Military Service* card. He was too young to register for the draft and instead elected to enlist in the National Army. He was not required to complete a draft registration card.

GERALD D. McINTYRE
1899 – 1939

Enlisting in the National Army on May 23, 1918, Gerald was nineteen when he reported to the Quartermaster Corps Recruit Depot at Fort Slocum, New York. On June 2, 1918, he transferred to Camp Johnston in Jacksonville, Florida, which was a specialized camp for the Quartermaster Corps. It was there that Gerald was assigned to the newly-organized Field Remount Squadron 322 on July 25, 1918. Gerald received a promotion to Private First Class on September 1, 1918, before leaving from Newport News, Virginia, aboard the Italian ship *Duca Degli Abruzzi* on September 8, 1918. He returned to Hoboken, New Jersey, from Brest, France, aboard the USS *Northern Pacific*, departing on November 3, 1919, and arriving on November 9, 1919. He was honorably discharged two days later on November 11, 1919.

Born in Spencerport, New York, to James and Tina (Darling) McIntyre in April 1899, Gerald graduated from Spencerport High School in 1917 and worked as an electrical inspector. He married Bertha Joanna Reynolds of Clarkson, New York, on September 12, 1922, and by 1930 they were living in Rochester, New York, where Gerald was a salesman for a bakery. He passed away on July 30, 1939, and is buried in Holy Sepulchre Cemetery in Rochester, New York.

Gerald McIntyre was not the only member of the *Honor Roll* in Spencerport High School's Class of 1917. Fellow veteran George Hochbrueckner is assumed to be the tall student in the center of the back row; Gerald McIntyre is suspected of being the boy on the far right of the back row.[274]

THE CLASS OF 1917.

FRESHMEN CLASS

Ethel Stearns	Wayland Payne
Wilhelmena Hill	Clarence Castle
Grace Warner	Austin Spencer
Gladys Bennett	Leslie Collins
Edna Dickinson	Percy Cromwell
Clara Palmer	Ivan Webster
Inez Stamp	Emily Corke
Lucy Adams	Vincent Ladd
Gertrude McIntyre	Clayton Cady
Mary Slayton	Louis Cleary
Eileen Hammer	Frank Sprong
George Hochbrueckner	Gerald McIntyre
Edward Cosgrove	

CLASS OFFICERS.

President - - - - - - -	Mary Slayton
Vice-President - - - - - -	Edward Cosgrove
Secretary - - - - - - -	Percy Cromwell
Treasurer - - - - - - -	George Hochbrueckner

Class Colors: Red and White.

Flower: Red Rose.

Class Motto: It is well to profit by the experience of others.

21

Form 1
REGISTRATION CARD 1784 No. 65

1 Name in full ..... George Miller   Age, in yrs. 22
(Given name)   (Family name)

2 Home address ..... Spencerport   N.Y.
(No.)   (Street)   (City)   (State)

3 Date of birth ..... November   2   1895
(Month)   (Day)   (Year)

4 Are you (1) a natural-born citizen, (2) a naturalized citizen, (3) an alien, (4) or have you declared your intention (specify which)? Natural born citizen

5 Where were you born? Rochester   N.Y.   U.S.A.
(Town)   (State)   (Nation)

6 If not a citizen, of what country are you a citizen or subject? .....

7 What is your present trade, occupation, or office? Farmer

8 By whom employed? ..... Self
Where employed? ..... Parma

9 Have you a father, mother, wife, child under 12, or a sister or brother under 12, solely dependent on you for support (specify which)? Father and mother

10 Married or single (which)? single   Race (specify which)? Caucasian

11 What military service have you had? Rank ..... none   ; branch .....
years .....   ; Nation or State .....

12 Do you claim exemption from draft (specify grounds)? .....

I affirm that I have verified above answers and that they are true.

If person is of African descent, tear off this corner   84

George Miller
(Signature or mark)

GEORGE B. MILLER
1895 – 1988

Private Miller was twenty-two when he was inducted into the United States Army from Rochester, New York, on August 7, 1918, and assigned to Battery F, 35th Field Artillery, at Camp McClellan, Alabama. He was promoted to Sergeant on October 21, 1918, and designated Stable Sergeant on October 23, 1918. George was discharged a little over three months later on February 5, 1919.

George B. Miller was born to Robert C. and Anna E. (Skuse) Miller on November 2, 1895, in Rochester. He grew up in Parma, New York, working alongside his father as a farm laborer. Four months after his discharge from military service he married Minerva Louise Webster on June 2, 1919, in Ontario, New York, and they settled in Parma.

George earned his living as a farm laborer and was a draftsman, continuing the same line of work when he moved his family to Canadice, New York. He moved to Rochester, leaving farming behind, and worked as an attendant at the State Hospital in Rochester. George passed away in the Batavia Veterans Medical Center on May 7, 1988, and is buried in Boughton Hill Cemetery in Victor, New York.

George Miller's World War II Draft Registration Card.[275]

Form 1   2053   REGISTRATION CARD   No. 2

1 Name in full   Edgar Roy   Murrell   Age, in yrs. 27
   (Given name)   (Family name)

2 Home address   LeRoy   N.Y.
   (No.)   (Street)   (City)   (State)

3 Date of birth   May   23   1890
   (Month)   (Day)   (Year)

4 Are you (1) a natural-born citizen, (2) a naturalized citizen, (3) an alien, (4) or have you declared your intention (specify which)?   Natural born

5 Where were you born?   Ogden N.Y.
   (Town)   (State)   (Nation)

6 If not a citizen, of what country are you a citizen or subject?

7 What is your present trade, occupation, or office?   Farmer

8 By whom employed?   Eli Bolt
   Where employed?   LeRoy N.Y.

9 Have you a father, mother, wife, child under 12, or a sister or brother under 12, solely dependent on you for support (specify which)?   no

10 Married or single (which)?   Single   Race (specify which)?   American

11 What military service have you had? Rank   none ; branch
   years   ; Nation or State

12 Do you claim exemption from draft (specify grounds)?

   I affirm that I have verified above answers and that they are true.

   Edgar Roy Murrell
   (Signature or mark)

186

★ EDGAR ROY MURRELL ★
1890 – 1918

Edgar was inducted into the United States Army at the age of twenty-seven from Batavia, New York, on September 25, 1917. He was assigned to Battery D, 307th Field Artillery, 78th Division, and sent to Camp Dix, New Jersey. Edgar was detached from the 78th Division and embarked Hoboken, New Jersey, on March 4, 1918, aboard the USS *Leviathan* as part of the replacement draft.[P]

The journey across the Atlantic Ocean was not without risk. Transport of troops and supplies faced many challenges and dangers; significant efforts were made to ensure safe arrival at European ports. Like many transport ships, the USS *Leviathan* experienced its share of excitement and close calls, as described in this excerpt of history of the vessel, from the ship's log:

> THE U. S. S. LEVIATHAN
> Second Trip to Liverpool
> After a stay of thirteen days in New York, during which time our supplies were replenished and minor repairs and alterations were made, we steamed out of New York Harbor on March 4th, for our second trip overseas. On board we had 8,242 troops, with the following organizations:
> 120th Field Artillery, 121st Field Artillery, 2nd Motor Mechanics, 9th and 10th Brigades, 20th F. A., 5th Div. School; Maj. Gen. J. T. Dickman. Accompanying us was H. B. Davison, Chairman of the War Council, American Red Cross. After passing out of the channel we dropped our Pilot at Sandy Hook and once more set our course at 90 degrees headed due east. Fire Island Light was passed abeam at 2.43 the same afternoon. We were making a standard speed of 20 knots which was maintained throughout the day while the weather remained clear and the sea smooth. After sundown the ship was darkened with the exception of a few blue lights, commonly known as battle lights, located at the various watertight doors and at the stairways. For two days following, the weather remained moderate with occasional rain squalls and light northeast winds. From this time on all of our watertight doors were kept closed while an army guard kept constant watch on all doors to see that they were not tampered with or opened. Abandon ships drills were held each day and it may be mentioned that there was ample lifeboat equipment for every soldier aboard. Each soldier was provided with a lifebelt. On the afternoon of March 7th smoke was sighted dead ahead, we discovered it was a British cruiser and a half hour later we passed her, on our starboard beam 15,000 yards distant. On this same day a soldier on board was placed in solitary confinement for making seditious

---

P Edgar's headstone in England lists his unit as the 78th Division, yet the division had not yet sailed from New York when he died on March 29, 1918.

remarks.

At 6.15 A. M., March 9th, the following radio message, which was sent broadcast to all ships, was received: "Vessels may meet three Allied submarines now proceeding from New London to Bermuda. Not escorted at present."

We entered the War Zone on the eight to twelve watch on the morning of March 11th, picking up our escort of destroyers, seven in number.

The rendezvous is previously arranged by cable and the destroyers are picked up by wireless from 24 to 36 hours before meeting. The times of arrival at the rendezvous are exchanged, and the meeting place arranged.

After picking up our escort, of which the Destroyer Manly was the senior ship, we proceeded on a zigzag course heading again for Liverpool. While passing through St. George's Channel the Manly was seen to suddenly swerve out of the formation and while only 800 yards from our port bow she commenced firing with her forward battery and fired a five-inch shell apparently at some suspicious object sighted. She immediately dropped a depth charge. It was so close that the Leviathan shook from stem to stern and many thought that we had struck a mine. What the object was we do not know, but if it was a sub, we extend our most heartfelt sympathies to the families of the crew. We proceeded on our trip without further event and the following afternoon found us in Liverpool once more. Immediately upon arriving the disembarking of troops and baggage was begun. The next morning, before all troops had left the ship, it was necessary for us to proceed to dry dock while the tide was high. One of the river ferry-boats unfortunately passed too close to us and suffered considerable damage, although she had been properly warned to give us right of way.

Safely moored in Gladstone Dock this same afternoon, the disembarking of troops was continued and completed the next morning. It was fine to see regiments of American troops, with flags unfurled and bands playing popular Yankee airs, marching to war. The boys aroused the admiration of the English.[276]

Edgar disembarked in Liverpool, England, on March 12, 1918, and was sent to a rest camp to await movement to the battlefields. He never made it to France. Edgar died from pneumonia and diphtheria in England two weeks after his arrival. This brings into question why the opposite was stated in the *Hilton (NY) Record* on April 4, 1918. [right][277]

—Edgar R. Murrell son of Mr. and Mrs. W. H. Murrell of Parma Center who left Churchville Sep. 20th, for Camp Dix and on Feb. 15th, was transferred to Camp Merritt, writes his people that he has safely arrived in France.

Edgar Roy Murrell, or Roy as he was known, was born on May 23, 1890, in Ogden, New York, to William Harvey and Phebe Ann "Annie" (Rogers) Murrell. By the time Roy was fifteen he had lived in the towns of Riga, Sweden, and Parma, New York. When he registered for the draft in 1917 he was working on a farm owned by Eli Bolt in LeRoy, New York.

Edgar listed his cousin, Mrs. Edgar Pimm, as his next-of-kin and person to notify when he was inducted. For this reason, Mrs. Pimm received all initial notifications and correspondence from the Army when Edgar died. Medical records suggest he succumbed to pneumonia and diphtheria, [278] possibly contracted during his voyage, and died on March 29, 1918; his cousin received the notification. Edgar was buried April 3, 1918,[279] in Magdalen Hill Cemetery located in Winchester, Hampshire, England.[280] Mrs. Pimm kept Edgar's parents informed of correspondence with the Adjutant General's Office. It was his parents who responded to a request for disposition intentions in 1920, not his cousin. On the facing page, a letter signed by his parents explains why Edgar listed his cousin as the point of contact, not his immediate family. When presented the option to have Edgar's remains returned to the United States, William and Annie simply responded, "our request is that his body is to remain where it now lays."[281] On May 2, 1922,[282] he was disinterred and reburied June 2, 1922, in Brookwood American Military Cemetery in Brookwood, Woking, United Kingdom.[283]

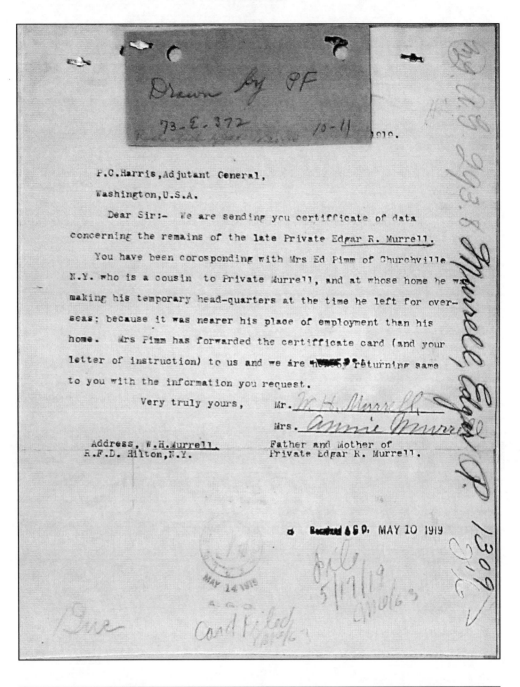

Drawn by PF

73-E-372   10-11   1919.

P.C.Harris,Adjutant General,

Washington,U.S.A.

Dear Sir:- We are sending you certificate of data
concerning the remains of the late Private Edgar R. Murrell.

You have been corosponding with Mrs Ed Pimm of Churchville
N.Y. who is a cousin to Private Murrell, and at whose home he was
making his temporary head-quarters at the time he left for overseas; because it was nearer his place of employment than his
home. Mrs Pimm has forwarded the certificate card (and your
letter of instruction) to us and we are hereby returning same
to you with the information you request.

Very truly yours,   Mr. W.H. Murrell,

                      Mrs. Annie Murrell

Address, W.H.Murrell,   Father and Mother of
R.F.D. Hilton,N.Y.   Private Edgar R. Murrell.

Received AGO. MAY 10 1919

Murrell, Edgar R. P. 1309

Mai. 28, 1920.

Received your notice to day in Regard to the
reburial of our Son Prigate Edgar Roy Murell
our request is that his body is to remain
where it now lays. Father. Wm H Murrell.
Mother. Annie Murrell

Name NEWCOMB- CARLYLE BRADLEY				Service Number 124-02-57

Enlisted at NAVY RECRUITING STATION ALBANY N.Y. Date 6-19-18

Age at Entrance 19 YRS.3 MO.   Rate SEAMAN 2ND CLASS

Home Address

XX X.XXX
U.S.N.R.F.

County MONROE   Town HILTON
                       State N.Y.

Q

Served at	From	To	Served as	No. Days
NAVAL TRAINING CAMP PELHAM BAY PARK NEW YORK N.Y.	6-21-18	11-11-18	SEAMAN 2ND CLASS	43
			SEAMAN	102

Remarks:

Date Discharge XX 12-1-18
Place Inactive Duty NAVAL TRAINING CAMP PELHAM BAY PARK NEW YORK N.Y.

Rating at Discharge QUARTERMASTER 3RD CLASS

Library Bureau 26-1533 -Δ

Carlyle Newcomb's *New York State Abstracts of World War I Military Service* card. He was too young to register for the draft and elected to enroll in the United States Naval Reserve Force. He was below the minimum age for all three draft registrations and was not required to submit a registration card.

CARLYLE BRADLEY NEWCOMB
1899 – 1967

Carlyle enrolled in the United States Naval Reserve Force at Albany, New York, on June 19, 1918, and was sent to Naval Training Camp, Pelham Bay Park, in Bronx, New York, until November 11, 1918. He was discharged at the rate of Quartermaster, Third Class, on December 1, 1918.

In July of 1942, as a newly-commissioned Navy Lieutenant, Carlyle returned to the Naval Reserve to work as a lawyer in Washington, DC, and served as a legal officer of the Eighth Fleet under Admiral H. Kent Hewitt in the Mediterranean.[284] He was promoted to the rank of Lieutenant Commander in October of 1944, and on July 1, 1951, Commander. Carlyle retired from the Naval Reserve Force in July of 1959.[285]

Carlyle Bradley Newcomb spent his life in service to others. Born to Z.W.J. and Adelaide D. (Judd) Newcomb in Hilton, New York, on March 18, 1899, Carlyle would first serve his community, at the age of fourteen, when he was sworn in as a member of the Lookout Mountain Patrol.[286] Graduating from Hilton High School in 1916, he was admitted to the University of Rochester (New York) and earned his bachelor of science degree in 1920, serving as president of the Students' Association.[287]

Carlyle began his career as a school teacher. He promoted to high school principal in Cato, New York, before assuming duties as superintendent of schools in Whitehall, New York.[288] He left the teaching profession to attend Yale University Law School in October of 1925, pursing of a bachelor of law degree, which he received on the 5th of November 1927.[289] After being admitted to the bar association in 1928, he was an assistant district attorney in Monroe County, New York.[290] [right] He was passionate about his service to the court, becoming infected by poison ivy during a manhunt. [left][291]

With over ten years in both private and public law,[292] Carlyle once again answered our nation's call after the United States' entry into World War II, returning to the United States Naval Reserve in 1942. [293] [next page] In July of 1946, Carlyle returned Rochester and opened his law office in the Genesee Valley Trust building. [next page][294]

Carlyle B. Newcomb Appointed Assistant to District-Attorney

District-Attorney William F. Love yesterday announced the appointment of Carlyle B. Newcomb, of Hilton, to fill an assistant's position in his office, at a salary of $3,150, effective August 1st. There has been a vacancy in the office since January 1st.

Charles S. Wilcox, who has held the position paying $3,150, was advanced to the position paying $3,475 a year. Mr. Wilcox will be transferred from City Court, criminal branch, to the main office in the Court House and assigned to Grand Jury and trial work.

Mr. Newcomb is 29 years old and a graduate of the University of Rochester in 1920 and the Yale Law School in 1927. He was a school teacher for several years after leaving the University of Rochester and served as principal of Cato High School from 1920 to 1922 and of Whitehall High School from 1923 to 1925. In his senior year at the University of Rochester he was president of the Students' Association.

Since leaving law school Mr. Newcomb has been in the office of Sutherland & Dwyer. Both Arthur E. Sutherland and Eugene J. Dwyer, senior partners in the firm, recommended Mr. Newcomb to Mr. Love.

Poison Ivy Infection Brings Delay in Trial

Recurrence of poison ivy infection received by Assistant District Attorney Carlyle B. Newcomb in May last year during the manhunt for Ross Caccamise, convicted slayer, in a woods near Lakeside caused a criminal trial to be put over the term in County Court yesterday.

Newcomb was to have prosecuted Samuel Kravetz, 32, of Cleveland, on an indictment charging third-degree burglary, first-degree grand larceny and criminally receiving stolen property. Kravetz is accused of entering the Segelin Clothes Shop, 1000 Clinton Avenue North, last Nov. 21 and stealing overcoats and cloth valued at $1,540.

While a senior at the University of Rochester, Carlyle bet a classmate he would get accepted to a national honor society. Winning the bet, Carlyle finally "made good" on the payout. [right] [295]

Friends Give Navy Officer Travel Items

Wherever his duties with the Navy take Lieut. Carlyle B. Newcomb, his friends have seen that he won't be lacking for traveling equipment.

A veteran of World War service with the Navy, Lieutenant Newcomb, a former assistant district attorney and practising attorney here, will report for duty with the General Courts Martial today in Washington.

CARLYLE B. NEWCOMB

When he left for Washington Saturday, he had shipped most of his effects in a wardrobe trunk, gift of the Rochester Police Veterans Association, and carried other traveling units presented him by the Sargent Force Post, American Legion.

Lieutenant Newcomb received the gifts at meetings held in his honor by members of the association and the post last week. He had for two years been attorney for the association and was one of the organizers of the post.

While a senior, Carlyle B. Newcomb, '20, wagered a box of cigars with one of his classmates that the latter would receive a Phi Beta Kappa key. "Nab" lost the bet. Seventeen years later—in May, 1937—he recalled that he had never handed over the cigars, and hastened to make good. Although 10-cent cigars had been specified in the original bet, Nab felt that the slight delay called for a somewhat higher quality of smokes, and the box he purchased contained Coronas. (Thanks, Carlyle!)

Lawyer Veteran Opens New Office

Carlyle B. Newcomb, who in World War I served in the Navy as a quartermaster third class and in World War II rose to the rank of lieutenant commander, yesterday announced opening of his law office at 1009 Genesee Valley Trust Building. He returned home on terminal leave in November after serving in Northwest African waters as legal officer of the Eighth Fleet under Admiral H. Kent Hewitt.

A graduate in 1920 of the University of Rochester, where he was president of the Students' Association, Newcomb was principal for five years of high schools in Cato and Whitehall before attending Yale Law School, where he received his law degree in 1927. For six and a half years until 1935 he served as an assistant district attorney of Monroe County. He was commissioned lieutenant in the Naval Reserve in July, 1942, and attained the rank of lieutenant commander in October, 1944.

Entering the political arena, Carlyle served the Rochester community as chairman of the board of the Supervisors' Elections Committee, held a seat on the Public Works and Planning Committee, and was supervisor of the Fourth Ward in the city of Rochester. Active in many civic organizations, he was a life member of Clio Lodge No. 779, Free & Accepted Masons, in Hilton; the Elks; the Champlain Chapter of the Royal Arch Masons in Whitehall; the Cyrene Commandery (a Masonic organization);[296] the Monroe Bar Association; Veterans of Foreign Wars; and the American Legion. Carlyle passed away on August 4, 1967, never having married, and is buried in Parma Union Cemetery in Parma, New York.

In 1960, as a member of the Monroe County Board of Supervisors, Carlyle was leading the charge to replace aging voting machines in Monroe County.[297]

NEWEST STYLE IN VOTING—Supervisor George C. Stockmeister, left, 20th Ward Democrat, and Supervisor Carlyle B. Newcomb, 4th Ward Republican, study printed form which records voting results on new machine being considered for use here.

Supervisors See New Vote Machine

The county Board of Supervisors yesterday viewed a new-style voting machine designed to eliminate some possible errors in preliminary tabulations.

The board was told by an official of the manufacturer that at least 200 of the 571 voting machines here need replacing.

Alaric R. Bailey, vice president of Rockwell Manufacturing Co. of Jamestown, noted that the first voting machine in th enation was used here in 1895. He said there now are more than 200 pre-World War I machines still in use here, and that the city is using 100 machines bought in 1912, "among the oldest in the state."

Supervisor Carlyle B. Newcomb, 4th Ward Republican and chairman of the board's election committee, told his colleagues the towns and city own the voting machines now in use.

Newcomb said the proposal is for the Jamestown firm to give an allowance of $125 on each of the 378 voting machines older than 1940. On the newer machines, the firm will give a tradein allowance based on depreciation of 5 per cent per year.

The new machines cost $1,565 each, Newcomb said.

Newcomb said the firm promised to donate the pre-1940 machines to the city, towns or county for scrap or for use by schools. Bailey stipulated that the machines would not be donated if they were to be sold to other communities for use as voting machines.

Cost of the new machines to the county would be about $700,000, Newcomb said. The cost would be $900,000, less an allowance of $200,000.

Bailey told the supervisors the new machines eliminate blank votes of which there were approximately 8,400 last November for a statewide judgeship. The blanks mostly occur, it is thought, when voters press down the lever and then mistakenly raise it back. The lever must be left down for the vote to be recorded.

The new machine won't allow the curtains to be opened unless at least one voting lever is down. Bailey said the theory is that the voter will realize the levers must be down for the vote to be recorded. He noted that the 8,400 votes was approximately 4 per cent of the votes cast here. Control of the city was retained by the Republicans by 52 votes.

The new machine also makes a printed record of the votes cast. This printed sheet, from which unofficial results can be tabulated, eliminates possibility of error in copying results from the machine, Bailey said.

Name NEWCOMB- DOUGLAS ALEXANDER 951	Service Number 124-02-62

Enrolled at NAVY RECRUITING STATION BUFFALO N.Y. Date - 4-16-18

Age at Entrance 20 YRS. 11 MO.   Rate SEAMAN 2ND CLASS   U.S.N.R.F.

Home Address ---   Town HILTON

Q   County ---   State N.Y.

Served at	From	To	Served as	No. Days
NAVAL TRAINING STATION GREAT LAKES ILL.	6-7-18	8-29-18	SEAMAN 2ND CLASS	209
NAVAL AUXILIARY RESERVE SCHOOL CHICAGO ILL.	8-29-18	10-3-18		
NAVAL AUXILIARY RESERVE CLEVELAND OHIO	10-3-18	11-11-18		

Remarks: APPOINTED OFFICER 3-1-19

Date Discharge 2-28-19   QUARTERMASTER

Place Inactive Duty NAVAL AUXILIARY RESERVE NEW YORK N.Y. Rating at Discharge 3RD CLASS

Library Bureau 26-1533 -A

Douglas Alexander Newcomb's *New York State Abstracts of World War I Military Service* card. Doug was too young to register for the first draft and elected to enroll in the United States Naval Reserve Force at the time of the second draft. Since he was on active duty, he was not required to complete a draft registration card for either the second or third drafts.

DOUGLAS ALEXANDER NEWCOMB
1897 – 1979

Douglas, age twenty, enrolled in the Naval Reserve Force at the Recruiting Station in Buffalo, New York, on April 16, 1918. As a Seaman Second Class he was stationed at the Naval

> Douglas Newcomb, who is attending Ensign school in Chicago, expects to go on a cruise on an ore boat to Duluth, next week.

Training Station in Great Lakes, Illinois, from June 7 until August 29, 1918; then attended the Naval Auxiliary Reserve School in Chicago, Illinois, until October 3, 1918. [left][298] His new assignment placed him at the Naval Auxiliary Reserve in

> —Ensign Douglas Newcomb has been honorably discharged from the Navy and returned to this village last week.

Cleveland, Ohio, until November 11, 1918. He was discharged as a Quartermaster Third Class on February 28, 1919, and appointed the rank of Provisional Ensign on March 1, 1919. He remained in the Naval Auxiliary Reserve until April 22, 1919, and placed on the Inactive Duty rolls. [left][299]

Douglas Alexander Newcomb was born on May 1, 1897, in Hilton, New York, to Z.W.J. and Adelaide (Judd) Newcomb. Graduating from Hilton High School, Douglas worked for the New York Central Railroad at the Hilton depot in 1913[300] and was Director of the Boy's Club of Rochester (NY) at School No. 6 by 1917.[301]

He received his post-secondary education from multiple universities. A member of the Rochester Chapter of Delta Upsilon Fraternity, Douglas received his bachelor's degree from the University of Rochester in 1918. He earned a master's degree from Stanford University (CA) in 1927, followed by a law degree from the University of Southern California in 1938. He never pursued the bar exam, instead dedicating himself to education.

After graduating from the University of Rochester, he taught in Ohio, [302] before starting his tenure in Long Beach, California, where he was revered for his work in education. Douglas taught math in 1923 at Franklin Junior High School in Long Beach and would later serve as the school's vice principal. Accepting the position of principal at both Seaside Park and Lowell elementary schools, he was named the Elementary Director of the district in 1941; and by 1947 was the school district's superintendent.[303] [right][304]

He married Helen Gertrude Dutton in Los Angeles, California, on December 17, 1931, and together they raised their family in Long Beach, California. Douglas spearheaded local Long Beach support for the armed forces during World War II, bridging the gap between the school district, the local community, and the war effort through distribution of ration books and the collection of scrap metal.

Douglas was credited for starting the remedial reading program with clinics, an FM educational radio station, an

Beach Schools Head Selected

LONG BEACH, June 23.— Douglas A. Newcomb, 50, today was appointed superintendent of Long Beach schools, succeeding Dr. Kenneth E. Oberholtzer, 44, whose resignation becomes effective July 31 when he will take

Douglas A. Newcomb

the post of superintendent of Denver (Colo.) city schools.

Newcomb, a veteran of 24 years with the Long Beach school system, is the first local teacher ever to become superintendent here. His appointment was announced by Eugene Tincher, president of the Board of Education.

outdoor science program, and the state's first school devoted to the mentally handicapped.[305] In 1960, construction started on a new elementary school, named the Douglas A. Newcomb Elementary School. It was the first of its kind in the area to encompass grades Kindergarten through eighth, eliminating the need for separate elementary and junior high schools. In 1963, a year after his retirement, the new school opened to all public school children in the district of Long Beach.

A reconstruction of the Newcomb Academy For Academic Excellence was started in 2012 and was completed in 2015. The revised facility encompassed six new buildings "surrounding a 'main-street/quad' in the campus center."[306] The Newcomb Academy Foundation was created to supplement any financial shortfall that may exist from state funding[307] and provide monetary support for programs no longer supported by the Long Beach Unified School District for the students of the Newcomb Academy.[308]

Douglas was "considered the architect of the modern Long Beach school system," as cited in two separate articles in the *Independent Press Telegram* (Long Beach, CA).[309] In an editorial following the announcement of his retirement, the same newspaper stated, "Superintendent Newcomb enters the record as one of the remarkable schoolmen of modern times." Douglas passed away on September 29, 1979, in Los Angeles, California, but his name and his legacy will live on.

School Name Is Newcomb Tribute

Another new elementary school will be constructed in the Long Beach Unified School District during the coming fiscal year.

It is the Douglas A. Newcomb school named in honor of the superintendent who has served as the executive head of the local public instruction program during the postwar years.

In deciding to name the school in honor of the superintendent, the Board of Education declared that it was fitting tribute to the man who had provided outstanding leadership in helping to build one of the outstanding school systems in America.

* * * *

THE NEW school, to be constructed on a 13-acre site a quarter mile north of Spring St. and a half mile west of Pioneer Blvd., will provide instruction in the kindergarten and the first eight grades of school for youngsters who will reside in the new El Dorado Park Estates section east of the Long Beach city park which has the same name.

Newcomb began his public school work 40 years ago as a teacher in Ohio and New Jersey from 1920 to 1923. In 1923 he came to Long Beach as a mathematics teacher at Franklin Junior High and has remained here since this time.

* * * *

HIS SCHOOL assignments included vice principal at Franklin, 1924-1925; principal at Seaside Elementary, 1925-1927; principal at Rogers Junior High, 1936-1941; director of elementary schools, 1941-1943; assistant superintendent, 1943-1944; deputy superintendent and acting superintendent, 1944-end of 1945; deputy superintendent, 1946-1947, and superintendent since 1947.

Newcomb attended high school in Hilton, N. Y., received his bachelor of science degree from the University of Rochester in 1916; his master of arts degree from Stanford University in 1927; and a bachelor of laws degree from the University of Southern California in 1938.

DOUGLAS NEWCOMB
Honored for Leadership

"If I have achieved anything, I owe it to the people with whom I work. No man achieves alone."

-Douglas Alexander Newcomb

Newcomb School Offers 'First'; Kindergarten and Eight Grades

The new $1.16 million Douglas A. Newcomb Elementary School will establish two "firsts" when it opens Monday to an initial enrollment of 300.

It will be the first Long Beach school located east of the San Gabriel River and the only school in the system serving pupils from kindergarten through eighth grade.

Located at 3351 Birdwell Ave., Newcomb will be the 55th grade school in the Long Beach Unified School District and the first school to be opened since 1960.

IT IS NAMED in honor of Douglas A. Newcomb, long-time Long Beach superintendent of schools who retired in 1962.

The school will combine grade school with the first two years of junior high school, eliminating the neces- sity for constructing a separ- ate junior high school for a small enrollment, district offi- cials said.

Built to serve residence of the El Dorado Park area, the school is expected to have an eventual enrollment of more than 1,000. Its first principal is Robert E. Ellis, who previ- ously served as principal at Fremont and Avalon elemen- tary schools.

EIGHT GRADES IN NEXT NEW SCHOOL
Slated for construction to begin next month is the Douglas A. Newcomb Elementary School which will serve West Long Beach. It will contain the full eight grades plus kindergarten instead of the customary six grades. This is being done to save expenditures at this time for a new junior high school in the area. Here Thomas D. Elliott, head of the project division of the Unified School District (left), and Robert A. Buse, a member of his staff, check the plans.

Newcomb was a trailblazer in California when he pursued construction of a new elementary school that contained Kindergarten through eighth grades. Traditionally schools housed Kindergarten to fifth or sixth grade, with junior high grades seven and eight in a separate building. [top],[310] [above][311]

At right, an editorial in the *Independent Press-Telegram* (Long Beach, CA), published upon his retirement, praised the work Douglas Newcomb did to further education in southern California.[312]

EDITORIAL

A Great School Leader Retires

THE ANNOUNCEMENT BY Douglas A. Newcomb that he will retire at the end of June as Superin- tendent of the Long Beach Unified School District is received with mixed emotions. His retirement is well- earned, but the citizens of the school system regret losing his splendid leadership. He has been one of the truly outstanding school superintendents in the nation during one of the most difficult eras for school admin- istrators.

★ ★ ★

NEWCOMB INHERITED the job shortly after World War II, and it was his duty to guide the district through the staggering post-war years when the school-age population inundated the land.

While hundreds of school systems throughout the country had their students on half-day sessions be- cause of classroom shortages, the Long Beach district under Newcomb solved its shortage and provided a seat for every child.

He planned, directed, and implemented a $100,- 000,000 school construction program and, though many other districts were voting down school bonds, ob- tained voter approval of four major school bond is- sues. These feats were possible because the school system under his leadership had earned the confi- dence and support of the taxpayers.

★ ★ ★

IT WAS, ABOVE ALL, a leadership of good com- mon sense. It was progressive without being faddish. Newcomb instituted a remedial reading program with clinics, a special school for physically handicapped, an educational radio station, and child welfare serv- ices. It was a fundamental without being backward. (He emphasized the 3 R's and placed ever greater emphasis on foreign languages and science.) And it kept in touch with the people.

We doubt that any school system ever had a more intelligent public relations program. Newcomb stressed the importance of letting the citizens know at all times what their system is doing, and this infor- mation program has been expertly operated—not as a propaganda agency but as a public service.

Realizing that a school system can be no better than its teachers, he maintained a strong recruitment program that attracted the best teaching talent from all parts of the nation.

★ ★ ★

IN THE END, OF COURSE, the product must speak for itself. And we are proud to say that the Long Beach system ranks as one of the greatest school systems in the nation—a system that has solved its building problems, obtained good teachers, held its costs within reason, and produced students who can compete successfully with students of any system.

The man who has had the major responsibility of the system deserves the major part of the credit. Superintendent Newcomb enters the record as one of the remarkable schoolmen of modern times.

Form 1

REGISTRATION CARD *543* | No. *59*

1 Name in full ..... *James B. Nice* — — Age. in yrs. *25*
(Given name) (Family name)

2 Home address ..... *Spencerport* ..... *N.Y.*
(No.) (Street) (City)

3 Date of birth ..... *August* *17th* *1892*
(Month) (Day) (Year)

4 Are you (1) a natural-born citizen, (2) a naturalized citizen, (3) an alien, (4) or have you declared your intention (specify which)? *Natural born citizen*

5 Where were you born? *Philadelphia* *Penn.* *U.S.A.*
(Town) (State) (Nation)

6 If not a citizen, of what country are you a citizen or subject?

7 What is your present trade, occupation, or office? *Machinist*

8 By whom employed? *Frank Stoffle*
Where employed? *Adams Basin*

9 Have you a father, mother, wife, child under 12, or a sister or brother under 12, solely dependent on you for support (specify which)? *None*

10 Married or single (which)? *Single* Race (specify which)? *Caucasian*

11 What military service have you had? Rank *None* ; branch
years .... ; Nation or State

12 Do you claim exemption from draft (specify grounds)?

I affirm that I have verified above answers and that they are true.

CA *James B Nice*
(Signature or mark)

198

JAMES BUCHANAN NICE
1891 (1892)–1953

James was inducted into the United States Army on September 7, 1917, at Spencerport, New York, as a twenty-five-year-old Private. [right][313] He was assigned to Battery D, 309th Field Artillery, 78th Division, and trained at Camp Dix, New Jersey. On November 23, 1917, he transferred to Supply Company, 309th Field Artillery, and was designated a Cook and Wagoner by February 1, 1918. James was discharged on February 20, 1918, on a Surgeon's Certificate of Disability.

When exactly James Buchanan Nice was born is unclear as various Federal, State, and local documents list different birthdays: August 21, 1891;[314] November 17, 1891;[315] August 17, 1892;[316] and November 16, 1892.[317] All documents are consistent in the place of birth–Philadelphia, Pennsylvania–and list James as the son of James and Margaret (Boyle) Nice.

Employed in Adams Basin, New York, as a machinist, he married Rachel C. Learn in the Methodist parsonage of Perry, New York, on December 22, 1917.[318] The couple lived for a short time in Spencerport before moving to Wyoming County, New York, where together they became actively involved in their community, both in business and civic organizations.

James became a poultry farmer in 1923 when he purchased an existing poultry farm in Perry.[319] In 1924 he was appointed by the village board of Castile, New York, to the position of deputy chief of police[320] and in 1925 he was appointed chief of police.[321] [below]

In 1925 he purchased an existing real estate and auctioneering business, located above the town clerk's office in Castile.[322] Ever on the move, James and his family uprooted in 1933 to a furnished apartment in

SPENCERPORT WILL "WATCH" HER BOYS

First Contingent Leaves for Camp Friday.

Spencerport, Sept. 5.—The Fellowship Committee of the town of Ogden and supervisors and other town officials of the towns of Greece, Parma, Hamlin, Clarkson, Chili, Riga and Ogden, in the First County Draft District in Monroe county, met at Spencerport to make arrangements to give the boys who were drawn or volunteered in the first 5 per cent, a rousing send-off and patriotic farewell.

Program for the celebration will commence at 9 o'clock Friday morning and continue until 1:35, at which time the first contingent leaves for their training camp. There will be an address by George A. Benton, remarks by Howard Widener, patriotic songs by the school children and music by the Spencerport Citizens' Band.

At the conclusion of the exercises the parade will form, headed by the band and followed by the officials in automobiles, Boy Scouts, Red Cross units and veterans that are and those who soon will be. After the parade dinner will be served to the boys and their families and friends. Each town is expected to provide the food for the men and their families of their town. Dinner will be served in Masonic Temple auditorium.

Those who are to be honored by this demonstration are: William H. Beaney, Spencerport; Homer Chauncey Odell, Parma; Lewis Edward Kress, Chili; Albert B. Gordon, 157 Eastman avenue, Rochester; Neil T. Vickery, Spencerport; Wallace Ray Austin, Spencerport; James Buchanan Nice, Parma; Arthur Manley Smith, Parma; Leo R. Goodridge, Spencerport; Albert Hiram Davis, Chili.

VILLAGE COMMITTEES

At the regular meeting of the village trustees, held last week, the following standing committees were named for the ensuing year: Streets, Bentley and Crawford; lights, Hopkins and Hubbard. Frank E. Vining was re-appointed as superintendent of the electric light system. The office of street commissioner was declared vacant, and for the present will be in charge of the standing committee. James B. Nice was appointed chief of police, in place of Norman Phelps, who is now employed in Silver Springs.

Hornell, New York, so he would be in his "territory" representing his new employer, J. Edward Jones, in the production of oil royalties.[323]

In 1935 James and his wife purchased an established mercantile and grocery store in Rossburg, New York, that had been in business for fifty-three years, once again relocating the family.[324] In the United States Federal Census of 1940, James and his wife are listed as being grocery store owners in Hume, New York, and it is unclear whether the two businesses are the same.

James was a member of the Independent Order of Odd Fellows, Castile Lodge No. 370, and served as a trustee for the organization in 1924.[325] His wife was an active member of the Goodwill Rebekah Lodge–the ladies' equivalent of the Odd Fellows–and the two organizations would meet simultaneously, often hosted by husband and wife.

James was also an active member of the American Legion Wallace-Jeffers Post 753, elected to the positions of commander in 1925 and 1926,[326] and chaplain in 1931.[327] He presided over the dedication of the "Soldiers, Sailors and Marines Memorial" in Castile during a Memorial Day ceremony on May 31, 1926. A "Doughboy" statue, created by artist E.M. Viquesney (1876-1946),[q] was erected in the town center.[328] [below]

Mirroring their Odd Fellows and Rebekah Lodge joint meetings, the same would occur as members of the American Legion and the American Legion Ladies' Auxiliary–the latter of which Rachel was a member–with concurrent meetings of the two organizations sponsored in the couple's home.[329]

In 1939, James was a patient in the Sunmount Veterans Administration Hospital in Tupper Lake, New York, which was a facility for the treatment of veterans with tuberculosis.[330] He passed away on November 19, 1953, and is buried in Grace Cemetery in Castile, New York.

CEREMONIAL PROGRAM OF DOUGHBOY MEMORIAL DEDICATION ON MONDAY

The local committee present to the public their completed program for the ceremonial dedication of the Soldiers', Sailors' and Marines' Memorial which will take place Monday morning at 11 o'clock.

Headed by the Perry Drum Corps, the parade of the Wallace-Jeffers Post, Legionaires from Warsaw and Silver Springs with the local Boy Scouts and Troops from surrounding towns will leave the High School grounds at 10:30, a. m., proceeding to the corner of Washington on Main where the monument is situated. The assembly will be called to order at the hour stated by Post Commander James B. Nice, after which the program will be carried out as follows:

Invocation.

Unveiling and Dedication of Memorial by Rev. William Blankley, Chaplain Wallace-Jeffers Post.

Singing, "America The Beautiful," by school children.

Address by Hon. James W. Wadsworth, Jr. of Geneseo, United States Senator.

Singing, "The National Anthem."

Benediction.

Children wishing to take part in the parade will meet at the school at 10:15.

The State Senator, Congressman, Assemblyman and Wyoming County Board of Supervisors will be guests of our community at the dedication, later being entertained at a luncheon under the auspices of the Castile Community Club in the dining room of the Presbyterian church.

Members of the Club wishing to attend the luncheon may secure tickets Friday and Saturday at the Cummings Pharmacy.

The monument was placed in position yesterday by the Sutherland Granite Works of Perry, with a copper box set in the concrete base containing the names of members of the Wallace-Jeffers Memorial Association, who have subscribed towards its erection, together with data concerning the various organizations of the community, its officials and public buildings, churches, also postage stamps, coins, etc.

A special base ball game is scheduled for Monday afternoon at two o'clock here, when Canaseraga will play against Castile.

q https://doughboysearcher.weebly.com/castile-new-york.html

PLAN MEMORIAL FOR DOUGHBOYS OF WORLD WAR

Castile Church Donates Land; Legion Will Start Drive.

Castile, Jan. 17.—Final plans have been made for the erection of a Soldiers', Sailors' and Marine Memorial in this village, the contract for a bronze life-size statute of an American Doughboy having already been let.

The local American Legion Post has been working for a memorial for the last two or three years. One difficulty that has confronted the post has been a suitable place for the erection of the monument. However, the trustees of the Presbyterian Church recently have given consent to its being placed on the plot at Main and Washington streets.

The Memorial will have a marble base set on a concrete foundation. The statute depicts an American Doughboy in action with a hand grenade in one hand and a rifle in the other. Other details are perfect even to the barbed wire. A replica of this memorial is now on display in the windows of the Cummings Pharmacy.

The date of unveiling has been set for Memorial Day. The amount raised through the activities of the Wallace-Jeffers Post and other contributions will require an additional $1,400 to complete the purchase. For this purpose, a drive will be made next week when a well-organized committee will canvas the town and vicinity.

A popular subscription of $1 has been thought the most advisable plan, each subscriber being given a certificate of membership in the Wallace-Jeffers Memorial Association, with no further dues or assessments to be levied. Ample provision will be made for the perpetual care of the plot.

The Soldiers, Sailors, and Marines Memorial at the corner of North Main Street and Washington Street in Castile.[331]

Form 1	**REGISTRATION CARD** 302 No. 26	Age, in yrs.

1 Name in full *Homer Chauncey Odell*   21
(Given name) (Family name)

2 Home address *Spencerport*   *N.Y.*
(No.) (Street) (City) (State)

3 Date of birth *Sept*   *7*   *1890*
(Month) (Day) (Year)

4 Are you (1) a natural-born citizen, (2) a naturalized citizen, (3) an alien, (4) or have you declared your intention (specify which)? *Natural Born*

5 Where were you born? *Parma*   *N.Y.*   *U.S.A.*
(Town) (State) (Nation)

6 If not a citizen, of what country are you a citizen or subject?

7 What is your present trade, occupation, or office? *Farmer*

8 By whom employed? *A S Odell*
Where employed? *Parma*

9 Have you a father, mother, wife, child under 12, or a sister or brother under 12, solely dependent on you for support (specify which)? *No*

10 Married or single (which)? *Single*   Race (specify which)? *Caucasian*

11 What military service have you had? Rank *none* ; branch ____ years ____ ; Nation or State ____

12 Do you claim exemption from draft (specify grounds)? ____

I affirm that I have verified above answers and that they are true.

C A

Homer Chauncey Odell
(Signature or mark)

302 If person is of African descent, tear off this corner

HOMER CHAUNCEY ODELL
1895 – 1966

Twenty-two-year-old Homer was inducted into the United States Army at Spencerport, New York, on September 7, 1917. He was sent to Camp Dix, New Jersey, [below][332] and assigned to Battery D, 309th Field Artillery, 78th Division; promoting from Private Odell to Corporal Odell on November 15, 1917. He went overseas with Battery D on May 28, 1918, departing from Boston, Massachusetts, aboard the SS *Arawa*. Homer participated in the campaigns at Lorraine, Saint-Mihiel, and Meuse-

> **PARMA CENTER**
> Homer Odell left Friday for Camp Dix, Wrightstown, New Jersey. He was acting Captain of the eleven boys who went from this district.

Argonne, earning a promotion to Sergeant on October 2, 1918. Homer and Battery D departed from Marseilles, France, on April 26, 1919, aboard the SS *Infanta Isabel* and arrived in Hoboken, New Jersey, on May 10, 1919. He reported back to Camp Dix and was discharged on May 17, 1919.

Homer Chauncey Odell was born in Parma, New York, to Chauncey A. and Louisa (Newton) Odell on September 4, 1895. A member of the Class of 1912 at Hilton High School, he played on the baseball team and in 1912 was elected team manager.[333] Homer attended Purdue University, studying agriculture for two years, between the fall of 1915 and the spring of 1917. He listed farming as his occupation on his June 5, 1917, draft registration card.

Returning to New York after his discharge, Ode, as he was nicknamed, attended Cornell University and participated in the Country Community Club, the Agricultural Economics Club, and the Round-Up Club, graduating with a bachelor of science in agriculture in 1922.[334]

His first job, with Nassau County Farm Bureau, was assistant to the agricultural agent and then principal agricultural agent by October 1922;[335] by 1925 he would become the farm bureau manager.[336] Homer and Gladys Bretsch were married on July 25, 1924, in her hometown of Hastings-on-Hudson, New York. The newlyweds left for a honeymoon in Bermuda and, after their return, made their home in Mineola, New York.[337]

In 1926, Homer moved his family to Glens Falls, New York, becoming the district representative for the Chevrolet Company in the Adirondack region.[338] He was an automotive company representative in West Hartford, Connecticut by 1930, but didn't remain in the automotive industry for long.

In 1932, Homer changed professions and began working in the insurance industry for the Federal Land Bank of Springfield, Massachusetts; moving the family once more to Longmeadow, Massachusetts. As assistant to the president of the bank, he was responsible for brokering real estate loans for farms.[339] Leaving his position in 1945, he accepted a position as sales manager with Farmers' Cooperative in Waltham, Massachusetts, [340] retiring as an appraiser for the Equitable Life Insurance Company.[341]

Homer was a member of the American Legion Doud Post 98 and the Cornell Alumni Association. He died in Melbourne, Florida, on April 4, 1966, and is buried in Parma Union Cemetery in Parma, New York.

Homer's graduation photo from Cornell University, published in the *Cornellian* in 1922.[342]

Form 1   **REGISTRATION CARD** 25   No. *105*

1. Name in full ___ *Edwin W. Oviatt* ___ Age, in yrs. **26**
(Given name)   (Family name)

2. Home address ___ *280* ___ *West ave* ___ *Rock* ___ *N.Y.*
(No.)   (Street)   (City)   (State)

3. Date of birth ___ *January 16* ___ *1891*
(Month)   (Day)   (Year)

4. Are you (1) a natural-born citizen, (2) a naturalized citizen, (3) an alien, (4) or have you declared your intention (specify which)? ___ *Natural Born*

5. Where were you born? ___ *Ironton* ___ *Ohio* ___ *U.S.*
(Town)   (State)   (Nation)

6. If not a citizen, of what country are you a citizen or subject? ___ *U.S.*

7. What is your present trade, occupation, or office? ___ *Clerk* 29

8. By whom employed? ___ *North East Co*
Where employed? ___ *Whitney St*

9. Have you a father, mother, wife, child under 12, or a sister or brother under 12, solely dependent on you for support (specify which)? ___ *No*

10. Married or single (which)? ___ *Single* ___ Race (specify which)? ___ *Caucasian*

11. What military service have you had? Rank ___ *No*; branch ___;
years ___; Nation or State ___

12. Do you claim exemption from draft (specify grounds)? ___ *No*

I affirm that I have verified above answers and that they are true.

Edwin W. Oviatt
(Signature of man)

If person is of African descent, tear off this corner.

EDWIN WATKINS OVIATT
1891 – 1979

Edwin enlisted in the United States Navy at the Recruiting Station in Rochester, New York, on June 25, 1917, at the age of twenty-six. According to his *New York State Abstracts of World War I Military Service* card, his first assignment was to a Receiving Ship in New York City until July 25, 1917. He transferred to another Receiving Ship in Boston, Massachusetts, for two weeks, before starting radio school in Cambridge, Massachusetts, on August 9, 1917, completing training on December 31, 1917. At this point the card states he transferred to a Receiving Ship in Philadelphia, Pennsylvania, for two weeks; then assigned to the USS *Carola* from January 17 until November 11, 1918.

According to the Naval History and Heritage Command the *Carola IV*, built in 1885, was purchased by the United States Navy in 1917 and assigned to the Second Division, Patrol Squadron, Atlantic Fleet.

> *Carola IV* cleared New York late in July 1917 for Saint John's, Newfoundland; the Azores; and Brest, France. Arriving 29 August, she served on patrol and escort duty along the coast of France. Her active service ended in October 1917, when she was fitted out for service as an auxiliary berthing ship. She served at Base Seven, Brest, until 27 December 1919, when she was decommissioned and sold.[343]

An entry on the same webpage includes another reference to Carola: "8 February [1918] The former French naval prison in Brest is established as Carola Naval Barracks, eventually housing more than 3,500 Bluejackets."[344]

Additional research uncovered a letter Edwin wrote to his maternal first cousin, Mrs. Mabel Norris Weber, in Springville, New York, and published in the *Journal and Herald* (Springville, NY) in June 1918. Edwin described his experiences in detail and being "out in a land station about fifteen miles out of Brest, way out in the country."[345] In closing, below his name, he includes the following: "Station T.S.F. de Mengam, par. Brest, France." The nomenclature "T.S.F. de Mengam" was also found in an article in the January 1934 issue of the *American Legion Monthly*. In the article, which included the photo below, the author relates a story from a United States Navy radio operator who was assigned to a French wireless station eight miles out from Brest, France.[346]

T. S. F. de Mengam, a French wireless station eight miles out from Brest, was shared by our Navy radio operators. Here were picked up S. O. S. calls from ships for relay to the Naval Office in Brest

The article explains that "T.S.F." stands for "Telegraphic sans fil" or "Telegraphy without wires" in English. At the close of the narrative, the former radio operator described how he was transferred to a ship in October 1918, and while glad to be back on a ship, he "hated to leave the gang–old Dixon from Georgia, Oviatt from Rochester, New York, the chief from Chicago and the other man, whose name I've forgotten, from Oklahoma."[347]

It is certain that Electrician Third Class Radio Oviatt was never assigned to the USS *Carola* as his abstract card states, given the ship was already in France and deemed unserviceable when he finished radio school. It is probable that he was assigned to the Carola Naval Barracks in Brest, France, instead of the actual ship. It is presumed that he didn't end his affiliation with the station on the armistice, as his abstract card indicates. He likely remained at the station until either spring or summer of 1919, at which time he would have returned to the United States to be discharged, like his abstract card states: Electrician First Class 'Radio' Edwin Oviatt was discharged on August 27, 1919, from a Receiving Ship in New York City. [below]

Born in Ironton, Ohio, on January 16, 1891, to Elias W. and Hattie (Norris) Oviatt, Edwin Watkins Oviatt migrated with his family to Parma, New York by 1910, spending a few years in Springville, Erie County, New York, around 1905. His father purchased a fruit farm in Parma and Edwin spent his teenage years and his time following military service working on the family farm. Around 1925, Edwin found employment as a production engineer in Rochester.

Edwin was enthusiastic about the sport of golf and not just improving his handicap. In 1926 he was a business partner, with his brother and others, in the creation and development of Westridge Country Club in Parma–a nine-hole course that opened in July of 1928–with Edwin as the secretary-treasurer for the organization.[348] Westridge Country Club became what is now known as Braemer Country Club.[349]

Miss Florence Ogden Roberts of Allison Park, Pennsylvania, married Edwin on January 22, 1930, in East Aurora, New York.[350] The couple established their home in Brighton, New York, while Edwin continued to work as a production engineer for the American Laundry Machine Company; he was later promoted to foreman.

Edwin passed away in Sarasota, Florida, on January 30, 1979, and is buried in Meadowlawn Memorial Garden in New Port Richey, Florida.

The letter below was sent from Edwin to his cousin, Mabel, in late spring 1918, after he had been at the radio station for a few months.[351] The description he provides is nearly identical to the story described by J.F. Parrish in the *American Legion Magazine*.[352]

Letter From France

The following letter was received by Mrs. Mabel Norris Weber from Edwin Oviatt, a former Springville boy, who is doing his bit in France:

May 13, 1918.

Dear Cousin Mabel :—

Mother has written me that you have knitted me a pair of wool socks and sent them to her. I thank you very much for them and will certainly send for them if I am here next winter. We all appreciate the woolen socks, jackets, etc., as they are very comfortable when cold.

I thought I had written you a postal just before I left the states. I have been over here since February 1st. Had a good trip over but quite rough altho I didn't get the least bit sea sick. I have been very fortunate in so far as getting a good place to work. I am out in a land station about fifteen miles out of Brest, way out in the country. We are right on the sea shore on a great high bluff. The views around here are great. The country is quite wild and the shore is very rocky. We have a small kodak that we have had out here for two or three days and hope to get some good pictures to take home. Our station is in an old fort that was built by Louis the Fourteenth and has a moat and all the rest of the old-time appliances, such as a draw bridge, etc. We stand our watches in an old tower that is always damp. The walls are four feet thick and never any fire in it.

The French don't believe in being comfortable, at least not the way we are used to. There are six of us out here besides the French. We have a chief, four radio men and a cook. Our rooms consist of one large room where five of us sleep, one room for the chief, wash room, lounging room, dining room and kitchen. The dining room and galley are in a separate building. We worked out here a week, painting, washing windows, etc. Have matting on the floors. In the lounging room we have four large upholstered chairs, a large couch and two writing tables and heating stove. Dining room has a good table, sideboard and looks quite like home. Our bunks are very comfortable. In the wash room we have three wash stands. We are very comfortable out here. Our officer told us when we were sent out here that it would be lonesome, but that he would try and make that up by making us comfortable, and he has. Our cook, a navy cook, is pretty good. We have good food and take it as a whole, I like it fine. We have some books and magazines and get two daily papers every day. The New York Herald and Daily Mail, both published over here. They are two -sheet affairs, but enjoy them a great deal.

Give my love to the boys and remember me to Mr. Weber. Hope you are all enjoying good health.

Your affectionate cousin,

Edwin Oviatt

Station T. S. F. de Mengam, par, Brest, France.

Form 1   REGISTRATION CARD   No. **70**

1. Name in full _Selden Harold Oviatt_
   (Given name)   (Family name)   Age, in yrs. **30**

2. Home address _280 Westave Roch N.Y_
   (No.) (Street) (City) (State)

3. Date of birth _July 10 1887_
   (Month) (Day) (Year)

4. Are you (1) a natural-born citizen, (2) a naturalized citizen, (3) an alien, (4) or have you declared your intention (specify which)? _Natural Born_

5. Where were you born? _Springville N.Y U.S._
   (Town) (State) (Nation)

6. If not a citizen, of what country are you a citizen or subject? _U.S._

7. What is your present trade, occupation, or office? _Tool Draftman_

8. By whom employed? _North East_
   Where employed? _Electric Co_

9. Have you a father, mother, wife, child under 12, or a sister or brother under 12, solely dependent on you for support (specify which)? _No_

10. Married or single (which)? _Single_ Race (specify which)? _Caucasian_

11. What military service have you had? Rank _No_ ; branch _____ ;
    years _____ ; Nation or State _____

12. Do you claim exemption from draft (specify grounds)? _No_

I affirm that I have verified above answers and that they are true.

Selden H. Oviatt
(Signature or mark)

If person is of African descent, tear off this corner

SELDEN HAROLD OVIATT
1887 – 1981

Accepting an appointment with the United States Naval Academy at Annapolis, Maryland, on July 26, 1906, Midshipman Oviatt was known as Ovie to his classmates.[353] He resigned his commission on the 11th of February 1907 because he was "deficient in the recent semi-annual examinations."[354]

When the United States called for volunteers to serve during World War I, Harold enrolled in the United States Naval Reserve Force at the Rochester, New York, Recruiting Station on July 10, 1917, at the age of thirty. He was assigned to the Summerville Armory in Summerville, New York,[r] until November 2, 1917; Pelham Bay Park, Bronx, New York, until November 28, 1917; and a Receiving Ship in Washington, DC, until May 15, 1918. Entering the Naval Reserve Force as a Quartermaster Third Class, he made rate to Quartermaster Second Class and then Chief Quartermaster in seven-and-a-half months. He was discharged on May 15, 1918, to accept a Naval Reserve Force commission as an Ensign.

Ensign Oviatt was assigned to duty at the Navy Yard in Washington, DC, from May 16 to June 9, 1918. Two days later he started his course of instruction at the Naval Academy, completing all requirements on September 18, 1918.

He was assigned temporary duty, for twelve days, with the Flagship of Commander Cruiser and Transport Forces, completing his assignment on September 29, 1918. Ensign Oviatt was assigned duty aboard the USS *Rochester* on September 30, 1918, where he served until December 18, 1918. Selden resigned his commission with the United States Naval Reserve Force on September 28, 1919.

Selden Harold Oviatt, Harold as he was called, was born in Springville, New York, on July 10, 1887, to Elias W. and Harriet (Norris) Oviatt. Harold was seventeen-years-old in 1905, and living in Concord, New York, when he accepted his appointment to the United States Naval Academy. After leaving the academy he moved to Rochester and, in 1910, was employed by Eastman Kodak Company as a machinist performing "camerawork." By 1915, Harold was living in Parma, New York, working on the family farm.

In 1919, after resigning his commission, Harold returned to Rochester. By 1925, he is living with his parents on the family farm, working as a draftsman. Like his brother Edwin, Harold was an avid golfer. In September 1926 the brothers, with business partners, received Certificate of Incorporation documents for the development of Westridge Country Club, Inc. "for the purpose to maintain facilities suitable for recreational purposes."[355] With Harold as president of the club, the directors oversaw the development of a golf club whose members competed against such organizations as the Canandaigua Country Club and Lakeside Country Club.

On May 14, 1936, Harold married Edith Marie Nusbickel. Returning from their honeymoon in White Sulphur Springs, West Virginia, the couple made their home in Brighton, New York. Harold was working as a production manager for Ritter Company, a manufacturer of dental equipment. In the 1930 United States Federal Census his occupation was listed as "industrial economist" in the field of dental manufacturing.[356] By 1940 Harold changed professions and was working as a sales representative for an insulation company.

Harold and his wife were very busy members of the Brookside Garden Club, with Harold taking the reigns as president in 1940. Often, he and his wife opened their home to fellow gardening enthusiasts with topics and projects for both men and women. Christmas of 1940 saw the men tackling how to "wrestle with the problem of making wreaths and other outside decorations" while the women of the club focused on interior decorations to include mantle

---

[r] Summerville is in the present-day town of Irondequoit, NY, at the mouth of the Genesee River.

pieces and tables arrangements.[357] Harold passed away on June 1, 1981, and is interred at Mount Hope Cemetery in Rochester, New York.

Westridge Country Club Will Open Tees, Greens To-morrow

Another addition to the golfing facilities of Rochester, which is an excellent position in this regard, will be opened for play to-morrow. At that time the Westridge Country Club, on Ridge road, in Spencerport, will allow members to tee off over the nine holes of the course, still rough, but advanced surprisingly well in its months of construction.

The course is situated just seven miles from Lake avenue on the Ridge, on the sloping lands toward the lake, and is just thirty minutes by automobile from Main and State streets. The clubhouse and grounds were started last fall and the heavy rains of the past month have enabled the officers of the club to move the starting date forward quite some period of time over their first estimate.

Par for the nine holes will be 36, with a total yardage of 3,270 yards. There are seven four holes, two of five par and two that call for three strokes for perfect figures. The shortest hole, the eighth, is 139 yards long, while the longest is the sixth, skirting the edge of the club property for a distance of 521 yards.

Tourney Listed

Lounge rooms, lockers, showers and sun porch are incorporated into the club house, a purely golf headquarters. The motive of the club is seen in the clubhouse, which is built to give golfers' conveniences, without great preparation for social activity.

A kickers' tourney will start the competitions at the new lay-out, with a golf bag for first prize, one dozen balls, second; and one-half dozen balls, third. Cards will be turned in and a handicap rating established as soon as possible.

Membership in the club has been subscribed at a rapid rate, and the full limit is expected before the end of the month. Seldon H. Oviatt is president of the organization; Edmund W. Oviatt, secretary-treasurer; Cameron Shutt, chairman of By-law Committee and William H. Cook chairman of Membership Committee. With these officers, Fred Scholand, Ray Bauman, Sidney Drumheller and Dr. George Sanders form the Board of Directors. Billy Falls has been appointed as pro and he will be assisted by Ed Burkin.

The opening of Westridge Country Club was big news in 1928, as shown in the *Democrat and Chronicle* (Rochester, NY) at left–Harold was president.[358]

Ten years later the club was in dire straits facing a tax foreclosure. By this time, only Edwin Oviatt, Harold's brother, was on the board of directors.[359] [below]

Golf Club Faces Tax Foreclosure

Because of unpaid county taxes, the Parma Golf Club Inc. yesterday was named defendant in a suit to foreclose on the nine-hole Westridge golf course, comprising nearly 14 acres in Ridge Road near Spencerport.

The action was filed by the Larpeg Realty Corporation of New York City. Its attorney, William S. Zielinski, said that firm as owner of tax certificates sold by the county seeks sale of the golf course on the Courthouse steps to recover $161.44 plus interest, representing unpaid taxes for the years 1932 through 1935.

RIT grant provides money for student travel

About 50 students at Rochester Institute of Technology and RIT's National Technical Institute for the Deaf will travel to Toronto in December, thanks to a $100,000 grant.

The grant was recently awarded to RIT for the establishment of the Edith N. and Selden H. Oviatt Memorial Endowment Fund.

Income from the fund will be used to finance programs designed to enhance relationships between deaf and hearing students.

The first program to receive funds from the Oviatt Endowment is RIT's educational travel program.

Between 400 and 500 RIT students will travel to Pennsylvania; New York City; Provincetown, Mass.; and other areas.

"Income from the Oviatt Memorial Fund will help to provide notetakers on the trips, underwrite some student travel costs and subsidize the teach-ins that are held in preparation for each trip," said Elaine Spaull, director of RIT's complementary education program.

Selden Oviatt, a consulting industrial engineer, died in June. He first became interested in assisting students at NTID after suffering a severe hearing loss in his later years.

Edith Oviatt, who bequeathed the fund to RIT, died in 1978.

In 1981 money from the estate of Harold and Edith Oviatt was bequeathed to Rochester Institute of Technology (NY), establishing the Edith N. and Selden H. Oviatt Memorial Endowment Fund. A grant from the endowment was used to support education travel expenses for the National Technical Institute for the Deaf at the school.[360] [above]

Harold and Edith enjoyed traveling in their later years, as depicted in this *Democrat and Chronicle* (Rochester, NY) picture from the April 1, 1958 edition. This was their second visit to Kauai in the Hawaiian Islands.[361]

Harold suffered a broken leg and was in the hospital after a shoplifter "resisted violently" while being arrested on East Main Street in downtown Rochester in October 1980.[362] [below]

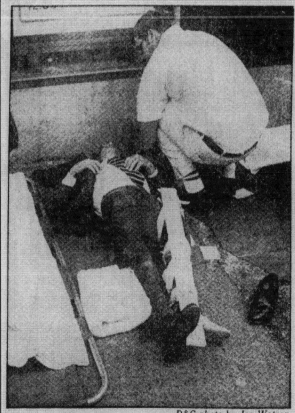

Man, 93, knocked down, hurt

By MICHAEL WINTER

A 93-year-old Brighton man suffered head injuries and a broken left leg yesterday when he was knocked down on East Main Street by a man Rochester police and store security guards were trying to arrest for shoplifting.

Selden Oviatt of 222 Roosevelt Road was listed in satisfactory condition last night at Strong Memorial Hospital.

Police charged Wardell Mitchell, 25, of 118 Van Auker St., with second-degree assault, petit larceny, resisting arrest and possession of a hypodermic instrument.

Police said a guard at McCrory's department store, 196-212 E. Main St., spotted a man leaving the store about 1:40 p.m. without paying for two steam irons valued at $50.

Rochester police Officer Richard Vigilante, driving past, spotted two guards chasing the man and stopped to assist. As Vigilante and the guards tried arresting the man in front of 183 E. Main St., police said, the suspect resisted violently, knocking Oviatt to the sidewalk.

D&C photo by Joe Watson

Ambulance attendants care for Selden Oviatt, 93

... knocked down on Main Street by a man resisting arrest

Form 3721 **REGISTRATION CARD** No 912

1. **231** Name in full George J. Paulsen   Age, in yrs. **27**
   (Given name)   (Family name)

2. Home address 657 Classon ave Brooklyn N.Y.
   (No.)   (Street)   (City)   (State)

3. Date of birth November 10 1889
   (Month)   (Day)   (Year)

4. Are you (1) a natural-born citizen, (2) a naturalized citizen, (3) an alien, (4) or have you declared your intention (specify which)? natural

5. Where were you born? New York N.Y. U.S.
   (Town)   (State)   (Nation)

6. If not a citizen, of what country are you a citizen or subject?

7. What is your present trade, occupation, or office? Automobile Helper

8. By whom employed? Edison Electric Co
   Where employed? 7 Quincy St Brooklyn

9. Have you a father, mother, wife, child under 12, or a sister or brother under 12, solely dependent on you for support (specify which)? 1 mother

10. Married or single (which)? Single   Race (specify which)? Caucasian

11. What military service have you had? Rank none ; branch
    years ; Nation or State

12. Do you claim exemption from draft (specify grounds)? none

C-A I affirm that I have verified above answers and that they are true.

If person is of African descent, tear off this corner.

ORDER George H Paulsen
2181   (Signature or mark)

GEORGE PAULSON
1889 – 1954

George enrolled in the United States Naval Reserve Force on February 3, 1908, and assigned the duties of a stenographer before he was discharged from service on February 2, 1912. At twenty-seven, he re-enlisted on May 11, 1917, and George served aboard the USS *Corsair*[s]. George was discharged on January 11, 1919, as a Chief Yeoman.

> **To Rejoin the Navy.**
>
> George Paulson who has assisted his brother, D. A. Paulson, in this village for several months past during which time he has made many friends, left Wednesday for New York to rejoin the Navy. Mr. Paulson left the Navy five years ago after a term of four years service, during which time he was on the "Montana" and traveled to parts all over the world. He was Yeoman for a long time and at the time he left the service was Chief Yeoman. He expects to receive an appointment as Yeoman after he re-enlists.

George Paulson was born in Arlington, New Jersey, on November 10, 1889, to Swedish-born parents Charles C. and Wilhelmina (Starr) Paulson. Growing up in Kearny, New Jersey, George was fifteen-years-old and employed as a clerk. After his first navy discharge he worked as a stone setter.

Leaving his job as a stone setter, George moved to Hilton, New York, and joined his brother, David Arthur Paulson, in a successful meat market and grocery business known as Paulson's Market, which had opened for business April 19, 1913.[363] George was a wholesale supplier of produce,[364] eggs, and butter.[365]

He married Florence F. Hoover on February 20, 1922, in Rochester, New York, and the newlyweds made their home in Parma, New York. George started working for Eastman Kodak Company in 1937, in the photographic emulsions division at Kodak Park.[366] The meat market and grocery business remained in the brothers' control until it was sold in June of 1943.[367]

George was a member of the Clio Lodge No. 779, Free & Accepted Masons, and was very active as a member of the American Legion Hiscock-Fishbaugh Post 788. In the latter, George was elected to the positions of treasurer and adjutant and served on committees that organized events. He was named a delegate from the post and attended both the New York State convention held in Buffalo, New York, in 1934, and the National Convention in Cleveland, Ohio, in 1936.

George retired and moved to Florida with his wife in 1945, living in the communities of Clearwater Beach and Saint Petersburg. George passed away in the Bay Pines Veterans Hospital February 24, 1954, and is interred in Bay Pines National Cemetery in Saint Petersburg, Florida.

Hilton Legionaries to Have Clambake Today

GEORGE PAULSON

Hilton, Oct. 8 — Hiscock-Fishbaugh Post, American Legion, will have its annual clambake tomorrow at Randall's Grove. The committee in charge includes Alton Sleight of Ridge Road, Greece, and George Paulson of Hilton. Complimentary tickets have been sent to the supervisor, mayor and various other officials. The post has been having clambakes for the past 10 years.

---

[s] The USS *Corsair* was a 1600-ton steam yacht owned by J.P. Morgan and had been christened 'Corsair'. The yacht was pressed into service in May of 1917, for use by the U.S. Navy.

Form 1   **REGISTRATION CARD**   No. 49

1   Name in full   *Bert Jason Perry*   Age, in yrs. 21
    (Given name)   (Family name)

2   Home address _____   *Hilton*   *N.Y.*
    (No.)   (Street)   (City)   (State)

3   Date of birth   *April*   *17*   *1896*
    (Month)   (Day)   (Year)

4   Are you (1) a natural-born citizen, (2) a naturalized citizen, (3) an alien, (4) or have you declared your intention (specify which)?   *Natural born*

5   Where were you born?   *Parma*   *N.Y.*   *U.S.A.*
    (Town)   (State)   (Nation)

6   If not a citizen, of what country are you a citizen or subject?

7   What is your present trade, occupation, or office?   *Lineman 24*

8   By whom employed?   *Hilton Telephone Co*
    Where employed?   *Hilton*

9   Have you a father, mother, wife, child under 12, or a sister or brother under 12, solely dependent on you for support (specify which)?   *no*

10 Married or single (which)?   *Single*   Race (specify which)?   *White*

11 What military service have you had? Rank   *no*   ; branch _____
    years _____ ; Nation or State

12 Do you claim exemption from draft (specify grounds)?   *no*

I affirm that I have verified above answers and that they are true.

Bert Jason Perry
(Signature of registrant)

If person is of African descent, tear off this corner

BERT JASON PERRY
1896 – 1971

Bert was inducted into the United States Army at Spencerport, New York, on February 24, 1918, as a twenty-one-year-old Private assigned to 30th Company, 8th Training Battalion, 151st Depot Brigade. He was promoted to Corporal on March 11, 1918, and discharged a month later from Camp Devens, Massachusetts. He received an honorable discharge with a Surgeon's Certificate of Disability on April 19, 1918.[368] [right, top]

—Bert J. Perry returned to Hilton last Saturday from Camp Devens, Mass., having been honorably discharged on account of physical disability.

He entered the service again from Rochester, New York, on October 4, 1918, and was assigned to the 10th Recruit Company, General Service Infantry, at Columbus Barracks, Ohio. He was discharged on November 29, 1918.[369] [right, bottom]

—Bert Perry, who has been in the U. S. Army, stationed at Columbus, Ohio, has been honorably discharged and arrived at his home in this village the first part of the week. He is looking and feeling fine having gained in flesh.

Bert Jason Perry was born in Hilton, New York, on April 17, 1896, to Joseph T. and Myra (Van Dorn) Perry. By 1915, Bert was working as a lineman for Hilton Telephone Company and Hilton Electric Light, Power and Heat Company. In an agreement authorized in 1925, Rochester Gas & Electric Corporation (RG&E) purchased the latter. Bert became an employee of RG&E in 1932 when they officially took ownership.[370]

While with RG&E, he worked as a troubleman in the line operating department, promoting to inspector. Bert married Margaret R. McGraw on July 7, 1927, in Monroe County, New York, and together they made their home in Hilton, moving to Rochester by 1940. In 1958, Bert was recognized for his thirty-eight years of service with RG&E;[371] [below] he retired three years later in May 1961.[372]

Bert was a member of the Clio Lodge No. 779, Free & Accepted Masons. In 1921, he was elected second vice commander of the newly-chartered American Legion Hiscock-Fishbaugh Post 788 and served as its historian.[373] Bert passed away on June 11, 1971, and is interred in Parma Union Cemetery in Parma, New York.

Bert Perry Honored, Early Local Lineman

Bert Perry, a former resident who worked for the village's first electric company, was honored last week by the Rochester Gas & Electric Corporation, when he was presented with a 40-year pin.

Mr. Perry, who now lives at 301 Selye Terrace, Rochester, has been a troubleman in the Line Operating Department. He first began working in Hilton for the Hilton Power & Light Company, and the Hilton Telephone Company, and was automatically transferred to the R. G. & E. payroll when that company assumed ownership of the Hilton Power & Light in 1932.

Bert formed up with other "Hilton Boys" as they marched in a post-war parade in Hilton.[374] [right]

REGISTRATION CARD X 1929 No. 33.

1 Name in full George W. Quinn   Age, in yrs. 27
(Given name) (Family name)

2 Home address Charlotte N.Y.
(No.) (Street) (City) (State)

3 Date of birth Sept, 3 1889
(Month) (Day) (Year)

4 Are you (1) a natural-born citizen, (2) a naturalized citizen, (3) an alien, (4) or have you declared your intention (specify which)? a natural born Citizen

5 Where were you born? Sweden N.Y. U.S.A.
(Town) (State) (Nation)

6 If not a citizen, of what country are you a citizen or subject?

7 What is your present trade, occupation, or office? Farm Labor

8 By whom employed? William Kenty
Where employed? Greece

9 Have you a father, mother, wife, child under 12, or a sister or brother under 12, solely dependent on you for support (specify which)? No,

10 Married or single (which)? Single Race (specify which)? Caucasian

11 What military service have you had? Rank None branch
years ; Nation or State

12 Do you claim exemption from draft (specify grounds)? No.

I affirm that I have verified above answers and that they are true.

39 C George W. Quinn

If person is of African descent tear off this corner

★ GEORGE WILLIAM QUINN ★
1889 – 1918

George William Quinn was the first child born to Nicholas and Caroline (Wohlers) Quinn in Sweden, New York, on the 3rd of September 1889. In a span of ten years, George and his family lived in towns of Hamlin and Greece, eventually settling on West Town Line Road in Parma, New York. When he was of age, he began working on farms as a laborer, first for his family and then for William Kentz of Greece, where he was employed when he filled out his draft registration card in 1917.

George was twenty-eight when he was inducted into the United States Army at Spencerport, New York, on February 24, 1918; reporting to Camp Devens in Ayer, Massachusetts. Private Quinn was assigned to Company D, 308th Infantry, 77th Division, joining the division at Camp Upton in Yaphank, Long Island, New York, before embarking on the 6th of April 1918, aboard the vessel SS *Lapland*.

> Word has been received by Mr. and Mrs. Nicholas Quinn, of Charlotte, of the safe arrival in France of their son, private George W. Quinn, of Company D, 308th Infantry. He entered the service on February 25, 1918, and was stationed at Camp Devens in the depot brigade for about three weeks. He was then transferred to Camp Upton.

The Meuse-Argonne offensive began the morning of September 26, 1918.[375] On the 28th of September, George William Quinn and two other soldiers were assigned to battalion adjutant Lieutenant Arthur McKeogh as escorts and "runners." Lieutenant McKeogh scribbled a quick message for the battalion commander, Major Charles Whittlesey, and gave it to Private Quinn to deliver, but the message was never received. George Quinn was listed as killed in action, date unknown, and would remain that way for another four months.[376]

While registering graves in the Argonne forest in January 1919, Captain Jack S. Grady, Commander, Company E, 805th Pioneer Infantry, discovered the remains of George Quinn and three German soldiers surrounding his body. After the war, former Captain Grady wrote to McKeogh about discovering Private Quinn's body, details of the scene, and analysis of the events that must have transpired. It was later determined that George may have killed the three German soldiers found near him before dying of a bullet wound to the head. This fact was noted by the Graves Registration Service when his body was discovered.[377] George was buried on January 24, 1919, in an "American Cemetery three-and-a-half kilometers from Binarville on main road to Apremont with 'Lost Battalion' graves," as reported by First Lieutenant Orley E. Ooley of the 805th Pioneer Infantry.[378] The undelivered message written by Lieutenant McKeogh to Major Whittlesey was found in George Quinn's pocket, along with letters George had written to his mother and aunt, both of which were illegible.

Once the Army determined the true circumstances behind Quinn's disappearance and death, they attempted to contact George's mother, Caroline Quinn, in February of 1919 about the discovery of her son. They were unable to reach her at her Charlotte, New York, address because she had moved.[379]

After the war, Arthur McKeogh wrote about Quinn in *Colliers* and authored a poem titled "Runner Quinn" which was published in the *Saturday Evening Post* on August 16, 1919. Since the Army had been unsuccessful in contacting her in February 1919, and it had been fourteen months from George's last letter (dated June 2, 1918), the poem may have been Caroline Quinn's first exposure to her son's death on the battlefield.[380] Private Quinn was listed on a revised, official casualty list in July of 1919, which was reported in the July 10, 1919 edition of the *Democrat and Chronicle* (Rochester, NY).[381] [left] Subsequent correspondence between Caroline and Arthur McKeogh enabled the former to connect with United States Army personnel and the latter to finally inform a grieving mother of her son's heroic behavior.[382]

ROCHESTERIAN IS KILLED

War Department Reports Death of George W. Quinn.

The official casualty list issued by the War Department and published in part on another page of this paper to-day contains the name of George W. Quinn, of Charlotte, as killed.

Private Quinn was sent on his mission the 28th of September 1918. Military reports and forms found in his personnel records at the National Archives and Records Administration confirm the same as his official date of death. George was buried in the "Battle Area Cemetery" in Charlevaux, Ardennes, France on January 24, 1919. [383] He was disinterred on March 26, 1919, and relocated to Meuse-Argonne American Military Cemetery located in Romagne-sous-Montfaucon, France.[384] George was disinterred once more and moved to a different grave within Meuse-Argonne Military Cemetery on March 7, 1922.[385]

POEM IMMORTALIZES DEED OF CHARLOTTE SOLDIER IN ARGONNE BATTLE OVERSEAS

Arthur McKeogh's poem "Runner Quinn" appeared in the August 16, 1919, edition of the *Saturday Evening Post*. [386] [below] The story of the poem and Mrs. Quinn's revelation was given a three-fourths page spread in the September 7, 1919, *Democrat and Chronicle*.[387] [left]

The following passages are excerpts from Arthur McKeogh's letter to Mrs. Caroline Quinn after she read about her son's death in McKeogh's poem, "Runner Quinn," that was published in the *Saturday Evening Post*. The full text of the letter is found in *World War Service Record of Rochester and Monroe County New York–Volume I Those Who Died for Us.*[388]

"I have your letter with inquiries concerning Private Quinn, whose gallant conduct in France I tried to extol recently in the Saturday Evening Post. It is a source of real gratification to me that this caught your eye because since learning of his death I have been eager to communicate with his Mother or some of his relatives as I know how keen their anxiety would be."

"I have only the finest things to say of your boy, I met him first some time in August, 1918 when as Battalion Adjutant, I asked Lieutenant Paul Knight, then in Command of Company D, for advance runners inasmuch as we had suffered considerable casualties from previous engagements. At the time George reported to me, we were in the second line of the Aisne Front, burrowed away in little holes on the protected side of a hill, which afforded us some protection from the German shells. I soon found that your son could be depended upon to discharge most satisfactorily any job given to him; he was one of my most dependable men, intelligent in the matter of forwarding messages, sometimes of very great importance, and the kind who could be counted upon to fulfill his mission where others might fail. He was serenely indifferent under shellfire and, quite frankly watching his coolness in moments of stress, served as an inspiration to me."

"...George suddenly looked sharply over my shoulder, picked up his rifle and fired. I turned, quickly, having had my pistol in my hand since early morning, to hear the unearthly scream that a man mortally wounded always gives. Together we ran over to the spot where he had fired and found a German infantryman already dead, with his knees hunched up in way that would have been funny if it were not tragic."

"It was by an odd coincidence that I learned of your son's death, months later. I had inquired of the Regiment Infantry Association, but learned they knew nothing of him, then one day in April last, Captain Jack A. McGrady, who lives on Arkansas Avenue in Lorraine, Ohio, wrote to me through *Colliers*, in which I had published an article carrying a reference to your son. Captain McGrady had read the article and later while policing the area of the forest had found the body of Private Quinn."

"Private Quinn must have put up a very good fight before he went, to have taken along with him unaided as he was, three of the crack German Infantry. I am very proud of him. To me he typifies the kind of American doughboy who faithfully performed all his duties, without any grumbling, who took hardships as they came and who in the end gave everything he had without any blowing of trumpets."

"...I hope you have taken consolation so largely due you from the fact that your son did the finest thing it was possible for a man to do in service of his country. For myself I shall be one of those who, when I revisit France, will pay very reverent tribute at his grave, aware as I must be that it was much more than I could ever hope to do."

Form 1 | *1846* | REGISTRATION CARD *1458* | No. *39*

1 Name in full *Frank W. Randall* | Age, in yrs. *22*
(Given name) (Family name)

2 Home address *Hilton* *N.Y.*
(No.) (Street) (City) (State)

3 Date of birth *November* *10* *1894*
(Month) (Day) (Year)

4 Are you (1) a natural-born citizen, (2) a naturalized citizen, (3) an alien, (4) or have you declared your intention (specify which)? *Natural Born*

5 Where were you born? *Greece* *N.Y.* *USA*
(Town) (State) (Nation)

6 If not a citizen, of what country are you a citizen or subject?

7 What is your present trade, occupation, or office? *1 farmer*

8 By whom employed? *Father*
Where employed? *Greece*

9 Have you a father, mother, wife, child under 12, or a sister or brother under 12, solely dependent on you for support (specify which)? *none*

10 Married or single (which)? *Single* Race (specify which)? *White*

11 What military service have you had? Rank ____; branch ____
years ____; Nation or State ____

12 Do you claim exemption from draft (specify grounds)?

I affirm that I have verified above answers and that they are true.

Frank W. Randall
(Signature of person)

If person is of African descent, tear off this corner. *1458*

FRANK WEBSTER RANDALL
1894 – 1972

Frank enlisted in the New York National Guard in Rochester, New York, on June 5, 1917, as a twenty-two-year-old Private. He reported to the 2d Ambulance Company on July 17, 1917. Upon federalization of the New York National Guard, the unit was reclassified from the 2d Ambulance Company to Ambulance Company 106, 102d Sanitary Train, 27th Division, on July 20th, 1917; he was promoted to Private First Class and appointed Dispensary Assistant on October 1, 1917. The division organized and trained at Camp Wadsworth, in Spartanburg, South Carolina, before going overseas.[389] [right]

> —The 2nd Ambulance Company of Rochester, of which Dr. Walton Hovey of this village is lieutenant and Frank Randall a member, has received orders to be prepared to move to a southern concentration camp by Saturday of this week. It is not known just what camp they will be sent to but it is expected that it will be at Asheville, N. C.

Frank left for overseas duty from Newport News, Virginia, aboard the USS *Huron* on June 30, 1918. He returned aboard the USS *Mount Vernon*, leaving Brest, France, on March 3, 1919, arriving in Hoboken, New Jersey, on March 11, 1919. He was honorably discharged on March 31, 1919, from Camp Merritt, New York.

Frank Webster Randall was born in Greece, New York, on November 10, 1894, to William J. and Elizabeth "Libby" (Williams) Randall. By 1900, Frank and his family were living in Parma, New York, but returned to Greece by 1910. Four days after enlisting in the New York National Guard, Frank married Pearl M. Henthorn in Rochester on June 9, 1917. The couple, along with Alton B. Sleight (a fellow World War I soldier) and his new bride honeymooned together.[390] [right]

Frank and Pearl settled in Hilton, New York, where he worked as caretaker of a home and as a farmer. By 1930 he was working as an insurance agent for Prudential Insurance

> **MARRIED SAME DAY, ON TRIP TOGETHER**
> Two Young Couples United by Same Clergyman.
>
> Ida L. Hall and Alton V. Sleight were married on Saturday afternoon at 4 o'clock at the home of the bride's parents, Mr. and Mrs. Fred E. Hall, No. 438 Plymouth avenue. Rev. James M. Hutchinson officiated. The attendants were Frank W. Randall, of Hilton, and Pearl M. Henthorn, of this city.
> The marriage of Frank W. Randall to Pearl M. Henthorn took place on Saturday afternoon at 5 o'clock at the home of the officiating clergyman, Rev. Mr. Hutchinson, who is pastor of Calvary Baptist Church, No. 378 Genesee street. The attendants were Mr. and Mrs. Sleight.
> Mr. and Mrs. Randall, after a wedding dinner at the home of Fred E. Hall, left for a Western trip with Mr. and Mrs. Sleight.

in Brockport, New York. He ran on the Republican ticket in both 1953 and 1957, seeking back-to-back, four-year terms as assessor for the Town of Parma; he won both elections.[391] [left]

Frank was a member of the Hilton Baptist Church and the Clio Lodge No. 779, Free & Accepted Masons. As a member of the American Legion Hiscock-Fishbaugh Post 788, he was elected to the position of financial secretary. Frank W. Randall passed away on September 24, 1972, and is buried in Riverside Cemetery in Rochester, New York.

Let's Keep Good Local Government!
Vote Republican
Supervisor - John Crook
Town Clerk - Arthur Kirchgessner
Supt. of Highways - Anthony Schalk
Justice of Peace - Seeley Adams
Councilman - Luther Pisher
Assessor - Frank Randall
Assessor - E. B. Hendershot
Tax Collector - Henry Carter

These experienced men have given you good government. They are prepared to meet the needs of this growing town and will continue to give you the best administration possible with a continued low tax rate.
Vote Republican
— ROW "A" ALL THE WAY —

To Ex-Soldiers from Canisteo

The Department of Education at Albany requires that the records of all men in the army or navy during the recent war shall be compiled and kept on file

Will you kindly fill out this blank and return immediately, enclosing a photograph taken, if possible, during the war? It is imperative that this record be correct and complete in every particular. No one can correctly estimate the value it may have in the future.

1. Full name *Clarence Elford Robinson*
2. Place of birth and date *Oshawa Ontario Canada June 6-1899*
3. Father's full name and place of birth *Oshawo Ont Canada May 3- 1877*
4. Mother's maiden name and place of birth *Mary Elizabeth Elford-Cornwall Eng*
5. Was your father ever in the army or navy of the U. S.; if so, when? *No.*
6. If you are married, give wife's maiden name, date and place of birth. and date of your marriage *Not married*
7. If you have children, give name and date of birth of each. *None*
8. Were you drafted, or did you enlist? 7½ Regiment and Division *4th Reg. Inf. 3rd Division*
9. Date of entry into service and camp where trained *Nov 23-1917- Camp Green Charlotte N.C. - Camp Stuart- Newport News Va,*
10. Date of going over seas and name of ship *April 15-1918 Madawaska -(formerly Kaiser Wilhelm II)*
11. Names of officers in command of regiment and company *Col. Dowyer commander. Capt Smith Co. commander*
12. Promotions and medals *none*
13. Where did you see service? *Chateau Thierry - St mihiel - Argonne Fores*
14. Were you wounded?; if so, at what fight? Give details. *Yes. In argonne Fores 3 times but not very serious*
15. Give date of release or discharge *Feb 22-1919*
16. Present address and occupation *Canisteo N.y. Segnalman Erie R.R.*
17. Write any of your interesting experiences on the back of this sheet. If you have a copy of any letter that you wrote while in camp or over seas, and which might be interesting, please enclose.

Return to *Wm. M. Stuart* Town, Historian

Clarence was too young to complete a draft registration card for the June 1917 draft. Following the war, he completed a New York State Department of Education-sponsored survey of war veterans as a resident of the town of Canisteo.[392] His *New York State Abstracts of World War I Military Service* card recorded that he was wounded "severely"[393] yet Clarence considered it "not very serious" in question fourteen on the survey form.

CLARENCE ELFORD ROBINSON
1899 – 1956

Clarence enlisted in the Regular Army at age eighteen at Columbus Recruit Barracks in Ohio on November 23, 1917. [below][394] Private Robinson was assigned to Company A, 4th Infantry, 3d Division, and trained at Camp

> —Clarence Robinson late of this town has enlisted and is at Columbus, Ohio, and is later to go to Alabama.

Green in Charlotte, North Carolina, before arriving at the Embarkation Camp at Camp Stuart in Newport News, Virginia. He left for his overseas assignment on April 15, 1918, aboard the USS *Madawaska*. While in France, Clarence participated in operations at Chateau-Thierry, Saint-Mihiel, along the Marne River, and the Meuse-Argonne. After intense fighting October 12-14, 1918, the 4th Infantry attacked on the morning of October 15th. During this all-day assault, Clarence received shrapnel wounds to his left leg that were classified as severe; he was awarded the Purple Heart.[395] (Conversely, Clarence reported to the historian of Canisteo, New York, that he was wounded "three times, but not very serious." See complete form, previous page.) Whatever the degree of his wounds, they were enough that he was pulled off the line and likely treated at a base hospital in the Paris district.[396] [bottom left] Clarence did not rejoin his unit. Instead he returned from France with Blois Casual Company No. 324, departing Brest, France, aboard the RMS *Celtic* on January 24, 1919. He was honorably discharged on February 22, 1919, at Camp Upton, New York.[397] [bottom right]

> Letter received by relatives and friends of Clarence Robinson of this place. who has been in France for several months, announces that he had been wounded, being struck in the leg by two pieces of shrapnel. He is in one of the base hospitals and is doing nicely.

> —Clarence Robinson of this town, son of Joseph Robinson, arrived in this country from France on February 1st and was mustered out at Camp Upton. He arrived here Monday. evening. His company was commended for good service in the great war. Clarence was wounded three times in the left leg, and at present walks with a slight limp.

Clarence Elford Robinson was born in Oshawa, Ontario, Canada on June 6, 1899, to parents Joseph Hiram and Elizabeth Mary (Elford) Robinson. The family immigrated to the United States in 1909, settling in Parma, New York, where his father supported the family by working on a farm. Clarence left home around the age of seventeen and lived in Elmira, New York, supporting himself by working for the Delaware, Lackawanna & Western Railroad[398] [below left] and the Erie Railroad.[399] [below right]

> . —Clarence E. Robinson former- ly of this village who works for the Delaware, Lackawanna & Western R. R. Co., at their depot in Elmira writes for the Record to be sent to him for the coming year.

> —Clarence Robinson formerly of this village who has been working at Elmira is now work- ing for the Erie Railroad Co., as signal man and telephone operator at Canisteo, N. Y.

After Clarence's discharge from the army he returned to Steuben County, New York, and supported himself by working for the Susquehanna Division of the Erie Railroad, which later merged with the Lackawanna and Western Railroad; Clarence had a combined forty years as a signalman and conductor.[400]

> # CAMERON
>
> ### AMERICAN LEGION AFTER MEMBERS
> The American legion which is being organized at Canisteo with a number of members in this village and vicinity wishes to enroll every service man in this vicinity. Clarence E. Robinson has been designated by the legion to enroll all members in this vicinity. There are about 16 service men here who are eligible.

Clarence immersed himself in the communities of Canisteo and Cameron Mills through civic organizations. Tasked by the American Legion in February of 1920 to organize the local post, he set about enrolling every eligible person in the local area.[401] [left] Through his efforts, the Canisteo Memorial Post 846 received its charter. He worked on fundraisers that benefited the Veterans Christmas Fund and was post commander and historian.[402] Clarence was also a member of the former Veterans of Foreign Wars Marion O. Freeland Post in Hornell, New York. Outside of veterans organizations, he participated on the salary committee for the County Civil Service Employees Association.[403]

He married Ruth (nee Dimick) Stillman on March 9, 1942, in Hornell, becoming a step-father to her children from her first marriage. In May of 1942, at the age of forty-two, Clarence was drafted for World War II service, but not accepted by the United States Army.[404]

On May 4, 1956, Clarence died unexpectedly at home and is buried in Town Line Cemetery of Cameron Mills, New York.

Clarence's work with the American Legion continued through the 1940s and 1950s. Clarence was post historian when the Canisteo Memorial Post 846 anticipated victory in World War II. They issued a resolution stating "that when V day comes, it shall be declared a day of reverence and thanksgiving." The post requested local churches remain open so "that all who so desire may enter and give thanks to God." Their plans were about seven months premature when the article was printed in the *Canisteo (NY) Times* in October 1944.[405] [below left]

Clarence and fellow Legionnaire Joseph Holley were thankful for donations from the merchants of Canisteo in December 1952. The pool of donations from across Steuben County provided $1,200 in Christmas presents for the patients at the Bath (NY) Veterans Hospital. [below right][406]

CANISTEO LEGION PLANS V-DAY

At a special meeting of Canisteo Post 846 of the American Legion. The following resolution was adopted:

That Canisteo Post 846 of The American Legion goes on record as desiring that when V day comes, it shall be declared a day of reverence and thanksgiving. The Post requests that the various churches of the community be kept open so that all who so desire may enter and give thanks to God.

The following officers were installed: Commander Clark Foote; 1st vice com., Howard Garman; 2nd vice commander, John Hunter; adjutant, Joseph Holley; treasurer, Glenn Roe. Delegate to county committee, Glenn S. Roe; alternate delegate to county committee, Joseph Holley.

The first meeting of the Post was held Thursday, Oct. 12. Commander Foote appointed the following committees: Sgt. at Arms, Fred Pulkowsky; Liason officer, Ross H. Cook; Americanism, Dr. J. E. Crossman; membership, Howard P. Garman; Service Officer, Otis W. Norton; Oratorical committee, Donald M. Gardner; Welfare, C. Howard Richardson; Mobilization and Defense, Herbert F. Adams; Boys' state, Donald M. Gardner; Juvenile Delinquency, Harold P. Stephens; Historian, Clarence E. Robinson.

Canisteo Aids Vets' Yuletide

Clarence E. Robinson and Joseph E. Holley, members of Canisteo American Legion and of Steuben Voiture 95, 40 & 8 report that the November response of Canisteo merchants and residents to the "Veterans Christmas Fund" totaled $100 in this village. The donations were pooled with others from throughout the county, and about $1,200 worth of Christmas presents were distributed Dec. 5th to veterans in Bath Facility who receive no compensation nor benefits.

In this manner the American Legion, Auxiliary and 40 & 8 canvassers made the giving of Christmas gifts possible for patients in the Bath Veteran's hospital, who otherwise would have no means to send Yule gifts to their loved ones.

Messers. Holley and Robinson, in charge of the Canisteo canvass, issued the following message of thanks:

"We wish to thank the merchants and individuals of Canisteo who donated so generously to the annual Christmas fund for the veterans in Bath who are compensation-less. This enabled them to pick out a gift to send home at Christmas time. This enabSo..

Christmas time. American Legion Auxiliary members spent Friday, Dec. 5th at the Bath Facility and wrapped and addressed the gifts, collected from throughout the county.

Form 1   1289   **REGISTRATION CARD**   No. 82

1 Name in full _George H Rowley_   Age, in yrs. 25
     (Given name)   (Family name)

2 Home address _Hilton_   _N. Y_
     (No.)   (Street)   (City)   (State)

3 Date of birth _September_   _4_   _1892_
     (Month)   (Day)   (Year)

4 Are you (1) a natural-born citizen, (2) a naturalized citizen, (3) an alien, (4) or have you declared your intention (specify which)? _Alien_

5 Where were you born? _Brighton_   _Prov ontario_   _British_
     (Town)   (State)   (Nation)

6 If not a citizen, of what country are you a citizen or subject? _Canada_

7 What is your present trade, occupation, or office? _Farming_

8 By whom employed? _Fred Rowley_
Where employed? _Parma_

9 Have you a father, mother, wife, child under 12, or a sister or brother under 12, solely dependent on you for support (specify which)? _none_

10 Married or single (which)? _Single_   Race (specify which)? _White_

11 What military service have you had? Rank _____; branch _____;
years _____; Nation or State _____

12 Do you claim exemption from draft (specify grounds)? _____

I affirm that I have verified above answers and that they are true.

George H Rowley
(Signature of man)

If person is of African descent, tear off this corner   1168

★ GEORGE HARLOW ROWLEY ★
1892 – 1918

George was twenty-five when he was inducted into the United States Army on February 24, 1918, at Spencerport, New York. He reported to 30th Company, 8th Training Battalion, 151st Depot Brigade, located at Camp Devens, Massachusetts. He remained there until March 15, 1918, when he transferred to Company D, 308th Infantry Regiment, 77th Infantry Division, at Camp Upton, New York. Leaving with Company D from New York City on April 6, 1918, aboard the SS *Lapland*, Private Rowley arrived in Europe April 19th, 1918.

George Harlow Rowley was born on September 4, 1892, in Brighton, Ontario, Canada, to parents Amos and Jane "Jennie" (McCready) Rowley. Leaving his parents in Canada, George, a machinist, emigrated to the United States on August 23, 1915, arriving in Charlotte, New York. When he registered for the draft in 1917, George was working on his brother's farm in Parma, New York.

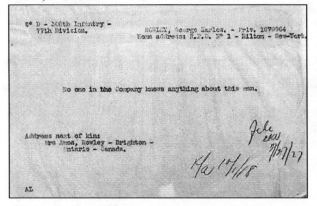

Private George H. Rowley was killed during the Meuse-Argonne offensive, the result of a gunshot wound in the "Forêt d'Argonne" (forest of Argonne) on October 1, 1918. He was buried in the "Battle Area Cemetery," Binarville, Marne, France, on October 3, 1918,[407] then disinterred and moved to Meuse-Argonne American Military Cemetery, Romagne-sous-Montfaucon, France, on June 19, 1919.[408]

George was cited under General Order No. 39, Headquarters 77th Division, and was posthumously awarded the Silver Star on November 14, 1918:

PRIVATE GEORGE H. ROWLEY, No. 1679964, Co. D, 308th Infantry, who was with a patrol of his company on their flank in the advance through the Argonne Forest southeast of Binarville. He stuck to his post under heavy machine gun and artillery fire with an absolute disregard for his personal safety until he was killed on September 29th, 1918.[409]

Unfortunately, as indicated in George's personnel file in the National Archives, little else was known about him or his service in the 77th Division.[410] [above, left]

Form 1   **REGISTRATION CARD 9** | **No. 12**

1. Name in full *Walter S. Ryder*   Age, in yrs. **25**
   (Given name)   (Family name)

2. Home address *Spencerport*   *N. Y.*
   (Street)   (City)

3. Date of birth *March*   *11*   *1892*
   (Month)   (Day)   (Year)

4. Are you (1) a natural-born citizen, (2) a naturalized citizen, (3) an alien, (4) or have you declared your intention (specify which)? *Natural Born*

5. Where were you born? *Boston Mass.*   *U. S. A.*
   (Town)   (State)   (Nation)

6. If not a citizen, of what country are you a citizen or subject?

7. What is your present trade, occupation, or office? *Christian Minister*

8. By whom employed? *Baptist Church*
   Where employed? *Parma Monroe N. Y.*

9. Have you a father, mother, wife, child under 12, or a sister or brother under 12, solely dependent on you for support (specify which)? *Wife*

10. Married or single (which)? *Married*   Race (specify which)? *Caucasian*

11. What military service have you had? Rank *None* ; branch
    years ; Nation or State

12. Do you claim exemption from draft (specify grounds)? *On Clergyman Exemption*

I affirm that I have verified above answers and that they are true.

Walter S. Ryder
(Signature or mark)

If person is of African descent, tear off this corner.

9

WALTER SCOTT RYDER
1892 – 1956

MONROE COUNTY MEN CALLED BY DRAFT LOTTERY

List Includes Those for First Quota.

SHULENBURG LEADS GREECE

Revised List for Town of Mendon Shows Heavy Roster for Honeoye Falls, with Henry G. Clark First Name Out from that Village

Spencerport, July 25.—The list of names from the first district which includes the following towns, Greece, Ogden, Parma, Hamlin, Clarkson, Riga and Chili, are sure to be summoned for the first quota. Headquarters, office and examining room for this division is the village building, Spencerport. The examining board is Dr. L. E. Slayton, secretary, Spencerport; H. H. Widner, chairman, Chili; Eugene Collamer, Hilton. The following list shows the order in which numbers were drawn for each town:

Parma—Walter S. Ryder, Ernest Leskeyawaski, Albert C. Bateman, Arthur M. Eller, Arthur M. Smith, Elmer Samuel Wadsworth, Frederick B. Wadsworth, Roy L. Brown, William Charles Lais, Fay M. Tenny, Frank C. Weston, Adolf Fred Diedrich, Grover C. Tracy, Herman Worden, Leslie C. Kettenberg, Roy B. Webster, John Henry Wright, Fred E. Ashbaw, William A. Peffer, Hartley S. Smith, Wilbur J. Dunbar, Merton S. Williams, John Conley, Jr., Harry Lee Fowler, Stanley Marcelan Smith, Charles Henry Ainsworth, Van Allen McKinney, James L. Adams, Franklin W. Wells, John E. Darling, Wilber F. King, John F. Donohue, Lester P. Hiscock, Homer Harmer, David H. Bronson, William A. Arnold, Burton L. Smith, Wilber W. Curtis, Clifford Welch, Irving G. Howe, Walter H. Hill, Bruce Ingham, William Neritt, Arthur Turgon, Alfred Turgon, Roy A. Talbot, Henry James Wise, Howard I. Ingham, Howard Lloyd Fowler, William Cyreus Hunt.

Walter Scott Ryder's number was the first one drawn from the town of Parma, New York, during the initial draft lottery in July 1917.[411] [left] Likely exempted by the 1st District Draft Board due to his status as a clergyman, Walter did not enter military service. Instead, twenty-six-year-old Walter chose to serve his country through the Young Men's Christian Association (Y.M.C.A.). Joining the war effort from Spencerport, New York, on August 1, 1918, he was a Physical and Recreational Director, spending the duration of his commitment at Fort Dupont, located in Delaware City, Delaware. He completed his service in January 1919.

Walter Scott Ryder was born outside Boston, Massachusetts, in the town of Norfolk, on March 11, 1892, to Charles E. and Bessie Alice (Duncan) Ryder, both parents emigrating from New Brunswick, Canada, in 1888. He returned to Canada fourteen years later to reside in Moncton, New Brunswick, Canada. Highly educated, Walter graduated from Acadia University in Wolfville, Nova Scotia, with a bachelor of arts degree in 1915,[412] the same year he married Alice Mae Storey of Moncton, New Brunswick, Canada, on August 18th.

Returning to the United States, he was leading the congregation of the Second Parma Baptist Church in Parma Corners as their minister by 1916.[413] Simultaneously he was studying for his bachelor of divinity from the Rochester Theological Seminary in Rochester, New York; he completed classwork in 1918, receiving his bachelor of divinity, in absentia, in 1920.[414][415] He left the United States in January of 1919, after completing his military Y.M.C.A. work. Walter moved to Vancouver, British Columbia, Canada, and served the congregation of Fairview Baptist Church[416] while attending the University of British Columbia (Vancouver, British Columbia, Canada). He studied economics and sociology,[417] and he wrote his thesis on the subject of "Canada's Industrial Crisis of 1919,"[418] earning his masters in anthropology in 1920.

Walter and his wife lived the remainder of their years in the Midwest, where Walter continued as a minister, was college professor at two colleges, earned his doctorate of philosophy from the University of Chicago, published two books, studied law, passed the bar exam in Michigan (though he never practiced), and worked as a life insurance salesman. He was granted a fellowship at the University of Michigan to further his education when he passed away on May 26, 1956. Walter S. Ryder is buried in Riverside Cemetery in Mount Pleasant, Michigan.

[far left][419] [left top][420] [left bottom][421]

Rev. W. S. Ryder went to New York, Wednesday evening of this week to take his examination in Y. M. C. A. work.

Rev. Ryder visited Harold Adams at the U. S. Naval Hospital at League Island, Phila., on Friday of last week and reports he is steadily improving and recovering his strength.

Herman Faulding Skinner's *New York State Abstracts of World War I Military Service* card. Herman was not old enough to register for any of the three World War I drafts, so he enlisted in the Regular Army, joining the Air Service. He was not required to complete a draft registration card.

HERMAN FAULDING SKINNER
1898 – 1983

Nineteen-year-old Herman enlisted in the United States Army on February 22, 1918, and reported to Fort Slocum, New York. Following initial screening he was sent to Kelly Field, Texas, before being assigned to the 614th Aero Squadron at Waco, Texas. The squadron relocated to Camp Greene, North Carolina, then Garden City, New York, where he transferred to the 309th Aero Squadron on July 6, 1918.[422] [left] He departed for Europe with the unit, leaving the port of New York on July 31, 1918, aboard the SS *Elpenor*, arriving in Liverpool, England, on August 11, 1918. The unit remained in England for the duration of the war.[423] [below] Herman returned to Camp Mills on Long Island, New York, aboard the SS *Mauretania* from Liverpool, England, on December 1, 1918; he was discharged less than two weeks later December 13, 1918.

Herman Faulding Skinner was born on April 7, 1898, to Frank and Mary (Hener) Skinner in Hilton, New York. Herman's mother passed away in 1900 and a year later his four-year-old sister died when fire erupted at the Rochester Orphan Asylum, killing thirty-one children and staff on January 8, 1901.[424] In 1910, twelve-year-old Herman was living with his aunt and uncle on Town Line Road in Greece, New York, while his father was living in Richfield, New York, working on a Skinner family farm.

—Herman F. Skinner arrived safely from over seas Dec. 22nd, coming on the S. S. Mauretania, after being 4 months in England, with the 309th Aero Squadron, which was stationed at Ladcaster, Yorkshire. Herman has had many interesting experiences, but says, "no place like good old U. S. A."

Mildred Leila Conklin and Herman were married on May 10, 1919, in Canandaigua, New York, and settled in Akron, Ohio. Herman earned a living in the building trade as a carpenter. Returning to Rochester, New York, by 1925, Herman worked for Eastman Kodak Company in the same line of work and would eventually retire from Kodak after twenty-nine years of service at Kodak Park.

In 1963, after forty-four years of marriage, Herman suffered the loss of his wife, Mildred, when she passed away in Rochester. Herman remarried, and with his second wife, Florence M. Corrigan, lived in Port Saint Lucie, Florida, where on June 29, 1983, he passed away. Herman is buried in Parma Union Cemetery in Parma, New York.

Herman Skinner is shown in his Air Service uniform in this undated photo.[425]

Alton Sleight was already serving in the New York National Guard and therefore did not have to complete a draft registration card. The top card is his *Abstracts of Muster Rolls For National Guard Units Mustered Into Federal Service During the 1916 Mexican Punitive Campaign*; the bottom is his *New York Abstracts of National Guard Service in WWI* card.

ALTON VICTOR SLEIGHT
1891 – 1980

On June 13, 1916, Alton enlisted in the New York National Guard in Rochester, New York, at the age of twenty-five. He mustered in on July 3, 1916, as a Private in the 2d Ambulance Company in response to the Mexican Punitive Campaign; he mustered out in Rochester on December 27, 1916, as a Mechanic with the same unit. Seven months later he mustered in again with 2d Ambulance Company, re-designated the 106th Ambulance Company, assigned to the 102d Sanitary Train, 27th Division. He transferred to the 108th Field Hospital on November 22, 1917, part of the same sanitary train. [right][426]

Alton left for Europe with the 27th Division, departing Newport News, Virginia, aboard the USS *Huron* on June 30, 1918. He returned with the same unit, sailing from Brest, France, on March 3, 1919, aboard the USS *Mount Vernon*, arriving in Hoboken, New Jersey, on March 11, 1919. He was honorably discharged on April 4, 1919.

Alton Victor Sleight, brother of Vernon Arthur, was born on January 21, 1891 to Arthur C. and Minnie (Lefler) Sleight in Jackson, Michigan. By 1909 the family was living in Rochester with both father and son employed in the railroad business— Alton as a train conductor.[427] Settling in Parma, New York, Alton found work as a farm laborer and became friends with Parma resident, and future fellow World War I soldier, Frank W. Randall.

Alton V. Sleight has arrived overseas, according to word received by his wife who lives at No. 456 Plymouth avenue.

ALTON SLEIGHT.

He is a member of 108th Field Hospital, 102d Sanitary Train. He joined the colors in September, 1917.

MARRIED SAME DAY, ON TRIP TOGETHER

Two Young Couples United by Same Clergyman.

Ida L. Hall and Alton V. Sleight were married on Saturday afternoon at 4 o'clock at the home of the bride's parents, Mr. and Mrs. Fred E. Hall, No. 438 Plymouth avenue. Rev. James M. Hutchinson officiated. The attendants were Frank W. Randall, of Hilton, and Pearl M. Henthorn, of this city.

The marriage of Frank W. Randall to Pearl M. Henthorn took place on Saturday afternoon at 5 o'clock at the home of the officiating clergyman, Rev. Mr. Hutchinson, who is pastor of Calvary Baptist Church, No. 378 Genesee street. The attendants were Mr. and Mrs. Sleight.

Mr. and Mrs. Randall, after a wedding dinner at the home of Fred E. Hall, left for a Western trip with Mr. and Mrs. Sleight.

Frank and Alton were witnesses at each other's weddings[428]–both taking place on June 9, 1917.[429] Alton married Ida L. Hall in Rochester and they would have forty-four years together before Ida passed on July 6, 1964.

Returning to Parma after the war, Alton worked in carpentry before joining General Railway Signal Corporation of Rochester as a foreman, promoting to supervisor.

Alton, one of 305 active members of the Clio Lodge No. 779, Free & Accepted Masons, was installed as a junior deacon in the lodge in 1930. The *Hilton (NY) Record* supposed that Clio Lodge had "the largest membership of any Masonic lodge in the state situated in a village of its size."[430] [next page, bottom right] He was also a member of Greece Baptist Church and was a general staff officer of the Federation of Men's Bible Classes.[431]

An active member of American Legion Hiscock-Fishbaugh Post 788, he was elected to the positions of secretary in 1932[432] and 1938;[433] taking the reigns as commander in 1935.[434] Alton attended both state[435] and county[436] conventions–

Local Legion Post Elects Officers

Alton V. Sleight New Commander— Delegates and Alternates Elected For County Convention.

Officers were elected at the meeting of Hiscock-Fishbaugh Post, American Legion, Tuesday evening, with Alton V. Sleight heading the list as Commander. Although Mr. Sleight and his family moved to Rochester from this vicinity several years ago, he has maintained his membership in the local post. He has seldom missed a meeting and, in fact, has been more active than many of the local veterans.

Other officers elected were: Albert Mehle, vice-commander; Geo. Paulson, adjutant; Henry A. Smith, treasurer; Frank Randall, financial secretary; Lucius Bagley, chaplain. The newly elected officers and other officers to be appointed by the new commander will be installed at the Post room at the regular August meeting by county officers.

Three delegates and three alternates to represent Hiscock-Fishbaugh Post at the Monroe County convention to be held July 20th at East Rochester were elected, as follows: Delegates, Wm. Kirk, A. V. Sleight and George Clift; Alternates, Frank Randall, Albert Mehle and J. Harlan Cooper.

Plans are being prepared for the Post's participation in the State convention to be held in Rochester next month. Members are having new insignia attached to their caps and uniform shirts and ties are being purchased. This will give the Post a much better appearance in the parade to be held during the three-day meet and also at future Legion functions.

1929 in Utica and 1935 in Monroe County, respectively—as a delegate from Hiscock-Fishbaugh Post. In 1935 he was named to the general committee planning a dinner for the National Commander in which more than six-hundred people were expected to attend.[437] [left][438]

Alton moved to Florida in 1968 and married former Rochester-native Mildred (Koehler) Judson; they lived in Largo, Florida. Alton was a member of the Orange Lake Village Interdenominational Church and his homeowners' association.[439] On July 9, 1980, Alton passed away in Largo, Florida, and is interred in Falls Cemetery in Greece, New York.

MASONIC OFFICERS INSTALLED

At the regular communication of Clio Lodge, F. & A. M., held Tuesday evening of this week, the following officers were installed by the retiring Master, Frank G. Blair, assisted by W. Bro. Fred Smith. Acting Grand Marshall:

W. M., J. Harlan Cooper; S. W., Howard Lewis; J. W., Fred B. Wadsworth; Sec'y, Wayne T Wolfrom; Treasurer, E. E. Wolfrom; S. D., Geo. Buckman; J. D., Alton V. Sleight; S. M. C., Charles Tubb; J. M. C, Henry Miller; Marshal, Raymond Verney; Pianist, Joseph Wagner; Tiler, Fay Taber.

Clio Lodge now has 305 active members. During the past year the five hundredth member was taken into the lodge. It is believed that Hilton now has the largest membership of any Masonic lodge in the state situated in a village of its size.

Charles Collamer has been engaged by the trustees as janitor for the ensuing year.

Men to Be Mobilized for Outing

General staff officers of the Federation of Men's Bible Classes inspecting plans to mobilize men for the annual Field Day, June 8, at Ellison Park, are, from left to right, Walter Sherman, Albert H. Lake and Alton V. Sleight.

In addition to the American Legion and the Masonic Lodge, Alton was an active member of his church and the Federation of Men's Bible Classes as shown in 1940.[440]

Alton is shown in his American Legion cap in this August 1935 article from the *Democrat and Chronicle* (Rochester, NY).[441]

Hiscock-Fishbaugh Post Sets Installation Rites August 13

Hiscock-Fishbaugh Post of Hilton is making elaborate preparations for the installation of officers in Hilton High School Tuesday, Aug. 13, at 8 p. m.

Officers to be inducted are: Alton V. Sleight, commander; Albert Mehle, vicecommander; Henry A. Smith, treasurer; Frank Randall, financial secretary, and Lucius Bagley, chaplain.

The installation will be in charge of William Bauer and the ritual team of Monroe Voiture III of the 40 and 8. The public is invited.

Commander Sleight has announced the following appointments: Sergeant-at-arms, William Kirk; service officer, Arthur Kirchgessner; welfare officers, George Paulson, Herman Worden and J. Harland Cooper; membership committee, John Crook, Albert Mehle and Merton Thompson.

Mr. Kirchgessner is post representative to the County Committee and Commander Sleight is alternate.

ALTON V. SLEIGHT

| Form 1 | 311 | REGISTRATION CARD | 3455 | No. 121 |

1. Name in full _Vernon A. Sleight_ (Given name) (Family name) Age, in yrs. **22**

2. Home address _395 Plymouth Rochester N.Y._ (No.) (Street) (City) (State)

3. Date of birth _May 3rd 1895_ (Month) (Day) (Year)

4. Are you (1) a natural-born citizen, (2) a naturalized citizen, (3) an alien, (4) or have you declared your intention (specify which)? _Natural born_

5. Where were you born? _Kalamazoo Mich. U.S.A._ (Town) (State) (Nation)

6. If not a citizen, of what country are you a citizen or subject? _____

7. What is your present trade, occupation, or office? _Chauffeur_

8. By whom employed? _Alling & Miles, Inc._ Where employed? _82 Stone St._

9. Have you a father, mother, wife, child under 12, or a sister or brother under 12, solely dependent on you for support (specify which)? _No_

10. Married or single (which)? _Single_ Race (specify which)? _Caucasian_

11. What military service have you had? Rank _None_; branch _____; years _____; Nation or State _____

12. Do you claim exemption from draft (specify grounds)? _No_

I affirm that I have verified above answers and that they are true.

V A Sleight
(Signature or mark)

If person is of African descent, tear off this corner

236

VERNON ARTHUR SLEIGHT
1895 – 1968

Enlisting in the New York National Guard on June 5, 1917, twenty-two-year-old Private Sleight joined his brother Alton in the 2d Ambulance Company, later re-designated the 106th Ambulance Company, 102d Sanitary Train, 27th Division. Mirroring his brother again, Vernon also transferred to the 108th Field Hospital, 102d Sanitary Train, on November 22, 1917. He was promoted to Private First Class but would never serve overseas. Vernon received a Surgeon's Certificate of Disability due to a diagnosis of pulmonary tuberculosis. He was discharged on January 24, 1918, reported as twenty percent disabled.

Vernon Arthur Sleight, brother of Alton Victor Sleight, was born on May 3, 1895, in Kalamazoo, Michigan, to Arthur C. and Minnie (Lefler) Sleight. The family moved to the Fifteenth Ward in Rochester, New York, and Vernon found work with General Railway Signal Corporation as an office assistant. On his off time, Vernon played semi-professional football from 1911 to 1914 for the Rochester Scalpers (1908-1925).[442] Games were played against other local and Western New York teams.[443]

Three weeks before joining the New York National Guard, Vernon married Flora H. Stuchfield on June 23, 1917, in Rochester. The newlyweds relocated around 1919, and, for the next ten years, were residents of Denver, Colorado.[444] Vernon worked for the Denver Cab Company in several capacities such as automobile mechanic, motor bus dispatcher, and superintendent.[445]

When they returned to Rochester in 1931,[446] Vernon drove a city bus for Rochester Transit Company, advancing his position over twenty-five years from a bus operator and driver-instructor, to director of safety, retiring in 1960.[447] [left][448]

Vernon and his wife participated in community fundraisers, helping to plus up the coffers of the American Red Cross as District Captains,[449] collecting clothes for the Salvation Army.[450] He was a member of Greece Baptist Church in Greece, New York, and a life member of Union Lodge No. 7, Free & Accepted Masons, of Denver, Colorado. Arthur passed away in Rochester General Hospital on February 12, 1968, and is interred in Falls Cemetery, Greece, New York.

As the Rochester Transit Corporation (RTC) Chief Instructor, Vernon developed a special training course for drivers, especially those who had just returned from World War II. Details of the training were reported in the *Democrat and Chronicle* (Rochester, NY) in November 1945.[451] [right]

The RTC figured, wisely, that a man could not merely come out of the Army and instantly become a good bus driver. To orient and make these ex-GI's just as efficient as possible, the bus company has set up an "exercise" course at the Main Street car barns. Any man who passes the course has to be good; take this reporter's word for it. Many a hot-shot cab driver would have his hands full getting through it.

Special Training

The idea—as expounded by Vernon Sleight, chief instructor who took a special course in cracker-jack bus driving at Syracuse—is to teach drivers how to stop on a dime, if necessary, or to stop quickly with a minimum of jolt; to train them so expertly that they instinctively know when their wheels are aligned with traffic strips or with the curb; to wheel between narrow passage areas without grazing anything.

This mechanical training is in addition to the expounding of courtesy, temper control (and anyone who ever has ridden a Rochester bus can appreciate that bus drivers must have the patience of a modern Job), and sound judgment.

No one yet has amassed more than 22 points over the "exercise" course. Sleight says it can't be done, but he says that any bus driver who can score 20 points over the course need never worry about being flagged by an irate cop or RTC checker.

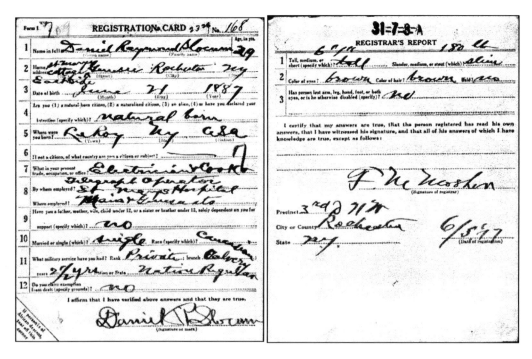

Daniel Slocum most likely registered twice for the same draft. The two draft cards have different addresses and different registrar signatures, indicating he filed with two different local boards. The top card was most likely submitted in the town of Ogden, New York, given the Adams Basin address. The bottom card was accepted in one of the local boards in the city of Rochester, New York, based on the precinct information provided.

DANIEL RAYMOND SLOCUM
1887 – 1929

Daniel enlisted in the United States Army in Rochester, New York, on August 30, 1905, and was sent to Troop A, 3d Cavalry, Camp Stotsenburg (also known as Fort Stotsenburg) in Pampanga, Philippine Islands. He was dishonorably discharged a year later on December 9, 1906; his character recorded as "not honest and faithful."

Two World War I draft registration cards were completed with Daniel's name, birthdate, and birth location being equal, the other entries varying slightly in response. Based on two different addresses listed, it is assessed Daniel registered twice for the June 5, 1917, draft at two different local draft boards—one responsible for the town of Ogden, New York, and the other, the city of Rochester.

He entered the United States Army a second time on February 24, 1918, being inducted at Spencerport, New York. Thirty-year-old Private Slocum was assigned to the 151st Depot Brigade, Camp Devens, Massachusetts, where he promoted twice: to Corporal on March 11, 1918, and Sergeant on July 21, 1918. On September 14, 1918, he transferred to Machine Gun Officers' Training School at Camp Hancock, Augusta, Georgia. When the war ended he elected to not continue training and was discharged on November 30, 1918.

Daniel Raymond Slocum was born in LeRoy, New York, on June 21, 1887, to James S. and Harriett E. (Campbell) Slocum. Daniel grew up in Buffalo, New York, and by the age of seventeen was employed by Kirk Printing Company. On May 7, 1904, he was accused of kicking a fourteen-year-old boy working at the same location; the boy later died as result of his injuries. Daniel was arrested but further details aside from newspaper accounts are unknown despite inquiries to several law enforcement agencies and government offices. Also unknown is whether the case went to trial.[452] [below]

The June 1905 New York State Census records indicate two entries for Daniel. In one his name was recorded as D. Raymond Slocum and he is living with his older brother, Herbert, in Rochester; listed on the census roll as Herbert's son. However, the same census taken in Freeville, New York, reported Daniel as a boarder in the George Junior Republic, an institution for disadvantaged youth.

ACCUSED OF MANSLAUGHTER.

On the charge of manslaughter in the second degree, Daniel R. Slocum, sixteen years old, of Niagara street, was arrested Saturday afternoon by Detectives Holmlund and Newton of police headquarters. The police had been searching for him for over a week.

It is alleged that Slocum kicked John Dotzler, fourteen years old, of 205 Strauss street, while the two were at work in an Eagle street printing shop. On May 21st Dotzler died at the German Deaconess Hospital from effects, it is said, of those kicks.

Slocum admitted to the police that he shoved Dotzler from a bench in the printing shop, but he denies having kickel him.

Exact dates on when the individual enumerations took place are unknown. It is theorized Daniel was treated as a minor for his 1904 infraction in Buffalo and sent to the institution in Freeville as a ward of the court. Then, during the summer of 1905, he left the George Junior Republic to live with his brother, where he joined the United States Army at the end of summer and departed for the Philippines. Without further details, this is the most likely scenario within the scope of the information obtained.

ARRESTED FOR MANSLAUGHTER.

Daniel R. Slocum Said to Have Inflicted Injuries Which Caused John Dotzler's Death.

After a week's search Detective-Sergeants Holmlund and Newton last night succeeded in locating Daniel R. Slocum, 17 years old, who, it is alleged, caused the injury which resulted in the death of John Dotzler, 14 years old, of 205 Strauss street, who died at the German Deaconess' Hospital, on Kingsley street, last Saturday. Blood poisoning, as the result of a kick in the stomach, was the cause of death.

Slocum was found in his home on Niagara street, near Ferry street, and was arrested on the charge of manslaughter, second degree. He was taken to Police Headquarters and locked up in the "freezer." He will have a hearing in Police Court tomorrow morning.

Slocum and the dead boy were employed by the Kirk Printing Company, at 73 West Eagle street, as type-cleaners. On the morning of April 23 Dotzler was suddenly stricken ill and, upon permission from the foreman of the shop, laid down under a bench to rest. Slocum came along and, seeing Dotzler asleep on the floor, he said:

"Get up out of there and go to work." Dotzler awoke, but was too ill to make any reply. As he did not move, Slocum, it is said, kicked him in the stomach. Dotzler, too weak to make an outcry, merely groaned.

Later in the day Dotzler grew worse and was finally taken to his home in a carriage. A physician was called and when he examined the boy he found that his right hip was terribly contused and swollen. He was treated at his home until May 7, when his condition became grave and he was removed to the hospital. Blood poisoning developed and he died.

Slocum admitted to Chief Taylor last night that he kicked Dotzler, but said he did it with no intent of injuring the boy, but just to awaken him, as he says he was shirking his work and leaving it for him to do.

When he registered for the draft, Daniel Slocum stated he was working at Saint Mary's Hospital in Rochester. However, he reported his occupation as "cook" on the card fill out for the Adams Basin, New York, address; and stated he was an electrician and telegraph operator for the "Genesee" address in Rochester. He married Gertrude L. McIntyre of Adams Basin on January 31, 1918, in Rochester before his induction. When he returned, he supported his family as a foreman in a tool business, a steamfitter, and a machinist. Daniel passed away on August 4, 1929, and is buried in Fairfield Cemetery in Spencerport, New York.

Above, an article from the *Evening News* (Buffalo, NY), May 30, 1904, describes the circumstances surrounding Daniel Slocum's altercation with his coworker.[453]

At right, almost twenty-one years later, Daniel is hit by an automobile and suffers hip and internal injuries after stepping off a curb in downtown Rochester as described in this May 7, 1925, article in the *Democrat and Chronicle*.[454]

DRIVER SPEEDS OFF AFTER PEDESTRIAN IS BADLY INJURED

Run down by an automobile while crossing Front street near Market late yesterday afternoon, Daniel Slocum, 38 years old, of Adams Basin, received a possible fracture of the hip and possible internal injuries. The motorist sped from the scene of the accident and was being sought by the police last night.

Slocum had just stepped from the curb when hit by the light touring car, witnesses reported. The police were unable to obtain the license number of the machine. Slocum was taken to the General Hospital in the ambulance where his condition was reported as serious.

In November of 1917, Daniel R. Slocum applied for a patent for his invention—a self-contained "apparatus for the raising of sponge used in the making of bread, by the utilization of artificial heat."

His invention also incorporated "a low grade of oil [used] in lamps for the purpose of providing heat, but preventing the fumes issuing from the lamp from coming into contact with the sponge."

Patent number 1,277,496 was granted September 3, 1918, while Daniel was serving in the Army at Camp Hancock, Georgia.[455]

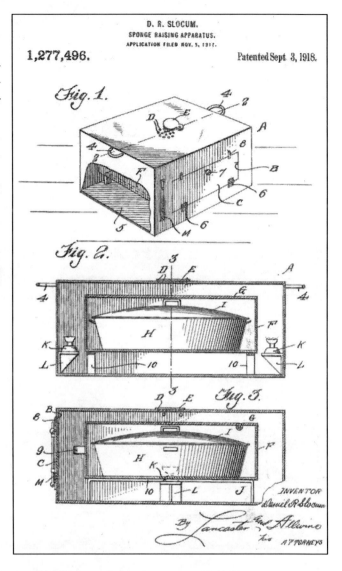

UNITED STATES PATENT OFFICE.

DANIEL R. SLOCUM, OF SPENCERPORT, NEW YORK.

SPONGE-RAISING APPARATUS.

1,277,496.   Specification of Letters Patent.   Patented Sept. 3, 1918.

Application filed November 5, 1917.   Serial No. 200,405.

To all whom it may concern:

Be it known that I, DANIEL R. SLOCUM, a citizen of the United States, and a resident of Spencerport, in the county of Monroe and State of New York, have invented a certain new and useful Improvement in Sponge-Raising Apparatus, of which the following is a specification.

My present invention relates to apparatus for the raising of sponge used in the making of bread, by the utilization of artificial heat.

The principal objects of my invention are to provide apparatus of the character described which is compact and easily manipulated; apparatus which will receive the usual ing, the container F including a lid G; H a pan for the sponge which may be provided with a lid I; J means for supporting the container F in spaced relation to the bottom of container A; K, heating devices, such as lamps; L supports for the devices K; and, M, a thermometer.

Referring first to the container A, it is preferably made of metal and may be provided with handles 4 extending from opposite sides, facilitating transportation of the apparatus. The lower margin of opening B is preferably at a substantial distance from the bottom 5 of the container, the door C being preferably hinged so as to swing about hinges 6, the pintles of which are

Form 1 REGISTRATION CARD

1 Name in full *Arthur M. Smith*
(Given name) (Family name)
Age, in yrs. *24*

2 Home address
(No.) (Street) *Hilton* (City) *New York* (State)

3 Date of birth *December 15* (Month) (Day) *1893* (Year)

4 Are you (1) a natural-born citizen, (2) a naturalized citizen, (3) an alien, (4) or have you declared your intention (specify which)? *Natural Born*

5 Where were you born? *Greece* (Town) *New York* (State) *U.S.A.* (Nation)

6 If not a citizen, of what country are you a citizen or subject?

7 What is your present trade, occupation, or office? *Labor on Farm*

8 By whom employed? *Fay Ducolon*
Where employed? *Parma Monroe Co New York*

9 Have you a father, mother, wife, child under 12, or a sister or brother under 12, solely dependent on you for support (specify which)? *No*

10 Married or single (which)? *Single* Race (specify which)? *Caucasian*

11 What military service have you had? Rank *None* ; branch
years ; Nation or State

12 Do you claim exemption from draft (specify grounds)?

I affirm that I have verified above answers and that they are true.

Arthur M Smith
(Signature or mark)

If person is of African descent, tear off this corner

242

ARTHUR M. SMITH
1892/1893 – 1977

Arthur was inducted into the United States Army in Spencerport, New York, on September 7, 1917, when he was twenty-three. Private Smith was sent to Camp Dix, New Jersey, and assigned to Battery D, 309th Field Artillery, 78th Division; he transferred to the Supply Company on November 23, 1917. He did not sail from Boston, Massachusetts, at the end of

> —Private Arthur M. Smith for the past four months has been guarding at the Standard Oil Works at Bayonne, N. J. Last week, while he was on guard one of the tanks exploded on his post, three girls being badly burned and several men killed, but he was lucky enough to escape unhurt. On Oct. 31, he was transferred to Metuchen, N. J., and is guarding an amunition factory.

May 1918 with his unit; instead he was assigned to Company D, 11th Battalion of United States Guards, on May 15, 1918. [left][456] He remained with the battalion at Metuchen, New Jersey, for the duration of his enlistment, promoting to Private First Class on May 1, 1918; Corporal on May 15, 1919; and Sergeant on May 23, 1919; before his discharge on July 3, 1919.

Arthur M. Smith was born to Henry T. and Alice (Reynolds) Smith in North Greece, New York, on December 15 of either 1892 or 1893. The Social Security Death Index, United States Federal Census Records, and his draft registration card (with his signature) indicate his birth year was 1893. However, the *New York State Abstracts of World War I Military Service* card and United States Department of Veterans Affairs Death File report his birth year as 1892. When he registered for the draft in 1917, he was employed as a farm laborer working for Fay Ducolon of Parma, New York; he continued in this line of work after his army discharge. He married Grace Marie Judd on November 29, 1923, making their home in Parma. In the 1930 United States Federal Census he listed his occupation as a painter; Grace worked as a shader in button manufacturing.

Arthur was a member of the American Legion Hiscock-Fishbaugh Post 788 and, in 1944[457] and 1946,[458] was elected financial secretary for the organization. Arthur passed away in Hilton, New York, on March 2, 1977, and is interred in Parma Union Cemetery in Parma, New York.

Arthur Smith is shown in the second row, behind the shoulder of George Dean. These soldiers were forming up in the village of Hilton on what is presumed to be the August 2nd Town of Parma "Welcome Home" celebration for the war veterans in 1919.[459]

Form 1   1227   REGISTRATION CARD   648   No. 18

1 | Name in full   Henry A Smith   Age, in yrs. 28
(First name) (Family name)

2 | Home address   Hilton   N Y
(Street) (City) (State)

3 | Date of birth   Sep   4   1888
(Month) (Day) (Year)

4 | Are you (1) a natural-born citizen, (2) a naturalized citizen, (3) an alien, (4) or have you declared your intention (specify which)?   Natural Born

5 | Where were you born?   Webster   N Y   USA
(Town) (State) (Nation)

6 | If not a citizen, of what country are you a citizen or subject?

7 | What is your present trade, occupation, or office?   29 Barber

8 | By whom employed?   Self
Where employed?   Hilton

9 | Have you a father, mother, wife, child under 12, or a sister or brother under 12, solely dependent on you for support (specify which)?   Mother

10 | Married or single (which)?   Single   Race (specify which)?   White

11 | What military service have you had? Rank _____; branch _____
years _____; Nation or State _____

12 | Do you claim exemption from draft (specify grounds)? _____

I affirm that I have verified above answers and that they are true.

Henry A Smith
(Signature or mark)

If person is of African descent, tear off this corner

244

HENRY ARTHUR SMITH
1888 – 1962

Henry was inducted into the United States Army at Camp Crane in Allentown, Pennsylvania, on April 20, 1918. At the rank of Private, he was assigned to Evacuation Ambulance Company No. 9 of the Medical Department at Camp Crane and promoted to Wagoner on June 20, 1918. He sailed from New York City aboard the USS *Plattsburg* on August 30, 1918, destined for France. His role in France is best described from United States Army Medical Department historical records: "Company No. 9 arrived September 14, 1918. Operated at Saint-Nazaire, Base Section 1. Detained there until ambulances were received; that is, until after the armistice. On November 25 Ambulance Company No. 144, with 121 men, and Evacuation Ambulance Company No. 9, with 37 men, were organized into an evacuation ambulance battalion which evacuated hospital trains to the transport and moved sick and wounded in and out of hospitals. The battalion moved 80,000 patients by July [1919]."[460] He returned aboard the USS *Iowan*† from Saint-Nazaire, France, on July 8, 1919, and arrived in Brooklyn, New York, on July 19, 1919. He was honorably discharged on July 29, 1919.

> —Messrs Henry A. Smith and Thomas Roberts will on Monday next open a tonsorial parlor in the center store in the new Green block on Main Street, Mr. Roberts having sold his building on Hovey street to Sarafino Panzarella, the shoemaker.

Henry Arthur Smith was born to Marcus J. and Sarah (Hynes) Smith on September 4, 1888, in Webster, New York. By 1900 his family had moved to Greece, New York, and by 1905 the family was living in Parma, New York, where Henry found work as a house painter. On February 15, 1926, Henry married Mary J. VanderMill in Newark, New York. He was a prominent businessman and opened a tonsorial parlor (a business offering shaves and haircuts) with Thomas Roberts in 1916.[461] [left] He operated this business in the village of Hilton for forty-eight years.[462]

"Hank" was a member of several civic organizations in Hilton. He was a fifty-year member of the Clio Lodge No 779, Free & Accepted Masons, the Independent Order of Odd Fellows Lodge, and was a social member of the Hilton Fire Department.[463] Henry was listed as a charter member of the American Legion Hiscock-Fishbaugh Post 788 when the post filed their organizing papers in 1919. Within the post, he was elected treasurer in both 1932 and 1935. Retiring in 1959, Henry would enjoy three years of retirement, passing away on May 4, 1962. He is buried in Parma Union Cemetery in Parma, New York.

Appeal Made for Old Records

You are asked to leave your old records, either disc or cylinders, at the Henry Smith Barber Shop. The drive for old, used and unwanted Victrola records is being sponsored by Hiscock-Fishbaugh Post, American Legion. All records collected are to be sold to manufacturers who will remake them into new records to be sent to the boys in the armed services. Money derived from the sale of the old records will go to purchase new records for the enjoyment of the U. S. Army, Navy, Marine and Air Forces.

Look over your collection. There must be a score of cracked, broken, scratched or worn out records, to say nothing of the many which are relics of days gone so far past that they no longer have any interest or pleasure for you. Make this a "MUST" on your list at once.

Henry's shop on Main Street was the perfect central location in the village for citizens to stop by when supporting home front efforts during World War II.[464][465]

World War Veterans Asked to Register at Barber Shop

All vicinity World War veterans are urged to go to the Henry A. Smith barber shop to fill out forms of registration for possible home defense.

The government is anxious to know the qualifications of each former service man. Filling out the form will not obligate the man in any way, but will make known to the government important data it is anxious to obtain concerning ability available.

At his earliest opportunity, each veteran of the last war is urged to comply with the request of the government.

---

† Read more about the USS *Iowan* at http://www.shipscribe.com/usnaux/ww1/ships/id3002.htm.

				1½
Smith, Kenneth I.		1,078,126	White	
(Surname)	(Christian name)	(Army serial number)	(Race: White or colored)	

Residence: _____ Hilton   Monroe   NEW YORK
　　　　　　(Street and house number)　(Town or city)　(County)　　(State)

* Enlisted in　NA at Columbus Bks Ohio Apr 24/17

† Born in　　　Hilton NY 18 2/12 yrs

Organizations:

　　　　24 Aer Sq to July 9/18; 883 Aer Sq to Disch

Grades:　　　Pvt

Engagements:

Wounds or other injuries received in action: None.

‡ Served overseas:　No

§ Hon. disch.　Jan 28/19　on demobilization

Was reported　0　per cent disabled on date of discharge, in view of occupation.

Remarks:

Form No. 724-1½, A. G. O.　　* Insert "R. A.", "N. G.", "E. R. C.", "N. A.", as case may be, followed by place and
　March 12, 1920.　　　　date of enlistment.　† Give place of birth and date of birth, or age at enlistment.
　3—7688　　　　　‡ Give dates of departure from and arrival in the United States.　§ Give date.

Kenneth I. Smith's *New York State Abstracts of World War I Military Service* card. Kenneth enlisted in the National Army immediately after the United States declared war. He was too young to register for any of the three drafts and was not required to complete a draft registration card.

KENNETH ISAAC SMITH
1899 – 1964

Kenneth enlisted in the United States Army from Columbus Barracks in Columbus, Ohio, on April 24, 1917. As an eighteen-year-old Private, he was initially assigned to the 24th Aero Squadron at Kelly Field in Texas. Kenneth remained at Kelly Field even though the 24th Aero

> —Word was received last week by Mr. and Mrs. W. I. Smith of this village that their son, Kenneth Smith of Kelly Field, Texas, was in the hospital to have an operation performed upon his knee, otherwise he would have left the previous Monday with his Squad for France.

Squadron moved to New York City in January 1918 for deployment to France. His parents relayed to the *Hilton (NY) Record* in December 1917 that he was in the hospital pending knee surgery.[466] [left] He eventually transferred to the 883d Aero Squadron on July 9, 1918–a part of Aviation Repair Depot #3 located at Montgomery, Alabama. He was discharged, never having served overseas, on January 28, 1919.

Kenneth Isaac Smith was born to William I. and Bessie (Ferguson) Smith in Hilton, New York, on February 23, 1899. He married Hazel Luella Kelly on September 4, 1920, and found

> GENEVA HARDWARE FIRM.
> Geneva, Jan. 28.—The Dorchester & Rose Hardware Company, of Geneva, has elected the following officers: President, Oswald J. C. Rose; vice-president, James J. Taney; secretary, Walter C. Rose; treasurer, Melvin S. Gaylord; head of the wholesale oil department, Kenneth I. Smith; head of the agricultural department, Arthur Smith.

employment as a salesman. Living in Geneva, New York, he worked for a wholesale distributor representing the Rae Oil Company.[467] In 1928 Kenneth was president of the Dorchester-Rose Oil & Chemical Corporation, a division of the Dorchester and Rose hardware store, also in Geneva. [left][468]

By 1932 he moved his family to Tonawanda, New York, going back to his roots as a salesman. By 1940 he was a clerk for the United States Postal Service; retiring after twenty-five years. On March 12, 1964, Kenneth died in Buffalo, New York, after being struck by a car.[469] [below] He is buried in Cold Springs Cemetery in Lockport, New York.

Kenneth's picture was in the *Hilton Record* in February 1918. He was home on furlough after his knee operation and before transferring to an aircraft depot in Alabama.[470]

> **BUFFALO FATALITY**
>
> BUFFALO (P)—Kenneth I. Smith, 65, of Buffalo, a retired post office clerk, was killed yesterday when struck by an automobile as he was crossing a street.

HILTON, N. Y. THURSDAY, FEB. 14, 1918.

KENNETH SMITH, son of Mr. and Mrs. W. I. Smith of this Village, home on a furlough from Kelly, Tex.

	REGISTRATION CARD	No. 72

Form 1

1 Name in full *Thomas L. Sovia* — Age, in yrs. *21*
(Given name) (Family name)

2 Home address *Hilton* *N.Y.*
(No.) (Street) (City) (State)

3 Date of birth *September 21* *1896*
(Month) (Day) (Year)

4 Are you (1) a natural-born citizen, (2) a naturalized citizen, (3) an alien, (4) or have you declared your intention (specify which)? *Natural Born*

5 Where were you born? *Ogdensburg* *N.Y.* *U.S.A.*
(Town) (State) (Nation)

6 If not a citizen, of what country are you a citizen or subject?

7 What is your present trade, occupation, or office? *Farm Laborer*

8 By whom employed? *Emmett Chatten*
Where employed? *Parma*

9 Have you a father, mother, wife, child under 12, or a sister or brother under 12, solely dependent on you for support (specify which)? *No*

10 Married or single (which)? *Single* Race (specify which)? *White*

11 What military service have you had? Rank *Private* ; branch *N. Guard* ;
years *2 mos.* ; Nation or State *New York*

12 Do you claim exemption from draft (specify grounds)? *No*

I affirm that I have verified above answers and that they are true.

Thomas Sovia
(Signature or mark)

If person is of African descent, tear off this corner

★ THOMAS D. SOVIA ★
1896 – 1918

Thomas enlisted in the United States Army at Camp Syracuse in Syracuse, New York, on August 3, 1917, as a Private. He was initially assigned to Company M, 50th Infantry Regiment, and was supposed to be a part of the 20th Division of the Regular Army. The 20th finally organized a year later in July 1918; it demobilized after the armistice and never served overseas.[471] Thomas had been transferred to Company M, 23d Infantry Regiment, 2d Division, on August 16, 1917, and sailed overseas with the unit on September 7, 1917, departing from Hoboken, New Jersey aboard the USS *Pocahontas*. Thomas was initially assigned to a division that never saw combat; instead he was in France just over a month after his enlistment.

Thomas D. Sovia was born to David J. and Celina (Mallett) Sovia on September 21, 1896, in Ogdensburg, New York. The family moved to Lisbon, New York, by 1905, but returned to Ogdensburg by 1910. The next move was to Carlton, New York, where Thomas found work on a farm as a hired man and lived independently from his family.[472]

Arriving in Parma, New York, around 1916, Thomas worked as a farm laborer for Emmett Chattin, listing his residence as Hilton, New York, on his draft registration card dated June 5, 1917. He moved with his parents and siblings to the hamlet of Sanborn, New York, (between Lockport and Niagara Falls, New York) and Thomas left to enlist.

Thomas was killed in action during the Battle of the Aisne, as the division advanced towards Vaux, France, to the south of Belleau Wood, on June 6, 1918. He was hastily buried on "Hill 192" near the battle area, only to be exhumed and re-buried two more times: first in American Cemetery at Essomes-Sur-Marne, and finally in Aisne-Marne American Cemetery, Belleau, France, on June 5, 1919, where many others from the 23d Infantry Regiment were buried.[473]

Details of Sovia's death were reported by a member from Co. M in March 1919. [right][474]

Co M 23 Inf	SOVIA Thomas Pvt

Sovia was killed June 6- We advanced a little and when we found we could not hold our line we fell back and left most of our wounded and killed on the field I saw him just after he died. We were in a wheat field About July 6 21 or 22 open were buried at night in the neighboring woods. I don't know if he was one because we were able to recognize only two of the number.

Informant: Kempa Gottlieb Cpl
Co M 23 Inf -Base hosp/ 111
March 29-1919

F/M.
E.P. Cooley Searcher.

Serial No. **122**   9   Registration No. **122**

1 Name in full **Floyd Arnold Sweeting**   Age, in yrs. **21**
(Given name) (Family name)

2 Home address **89 Pullman Ave Rochester N.Y.**
(No.) (Street) (City or town) (State)

3 Date of birth **Sept 25 1896**
(Month) (Day) (Year)

4 Where were you born? **Spencerport N.Y. U.S.A.**
(City or town) (State) (Nation)

5 I am
1. A native of the United States.
2. ~~A naturalized citizen.~~
3. ~~Analien.~~
4. ~~I have declared my intention.~~
5. ~~A noncitizen or citizen Indian.~~
(Strike out lines or words not applicable)

6 If not a citizen, of what Nation are you a citizen or subject?

7 Father's birthplace **Spencerport N.Y. U.S.A.**
(City or town) (State or province) (Nation)

8 Name of employer **Northeast electrical company**
Place of employment **Whitney St Rochester N.Y.**
(No.) (Street) (City or town)

9 Name of nearest relative **Father Frank Sweeting**
Address of nearest relative **Spencerport N.Y.**
(No.) (Street) (City or town) (State or N.)

10 Race— White, ~~Negro~~, ~~Indian~~, or ~~Oriental~~
(Strike out words not applicable)

I affirm that I have verified above answers and that they are true.

Floyd Arnold Sweeting
(Signature or Mark of Registrant.)

P.M.G.O. Form 1 (blue)

If person is of African descent, tear off this corner.

REGISTRATION CARD.

250

★ FLOYD ARNOLD SWEETING ★
1896 – 1918

Twenty-one-year-old Floyd enrolled in the United States Naval Reserve Force on July 17, 1918, at the Recruiting Station in Buffalo, New York. He completed initial training at the Naval Training Station in Great Lakes, Illinois, earning the rate of Fireman Third Class. He continued his training at the Naval Training Station, Hampton Roads, Virginia, from September 4th until September 27th, 1918. He transferred to Philadelphia, Pennsylvania, and was assigned to the USS *Iowa* according to military records, however the *Hilton (NY) Record* reported differently.[475] [below right] He became ill sometime on or before October 4, 1918, and was transferred to the hospital vessel USS *Solace*.

Floyd Arnold Sweeting was born to Frank Arnold and Mary L. (Peckham) Sweeting on the 25th of September 1896, in Spencerport, New York. His mother passed away in 1902[476] and Floyd was raised by his father in Parma, New York. After graduating from Spencerport High School in 1915,[477] Floyd moved to Rochester, New York, and was working for Northeast Electrical Company.[478]

On October 9, 1918, Floyd died of bronchial pneumonia while on the USS *Solace*. He was laid to rest in Parma Corners Cemetery in Parma, New York.

SPENCERPORT TOURISTS.

Party Leaves for Trip to Washington and Points of Interest.

Spencerport, April 2.—At 8 o'clock this morning the annual senior class excursion conducted by Principal F. Neff Stroup, left for Washington. This trip will include a five-day stay in Washington with a visit to Arlington, Mt. Vernon, public buildings of interest and the class will be greeted by President Wilson at the White House.

The members of the senior class to take this trip are Edna Allen, Mabel Smith, Irene Rollin, Pearl Sharp, Florence Dickinson, Merton Colby, Bernard Colby, Francis Ryan, Myron Adams, Ben Everett, Earl Adams, Willis Taylor, Jermian Titus, Floyd Sweeting and James Spencer.

The class will be accompanied by Mrs. Charles Rollin and Miss Green. In Washington they will meet Mr. and Mrs Brainard who have been spending the winter in North Carolina. Mr. Brainard was school commissioner in this district for a number of years.

Returning home the class will spend a day in Philadelphia, arriving at Spencerport Friday, April 9th.

PARMA CORNERS

Frank Sweeting received a telegram about midnight on Saturday last stating, his son Floyd was dead. He was serving his country as seaman 1st class on the Ohio, no information as to the cause of death has been received. Floyd enlisted early in the Summer and went to the Great Lakes Training Station and was recently transferred to Norfolk and to the above mentioned ship. He was 22 yrs. of age.

Form 1   **REGISTRATION CARD**   ✗7ℵ 27

1 Name in full   *William G Taylor*   Age, in yrs.   *21*
   (Given name)   (Family name)

2 Home address   *Hilton*   *N Y*
   (No.)   (Street)   (City)   (State)

3 Date of birth   *Feb*   *22*   *1896*
   (Month)   (Day)   (Year)

4 Are you (1) a natural-born citizen, (2) a naturalized citizen, (3) an alien, (4) or have you declared your intention (specify which)?   *Natural Born*

5 Where were you born?   *Hamlin*   *N Y*   *usa*
   (Town)   (State)   (Nation)

6 If not a citizen, of what country are you a citizen or subject?

7 What is your present trade, occupation, or office?   *3 0 Labor*

8 By whom employed?   *non*
   Where employed?   *now where*

9 Have you a father, mother, wife, child under 12, or a sister or brother under 12, solely dependent on you for support (specify which)?   *none*

10 Married or single (which)?   *Single*   Race (specify which)?   *White*

11 What military service have you had? Rank   *none*   ; branch
    years   ; Nation or State

12 Do you claim exemption from draft (specify grounds)?   *none*

I affirm that I have verified above answers and that they are true.

Wm D Taylor
(Signature of man)

If person is of African descent, tear off this corner   *77*

WILLIAM DEVLAMORE TAYLOR
1896 – 1960

William was twenty-two when he was inducted into the United States Army from Spencerport, New York, and sent to Camp Devens, Massachusetts. He was released from military service and sent home on March 19, 1918, due to a physical disability. [left][479]

> ˙ —Wm. Taylor, son of Horace Taylor of this town returned home Tuesday from Camp Devens, Mass., with an honorable discharge from the army on account of physical disability.

William Devlamore Taylor was born on February 22, 1896, to Horace George and Emma Josephine (Quiett) Taylor in Hamlin, New York. William worked on a farm prior to his entering the service.

He married Nellie L. Ladue on November 19, 1919, and they made their home in Rochester, New York, where William found employment working as a brakeman for a railroad company. Eastman Kodak Company employed him for thirty-two years, working some of those years as a train engineer at Kodak Park. [right][480]

He was active in many fraternal organizations such as the Charlotte Lodge, Free & Accepted Masons; the Rochester Consistory (a branch of the Free & Accepted Masons known as the Scottish Rite); the Stonewood Lodge, Independent Order of Odd Fellows; the Damascus Temple of the Shrine; Lake Avenue Methodist Church; Kodak Pioneer Club; and a Republican committeeman in Greece, New York.[481] William died on November 8, 1960, and is buried in Parma Union Cemetery in Parma, New York.

> ## Boys Answers Call.
>
> The young men from this village and town who left last Monday for Camp Devens, Ayers, Mass. were: William Taylor, Bert Perry, George Rowley, Lyman Hall, Samuel Flemming, George Dean, Noah Tascarrni and Arthur McNeil.

William was among eight men sent to Camp Devens in February 1918. [above][482]

Six months earlier, William was exempted from military service by the local draft board. [right] Since he was subsequently drafted, the district or regional board must have denied the exemption and ruled him eligible to serve.[483]

> ## Hilton Exemptions
>
> The local board for the First district, Monroe county has certified to the district board, Court house, Rochester the following names of Hilton persons who have been called by this board for military service and exempted or discharged in accordance with the rules and regulations prescribed by the President and approved by congress; Frederick B. Wadsworth, Wm. D. Taylor, Wm. C. Wagner, Wm. C. Lais, John H. Wright, Wm. A. Peffer, Geo. F. Weidman, Wilber J. Dunbar, Arthur Harmer, Orin C. Curtis, Harry King, Herbert Harradine, Jos. Marshall, Wilfred Horrex, Stanly Smith, Van Allen Mc-Kinned, Lloyd Burritt.

REGISTRATION CARD No. 42

Form 1

1 Name in full _Alfred Turgeon_ Age, in yrs. 24

2 Home address _Hilton N.Y._

3 Date of birth _July 5th 1893_

4 Are you (1) a natural born citizen, (2) a naturalized citizen, (3) an alien, (4) or have you declared your intention (specify which)? _an alien_

5 Where were you born? _Valleyfield_ _Canada_

6 If not a citizen, of what country are you a citizen or subject? _Canada_

7 What is your present trade, occupation, or office? _30 Labour_

8 By whom employed? _H. J. Heing Co._ Where employed? _Hilton_

9 Have you a father, mother, wife, child under 12, or a sister or brother under 12, solely dependent on you for support (specify which)? _none_

10 Married or single (which)? _Single_ Race (specify which)? _White_

11 What military service have you had? Rank _no_; branch ____; years ____; Nation or State ____

12 Do you claim exemption from draft (specify grounds)? _no_

I affirm that I have verified above answers and that they are true.

Alfred Turgeon

ALFRED JOSEPH TURGON
1892 – 1965

In Spencerport, New York, twenty-five-year-old Alfred was inducted into the United States Army on September 26, 1917, as a Private. He was initially assigned to Battery D, 309th Field Artillery, 78th Division, at Camp Dix, New Jersey, but later transferred to Company A, 325th Infantry, 82d Division, at Camp Gordon, Georgia, sometime in October or November 1917. He was honorably discharged on December 29, 1917, on a Surgeon's Certificate of Disability.[484] [right]

—Fred Turgon, son of Mr. and Mrs. Oliver Turgon of this village, who was drafted and been in the army for several months has returned home honorably discharged from the army on account of physical disability.

Alfred Joseph Turgon was born to Oliver and Martha (Goyette) Turgon on July 5th, 1892, in Valley Field, Quebec, Canada. When he registered for the draft on June 5, 1917, and throughout his service with the United States Army, Alfred was not a citizen of the United States. In fact, it wasn't until seventeen years after his draft registration that his status changed when he was granted United States citizenship in Naturalization Court in May of 1934.[485] [below left][486]

SAVE TIME AND MONEY

GET OUR PRICES ON

Drawing Your Fruit
TO STORAGE OR ELSEWHERE

Having Three Trucks in Operation, we are in shape to do

CARTING AT ANY TIME
Also Local and Long Distance Moving

Have It Shipped By Truck For Better Service

Turgon Bros.
Bell Phone 121-F-11   HILTON, N.Y.

He married Mary Elizabeth Buell on April 27, 1918, in Rochester, New York, and they made their home in Hilton, New York. Alfred and his brother, Arthur, were proprietors of a trucking business, calling themselves "Turgon Bros. Express."[487] [above right] In addition to supporting their families through their trucking operations, Arthur and Alfred volunteered their time, and the resources of their business, to aid the community in its support of civic organizations and the war effort.

21 Former Soldiers Given Citizenship

Admitted as 'Gift' for Service in War

Uncle Sam presented as a gift in recognition of service to the United States in the World War citizenship to 21 veterans, who came within terms of a special legislative act.

The group was admitted in Naturalization Court before Supreme Court Justice Marsh N. Taylor. Under the special act, aliens who served with United States forces in the last war may obtain citizenship upon submission of an honorable discharge and proper identification. Those who did not apply for the special dispensation before the act expired must follow the lengthy procedure required of other aliens.

Fruit pits and nut shells were a critical component needed in the manufacture of gas masks for troops overseas—a natural and effective filter against the chlorine gas used during German chemical attacks.[488] Five barrels of peach pits had been collected at the office of the *Hilton (NY) Record* and the barrels were transported by the Turgon brothers to the Rochester Chapter of the American Red Cross warehouse.[489] In addition, a successful clothing drive in the fall of 1918 once more called upon the charitable services of the Turgon brothers to transport the donations to the American Red Cross Chapter.[490]

The brothers built their business into a three-truck operation but a devastating fire in 1923 resulted in the loss of the three trucks and all equipment in the garage they built.[491] The fire was reported around New York State including Shortsville, Whiteville, Warsaw, Montour Falls, Ovid, and Castile newspapers.

Despite the loss of the garage and equipment, Alfred continued to support his family by driving trucks and working "odd jobs." In 1942 he listed his employer as the Hilton Milling and Warehouse Company.[492] On October 26, 1965, Alfred passed away and was buried in Parma Union Cemetery in Parma, New York.

89242   HES

TURGON,   Frank   (NNV)   White
        (Surname.)   (Christian name.)   (Army serial number.)
Residence: ___57 Sidney Street., Rochester,N.Y._____
              (Street and house number.)   (Town or city.)   (County.)   (State.)
Enlisted } in the United States Marine Corps at __Rochester,N.Y.__ on __4-7-1₺7.
Inducted }   (Place of application.)   (Date of oath.)
Place of birth: __Hamlin,N.Y._____ Date of birth: Nov.1,1883.
Organizations served in, with dates of assignments and transfers 60th co.New York,N.Y;
Portsmouth,N.H.6-6-17,bks.det.bks.det.N.Y.9-18-17;1st Prov.
Brig,Port au Prince,Haiti 9-26-17,jd hdqtrs det.1st brig.*
Grades, with date of appointment: _appointed corporal July 19,1917;_
reduced to private;reappointed corporal 2-15-18;appointed
sergt.1-23-19;reduced to corporal 3-3-19.

Engagements: _____
Four years of previous service._____

Wounds or other injuries received in action: _____
Served overseas from _____ to _____
Exit from service: _April 6,1920,character,excellent.__
Remarks:*constabulary det.10-13-17;jd 53rd co.2-15-18;
jd.bks.det.Norfolk,Va.Quantico,Va. 10-13-18,co."B"jd co.
"C"11th sep.batt.11-6-18;jd 185th co.12-1-18 Charleston,
N. M. C. 311b A&I.   (OVER)   4—5056

Frank Turgon's *New York State Abstracts of World War I Military Service* card. Frank was discharged from the United States Marine Corps in 1913 after four years of service. When the United States declared war on Germany, Frank signed up with the New York Naval Militia and joined the National Naval Volunteers. This latter organization was the forerunner of today's Marine Corps Reserve. He did not complete a draft registration card.

FRANK TURGON
1882 – 1943

Frank had a long, and somewhat interesting relationship with the military, to include the four years he served prior to World War I. On May 7, 1909, Frank Turgon enlisted from the Rochester, New York, Recruiting Station within the Buffalo, New York, District of the United States Marine Corps and was sent to the Marine Barracks of the Navy Yard in New York City. In August of 1909 he received ten extra days duty for a "rusty scabbard at Commanding Officers' inspection"[493] and in October of the same year received "extra duty labor" for reasons unknown. He was sent to the USS *Ohio* in November of 1909 after having been tried in "deck court"[u] for "suffering from effects of intoxicating liquor, while restricted, being unfit for guard mounting."[494] He was found guilty and sentenced to extra police duty for ten days and received a loss of five dollars pay.

He transferred in January 1910 to the USS *Montana* and, during his service aboard the vessel, would incur multiple reprimands, receiving multiple disciplinary actions until the middle of 1911. In his second month aboard the *Montana*, Frank found himself in court, tried and found guilty, for "allowing a prisoner to escape while a sentry over the ship's brig."[495] He was sentenced to twenty days of bread and water, with a full meal every third day, and a thirty dollar fine. Three months after completing his sentence, in July 1910, he is "absent over leave" (takes more days off than approved)[496] earning him extra labor and loss of four liberties. In September 1910 he repeats his antics, but this time the absence cost him sixteen dollars in lost pay.[497]

A somewhat minor infraction in October 1910 awards him three extra duty hours when he is cited for leaving his clothes around the quarters.[498] Getting through the holidays, Frank is once again "absent over leave" in February 1911[499] and is sent to deck court. A few months later, July to be exact, Frank is assigned to detached duty at the Rifle Range in Wakefield, Massachusetts, after transferring into the Marine Barracks in Boston, Massachusetts.[500]

In August 1911, Frank is assigned to Company D of the Marine Barracks in Boston. January of 1912 finds Frank guilty of being "neglect of duty" and must work two extra duty hours.[501] In February, Frank earns a total of four hours extra duty for "inattention to orders" and being "late for reveille."[502] Frank was in the hospital at the end of March and the first two weeks of April 1912. He was awarded a sharpshooter's badge for the 1911 target year after he was discharged from the hospital.[503]

Frank headed south to Key West, Florida, in May 1912 with Company D, 2d Regiment, 1st Provisional Brigade, onboard the USS *Mississippi*; in July he was transferred to Camp Meyer, Guantanamo Bay, Cuba.[504] He headed north to the Naval Magazine in Hingham, Massachusetts, onboard the USS *Celtic*. In August of 1912 he transferred from Company D to Marine Barracks of the Navy Yard, in Boston, Massachusetts,[505] and becomes a fireman in March 1913.[506] Frank is discharged in May of 1913, at the completion of his enlistment, but is retained two extra days to make up for unauthorized absences. His character was listed as "Very Good."[507]

---

[u] Deck Court is a small tribunal presided over by a commanding officer.

MARINES ARE SCATTERED

Rochester Men of Second Company Sent to Various Points.

Members of the Second Marine Company, Third Battalion, New York Naval Militia, mainly Rochesterians, have been transferred from the Fifty-ninth and Sixtieth companies, United States Marine Corps, stationed at the Marine Barracks, New York, as follows:

To Massachusetts—Privates C. B. Gottry, J. E. Begy, H. A. Bellows, M. A. Birmingham, C. E. Bosche, J. H. Brearley, J. H. Brigham, H. R. Brown, G. G. Brown, C. O. Brown, G. W. Brown, E. W. Hoerscher.

To the Third Battalion, Fifth Regiment, U. S. M. C.—Privates M. V. Fishbaugh, E. F. Greenman, Fred Hults, T. H. Imeson.

To ——, N. H.—Privates E. T. Joyes, Hyman Kaplan, W. L. Keefe, Carl Scroggs, P. T. Stahlbrodt, J. R. Keller, E. H. Laugthorn, Lloyd N. Reynolds, L. L. Reynolds, H. T. Marlon, F. A. Mortimer, Jr., A. L. Petty, Jr., J. P. Thompson, Frank Turgon.

All the other members of the Rochester unit of marines are carried on the rolls at the New York barracks, but about forty of them have to go to the rifle range in Maryland, leaving about ten in the barracks.

At the age of thirty-four Frank signs up with the Naval Militia of New York State and was simultaneously enrolled in the Second Marine Company, Third Battalion, National Naval Volunteers, on April 7, 1917; he remained on duty at the company armory in Rochester until May 6th. He reported for duty at Marine Barracks, Navy Yard, in New York City, on May 7, 1917, and was assigned to 60th Company.[508] On June 6, 1917, Frank transferred to Marine Barracks, Navy Yard, Portsmouth, New Hampshire.[509] [left] He was promoted to Corporal at Portsmouth on July 19th.[510] He transferred to the Navy Yard, New York City, on September 18, 1917, for further transportation to Port-au-Prince, Haiti. He sailed by USS *Kittery* from New York City, arriving on October 13, 1917, and was assigned to the Constabulary Detachment in Port-au-Prince.[511] On February 15, 1918, he joined 53d Company, Marine Barracks, Port-au-Prince, qualified as a marksman on the 7th of March, and received his pin on the 18th.[512] On April 8, 1918, he violates a post order and receives a three-week restriction. He returns to the United States on the 20th of July via the USS *Hancock* and joined the Marine Barracks, Navy Yard, Norfolk, Virginia, on August 16, 1918.[513] On the October 13th he transferred, with several others, to Company B, Overseas Depot, at Quantico, Virginia. On November 6, 1918, he joined Company C, 11th Separate Battalion, Marine Base, Quantico, Virginia, and was transferred to 185th Company, 15th Regiment, Marine Base, Quantico, Virginia, on December 1st. Frank was promoted to Sergeant on January 23, 1919, but on March 3rd is reduced from Sergeant to Corporal by order of the Regimental Commander.[514] He spends February 10-16, 1919, at the Navy Yard, Norfolk, Virginia, and on February 17th embarked on the USS *Hancock* for foreign shore service. He disembarked February 26th at San Pedro de Macoris, Dominican Republic; Frank and his unit returned to the Marine Barracks, Navy Yard, Charleston, South Carolina, via USS *Hancock*, on August 15th, 1919.[515] He moved north on September 3, 1919, and joined Company A, 2d Casual Detachment, Marine Barracks, Navy Yard, Philadelphia, Pennsylvania, from 185th Company. Two days later, on September 5th, he transferred to Company C, Navy Yard Guard Post, Philadelphia. On October 1st he moved to Headquarters, Eastern Reserve Division, in Philadelphia, where he remained until he was discharged on April 6, 1920, for the expiration of enrollment; his character was listed as "excellent."[516]

Frank Turgon was born on November 1, 1882, in Hamlin, New York, to Louis Abraham and Sarah M. (Taylor) Turgon. Before entering the service in 1909, Frank worked in Parma, New York, as a farm laborer, a job he returned to when he moved in with his sister in New Haven, New York. After the death of his father in 1926, Frank shared a home with his mother, commuting to his job as a polisher for a button manufacturer. In 1931, he purchased the Hilton Home Restaurant and, with his mother, made a go of serving meals seven days a week; the business closed by 1933.[517]

Frank was a member of the American Legion Hiscock-Fishbaugh Post 788 and in both 1932 and 1942, was a member of the color guard. By 1942, at the time of the World War II draft, Frank was an unemployed resident at the Veterans Hospital in Batavia, New York. Frank passed away on August 1, 1943, and is buried in Parma Union Cemetery in Parma, New York.

Local Restaurant Sold

The Hilton Home Restaurant, which has been conducted for a number of years by Mr. and Mrs. Edw. Hurley, has been purchased by Frank Turgon, and possession was given yesterday.

Mr. Turgon will be assisted in the kitchen by his mother and by Mrs. Wm. Buell, both of whom are considered as excellent cooks.

In addition to transient trade, Mr. Turgon expects to have regular boarders, who can be furnished rooms above the restaurant.

ANNOUNCEMENT

Having purchased Hilton Home Restaurant, I wish to announce that we will be open every day, including Sundays. Patrons will be served during the evening as well as during the day time.

FRANK TURGON

Frank was active in the American Legion during the 1930s, serving as part of the color guard[518] [below] and supporting the Monroe County Convention, held in Hilton, in July 1938.[519] [right]

HILTON

Newly installed commander John L. Crook of Hiscock-Fishbaugh Post, American Legion, has appointed the following officers and members of committees for the year: County committee, A. V. Slaight, Norman Worden, Bert Perry; finance, Merton Thompson, George Clift, A. J. Wadsworth; membership, Herman Worden, Frank Randall, Henry A. Smith; welfare, George Paulson, William Kirk, A. Kirchgessner, Frank Randall; service officer, George Bigger; sergeant-at-arms, Dewey DeHey; color bearers, William Langswager and John Morehouse; color guards, William Pilon and Frank Turgon.—William

1,200 Vets Expected At Hilton

Hilton—Preparations for the entertainment of 1,200 Monroe County American Legion members at their annual convention here Saturday were being rushed today.

George Paulson heads the committee which consists of the following:

George Clift, Herman Worden, William Kirk, Bert Perry, Frank Randall, J. Harlan Cooper, John Crook, Frank Henthorn, Charles Tubb, Albert Mehle, Al Sleight, William Langswager, Clarence Davenport, Dewey de Hey, Henry A. Smith, Charles Merritt, J. H. Cooper, Walter Kinfehn, Frank Turgon, William Lortz and A. G. Kirchgessner.

Form 1 *1813* **REGISTRATION CARD** X 72 No. *441*

Age, in yrs.

1 Name in full *Fred H Turgon*
(Given name) (Family name) *21*

2 Home address *Hilton N.Y.* *N.Y. State*
(No.) (Street) (City) (State)

3 Date of birth *July 26 - 1896*
(Month) (Day) (Year)

4 Are you (1) a natural-born citizen, (2) a naturalized citizen, (3) an alien, (4) or have you declared your
intention (specify which)? *Natural Born Citizen*

5 Where were you born? *Hamlin N.Y.*
(Town) (State) (Nation)

6 If not a citizen, of what country are you a citizen or subject? ....

7 What is your present trade, occupation, or office? *Just Rec. Hon. Disability Disc*

8 By whom employed? *Eastman Kodak Co*
Where employed? *"* *"* *"*

9 Have you a father, mother, wife, child under 12, or a sister or brother under 12, solely dependent on you for
support (specify which)? *Mother + Father - Partly*

10 Married or single (which)? *Single* Race (specify which)? ....

11 What military service have you had? Rank *Militia* branch *1st C. Put*
years *1 yr. 7 mo.* Nation or State *N.Y. State*

12 Do you claim exemption from draft (specify grounds)? *Pronation of the Fut*

I affirm that I have verified above answers and that they are true.

7a *Fred H Turgon*
(Signature or mark)

If person is of African descent, tear off this corner.

FREDERICK HENRY TURGON
1896 – 1965

Fred enlisted in the New York National Guard on June 21, 1916, when he was eighteen years old. He joined Company H, 3d New York Infantry, on July 5, 1916, at the rank of Private. The 3d Infantry served on the Mexican Border from July 15 until September 8, 1916. On October 5, 1916, Fred mustered out at Camp Whitman in Green Haven, New York.[520] [right] Five months later Fred would muster back in with Company H, on April 17, 1917, when the New York National Guard was called up for service in World War I; he was appointed Private First Class on April 24. Fred remained with the unit, re-designated the 108th Infantry, until January 13, 1918, when he was discharged on a

> —Fred Turgon of this village who has been in Texas with the U. S. troops for several months, took cold while at Camp Whitman and on Friday was brought here by auto and has been ill at the home of his parents, Mr. and Mrs. Louis Turgon.

Surgeons Certificate of Disability for pronated feet.

Despite his honorable discharge with a disability, Fred completed and submitted a draft registration card on January 28, 1918. A little over two months later Fred was inducted into the United States Army on April 2, 1918, at Rochester, New York. He was assigned to the 153d Depot Brigade, Camp Dix, New Jersey, where he served until his discharge on March 4, 1919.[521] [left]

Born on July 26, 1896, to Louis Abraham and Sarah M. (Taylor) Turgon in Hamlin, New York, Frederick Henry Turgon was raised in Parma, New

> **RETURNS TO ARMY.**
>
> **Honorably Discharged from Service, Hilton Man Is Accepted in Draft.**
>
> Hilton, March 29.—Fred Turgon, who has an honorable discharge from the army, is again called into service. He enlisted in Rochester and served with the Rochester troops while at the border and was in the service until a few weeks ago, when he was given an honorable discharge because of flat feet.
>
> After arriving home he registered for the draft, passed and will be sent with the next quota from this county.

York. He was working for Eastman Kodak Company before the war, specifically as a film packer, when he joined the New York National Guard in June 1916.

Genevieve T. Sinclair and Fred Turgon were married on January 22, 1920, making Rochester their home before uprooting the family and moving to Los Angeles, California, in 1926. Fred supported his family as a salesman in the retail furniture business and relocated to San Diego, California, in 1934. Fred and his wife purchased half of the Chula Vista Furniture Company in 1945,[522] [right] and became sole owners in 1949.[523] They operated the business until it was sold on June 4th, 1953.[524] [next page]

Chula Vista Furniture Co.
Under New Management

IT IS WITH much pleasure that we announce that we have purchased the Chula Vista Furniture Store and have now taken possession. With this transaction we are mindful of our new responsibilities and wish to assure each and everyone in Chula Vista and the South Bay region that it will be our full aim and intention to bring you the best the market affords in furniture and home appliances.

Our many years of experience with some of the foremost home-outfitters in the area over a period of upwards to twenty years, has enabled us to be abreast with the wishes of the people of this region . . . and that you may be assured we will exert every effort possible to bring you the kind of merchandise you wish and at a price you will care to pay.

We are mindful that we do not have the high overhead expense of some of the larger stores, and hope that we may merit your patronage and support on the basis of quality, modern merchandise at a saving. Our service will be complete with delivery and in addition we stand behind each transaction just as it is represented.

We trust that this store can play an important part in the growth and development of Chula Vista . . . that you will learn to consider this store your headquarters for all home furnishings.

FRED H. TURGON
DR. L. A. SAUSSER

In taking possession we have rearranged the entire stock; thus you will find many items Reduced Far Below Their Invoice Price.

ACROSS FROM CITY HALL

Turgon Now Sole Owner Of Store

Fred H. Turgon announced early this week that he has purchased the interest of Louis M. Barrak in the Chula Vista Furniture Store, 286 Third avenue, and is now sole owner of the Chula Vista business establishment. The consideration was not divulged.

Mr. Barrak, a San Diego resident, had purchased his interest recently from Dr. Lew Sausser, who had been part owner for the last three years.

Mr. Turgon who has served as manager since the start of the business, came to Chula Vista in 1944. A native of Rochester, New York, he settled in Los Angeles in 1927, moving in 1932 to the San Diego area where he went into business at that time.

He will continue active management of the furniture company, assisted by his son, Richard Turgon.

Turgon Sells Furniture Store To San Diego Pair

Fred H. Turgon yesterday announced that he has sold his Chula Vista Furniture to Frank Winicki and Lloyd L. Boles, both of San Diego. Possession is to be given as of this morning. Although the announcement comes as somewhat of a surprise to many, Turgon stated today that he has been negotiating with the buyers for several weeks.

The new owners, both experienced furniture merchants, stated today that they do not contemplate any major changes in the store. They will continue the name of the store with no change in personnel. Boles commented that he and his partner have long been interested in Chula Vista and when this opportunity made it possible for them to buy Chula Vista's oldest furniture store, they couldn't resist.

Turgon stated today that he does not have any plans for the immediate future, other than he and Mrs. Turgon plan to continue to live in Chula Vista.

The Turgons came to Chula Vista eight years ago from San Diego, during which time, they have taken an active part in community life and have a wide acquaintance. He is a past director of chamber of commerce and a member of the Kiwanis (Continued on page 5-A)

FRED H. TURGON
. . . sells business

Fred was very involved in his community in both civic and social roles. He was a member of the Lions Club,[525] Kiwanis Club,[526] and the Masons.[527] He was elected to the board of directors of the San Diego Better Business Bureau[528] and was director of the Chula Vista Chamber of Commerce.[529] He was a charter member of the Chula Vista Mounted Patrol, occupying the positions of secretary and treasurer.[530] Fred passed away on May 18, 1965, and Masonic services were held by Chula Vista Lodge No. 626, Free & Accepted Masons.[531] He was interred at Greenwood Memorial Park in San Diego, California.

Chula Vista Furniture To Present Senior Girls With Gifts

Chula Vista Furniture, as has been the practice for the past several years, will present miniature Lane cedar chests to all girls graduating from Chula Vista high school this year, Dick and Fred Turgon of Chula Vista Furniture, announced today.

The furniture company, thru the cooperation of the Lane cedar chest people, have mailed out cards to all of the graduating girls. Turgon said.

An example of Fred's community focus is found in this May 1952 article from the *Chula Vista Star* (CA). Coordinating with the Lane Company, Fred and his son, Dick, saw to it that miniature cedar chests were presented to all girls graduating from Chula Vista High School.[532]

It Was A Great Party . . .

Yes, it was a great show, the formal opening of KFMB-TV on Monday night from the official throwing of the switch by Mayor Knox to the time the station signed off with the "Three Musketeers".

The response to the public invitation to our Television party was so great that it was necessary that we open our regular sales room and start a second show, with the crowd so large at times that it was impossible for all to get in.

May we suggest that you stop in most any evening at our store, when there is less confusion and really enjoy HOFFMAN TELEVISION at its best . . . or if you wish we will be pleased to make a demonstration in your home, where you can see and hear, realizing the many advantages of what is proclaimed to be the greatest development of all times, TELEVISION.

Sincerely yours,

FRED H. TURGON

Perhaps he was a fortune teller or just the consummate businessman? Fred opened his furniture store showroom when KFMB-TV went on the air for the first time in May 1949 for a "television party."

The event allowed the community to see first-hand, in the comfort of a pseudo living room, the experience of live television to realize "the many advantages of what is proclaimed to be the greatest development of all times, TELEVISION."[533]

Below left, one of the many Christmas ads Chula Vista Furniture Store ran in the local paper.[534] Below, a story about Fred's cross-country motor trip "home" to visit Rochester was big news in Chula Vista.[535]

Turgons Return From 7,000 Mile Trip

Mr. and Mrs. Fred Turgon, 545 Twin Oaks avenue, returned Tuesday from a five weeks, 7000 mile motor trip to their old home town, Rochester, New York. The trip was their first to the east coast in 14 years and although they had a wonderful time, Mr. Turgon stated that Chula Vista looked better than ever to them upon their return.

Form 1   1218   **REGISTRATION CARD** X11166. 91

1 Name in full	*William V Turgon*	Age, in yrs. **24**
	(Given name) (Family name)	

2 Home address *Hilton*   N Y
(No.) (Street) (City) (State)

3 Date of birth *Febuary 22 1893*
(Month) (Day) (Year)

4 Are you (1) a natural-born citizen, (2) a naturalized citizen, (3) an alien, (4) or have you declared your intention (specify which)? *natural Born*

5 Where were you born? *Hamlin N Y USA*
(Town) (State) (Nation)

6 If not a citizen, of what country are you a citizen or subject?

7 What is your present trade, occupation, or office? *30 Section Labor*

8 By whom employed? *Van Hoff*
Where employed? *Hilton*

9 Have you a father, mother, wife, child under 12, or a sister or brother under 12, solely dependent on you for support (specify which)? *none*

10 Married or single (which)? *Single*   Race (specify which)?

11 What military service have you had? Rank _____; branch _____;
years _____; Nation or State _____

12 Do you claim exemption from draft (specify grounds)? _____

I affirm that I have verified above answers and that they are true.

William V Turgon
(Signature or mark)

If person is of African descent, tear off this corner

WILLIAM VERNON TURGON
1893 – 1946

WILLIAM TURGON

William was twenty-five when he was inducted into the United States Army in Rochester, New York, on June 23, 1918, as a Private. He was assigned to 14th Company, Casual Detachment, Spruce Production Division, at the Vancouver Barracks in the state of Washington. He transferred to the 38th Spruce Squadron on July 10, 1918, at the same location. When the armistice was signed the Army moved quickly to demobilize the draftees, consolidating personnel at base camps and depots close to their hometowns. William was sent to Camp Meade, Maryland, and assigned to 2d Company, 1st Training Battalion, 154th Depot Brigade on December 28, 1918; he was discharged on January 11, 1919.

William Vernon Turgon was born on February 22, 1893, to Louis Abraham and Sarah M. (Taylor) Turgon in Hamlin, New York. He returned home to Hilton, New York, after his discharge from military service but moved to Akron, Ohio, to live with his brother and worked as a laborer in a rubber factory.[536] [left, top]

—William Turgon left Tuesday for Akron. Ohio. where he will be employed. His brothers, Fay and Oliver, reside in that city.

William Turgon is again in Hilton and employed at the button factory, after working for some months at Sea Breeze.

By 1925 he returned to Hilton, was living with his parents, and employed as a factory worker, to include the local button factory.[537] [left] William was a member of the American Legion Hiscock-Fishbaugh Post 788. Through the support of fellow Legionnaires, "Bill" was admitted to the Veterans Disabled Home in Bath, New York, on November 25, 1932. He remained at the facility, being treated for multiple health issues, until 1935 and occasionally returned home to Hilton in the summer months.[538] [below]

William was an elevator operator at the Hotel Hayward in downtown Rochester when he had an accident on November 13th, 1946. During his evening shift, he fell twenty-five feet down an elevator shaft and was killed. The story was carried in several newspapers across Western New York.[539] [below]

William is buried in Parma Union Cemetery in Parma, New York. His primary mission during the war, being in an aero squadron supporting the spruce production effort, is not mentioned on the headstone and reflects only the name of the depot brigade where he was discharged.

Plunges to Death

Rochester—(*P*)—William Vernon Turgon, 54, an elevator operator, was killed last night when he fell 25 feet down the shaft of a stalled elevator in a downtown hotel.

Hilton Veteran Admitted to Veterans' Home

William Turgon is now happily and comfortably located in the Veterans' Home at Bath, N. Y. He was taken there last Friday by John Crook, Commander, and Frank Randall, member of the Welfare Committee, of Hiscock-Fishbaugh Post, American Legion.

Unable to do much work on account of his physical condition, he had been assisted by the Legion Post and had been sleeping in the Post's room in the Village Building for some time. Through the assistance of George Clancy of Rochester, who has been active in Veterans' Relief Work for several years, the Legionnaires were able to procure a place for him in the home, where he will be well cared for.

The men were delighted upon reaching their destination to be greeted in the office by a former townsman, Walton Hovey, who holds the position of Secretary to the Adjutant at the Veterans' Home by Civil Service appointment. Mr. Hovey, who was a First Lieutenant in the U. S. Medical Corps during the war, cooperated in getting "Bill" admitted.

Form 1	**REGISTRATION CARD**	X 156	No. 2

1. Name in full _Arthur James Wadsworth_ — Age, in yrs. 29
   (Given name) (Family name)

2. Home address _Hilton_ _N.Y._
   (No.) (Street) (City) (State)

3. Date of birth _Nov_ _30_ _1887_
   (Month) (Day) (Year)

4. Are you (1) a natural-born citizen, (2) a naturalized citizen, (3) an alien, (4) or have you declared your intention (specify which)? _Natural Born_

5. Where were you born? _Hamlin_ _N.Y._ _U.S.A._
   (Town) (State) (Nation)

6. If not a citizen, of what country are you a citizen or subject?

7. What is your present trade, occupation, or office? _Farm Laborer_

8. By whom employed? _Eroy Anderson_
   Where employed? _Hill Road_

9. Have you a father, mother, wife, child under 12, or a sister or brother under 12, solely dependent on you for support (specify which)? _No_

10. Married or single (which)? _Married_ Race (specify which)? _Caucasian_

11. What military service have you had? Rank _Corporal_; branch _Coast Art_; years _3_; Nation or State _U.S.A._

12. Do you claim exemption from draft (specify grounds)? _No_

I affirm that I have verified above answers and that they are true.

Arthur James Wadsworth
(Signature or mark)

156 2

If person is of African descent, tear off this corner

ARTHUR JAMES WADSWORTH
1887 – 1935

Arthur was thirty when inducted into the United States Army on April 2, 1918, from Rochester, New York. He was sent to Camp Dix, New Jersey, and assigned to Company 11, 3d Training Battalion, 153d Depot Brigade. He transferred to Company B, 310th Infantry, 78th Division, at Camp Dix on April 25, 1918, promoted to Private First Class on May 1, 1918, then to Corporal on May 13, 1918. He sailed with Company B from New York City on May 19, 1918, aboard the HMAT *Beltana*, and arrived in Bordeaux, France. He was promoted to Sergeant on June 16, 1918. Records indicate he was assigned to prisoner escort duty with Prisoner of War Escort (P.W.E.) Company 69 on September 9, 1918, which is curious since the 78th Division remained in reserve until September 15, 1918. Further confusing matters, Arthur's 1935 obituary in the *Hilton (NY) Record* referred to him being "gassed during action," but no further details are provided. On December 11, 1918, he was assigned to Bordeaux Casual Company No. 1, and returned to the United States aboard the USS *Matsonia*, which arrived in Hoboken, New Jersey, on January 3, 1919. He was sent to Camp Meade, Maryland, and assigned to 3d Company, Convalescent Center, until his honorable discharge on January 21, 1919.

Arthur James Wadsworth was born on November 30, 1887, in Hamlin, New York, to Jasper and Rose (Patnode) Wadsworth. By 1893, Arthur's father had moved the family to Rochester. In 1905, at the age of nineteen, Arthur was employed as a tinsmith. Arthur and Mary L. Goodman exchanged vows in Rochester on January 1, 1907. His whereabouts until 1915 are unknown, but by then he is living in Parma, New York, with his brother on Hill Road, employed as a farm laborer.

"After being employed several years in the hardware store of Joseph Ingham, he opened a store and engaged in the hardware business in 1928, giving employment to several men during succeeding years."[540] The A.J. Wadsworth Hardware Store[541] was located in the "Wright block next to the IGA Store."[542]

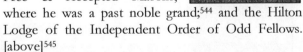

Window Display Uurges Legion Membership

Have you noticed the attractive display in a window of the A. J. Wadsworth hardware store?

Designed to help in the membership drive of Hiscock-Fishbaugh Post, American Legion, it appropriately appeared first on Armistice Day. In the center, rifles are stacked, flanked by the Legion standard and a membership cup which was won sometime ago by the local Post. At the back are drapes of red, white and blue crepe paper. An attractive placard urges ex-service men to join the American Legion. Mr. Wadsworth is a member of the local Post.

Hiscock-Fishbaugh Post has a membership quota of forty. As there were thirty-five members last year and one death during the year, the Post must retain all of the old members and gain six new ones. Three of these have been gained. They are Otto Johnson, T. J. Muntz and Lucius Bagley. John Crook is chairman of the membership committee.

His marriage to Mary ended in divorce on November 25, 1929. Arthur married Emma E. Newkirk on May 5, 1931, and the couple made their home in Hilton. Arthur was a member of the American Legion Hiscock-Fishbaugh Post 788 [left];[543] a member of Clio Lodge No. 779, Free & Accepted Masons, where he was a past noble grand;[544] and the Hilton Lodge of the Independent Order of Odd Fellows. [above][545]

He was a member of the Hilton Chamber of Commerce and both an exempt and honorary member of the Hilton Fire Department. Arthur passed away suddenly on March 24, 1935, in Hilton. He is buried in Parma Union Cemetery in Parma, New York.

Form 1   REGISTRATION CARD   No.

1 Name in full _Elmer Samuel Wadsworth_   Age, in yrs. **23**
(Given name)   (Family name)

2 Home
   Address _____ _Hilton_ _N.Y._
   (No.)   (Street)   (City)   (State)

3 Date of birth _March_ 7 _5 4_
   (Month)   (Day)   (Year)

4 Are you (1) a natural-born citizen, (2) a naturalized citizen, (3) an alien, (4) or have you declared your
   intention (specify which)? _Natural-born_

5 Where were
   you born? _Parma_ _New York_ _U.S.A._
   (Town)   (State)   (Nation)

6 If not a citizen, of what country are you a citizen or subject?

7 What is your present
   trade, occupation, or office? _Farm Laborer_

8 By whom employed? _William Roberts_
   Where employed? _Hilton_ _N.Y._

9 Have you a father, mother, wife, child under 12, or a sister or brother under 12, solely dependent on you for
   support (specify which)? _No._

10 Married or single (which)? _Single_ Race (specify which)? _Canadian_

11 What military service have you had? Rank _____
   years _____ ; Nation or State _____

12 Do you claim exemption
   from draft (specify grounds)? _No._

   I affirm that I have verified above answers and that they are true.

   59 C   _Elmer Samuel Wadsworth_
                        (Signature or mark)

ELMER SAMUEL WADSWORTH
1894 – 1978

Elmer was inducted into the United States Army at Spencerport, New York, on the 22nd of November 1917, as a twenty-three-year-old Private. He was assigned to Company 18, 153d Depot Brigade, at Camp Dix, New Jersey, through December 14, 1917. At that time, he joined Machine Gun Company, 7th Infantry, 3d Division, as it organized, trained, and prepared for deployment overseas at Camp Greene, North Carolina. Beginning his overseas tour of duty on the 6th of April 1918, Elmer embarked in Hoboken, New Jersey, aboard the SS *America*. Elmer was slightly wounded October 29, 1918, but remained overseas and was re-assigned to 337th Infantry, 85th Division, on February 8, 1919–the 85th functioned as a regional replacement depot for Second Army. He returned from his overseas assignment with a detachment of the 337th Infantry on March 26, 1919, leaving Brest, France, aboard the USS *Leviathan* and arriving Hoboken, New Jersey, on April 2, 1919. Returning to Camp Upton, New York, on April 17, 1919, he received his discharge the same day.

Elmer Samuel Wadsworth was born to parents Samuel Wadsworth and Emma Turney in Parma, New York, on March 7, 1894. His 1894 birth year is recorded on the United States Department of Veterans Affairs Beneficiary Identification Records Locator,[546] his headstone,[547] and his World War I draft registration card.[548] However, the registry of marriages recorded in New York State county clerk records[549] and Elmer's own handwriting on his World War II draft registration card[550] (which he signed), show 1896.

While serving in France his family moved to Boylston, New York, and he joined them at their dairy farm when he returned. He married Vada B. Coffey on April 30, 1921, in Oswego County, New York. Census data indicates that Elmer supported his family as a foreman working on county roads and, for a brief period, he worked in a lumber mill. Elmer and his family lived in the towns of Williamstown, Richland, and Fernwood, New York.

Elmer was a charter member of the American Legion Williamstown Post and served as its vice commander[551] and sergeant-at-arms.[552] He passed away on November 26, 1978, and is buried in Evergreen Cemetery in Orwell, Oswego County, New York.

CALL FIRST DISTRICT MEN

Ten Will Be Sent to Camp Dix to Fill Vacancies.

Spencerport, Oct. 29.—Ten men from the first county district of Monroe county will leave Spencerport for Camp Dix, Wednesday morning. Dr. C. S. Woolston, Supervisor O. B. Wood and Chauncey Brainard, of the Fellowship League, are making arrangements for the farewell.

These men are to fill out the second quota sent from this district. The vacancies were caused by five men failing to appear after having been summoned, and five having been rejected after arriving at Camp Dix. The men ordered to report Wednesday are: Clifford Wass, Clarkson; Elmer Samuel Wadsworth, Hilton; Charles M. Heiser, Walker; Irving Henry Ford, Chili; John D. McDonald, Greece; Frank Lambe, Chili Station; Everett Guy Shores, Greece; Lee Worden, Chili; Michael J. Daly, Greece; Macarius V. Kelly, Greece. Alternates, Edward Volkmer, Barnard; Martin Carl Langschwager, Hamlin; Charles John Blowers, Chili Station; Raymond John Quinlin, Greece; George Lehme Murray, Hamlin.

Williamstown Honors 134 Servicemen

When a monument was erected in Williamstown this spring to honor the town's service men and women, it had the names of 134 persons on its roster.

Names listed under World War I are: Lewis Bray, Charles Burns, Stanley Cox, Anthony Edick, Owen Finnerty, Harry Grant, Sergeant Hall (both World War I and II), John Hastings, Leo Healy Sr., Foster Kaine, George McCullagh, Glenn Spink, Addison Stearns, Ernest Sweatland, Elmer Wadsworth Sr.

Form 1   1985   REGISTRATION CARD 27651 No. _150_

1. Name in full _F Lester Welch_   Age, in yrs. _24_
(Given name)   (Family name)

2. Home address _137_ _Ontario_ _Rochester_ _NY_
(No.)   (Street)   (City)   (State)

3. Date of birth _Nov_   _6_   _1893_
(Month)   (Day)   (Year)

4. Are you (1) a natural-born citizen, (2) a naturalized citizen, (3) an alien, (4) or have you declared your intention (specify which)? _Natural born_

5. Where were you born? _Greece_ _NY_ _USA_
(Town)   (State)   (Nation)

6. If not a citizen, of what country are you a citizen or subject? _USA_

7. What is your present trade, occupation, or office? _Expressman 25_

8. By whom employed? _Am Express C_
Where employed? _____

9. Have you a father, mother, wife, child under 12, or a sister or brother under 12, solely dependent on you for support (specify which)? _Wife & Mother_

10. Married or single (which)? _Married_   Race (specify which) _Caucasian_

11. What military service have you had? Rank _None_   branch _____
years _____   Nation or State _____

12. Do you claim exemption from draft (specify grounds)? _Dependent_

I affirm that I have verified above answers and that they are true.

F Lester Welch
(signature or mark)

If person is of African descent, tear off this corner.

270

FRANCIS LESTER WELCH
1893 – 1982

Francis Lester Welch enrolled in the United States Naval Reserve Force from the Recruiting Station in Buffalo, New York, on June 11, 1918, at age twenty-four and was assigned to Great Lakes Training Station, Illinois. He transferred to the Training Station in Hampton Roads, Virginia, on August 13, 1918, remaining there until placed on inactive duty January 13, 1919. During his service he was promoted from Seaman Second Class to Seaman.

Francis Lester Welch, or Jack as he was known, was born to John L. and Luella (Breeze) Welch in Greece, New York, on November 6, 1893. Growing up in Parma, New York, Lester worked on the family farm. Before the war, he became a resident of Spencerport, New York, and was active in the local Ogden, New York, community through his membership in the Ogden Grange. He helped plan the town's Fourth of July celebration in the village of Spencerport and participated in activities of the Congregational Church.

Clara A. Winslow and Jack were married in her family's Spencerport home on June 2, 1917, and the couple made their first home in Rochester, New York. Over the years Lester supported his family through skilled jobs—construction mason,[553] auto mechanic, and as a mechanic with the Standard Brewing Company in Rochester. He retired as a custodian for the Spencerport Central School District in 1967.[554] [below]

Lester was a charter member of the Tenth Ward Garrison of the Army and Navy Union;[v] he served as "paymaster" for the organization.[555] [left] Francis Lester Welch passed away on August 28, 1982, and is interred in Parma Corners Cemetery in Parma, New York.

Charter Application Made for Garrison In 10th Ward

First step in the creation of a new unit in the Army and Navy Union was taken last week when the charter application of the 10th Ward Garrison was made by W. Earl Smith and Alvin Pfahl, provisional commander and vicecommander, respectively, appointed by County Commander Marine DeLee.

According to Smith, Rochester attorney and major in the United States Army Reserves, it is intended that the new unit shall be composed of former service men "who have the services of the United States first at heart." Although the new unit bears a geographical name, it nevertheless is intended to take in a larger area than just the 10th Ward.

Former service men who have submitted their applications for membership to date comprise several peacetime as well as wartime men. Taken from the Army, Navy, Marine Corps and National Guard, those who have signed and who will be regarded as charter members along with others who are expected to sign before the charter is sent in are Robert B. Shaw, Darwin B. Sherman, William C. Taylor, Fred Dutcher, Joseph Guzzetta, Austin W. Smith, Ralph Geer, Jacob Gerling, James D. Wood, Lester Welch, James P. Magee, William A. Tracy and Felix Rogowitz.

MR. AND MRS. F. LESTER
Welch, of 2324 West Side Drive, Ogden, formerly of 25 Mayflower St., celebrated their 50th wedding anniversary last Friday. A family dinner is planned for the couple today in their daughter's home at the West Side Drive address. Welch worked for many years for the old Standard Brewing Co. and recently retired as a custodian from the Spencerport Central School District.

---

v The Army and Navy Union is a federally chartered organization founded in 1886; their fundamental objective is to "continue National Defense and National Security." https://sites.google.com/site/armynavyunionusa/home

Form 1 **1552** REGISTRATION CARD 2852 No. 5

1 Name in full Wells (Lyndon Hawkins) 24
   (Christian) (Family) yr. to yr.

2 Home address 166 No Goodman Rochester N.Y.
   (No.) (Street) (City) (State)

3 Date of birth Sept 9 1892
   (Month) (Day) (Year)

4 Are you (1) a natural-born citizen, (2) a naturalized citizen, (3) an alien, (4) or have you declared your
   intention (specify which)? Natural Born

5 Where were you born? Estherville Iowa USA
   (Town) (State) (Nation)

6 If not a citizen, of what country are you a citizen or subject?

7 What is your present trade, occupation, or office? Yawman & Erbe Nyr. [?]

8 By whom employed? Yawman & Erbe
   Where employed? 424 St Paul St.

9 Have you a father, mother, wife, child under 12, or a sister or brother under 12, solely dependent on you for
   support (specify which)? Mother

10 Married or single (which)? Single Race (specify which)? Caucasian

11 What military service have you had? Rank No ; branch
    years ; Nation or State

12 Do you claim exemption from draft (specify grounds)? Support of Mother

I affirm that I have verified above answers and that they are true.

Lyndon H. Wells.
(Signature or mark)

If person is of African descent, tear off this corner.

LYNDON HAWKINS WELLS
1892 – 1968

Private First Class Lyndon entered the Enlisted Reserve Corps at the age of twenty-four in Ithaca, New York, on December 7, 1917. He was assigned to the School of Military Aeronautics at Cornell University (Ithaca, NY) for ground training until April 12, 1918. His ground training complete, Lyndon transferred to Camp John Dick in Dallas, Texas, where aviation cadets were sent while they awaited assignment to an aviation training field–Lyndon's assigned field unknown. Lyndon transferred to Garden City on Long Island, New York, on July 18, 1918–another holding camp–and was discharged on July 30, 1918, to accept a commission as a Second Lieutenant in the Air Service, United States Army. He was sent to Camp Dix in Wrightstown, New Jersey, in preparation for overseas movement.

Second Lieutenant Wells left from Hoboken, New Jersey, aboard the SS *President Grant* for his overseas assignment on August 22, 1918; his unit listed as "Fighting Observers" on the ship's manifest. He participated in the Meuse-Argonne campaign while in France. He returned home on February 8, 1919, from Brest, France, aboard the SS *Northland*, and arrived in Philadelphia, Pennsylvania, on February 21, 1919; he was discharged five days later on February 24, 1919.

Born in Estherville, Iowa, to Howell Franklin and Ellen (Hawkins) Wells on September 9, 1892, Lyndon Hawkins Wells moved to Rochester, New York, with his mother and siblings after the death of his father in 1908. Lyndon graduated from East High School in 1914 and was registered to attend Cornell University that fall. After he returned from the war, Lyndon settled in Parma, New York, with his brothers and mother and worked on their fruit farm, called the Elmwood Fruit Farm.[556] Lyndon and Rochester-native Margaret Deland Hubbell traveled to San Francisco, California, to exchange marriage vows on October 31, 1921.

LYNDON H. WELLS announces the opening of the GULF FLOUR MILL for all kinds of feed grinding--including "Cob and All." You can now be supplied with the following HIGH GRADE Clover Leaf Feeds--Sweet 16 Dairy feeds, Advanced Registry Dairy Feed, Scratch Grains, Developing Feed, Growing Mash (with buttermilk), Egg Mash (with buttermilk), Gulf Meal, Extra Fancy Cracked Corn, Recleaned Yellow Corn.

Clover Leaf Feeds cost more to buy because they cost more to make, but adding a few dollars to price MULTIPLIES RESULTS. Remember the cheap suit and the first rain? Same logic here.

GULF FLOUR MILL On the Ridge Road at Salmon Creek.
Service with us is a condition—not a name

In 1922, Lyndon purchased a flour mill in Parma, once known as the Gulf Milling Company.[557] [left][558] Annexing the surrounding farm, he relocated his family to the property and called his home "Gulf Mills Farms."[559] The mill supplied flour and feed to nearby towns but in 1925, after a significant renovation, a fire destroyed the building and business.[560]

By 1927, Lyndon and his family moved to Rochester where he was president and treasurer of Lyndon H. Wells, Inc., a manufacturer of platform and warehouse trucks.[561] [below]

Lyndon and his wife were active participants of the Tenth Twig, one of several "branches" of a fundraising organization affiliated with Rochester General Hospital, which provided financial support for the institution.

He was a member of Third Presbyterian Church, Genesee Valley Club, and Rochester Country Club.[562] Lyndon passed away on June 7, 1968, in Rochester and was interred on June 14, 1968, in Mount Hope Cemetery in Rochester, New York.

Lyndon H. Wells Incorporated 100-108 PLATT STREET Manufacturer of INDUSTRIAL TRUCKS

Form 1   **REGISTRATION CARD**   No. **27**

1. Name in full _Chester Burritt Williams_ | Age, in yrs. **26**
   (Given name)   (Family name)

2. Home address _Hilton_ _N.Y._
   (No.) (Street) (City) (State)

3. Date of birth _July_ _30_ _1891_
   (Month) (Day) (Year)

4. Are you (1) a natural-born citizen, (2) a naturalized citizen, (3) an alien, (4) or have you declared your intention (specify which)? _Natural born citizen_

5. Where were you born? _Parma_ _N.Y._ _U.S.A._
   (Town) (State) (Nation)

6. If not a citizen, of what country are you a citizen or subject?

7. What is your present trade, occupation, or office? _Farmer_

8. By whom employed? _Self_
   Where employed? _Town of Parma_

9. Have you a father, mother, wife, child under 12, or a sister or brother under 12, solely dependent on you for support (specify which)? _No_

10. Married or single (which)? _Single_ Race (specify which)? _Caucasian_

11. What military service have you had? Rank _none_; branch _____ years _____; Nation or State _____

12. Do you claim exemption from draft (specify grounds)? _Yes_

I affirm that I have verified above answers and that they are true.

Chester Burritt Williams
(Signature or mark)

If person is of African descent, tear off this corner

CHESTER BURRITT WILLIAMS
1891 – 1979

Enlisting in the United States Navy at the Recruiting Station in Buffalo, New York, on December 15, 1917, twenty-six-year-old Chester began his service and initial training at Naval Air Station Bay Shore, Long Island, New York. As a Landsman Quartermaster, he transferred to Norfolk Naval Air Station in Norfolk, Virginia, on February 8, 1918. He remained at Norfolk for almost three months, earning his Quartermaster Second Class Aviation rating. He returned to New York on April 25, 1918, stationed at Naval Air Station, Rockaway, New York, until his discharge on December 7, 1918.

Chester was born in Hilton, New York, to William Wilbur and Loretta (Burritt) Williams on July 30, 1891. He attended Brockport Normal School and Peekskill Military Academy, graduating from the latter in 1911.[563] Chester attended Cornell University and took summer classes between 1909 and 1911; he completed a non-degree, special course in agriculture.[564]

In May 1913, Chester offered a complete farm in Orleans County, New York, for sale through an advertisement in the *Hilton (NY) Record*.[565] [right] Chester married Lillian Madeline Simpson of Peekskill, New York, on October 20, 1913; they made their home on South Avenue in Hilton. The couple later divorced in Rochester on July 31, 1916.[566]

For SALE—Farm in fruit belt of Orleans Co. 110 acres: 6 acres bearing apple orchard, 10 of mixed apple and peach 6 years old. Good 10 room house with woodshed. Grain and stable 40x40, stock barn 30x80, shed 24x50, hen house 16x30. Soil about half clay loam, balance sandy loam with some black loam. Well fenced, within one mile of station, and two of two good markets, several schools, churches and high school. Will offer for a few days at $100 per acre and on easy terms.
CHESTER B. WILLIAMS,
Hilton, N. Y.

After his discharge in 1918, Chester lived in New York City and found work as a salesman for a shipping tag company. By 1922 he had returned to Hilton and on February 26, 1928, Chester married Dorothy Rogers Hickey in Niagara Falls, New York, listing his residence on his marriage license as the "Richford Hotel when in Rochester, New York." Chester worked as a commercial traveling salesman for a wholesale tobacco company while in Rochester. In late 1940 he joined the Curtiss Airplane Division of the Curtiss-Wright Corporation in Buffalo, spending eight months in London for the company in 1942.[567] [below] Chester passed away on July 25, 1979, and is buried in Holy Sepulchre Cemetery in Rochester, New York.

—Chester Williams who has been a traveling salesman for the Dennison Bros. of New York, for several months past, sailed last Monday on a six months' trip for Havana, and South America and he is to have six weeks vacation during that time for pleasure.

Chester Williams of Rochester, son of Mrs. W. W. Williams, who has been employed at the Rochester Municipal Airport, began work this week for the Curtis-Wright Airplane Company in Buffalo.

Chester was an international traveling salesman as shown in these *Hilton (NY) Record* clips from January 1920 [above],[568] October 1940 [above right],[569] and 1942 [right].[570]

Chester B. Williams, who has been in London for the past eight months, representing Curtis-Wright Airplane Corporation, returned last week to his home in Rochester.

	REGISTRATION CARD	690 12 No.
Form 1		Age, in yrs. 23

1 Name in full *Willis Winters*
    (Given name)   (Family name)

2 Home address   *Kenysville, Tenn.*
    (No.)   (Street)   (City)   (State)

3 Date of birth *December 6. 597*
    (Month)   (Day)   (Year)

4 Are you (1) a natural-born citizen, (2) a naturalized citizen, (3) an alien, (4) or have you declared your intention (specify which)? *Natural born*

5 Where were you born? *Kenysville*   *Tennessee*   *U.S.A.*
    (Town)   (State)   (Nation)

6 If not a citizen, of what country are you a citizen or subject?

7 What is your present trade, occupation, or office? *Farm Laborer.*

8 By whom employed? *Otto Hafner*
    Where employed? *Hilton Pt Parma N.Y.*

9 Have you a father, mother, wife, child under 12, or a sister or brother under 12, solely dependent on you for support (specify which)? *No*

10 Married or single (which)? *Single*   Race (specify which)? *Caucasian*

11 What military service have you had? Rank *None*; branch
    years   ; Nation or State

12 Do you claim exemption from draft (specify grounds)? *No*

I affirm that I have verified above answers and that they are true.

Willis Winters
(Signature or mark)

If person is of African descent, tear off this corner

276

WILLIS WINTERS
1894 – 1930

Willis, twenty-two, was inducted into the United States Army at Spencerport, New York, on October 31, 1917. He was sent to Camp Dix, New Jersey, and was assigned to Battery D, 309th Field Artillery, 78th Division. Promoted to Private First Class on May 21, 1918, Willis started his overseas service when he left on May 28, 1918, from Boston, Massachusetts, aboard the vessel SS *Arawa*. His service in France unclear, he was either gassed, wounded in the chest, or became sick (pneumonia) in France as he does not return to the United States with Battery D or the 78th Division. Willis embarked from Saint-Nazaire, France, on May 6, 1919, aboard the USS *Powhatan* with Convalescent Detachment No. 190. The ship's manifest lists him in the class of "walking cases requiring dressings," with a Major from the Medical Corp in charge of his detachment. He was diagnosed with "empyema"–a thickening of the chest cavity due to a bacterial infection as a result of chest trauma. The ship arrived in Newport News, Virginia, on May 20, 1919. Willis was discharged on June 4, 1919, reported by the *Hilton (NY) Record* to have been wounded twice during the war. [571]

Willis Winters was born on December 6, 1894, to Thomas and Minnie (Gosse) Winters in Henryville, Tennessee. He moved to Hamlin, New York, by 1915

> **Willis Winters who has been on a visit to Tennesee is back to Otto Hafner's.**

and found work as a servant for the LaDue family. Willis, known in the community as "Preacher," was working for Otto Hafner of Parma, New York, at the time of the draft registration. [572]

> **TWILIGHT LEAGUE ORGANIZED**
>
> So much interest has been manifest in the baseball games played evenings at Firemen's Park, using an indoor ball, that on Monday evening managers of six teams met and organized a league. The following officers were elected: President, Frank Pickett; 1st vice-president, Dale Clapper; 2nd vice-president, Fred Jenneiahn.
>
> The teams composing the league are: Hilton Service Co., Lutherans, Firemen, American Legion, Cardinals and Suburbanites. A game is scheduled for tonight between the Firemen and Lutherans, and it is planned to play each evening, weather permitting, beginning Monday. Games scheduled so far for next week are: Monday, Service vs. Firemen; Tuesday, Legion vs. Lutherans; Wednesday, Suburbanites vs. Cardinals. Loyd Burritt has consented to be the target for the pop bottles; in other words, he will umpire the games.
>
> Tentative squads of the teams composing the league are as follows:
>
> Hilton Service Co.—G. Huff, mgr.; C. MacDougal, Homer Harmer, Earl Hubble, R. Heffron, B. Hugaboom, W. Pfarrer, C. Skinner, Avery LaDue, Willis Winters, F. Huff, W. Hugaboom, Maurice Lee, Bert Cox, W. Heffron.

Finding work as a painter, Willis moved to New Philadelphia, Ohio, where he met his future wife, Mildred Evelyn Boyer, of Dover, Ohio. [573] The couple married on October 15, 1923, in Monroe County, Michigan. Returning to Hamlin, Willis supported his family as a laborer working "odd jobs." [574]

Willis died on July 9, 1930, at Brockport Hospital (NY) following surgery for appendicitis and peritonitis; [575] he is buried in Parma Union Cemetery in Parma, New York.

Six days before his death, the *Hilton (NY) Record* reported on a new twilight baseball league formed in the village. Willis is listed as a member of the Hilton Service Company team with other Hilton-Parma residents. [576]

REGISTRATION CARD

Form 1

1. Name in full _Herman Worden_   Age, in yrs. 25
   (Given name) (Family name)

2. Home address _14 Litton_ _N.Y._
   (No.) (Street) (City) (State)

3. Date of birth _Apr._ _4_ _1892_
   (Month) (Day) (Year)

4. Are you (1) a natural-born citizen, (2) a naturalized citizen, (3) an alien, (4) or have you declared your intention (specify which)? _Natural-born_

5. Where were you born? _Greece_, _N.Y._ _America_
   (Town) (State) (Nation)

6. If not a citizen, of what country are you a citizen or subject?

7. What is your present trade, occupation, or office? _Produce_ 30

8. By whom employed? _Mrs. D. L. Morgan_
   Where employed? _Brockport, N.Y._

9. Have you a father, mother, wife, child under 12, or a sister or brother under 12, solely dependent on you for support (specify which)? _No_

10. Married or single (which)? _Single_ Race (specify which)? _Caucasian_

11. What military service have you had? Rank _None_; branch _____;
    years _____; Nation or State _____

12. Do you claim exemption from draft (specify grounds)? _No_

I affirm that I have verified above answers and that they are true.

Herman Worden

(Signature or mark)

HERMAN GARDNER WORDEN
1892 – 1969

At twenty-five-years-old, Herman was inducted into the United States Army on March 4, 1918, at Rochester, New York, and assigned to Headquarters, Casual Detachment, Vancouver Barracks, in Vancouver, Washington. On March 22, 1918, he was assigned to 3d Casual Riving[w] Company, transferring on April 9, 1918, to the 16th Provisional Squadron–renamed the 82d Spruce Squadron in July 1918. He remained with this unit until honorably discharged on January 28, 1919. [right][577]

Herman Gardner Worden was born on April 4, 1892, in Greece, New York, to Lewis C. and Emma S. (Mosley) Worden. His family moved to Curtis Road in Parma, New York, and Herman worked as a farm laborer and painter.

Mabel Harriett Perry and Herman exchanged marriage vows on February 28, 1918, and made their home in Hilton, New York. Herman earned a living as foreman for the cold storage division of the Hilton Milling and Warehouse Company.[578] He promoted to manager and secretary, [579] [right] then vice-president and general manager, of the company,[580] located on Upton Street in Hilton. Herman retired in 1961 after forty-six years with the company.[581]

Herman was a member of the Republican Party of Parma for thirty years[582] and elected town supervisor, serving consecutively from 1946 until 1958.[583] During his tenure as supervisor, Herman served on multiple committees in Monroe County, including the Highway committee, Public Health and Sanitation committee,[584] and Public Works and Planning Committee.[585]

Herman was a charter member of the American Legion Hiscock-Fishbaugh Post 788,[586] a member of Clio Lodge No. 779, Free & Accepted Masons,[587] and a member of Hilton Baptist Church. Herman passed away on January 18, 1969, while spending the winter in Saint Petersburg, Florida; he was buried in Parma Union Cemetery in Parma, New York.

Officer Promoted By Hilton Company

HERMAN WORDEN

Hilton, June 7—Herman Worden has been made manager and secretary of the Hilton Milling & Warehouse Company. He takes the position of John Way, resigned. Mr. Worden, a veteran of the World War, has been in charge of the cold storage division of the company for the past 14 years.

Officers elected at the annual meeting were: President, M. G. Newcomb of Springfield, Mass.; vicepresident, Chester Fraser, and treasurer, Mrs. A. B. Fraser. Besides the officers, the members of the board are William V. Newcomb, John Way and Howard Crumb.

When the 43-member Board of Supervisors convenes, there'll be 11 newly elected officials sitting for the first time in the Courthouse board room. They include Republicans Carlyle B. Newcomb, 4th Ward, who replaces Clifford H. Tarrant who resigned; Arthur J. Muoio, 16th Ward, succeeding James G. D'Amico who also resigned; John L. Crook, Parma, succeeding retired Herman G. Worden;

At left, an article from December 1957 highlighted three men from the *Honor Roll* and their service on the Monroe County (NY) Board of Supervisors.[588] At right, a United States Forestry Service archival photo showing spruce riving in World War I.[589]

---

[w] Riving is splitting wood in the direction of its long fibers and was done in the field to save time during the war.

NOTES
Chapter 2–Honor Roll

A significant part of the research for these biographies was done through newspaper articles, columns, and advertisements. Archive copies were accessed using online, digitized repositories, some requiring a subscription to access the pages. Deviating slightly from the Chicago Manual of Style, citations from the *Greece Press*, *Hilton Record*, Rochester *Democrat and Chronicle*, Rochester *Times-Union*, and the *Suburban News* list the page number of the cited material instead of the headline, column name or author's name. In some instances, the page number presented in the online result was not the same as the page number in the original printed newspaper. When this occurred, both pages numbers are provided in the notes below. The original published page number is listed first, the online repository is second in parenthesis. If only one page number is shown, the published page number matched the online search page number.

1. *Democrat and Chronicle*, October 3, 1918, 18.

2. *Hilton Record*, August 1, 1918, 1.

3. Joseph P. Roth and Robert L. Wheeler, *History of Company "E" 303rd Engineers of the 78th Division 1917-1919*, (Rochester, NY: John P. Smith printing company,1919), 204.

4. Hilton Central, *Hiltonian*, 1.

5. *Democrat and Chronicle*, June 17, 1920, 25.

6. Ancestry.com, *New York, Passenger Lists, 1820-1957*, Year: 1924; Arrival: New York, New York; Microfilm Serial: T715, 1897-1957; Microfilm Roll: Roll 3580; Line: 21; Page Number: 139

7. *Democrat and Chronicle*, August 3, 1935, 10.

8. *Hilton Record*, December 3, 1964, 1.

9. *Greece Press*, September 25, 1942, 1.

10. Village of Hilton Historian, World War I Photograph Collection.

11. *Greece Press*, May 21, 1943, 3.

12. *Democrat and Chronicle*, August 26, 1918, 7; *Democrat and Chronicle*, September 25, 1934, 23.

13. Burial Case Files, Clarence S. Baxter, Box 294.

14. Burial Case Files, Clarence S. Baxter, Box 294.

15. Burial Case Files, Clarence S. Baxter, Box 294.

16. Burial Case Files, Clarence S. Baxter, Box 294.

17. *Democrat and Chronicle*, April 26, 1922, 18.

18. *New York State Abstracts of World War I Military Service*, Name Range: Benk-Benson, C (Box 39).

19. "Lyndonville News," *Daily Register* (Medina, NY), April 30, 1913, 2. http://nyshistoricnewspapers.org/

20. *Democrat and Chronicle*, October 12, 1922, 5; *Democrat and Chronicle*, March 31, 1927, 23; *Democrat and Chronicle*, November 11, 1924, 5; *Democrat and Chronicle*, May 3, 1926, 6.

21. *Democrat and Chronicle*, September 10, 1928, 17.

22. Village of Hilton Historian, Family Histories Collection.

23. Village of Hilton Historian, World War I Photograph Collection.

24. *British Army WWI Pension Records 1914-1920, WO364; Piece: 388*, 3.

25. *1911 England Census*, Class: RG14; Piece: 10661; Schedule Number: 72; Enumeration District: 12

26. *New York, Passenger and Crew Lists, 1820-1957*, Year: 1912; Arrival: New York, New York; Microfilm Serial: T715, 1897-1957; Microfilm Roll: Roll 1823; Line: 20; Page Number: 38

27. *British Army WWI Pension Records 1914-1920, WO364; Piece: 388*, 4.

28. "Obituaries–Bridgeman, B. Margaret," *The Times Colonist* (Victoria, BC), January 29, 2009. http://www.legacy.com/obituaries/timescolonist/obituary.aspx?n=b-margaret-bridgeman -marg&pid=123415294

29. Ancestry.com. Public Member Trees [database on-line]. Provo, UT, USA: Ancestry.com

Operations, Inc., 2006, Original data: Family trees submitted by Ancestry members.

30. *Democrat and Chronicle*, July 19, 1918, 5.

31. *Democrat and Chronicle*, September 27, 1921, 22.

32. "News of State," *Western New Yorker* (Warsaw, NY), October 5, 1922. http://fultonhistory.com

33. *Democrat and Chronicle*, March 28, 1919, 19.

34. "Daytime Broadcasts Include Recipes, Beauty Hints, Home Suggestions," *The Binghamton (NY) Press*, October 25, 1928, 19. http://fultonhistory.com

35. "Off The Beaten Track," *News-Press* (Fort Myers, FL), July 7, 1930, 4. https://www.newspapers.com/title_4572/newspress/

36. "Farm & Grove Section 2," *Orlando Evening Star* (Orlando, FL), December 2, 1928, 5 (35). https://www.newspapers.com/title_5488/orlando_evening_star/

37. "Step-by-step fight," *Journal News* (White Plains NY), March 25, 1975, 16A (16). https://www.newspapers.com/title_3726/the_journal_news/

38. "Members Talk At Stamp Club," *Daily Argus* (Mount Vernon, NY), December 8, 1934. http://fultonhistory.com.

39. "Members Talk At Stamp Club," *Daily Argus* (Mount Vernon, NY), December 8, 1934. http://fultonhistory.com.

40. *Democrat and Chronicle*.

41. *Democrat and Chronicle*, January 12, 1936, 15D (55).

42. Village of Hilton Historian, Family Histories Collection.

43. United States Army, *108th Infantry*, 34.

44. *Democrat and Chronicle*, September 11, 1929, 14.

45. *Democrat and Chronicle*, August 17, 1927, 25.

46. *Democrat and Chronicle*, December 21, 1934, 20.

47. *Democrat and Chronicle*, January 9, 1935, 17.

48. *Democrat and Chronicle*.

49. *Democrat and Chronicle*.

50. *Democrat and Chronicle*, December 21, 1934, 21.

51. *Democrat and Chronicle*, January 9, 1935, 17.

52. *Democrat and Chronicle*, March 17, 1935, 5B (19).

53. *Hilton Record*, March 27, 1919, 5.

54. Burial Case Files, Willard Edward Bush, Box 721.

55. Burial Case Files, Willard Edward Bush, Box 721.

56. *Democrat and Chronicle*, September 25, 1923, 19.

57. *New York State Abstracts of World War I Military Service*, Name Range: Chappell, F-Cherry, P (Box 99).

58. Grandson of Leonard Kenneth Church, email correspondence with author, March 2018.

59. *Times-Union*, September 19, 1941, 3-A.

60. *Hilton Record*, February 25, 1960, 1.

61. *Suburban News*, August 2, 1962, 6.

62 *New York State Census, 1925*, Election District: 02; Assembly District: 05; City: Parma; County: Monroe; Page: 1

63. *New York State Abstracts of World War I Military Service*, Name Range: Clayton, J - Clinon, H (Box 106).

64. *Hilton Record*, January 9, 1919, 5.

65. *Times-Union*, August 29, 1932, 21.

66. Leith L. Wright, *Hilton-U.S.A., An Illustrated History of the Settlement, Growth and Development of the Village of Hilton 1805-1981* (Rochester, NY: Genesee Printers, 1984), 145

67. *Hilton Record*, May 22, 1919, 7.

68. *Hilton Record*, October 29, 1942, 1.

69. "One Dead, Train Hits Hamlin Truck," *Brockport (NY) Republic*, October 11, 1945. http://nyshistoricnewspapers.org/lccn/sn88074072/1945-10-11/ed-1/seq-1/

70. United States Army, CMH Publication 23-2, 347-355.

71. *Democrat and Chronicle*, July 29, 1927, 19.

72. *Hilton Record*, August 23, 1917, 5.

73. *Hilton Record*, January 31, 1918, 1.

74. *Democrat and Chronicle*, June 7, 1918, 13.

75. Village of Hilton Historian, Family Histories Collection.

76. *Hilton Record*, March 27, 1919, 5.

77. *Hilton Record*, April 24, 1919, 1.

78. *The Senior Annual*, East High School, Rochester(NY): Ontario Press, 1911. http://www.libraryweb.org/~digitized/yearbooks/East/1911.pdf

79. *Hilton Record*, September 5, 1912, 5.

80. *Hilton Record*, September 7, 1911, 3.

81. *Purdue Debris*, 292,West Lafayette (IN): Senior Class of Purdue University, 1912. https://archive.org/details/purduedebris00purd_9/page/n9; and
    Purdue Debris, 268,West Lafayette (IN): Senior Class of Purdue University, 1914. https://archive.org/details/purduedebris00purd_7/page/10

82. *Purdue Debris*, 1912, 343.

83. Purdue University Alumni Affairs Office, telephone interview, October 2017.

84. *State Population Census Schedules, 1915*; Election District: 03; Assembly District: 05; City: Parma; County: Monroe; Page: 12.

85. *Hilton Record*, September 14, 1916, 1.

86. *Democrat and Chronicle*, February 16, 1932, 8.

87. *Democrat and Chronicle*, December 17, 1931, 18; *Democrat and Chronicle*, July 16, 1938, 21.

88. *Democrat and Chronicle*, February 2, 1949, 20.

89. *Democrat and Chronicle*, May 19, 1953, 1.

90. "Cooper is installed by World War I vets," *Tampa Bay Times* (St. Petersburg, FL), June 3, 1974. https://www.newspapers.com/title_5744/tampa_bay_times/

91. *Democrat and Chronicle*, January 21, 1936, 16.

92. *Democrat and Chronicle*, May 21, 1945, 15.

93. *Times-Union*, June 2, 1934, 7. Original copy available Hilton Village Historian Family Histories Collection.

94. United States Army, 3d Division, *Third Division citations* (Andernach on the Rhine: 3d Division, 1919), 61. http://cdm16635.contentdm.oclc.org/cdm/search/searchterm/4986216

95. *Democrat and Chronicle*, September 24, 1944, 3B (19).

96. *Democrat and Chronicle*, April 14, 1944, 17 (31).

97. *Democrat and Chronicle*, May 30, 1932, 6.

98. *Democrat and Chronicle*, July 6, 1932, 13.

99. *Democrat and Chronicle*, April 14, 1944, 17 (31).

100. *Hilton Record*, January 23, 1919, 1.

101. *World War II Draft Cards (Fourth Registration) for the State of New York;* Record Group Title: *Records of the Selective Service System, 1926-1975;* Record Group Number: 147; Box or Roll Number: 121

102. Village of Hilton Historian, World War I Photograph Collection.

103. *Suburban News*, October 10, 1963, 1.

104. *Democrat and Chronicle*, November 13, 1932, 12A (12).

105. *Hilton Record*, July 23, 1959, 1.

106. *Democrat and Chronicle*, October 17, 1963, 5D (18).

107. *Hilton Record*, May 3, 1917, 5.

108. *Hilton Record*, September 18, 1924, 5.

109. Edward Gable, Email query and response, January 7, 2018.

110. *Democrat and Chronicle*, January 1, 1959, 32 (29).

111. *Hilton Record*, March 18, 1948, 1.

112. *Hilton Record*, February 26, 1925, 5.

113. *Hilton Record*, September 18, 1924, 5.

114. *Democrat and Chronicle*, January 1, 1959, 32 (29).

115. *Hilton Record*, December 31, 1958, 1.

116. *Pennsylvania, Federal Naturalization Records, 1795-1931*, Description: (Roll 145) Petition Numbers 27461-27840.

117. *Hilton Record*, August 11, 1932, 1.

118. Village of Hilton Historian, World War I Photograph Collection.

119. "Fort Hancock & Sandy Hook Proving Grounds," Military Railroads of The New York Metropolitan Area, updated March 14, 2015, http://members.trainweb.com/bedt/milrr/fthancock.html

120. *Hilton Record*, May 29, 1919, 4.

121. *Democrat and Chronicle*, November 17, 1944, 42.

122. *Democrat and Chronicle*, October 1, 1959, 12.

123. *Democrat and Chronicle*, April 17, 1952, 14.

124. United States Army, CMH Publication 23-4, 648.

125. *Hilton Record*, December 19, 1929, 1.

126. *Democrat and Chronicle*, February 6, 1915, 5.

127. *New York Abstracts of National Guard Service*; Series: 13721; Box: 5; Volume: 13 108th Infantry (3rd Inf NYNG) F-I

128. Burial Case Files, Glenn W. Fishbaugh, Box 1642.

129. *New York Abstracts of National Guard Service*; Series: 13721; Box: 5; Volume: 13 108th Infantry (3rd Inf NYNG) F-I

130. Burial Case Files, Glenn W. Fishbaugh, Box 1642.

131. *Hilton Record*, September 9, 1965, 8.

132. Village of Hilton Historian, Family Histories Collection.

133. Burial Case Files, Glenn W. Fishbaugh, Box 1642.

134. Kyle Mullen, *Glenn Fishbaugh Headstone*, 2017, personal photograph.

135. Village of Hilton Historian, World War I Photograph Collection.

136. *New York Abstracts of National Guard Service*; Series: 13721; Box: 5; Volume: 13 108th Infantry (3rd Inf NYNG) F-I

137. Village of Hilton Historian, World War I Photograph Collection.

138. *Democrat and Chronicle*, July 5, 1918, 5.

139. *Abstracts of Muster Rolls For National Guard Units Mustered Into Federal Service During the 1916 Mexican Punitive Campaign, 1916-1917*, Series B0802 (38 volumes), Unit: *3rd Infantry: A-F*, New York , Adjutant General's Office, New York State Archives, Albany, New York.

140. *Hilton Record*, June 22, 1967, 3.

141. *Democrat and Chronicle*, October 11, 1933, 10.

142. *Hilton Record*, June, 13, 1918, 7.

143. *Hilton Record*, September 25, 1947, 8.

144. *Hilton Record*, December 26, 1963, 1.

145. *Greece Press*, December 23, 1938, 10.

146. *Hilton Record*, December 26, 1963, 1.

147. *Hilton Record*, April 11, 1918, 9.

148. *Hilton Record*, April 15, 1943, 4.

149. Albert R. Stone, *Iola Sanatorium (Rochester, NY)*, 1916?, Photograph, From the Albert R. Stone Negative Collection, Rochester Museum & Science Center Rochester, NY. http://collections.rmsc.org/StoneCollection/08/scm08671.jpg Originally published in *Rochester Herald*, July 12, 1916; reprinted *Rochester Herald*, January 28, 1923. http://www.uer.ca/locations/viewgal.asp?picid=48071

150. *Hilton Record*, October 21, 1921, 5.

151. *Hilton Record*, June 6, 1918, 10.

152. United States Army, CMH Publication 23-4, 82-83.

153. *Hilton Record*, September 27, 1917, 4.

154. *Democrat and Chronicle*, September 25, 1917, 15.

155. *Democrat and Chronicle*, December 29, 1918, 8.

156. *Hilton Record*, December 4, 1919, 1.

157. Village of Hilton Historian, Local History Collection.

158. Family of Fred C. Hall, Email correspondence, September 28, 2018.

159. "Legal Notices," *Rochester Daily Record* (NY), April 17, 1926. http://fultonhistory.com

160. *Times-Union*, May 23, 1932, 16.

161. "Certificate to do Business Under an Assumed Name," *Rochester Daily Record* (NY), June 28, 1945. http://fultonhistory.com

162. *Democrat and Chronicle*, August 8, 1947, 29.

163. American Expeditionary Forces, *A History of United States Army Base Hospital No. 19*, (Rochester, NY: Wegman-Walsh Press, 1922. http://resource.nlm.nih.gov/14230610R

164. *Hilton Record*, February 28 1918, 1.

165. *Hilton Record*, July 17, 1918, 5.

166. *Hilton Record*, February 10, 1916, 1.

167. *Hilton Record*, September 14, 1916, 5.

168. *Democrat and Chronicle*, July 23, 1924, 21-22.

169. *Democrat and Chronicle*, June 11, 1925, 21; *Democrat and Chronicle*, June 28, 1925, 35; *Democrat and Chronicle*, June 20, 1925, 19.

170. "Will Deport Parma Man," *Buffalo Evening News* (NY), April 27, 1927, 44; *Democrat and Chronicle*, June 9, 1936, 30; *Hilton Record*, January 13, 1955, 5.

171. *Hilton Record*, April 26, 1917, 8.

172. *Lists of Incoming Passengers, 1917-1938*. Textual records. 360 Boxes. NAI: 6234465. Records of the Office of the Quartermaster General, 1774-1985, Record Group 92, Roll or Box Number: 92, Date Range: 29 Oct 1919-4 Sep 1919.

173. *Hilton Record*, April 22, 1920, 7.

174. Ancestry.com. *U.S. Army, Register of Enlistments, 1798-1914* [database on-line]. Provo, UT, USA: Ancestry.com Operations Inc, 2007.
Original data: Register of Enlistments in the U.S. Army, 1798-1914; (National Archives Microfilm Publication M233, 81 rolls, Surname Letter Range or Title: E-K); Records of the Adjutant General's Office, 1780's-1917, Record Group 94; National Archives, Washington, D.C.

175. *Hilton Record*, March 14, 1918, 5.

176. *Hilton Record*, April 25, 1918, 8.

177. *Hilton Record*, May 2, 1918, 5.

178. *Hilton Record*, August 21, 1919, 5.

179. *Democrat and Chronicle*, November 3, 1934, 13.

180. *Times-Union*, November 3, 1934, 9.

181. United States Army, CMH Publication 23-4, 565.

182. *Democrat and Chronicle*, December 28, 1931, 10.

183. "Red Jacket's Wooden Anniversary," *Fairport Herald=Mail* (NY), March 2, 1939.

184. *Democrat and Chronicle*, December 31, 1939, 17 (57).

185. *Greece Press*, March 8, 1940, 7.

186. *Democrat and Chronicle*, June 12, 1938, 10A (10).

187. Burial Case Files, Lester Peter Hiscock, Box 2290.

188. Burial Case Files, Lester Peter Hiscock, Box 2290.

189. Burial Case Files, Lester Peter Hiscock, Box 2290.

190. Burial Case Files, Lester Peter Hiscock, Box 2290.

191. *Hilton Record*, September 22, 1921, 1.

192. *New York State Abstracts of World War I Military Service*, Name Range: Hillary-Hogan (Box 35).

193. *Democrat and Chronicle*, November 6, 1929, 12.

194. *Democrat and Chronicle*, January 19, 1936, 2B (16).

195. *Democrat and Chronicle*, September 23, 1939, 12.

196. *New York State Abstracts of World War I Military Service*, Name Range: Holley, C-Holtyn, S (Box 279).

197. *Hilton Record*, July 4, 1918, 1.

198. *Democrat and Chronicle*, September 21, 1918, 21.

199. *Democrat and Chronicle*, April 6, 1930, 20.

200. *Democrat and Chronicle*, December 29, 1929, 9.

201. *New York State Abstracts of World War I Military Service,* Name Range: Hones, W-Hunter, R (Box 693).

202. *New York State Abstracts of World War I Military Service,* Name Range: Hones, W-Hunter, R (Box 693).

203. Ibid.

204. *Hilton Record,* June 7, 1917, 5.

205. *Hilton Record,* January 10, 1918, 5.

206. *Hilton Record,* January 16, 1919, 5.

207. *Democrat and Chronicle,* April 22, 1927, 42.

208. *Democrat and Chronicle,* March 28, 1934, 9.

209. Harvard University Archives, Pusey Library-Harvard Yard, Cambridge, MA, email correspondence with author, May 2017.

210. *World War I Veterans' Service Data and Photographs,* Series A0412, Reel Number: A0412:18, Residence City: Parma, Residence County: Monroe, New York State Education Dept. Division of Archives and History, New York State Archives, Albany, New York.

211. *Times-Union,* September 19, 1933, 1.

212. *Hilton Record,* February 20, 1964, 1.

213. "Kendall," *Holley Standard* (NY), July 4, 1907.

214. "Escaped Patient Killed on C.N.E.," *Poughkeepsie Daily Eagle* (NY), November 22, 1911; *Forty-Sixth Annual Report of the Hudson River State Hospital at Poughkeepsie, N.Y. to the State Hospital Commission For the Year Ending September 30, 1912,* 5, http://books.google.com.

215. *Hilton Record,* June 4, 1914, 1.

216. "Tells Fairport Merchants They Should Advertise," *Fairport Herald* (NY), February 24, 1915.

217. *Hilton Record,* January 11, 1917, 5.

218. *Hilton Record,* September 9, 1965, 8.

219. *Historical Register of National Homes for Disabled Volunteer Soldiers, 1866-1938;* (National Archives Microfilm Publication M1749, 282 rolls); Records of the Department of Veterans Affairs, Record Group 15; National Archives, Washington, DC

220. *Hilton Record,* November 24, 1932, 1.

221. "Doctor at CGW Joins Med Group," *Evening Leader* (Corning, NY), April 8, 1943.

222. *Hilton Record,* January 26, 1968, 7.

223. *Democrat and Chronicle,* June 16, 1917, 17.

224. Cochrane, *Gas Warfare,* 52.

225. Cochrane, *Gas Warfare,* 59.

226. *Democrat and Chronicle,* September 21, 1918, 2.

227. *Hilton Record,* October 31, 1918, 5.

228. *Hilton Record,* January 10, 1946, 8.

229. *Democrat and Chronicle,* September 22, 1967, 4D (40).

230. *Times-Union,* July 3, 1931, 7.

231. "American Casualties," *Plattsburg Sentinel* (NY), November 26, 1918.

232. *State Population Census Schedules, 1915;* Election District: 03; Assembly District: 05; City: Parma; County: Monroe; Page: 21

233. *Hilton Record,* April 11, 1940, 1.

234. The National Archives of the UK; Kew, Surrey, England; *Board of Trade: Commercial and Statistical Department and successors: Inwards Passenger Lists.;* Class: BT26; Piece: 603; Ancestry.com. UK, Incoming Passenger Lists, 1878-1960 [database on-line]. Provo, UT, USA: Ancestry.com Operations Inc, 2008.

235. *New York, Passenger and Crew Lists, 1820-1957,* ear: 1919; Arrival: New York, New York; Microfilm Serial: T715, 1897-1957; Microfilm Roll: Roll 2695; Line: 1; Page Number: 129.

236. *Hilton Record,* September 12, 1946, 4.

237. *Hilton Record,* December 2, 1937, 1.

238. *Democrat and Chronicle,* July 22, 1946, 13.

239. *Hilton Record,* May 5, 1915, 1.

240. *Hilton Record,* May 25, 1911, 3.

241. *Hilton Record*, January 18, 1968, 2.

242. *Hilton Record*, December 2, 1920, 4.

243. *Hilton Record*, January 30, 1919, 1.

244. *Democrat and Chronicle*, January 26, 1951, 27 (29).

245. *Democrat and Chronicle*, January 26, 1951, 27 (29).

246. "Dog's Life Saved as Marine Corps Accepts Him," *Star-Gazette* (Elmira, NY), July 22, 1944.

247. *Hilton Record*, July 4, 1918, 7.

248. *Hilton Record*, January 9, 1913, 1.

249. University of Rochester, *General Catalogue of The University of Rochester 1850-1928*, 266, Rochester, NY: University of Rochester, 1928. https://hdl.handle.net/2027/nnc1.1002290464

250. "Long Island Society," *Brooklyn Daily Eagle* (NY), January 27, 1930.

251. "Roosevelt – Weddings," *Nassau Daily Review* (NY), July 14, 1930.

252. Smucker, *Ambulance Service*, Appendix C.

253. *Pennsylvania, Federal Naturalization Records, 1795-1931*, Description: (Roll 145) Petition Numbers 27461-27840.

254. *Hilton Record*, June 6, 1918, 7.

255. Smucker, *Ambulance Service*, Appendix C.

256. *Hilton Record*, August 16, 1917, 5.

257. *New York State Census, 1925*, Election District: 02; Assembly District: 05; City: Parma; County: Monroe; Page: 1

258. *Hilton Record*, February 22, 1912, 1.

259. *Democrat and Chronicle*, September 2, 1959, 7 (2).

260. *Democrat and Chronicle*, August 13, 1949, 17.

261. *Democrat and Chronicle*, October 22, 1936, 9.

262. *Democrat and Chronicle*, March 30, 1918, 9.

263. "On The Field Of Honor," *Buffalo Morning Express and Illustrated Buffalo Express*, October 20, 1918.

264. *Hilton Record*, April 17, 1919, 5.

265. *Hilton Record*.

266. *Hilton Record*.

267. *Buffalo Morning Express*, October 20, 1918.

268. "Jamestown Democrats To Support McCarty," *Dunkirk Evening Observer* (NY), August 5, 1938.

269. "Dr. Frederick McCarty Is Named Alternate," *The Olean Times-Herald* (NY), February 17, 1936.

270. "Dr. F. E. McCarty Dies Here; Funeral Rites Tuesday Morning," *Wellsville Daily Reporter* (NY), January 12, 1942, 3.

271. *Democrat and Chronicle*, September 26, 1947, 23 (41).

272. *Hilton Record*, July 11, 1918, 5.

273. *Hilton Record*, August 29, 1918, 5.

274. Ancestry.com. *U.S., School Yearbooks, 1900-1990* [database on-line]. Provo, UT, USA: Ancestry.com Operations, Inc., 2010.

275. *World War II Draft Cards (Fourth Registration) for the State of New York;* Record Group Title: *Records of the Selective Service System, 1926-1975;* Record Group Number: 147; Box or Roll Number: 417.

276. Crew of USS *Leviathan*, *History of the USS Leviathan*, Brooklyn, NY: Brooklyn Eagle Press, 1919, 67-69, https://archive.org/details/historyofusslevi00broo/page/66.

277. *Hilton Record*, April 4, 1918, 5.

278. Burial Case Files, Edgar Roy Murrell, Box 3519.

279. Burial Case Files, Edgar Roy Murrell, Box 3519.

280. Burial Case Files, Edgar Roy Murrell, Box 3519.

281. Burial Case Files, Edgar Roy Murrell, Box 3519.

282. Burial Case Files, Edgar Roy Murrell, Box 3519.

283. Burial Case Files, Edgar Roy Murrell, Box 3519.

284. *Democrat and Chronicle*, January 21, 1946, 15 (27).

285. Navy Department Library - Naval History and Heritage Command; Washington, DC; Navy Register: Retired Officers of the U.S. Navy; Year: 1964 (v.1)

286. *Hilton Record,* January 13, 1938, 4.

287. *Democrat and Chronicle,* January 21, 1946, 15 (27).

288. *Democrat and Chronicle,* August 6, 1967, 14B (39).

289. Yale University Registrar's Office, Degree Verification request via email correspondence 16 February 2018

290. *Democrat and Chronicle,* July 28, 1928, 13.

291. *Democrat and Chronicle,* June 7, 1934, 19.

292. *Democrat and Chronicle,* July 28, 1928, 13.

293. *Democrat and Chronicle,* August 10, 1942, 16.

294. *Democrat and Chronicle,* January 21, 1946, 15 (27).

295. University of Rochester, "Meanderings," *Rochester Alumni Review* 15, no. 4 (April-May 1937): 21, https://www.lib.rochester.edu/IN/RBSCP/Databases/Attachments/Reviews/1937 /15-4/1937_April.pdf

296. "Cyrene Commandery No. 39," 1873 Rochester Time Capsule, accessed March 2018, http://www3.rmsc.org/capsule/2000%201%20273.html.

297. *Democrat and Chronicle,* August 2, 1960, 19.

298. *Hilton Record,* September 26, 1918, 4.

299. *Hilton Record,* May 1, 1919, 5.

300. *Hilton Record,* September 4, 1913, 5.

301. *Hilton Record,* February 1, 1917, 5.

302. *Hilton Record,* September 2, 1920, 5.

303. *Hilton Record,* June 24, 1943, 1.

304. "Beach Schools Head Selected," *Los Angeles Times,* June 24, 1947, https://www.newspapers.com/title_4312/the_los_angeles_times/.

305. "A Great School Leader Retires," *Independent Press Telegram* (Long Beach, CA), June 17, 1962, https://www.newspapers.com/title_694/independent_presstelegram/

306. "Newcomb K-8 Academy New Construction," Long Beach Unified School District, last updated July 19, 2018, http://lbschoolbonds.net/newcombacademy.cfm

307. "About Us," Newcomb Academy Foundation, accessed May 2018, http://newcombacademyfoundation.com/about-2/

308. "Education," Newcomb Academy Foundation, accessed May 2018, http://newcombacademyfoundation.com/education-programs/

309. "3 distinguished citizens judge Witness awards," *Independent Press-Telegram* (Long Beach, CA), June 11, 1972, https://www.newspapers.com/title_694/independent_presstelegram/.

310. "Newcomb School Offers 'First'; Kindergarten and Eight Grades," *Independent Press-Telegram* (Long Beach, CA), September 13, 1963, https://www.newspapers.com/title_694/independent_presstelegram/.

311. "Eight Grades in Next New School," *Independent Press-Telegram* (Long Beach, CA), August 23, 1962, https://www.newspapers.com/title_694/independent_presstelegram/.

312. "L.B. Superintendent of Schools Retiring," *Independent Press-Telegram* (Long Beach, CA), June 17, 1962, https://www.newspapers.com/title_694/independent_presstelegram/.

313. *Democrat and Chronicle,* September 6, 1917, 3.

314. *New York State Abstracts of World War I Military Service,* Name Range: Newcomb, C-Nichol, C (Box 440); "Pennsylvania Births and Christenings, 1709-1950," database, *FamilySearch* (https://familysearch.org/ark:/61903/1:1:V2J4-8WR : 11 February 2018), James Nice, 21 Apr 1891; Birth, citing Philadelphia, Philadelphia, Pennsylvania; FHL microfilm 1,289,330.; Birth, citing Philadelphia, Philadelphia, Pennsylvania; FHL microfilm 1,289,330.

315. *Applications for Headstones compiled 01/01/1925 - 06/30/1970, documenting the period ca. 1776 - 1970* ARC: 596118, Record Group 92, 1951-1954, Surname Range: Nelsen, Berner M - North, Carl E.

316. *World War II draft cards (Fourth Registration) for the State of Pennsylvania;* Record Group Title: *Records of the Selective Service System, 1926-1975;* Record Group Number: 147; Series Number: M1951; Name Range: All.

317. *U.S., Social Security Applications and Claims Index, 1936-2007*.

318. "Nice–Learn," *Perry Record* (NY), December 27, 1917. http://fultonhistory.com

319. "Castile Chronicle; The News in Tabloid Form," *Perry Record* (NY), January 24, 1923. http://fultonhistory.com

320. "Castile Department," *Perry Record* (NY), April 3, 1924. http://fultonhistory.com

321. "Castile Department; Items In Brief," *Perry Record* (NY), April 16, 1925. http://fultonhistory.com

322. "Castile Department; Personals," *Perry Record* (NY), July 23, 1925. http://fultonhistory.com

323. "Personal Mention," *The Wyoming County Times* (Warsaw, NY), October 19, 1933. http://fultonhistory.com

324. "Castile Department," *The Wyoming County Times* (Warsaw, NY), October 17, 1935. http://fultonhistory.com

325. "I.O.O.F. Officer," *The Castilian* (Castile, NY), January 3, 1924. http://fultonhistory.com

326. "A. L. Post Re-elect Officers," *Perry Record* (NY), October 6, 1926. http://fultonhistory.com

327. "Castile," *The Wyoming County Times* (Warsaw, NY), October 8, 1931. http://fultonhistory.com

328. "Ceremonial Program of Doughboy Memorial Dedication On Monday," *The Castilian* (Castile, NY), May 27, 1926. http://fultonhistory.com

329. "Castile Department; Local Paragraphs," *The Wyoming County Times* (Warsaw, NY), May 19, 1932. http://fultonhistory.com

330. "Castile," *The Sheldon Democrat* (Varysburg, NY), August 30, 1939. http://fultonhistory.com

331. Kyle Mullen, *Soldiers Sailors Marines Memorial*, Castile, NY, 2017, personal photographs.

332. *Hilton Record*, September 13, 1917, 8.

333. *Hilton Record*, February 22, 1912, 1.

334. Cornell University, *The Register 1920-1921* 12, no. 17 (1921): 281. https://hdl.handle.net/1813/41893;
Cornell University, *The Register 1921-1922* 13, no. 17 (September 1922): 222. https://hdl.handle.net/1813/22353

335. *Hilton Record*, October 12, 1922, 7.

336. "School Children Striving to Wipe Out Caterpillar," *The Daily Review* (Freeport, NY), March 21, 1925. http://fultonhistory.com

337. "Miss Gladys Bretsch Weds Homer C. Odell in Hastings," *The Yonkers Statesman* (NY), July 28, 1924.

338. Cornell University, *Cornell Alumni News* 30, no. 26 (March 29, 1928): 323 (9). https://hdl.handle.net/1813/26878

339. *Hilton Record*, August 31, 1944, 8.

340. *Hilton Record*, December 14, 1944, 3.

341. "Farm Loan Appraisers," *Fredonia Censor* (NY), September 29, 1960.

342. Cornell University, *The 1922 Cornellian* 54 (1922): 151. https://hdl.handle.net/2027/coo.31924078965104

343. Blazich Jr., "1914-1922."

344. Blazich Jr., "1914-1922."

345. "Letter From France," *Journal and Herald* (Springville, NY), June 27, 1918.

346. "This is Station GOB Broadcasting," *American Legion Monthly*, 16, no. 1 (January 1934): 36. https://hdl.handle.net/20.500.12203/3413

347. "GOB Broadcasting," 37.

348. *Democrat and Chronicle*, July 21, 1928, 5.

349. *Democrat and Chronicle*, April 20, 1938, 24.

350. *Democrat and Chronicle*, January 25, 1930, 8.

351. "Letter From France," *Journal and Herald* (Springville, NY), June 27, 1918.

352. "GOB Broadcasting," 36-37.

353. United States Naval Academy, "Past Midshipmen," *The Lucky Bag, The Yearbook of the United States Naval Academy* 15, no. 1 (1910): 197. http://cdm16099.contentdm.oclc.org/cdm/singleitem/collection/p16099coll7/id/6/rec/1

354. "Thirty-Five Must Resign," *Baltimore Sun* (MD), February 10, 1907.

355. "Business Papers Recorded; Certificate of Incorporation," *Daily Record* (Rochester, NY), September 2, 1926.

356. *1930 United States Federal Census*, Census Place: Parma, Monroe, New York; Page: 6B; Enumeration District: 0236; Description: Parma Town (South Part); FHL microfilm: 2341182.

357. *Times-Union*, December 10, 1940, 6A.

358. *Democrat and Chronicle*, July 21, 1928, 5.

359. *Democrat and Chronicle*, April 3, 1937, 14.

360. *Democrat and Chronicle*, November 15, 1981, 9B (36).

361. *Democrat and Chronicle*, April 1, 1958, 25 (14).

362. *Democrat and Chronicle*, October 18, 1980, 1B (13).

363. *Hilton Record*, April 15, 1943, 1.

364. *1930 United States Federal Census*, Census Place: Parma, Monroe, New York; Page: 1B; Enumeration District: 0234; Description: Hilton Village; FHL microfilm: 2341182.

365. *Democrat and Chronicle*, February 26, 1954, 22.

366. *Hilton Record*, September 2, 1937, 5.

367. *Hilton Record*, June 21, 1945, 4.

368. *Hilton Record*, April 25, 1918, 5.

369. *Hilton Record*, December 5, 1918, 5.

370. *Hilton Record*, April 23, 1925, 1.

371. *Hilton Record*, April 10, 1958, 1.

372. *Democrat and Chronicle*, May 1, 1961, 19.

373. *Hilton Record*, December 15, 1921, 1.

374. Village of Hilton Historian, World War I Photograph Collection.

375. United States Army, CMH Publication 23-2, 303.

376. Burial Case Files, George William Quinn, Box 3978.

377. Burial Case Files, George William Quinn, Box 3978.

378. Burial Case Files, George William Quinn, Box 3978.

379. *Democrat and Chronicle*, September 7, 1919, 24.

380. *Democrat and Chronicle*.

381. *Democrat and Chronicle*, July 10, 1919, 15.

382. Rochester City Historian, *World War Service vol. 1*, 333-336.

383. Burial Case Files, George William Quinn, Box 3978.

384. Burial Case Files, George William Quinn, Box 3978.

385. Burial Case Files, George William Quinn, Box 3978.

386. *The Saturday Evening Post*, August 6, 1919, cover, https://hdl.handle.net/2027/umn.31951001459150j?urlappend=%3Bseq=319

387. *Democrat and Chronicle*, September 7, 1919, 24.

388. Rochester City Historian, *World War Service vol. 1*, 333-336.

389. *Hilton Record*, July 12, 1917, 13.

390. *Democrat and Chronicle*, June 11, 1917, 11.

391. *Hilton Record*, October 24, 1957, 4.

392. *World War I Veterans' Service Data and Photographs*, Series A0412, Reel Number: A0412:40; Residence City: Canisteo; Residence County: Steuben, New York State Education Dept. Division of Archives and History, New York State Archives, Albany, New York.

393. *New York State Abstracts of World War I Military Service*, Name Range: Robinson, C-Roche (Box 507).

394. *Hilton Record*, November 29, 1917, 3.

395. *Applications for Headstones, compiled 01/01/1925 - 06/30/1970, documenting the period ca. 1776 - 1970* ARC: 596118, Record Group 92, 1951-1954, Surname Range: Rivers, Frederick Elliott - Roseberry, William L.

396. *Hilton Record*, November 28, 1918, 1.

397. *Hilton Record*, March 6, 1919, 1.

398. *Hilton Record*, May 17, 1917, 4.

399. *Hilton Record*, September 6, 1917, 5.

400. "Obituaries," *Canisteo Times* (NY), May10, 1956. http://fultonhistory.com

401. "American Legion After Members," *Canisteo Times* (NY), February 25, 1920.

402. "Canisteo Aids Vets' Yuletide," *Canisteo Times* (NY), December 11, 1952. http://fultonhistory.com

403. "County Civil Service Employees Officers," *Canisteo Times* (NY), October 3, 1946. http://fultonhistory.com

404. "Clarence Robinson Rejected by the Army," *Canisteo Times* (NY), May 28, 1942. http://fultonhistory.com

405. "Canisteo Legion Plans V-Day," *Canisteo Times* (NY), October 19, 1944.

406. "Canisteo Aids Vets' Yuletide," *Canisteo Times* (NY), December 11, 1952.

407. Burial Case Files, George H. Rowley, Box 4215.

408. Burial Case Files, George H. Rowley, Box 4215.

409. Miles, *308th Infantry*, 303.

410. Burial Case Files, George H. Rowley, Box 4215.

411. *Democrat and Chronicle*, July 26, 1917, 3.

412. "Rev. Walter S. Ryder To Occupy Pulpit At First Unitarian," *Ithaca Journal* (NY), May 24, 1935. http://fultonhistory.com

413. Colgate Rochester Divinity School, *Rochester Theological Seminary General Catalogue 1850 to 1920* (Rochester, N.Y.: E.R. Andrews Printing Co., 1920), 326. https://catalog.hathitrust.org/Record/100965685/Home

414. Colgate Rochester Divinity School, *Rochester Theological Seminary General Catalogue 1850 to 1920* (Rochester, N.Y.: E.R. Andrews Printing Co., 1920), 326. https://catalog.hathitrust.org/Record/100965685/Home

415. *Democrat and Chronicle*, May 19, 1920, 29.

416. "Purse of Gold Parting Gift," *Vancouver Daily World* (BC, Canada), September 24, 1921. https://www.newspapers.com/title_2408/vancouver_daily_world/

417. "Students' Successes At British Columbia University Exams," *Vancouver Daily World* (BC, Canada), May 6, 1920. https://www.newspapers.com/title_2408/vancouver_daily_world/

418. Walter S. Ryder, "Canada's Industrial Crisis of 1919" abstract (master's thesis, UBC, 1920), T. doi: http://dx.doi.org/10.14288/1.0088714.

419. "Local Clergyman Accepts Chair At St. Paul College," *The Daily Northwestern* (Oshkosh, WI), August 20, 1927. https://www.newspapers.com/title_3743/the_oshkosh_northwestern/

420. *Hilton Record*, June 6, 1918, 8.

421. *Hilton Record*, June 13, 1918, 8.

422. *Democrat and Chronicle*, August 25, 1918, 4.

423. *Hilton Record*, November 7, 1918, 5.

424. *Democrat and Chronicle*, January 9, 1901, 10 (11); *Democrat and Chronicle*, January 11, 1901, 10; *Democrat and Chronicle*, January 12, 1901, 14.

425. Village of Hilton Historian, World War I Photograph Collection.

426. *Democrat and Chronicle*, July 21, 1918, 28.

427. *Democrat and Chronicle*, May 21, 1909, 20.

428. *Democrat and Chronicle*, June 11, 1917, 11.

429. Ancestry.com. *New York, County Marriage Records, 1847-1849, 1907-1936* [database on-line]. Lehi, UT, USA: Ancestry.com Operations, Inc., 2016. Original data: *Marriage Records. New York Marriages.* Various New York County Clerk offices.

430. *Hilton Record*, January 9, 1930, 1.

431. *Democrat and Chronicle*, May 25, 1940, 6.

432. *Democrat and Chronicle*, November 13, 1932, 12A (12).

433. *Democrat and Chronicle*, July 16, 1938, 21.

434. *Times-Union*, July 15, 1935, 26.

435. *Democrat and Chronicle*, August 28, 1929, 15.

436. *Democrat and Chronicle*.

437. *Democrat and Chronicle*.

438. *Hilton Record*, July 11, 1935, 1.

439. "Obituaries," *St. Petersburg Times* (FL), July 11, 1980. https://www.newspapers.com/title_5744/tampa_bay_times/

440. *Democrat and Chronicle*, May 25, 1940, 6.

441. *Democrat and Chronicle*, August 4, 1935, 12.

442. "Rochester Jeffersons," Revolvy, accessed July 23, 2018, https://www.revolvy.com/main/index.php?s=Rochester%20Jeffersons.

443. "1912 Rochester Scalpers," The Pro Football Archives, accessed July 23, 2018, http://www.profootballarchives.com/1912rochs.html.

444. *Democrat and Chronicle*, February 14, 1968, 11C (41).

445. Ancestry.com. *U.S. City Directories, 1822-1995* [database on-line]. Provo, UT, USA: Ancestry.com Operations, Inc., 2011. Original data: *Denver, Colorado, City Directory, 1924; Denver, Colorado, City Directory, 1926; Denver, Colorado, City Directory, 1928; Denver, Colorado, City Directory, 1929; Denver, Colorado, City Directory, 1930.*

446. *Democrat and Chronicle*, February 14, 1968, 11C (41).

447. *Democrat and Chronicle*, January 21, 1957, 11.

448. *Democrat and Chronicle*, November 5, 1942, 22.

449. *Greece Press*, November 11, 1948, 1; *Greece Press*, March 17, 1949, 1; *Greece Press*, May 5, 1949, 4.

450. *Greece Press*, February 14, 1946, 1.

451. *Democrat and Chronicle*, November 26, 1945, 17.

452. "Accused of Manslaughter," *Buffalo Commercial* (NY), May 30, 1904. https://www.newspapers.com/title_5123/the_buffalo_commercial/

453. "Arrested For Manslaughter," *Buffalo Evening News* (NY), May 30, 1904. https://www.newspapers.com/title_5960/buffalo_evening_news/

454. *Democrat and Chronicle*, March 7, 1925, 17.

455. Daniel R. Slocum, Sponge-Raising Apparatus, US Patent 1,277,496, filed November 5, 1917, and issued September 3, 1918, available: http://patft.uspto.gov/netahtml/PTO/patimg.htm

456. *Hilton Record*, November 7, 1918, 5.

457. *Hilton Record*, July 13, 1944, 1.

458. *Hilton Record*, July 11, 1946, 1.

459. Village of Hilton Historian, World War I Photograph Collection.

460. Surgeon General, *Medical Department*, vol. 8, chap. 5. Also available online at: http://history.amedd.army.mil/booksdocs/wwi/fieldoperations/chapter5.html

461. *Hilton Record*, February 3, 1916, 8.

462. *Hilton Record*, May 10, 1962, 1.

463. *Hilton Record*.

464. *Hilton Record*, March 13, 1941, 1.

465. *Hilton Record*, August 6, 1942, 1.

466. *Hilton Record*, December 20, 1917, 4.

467. *Democrat and Chronicle*, March 15, 1964, 9C

468. *Democrat and Chronicle*, January 29, 1926, 8.

469. *Democrat and Chronicle*, March 13, 1964, 9C (46).

470. *Hilton Record*, February 14, 1918, 1.

471. United States Army, CMH Publication 23-4, 660-661.

472. *State Population Census Schedules, 1915;* Election District: 01; Assembly District: 01; City: Carleton; County: Orleans; Page: 20

473. Burial Case Files, Thomas D. Sovia, Box 4613.

474. Burial Case Files, Thomas D. Sovia, Box 4613.

475. *Hilton Record*, October 17, 1918, 8.

476. *Democrat and Chronicle*, December 29, 1902, 4.

477. *Democrat and Chronicle*, October 16, 1918, 11.

478. United States, Selective Service System. *World War I Selective Service System Draft Registration Cards, 1917-1918*, Registration State: New York; Registration County: Monroe; Roll: 1753844; Draft Board: 1

479. *Hilton Record*, March 21, 1918, 11.

480. Eastman Kodak retirement photo, provided by the family of William Taylor.

481. *Democrat and Chronicle*, November 9, 1960, 24.

482. *Hilton Record*, February 28, 1918, 1.

483. *Hilton Record*, August 30 1917, 1.

484. *Hilton Record*, January 3, 1918, 5.

485. *Democrat and Chronicle*, May 25, 1934, 23.

486. *Democrat and Chronicle*, May 25, 1934, 23.

487. *Hilton Record*, September 8, 1921, 1.

488. Brian Resnick, "What America Looked Like: Collecting Peach Pits for WWI Gas Masks," *The Atlantic*, February 1, 2012, https://www.theatlantic.com/national/archive/2012/02/what-america-looked-like-collecting-peach-pits-for-wwi-gas-masks/252294/.

489. *Hilton Record*, October 24, 1918, 5.

490. *Hilton Record*, October 10, 1918, 5.

491. *Democrat and Chronicle*, August 16, 1923, 4.

492. *1930 United States Federal Census,* Census Place: Parma, Monroe, New York; Page: 5A; Enumeration District: 0234; Description: Hilton Village; FHL microfilm: 2341182; *World War II Draft Cards (Fourth Registration) for the State of New York;* Record Group Title: *Records of the Selective Service System, 1926-1975;* Record Group Number: 147; Box or Roll Number: 623.

493. *U.S. Marine Corps Muster Rolls, 1893-1958, Roll 0069.*

494. *U.S. Marine Corps Muster Rolls, 1893-1958, Roll 0071.*

495. *U.S. Marine Corps Muster Rolls, 1893-1958, Roll 0073.*

496. *U.S. Marine Corps Muster Rolls, 1893-1958, Roll 0075.*

497. *U.S. Marine Corps Muster Rolls, 1893-1958, Roll 0076.*

498. *U.S. Marine Corps Muster Rolls, 1893-1958, Roll 0076.*

499. *U.S. Marine Corps Muster Rolls, 1893-1958, Roll 0078.*

500. *U.S. Marine Corps Muster Rolls, 1893-1958, Roll 0081.*

501. *U.S. Marine Corps Muster Rolls, 1893-1958, Roll 0084.*

502. *U.S. Marine Corps Muster Rolls, 1893-1958, Roll 0084.*

503. *U.S. Marine Corps Muster Rolls,* 1893-1958, *Roll 0085.*

504. *U.S. Marine Corps Muster Rolls, 1893-1958, Roll 0086* and *Roll 0087.*

505. *U.S. Marine Corps Muster Rolls, 1893-1958, Roll 0087.*

506. *U.S. Marine Corps Muster Rolls, 1893-1958, Roll 0093.*

507. *U.S. Marine Corps Muster Rolls, 1893-1958, Roll 0095.*

508. *U.S. Marine Corps Muster Rolls, 1893-1958, Roll 0122.*

509. *Democrat and Chronicle,* June 10, 1917, 35.

510. *U.S. Marine Corps Muster Rolls, 1893-1958, Roll 0124.*

511. *U.S. Marine Corps Muster Rolls, 1893-1958, Roll 0130.*

512. *U.S. Marine Corps Muster Rolls, 1893-1958, Roll 0136.*

513. *U.S. Marine Corps Muster Rolls, 1893-1958, Roll 0147.*

514. *U.S. Marine Corps Muster Rolls, 1893-1958, Roll 0166.*

515. *U.S. Marine Corps Muster Rolls, 1893-1958, Roll 0178.*

516. *U.S. Marine Corps Muster Rolls, 1893-1958, Roll 0189.*

517. *Hilton Record*, May 24, 1934, 1.

518. *Times-Union*, November 12, 1932, 20.

519. *Times-Union*, July 13, 1938, 1A.

520. *Hilton Record*, October 12, 1916, 5.

521. *Hilton Record*, March 30, 1918, 9.

522. "Chula Vista Furniture Company Under New Management," *Chula Vista Star* (CA), June 15, 1945. https://www.newspapers.com/title_3898/the_chula_vista_star/

523. "Turgon Now Sole Owner Of Store," *The Chula Vista Star* (CA), January 28, 1949. https://www.newspapers.com/title_3898/the_chula_vista_star/

524. "Legal Notices, Notice of Intention to Sell," *The Chula Vista Star* (CA), May 28, 1953. https://www.newspapers.com/title_3898/the_chula_vista_star/

525. "Lions Club Dedicate New Park Addition," *The Chula Vista Star* (CA), July 13, 1945. https://www.newspapers.com/title_3898/the_chula_vista_star/

526. "Turgon Sells Furniture Store To San Diego Pair," *The Chula Vista Star* (CA), May 21, 1953. https://www.newspapers.com/title_3898/the_chula_vista_star/

527. "Fred H. Turgon," *The Chula Vista Star-News* (CA), May 23, 1965. https://www.newspapers.com/title_3897/chula_vista_starnews/

528. "Turgon Director Better Business," *The Chula Vista Star* (CA), April 22, 1949. https://www.newspapers.com/title_3898/the_chula_vista_star/

529. "Turgon Sells Furniture Store To San Diego Pair," *The Chula Vista Star* (CA), May 21, 1953. https://www.newspapers.com/title_3898/the_chula_vista_star/

530. Ibid.

531. "Fred H. Turgon," *The Chula Vista Star-News* (CA), May 23, 1965. https://www.newspapers.com/title_3897/chula_vista_starnews/

532. "Chula Vista Furniture to Present Senior Girls With Gifts," *The Chula Vista Star* (CA), May 1, 1952., https://www.newspapers.com/title_3898/the_chula_vista_star/

533. "It Was A Great Party," *The Chula Vista Star* (CA), May 20, 1949. https://www.newspapers.com/title_3898/the_chula_vista_star/

534. "Merry Christmas To All," *The Chula Vista Star* (CA), December 20, 1951. https://www.newspapers.com/title_3898/the_chula_vista_star/

535. "Turgons Return From 7,000 Mile Trip," *The Chula Vista Star* (CA), October 15, 1948. https://www.newspapers.com/title_3898/the_chula_vista_star/

536. *Hilton Record*, November 13, 1919, 6.

537. *Hilton Record*, October 11, 1928, 5.

538. *Historical Register of National Homes for Disabled Volunteer Soldiers, 1866-1938*; National Archives Microfilm Publication M1749, 282 rolls; Bath Branch, Bath, New York, Historical Registers and Indexes to Historical Registers, 1876-1934, First Letter of Surname: T.

539. "Plunges to Death," *Binghamton Press* (NY), November 14, 1946. http://fultonhistory.com

540. *Hilton Record*, March 28, 1935, 1.

541. *Hilton Record*.

542. *Hilton Record*, October 26, 1944, 3.

543. *Hilton Record*, November 16, 1933, 1.

544. *Hilton Record*, March 28, 1935, 1.

545. Leith L. Wright, *Hilton-U.S.A., An Illustrated History of the Settlement, Growth and Development of the Village of Hilton 1805-1981* (Rochester, NY: Genesee Printers, 1984), 145.

546. *Beneficiary Identification Records Locator Subsystem (BIRLS) Death File*.

547. "Elmer S Wadsworth," Find A Grave, https://www.findagrave.com/memorial /148341759/elmer-s-wadsworth

548. United States, Selective Service System, *World War I Selective Service System Draft Registration Cards, 1917-1918*, Registration State: New York; Registration County: Monroe; Roll: 1753844; Draft Board: 1

549. Ancestry.com. *New York, County Marriage Records, 1847-1849, 1907-1936* [database on-line]. Lehi, UT, USA: Ancestry.com Operations, Inc., 2016. Original data: *Marriage Records. New York Marriages.* Various New York County Clerk offices.

550. *World War II Draft Cards (Fourth Registration) for the State of New York;* Record Group Title: *Records of the Selective Service System, 1926-1975;* Record Group Number: 147; Box or Roll Number: 639

551. "Williamstown Legion Post Officers Installed," *Oswego Palladium-Times* (NY), November 5, 1945. http://fultonhistory.com

552. "Williamstown – Legion Elects," *Oswego Palladium-Times* (NY), May 16, 1953. http://fultonhistory.com

553. *1930 United States Federal Census*; Census Place: Rochester, Monroe, New York; Page: 16B; Enumeration District: 0045; Description: Rochester City, Ward 10 (Part), Bounded By (N) City Limits; (E) Dewey Ave.; (S) Steko Ave., Aster, Knickerbocker Ave., Railroad Tracks, Ridgeway Ave., Ramona, Wheatland; (W) Mt. Read Blvd., Bancroft, City Limits; FHL microfilm: 2341185

554. *Democrat and Chronicle,* June 4, 1967, 13B (39).

555. *Democrat and Chronicle*, March 26, 1939, 12D (67).

556. *Democrat and Chronicle*, July 28, 1924, 22.

557. *Democrat and Chronicle*, August 7, 1925, 4.

558. "Lyndon H. Wells," *Brockport Republic* (NY), September 6, 1923. http://nyshistoricnewspapers.org/lccn/sn86053142/

559. *Democrat and Chronicle*, July 2, 1925, 26.

560. *Democrat and Chronicle*, August 7, 1925, 4.

561. Ancestry.com. *U.S. City Directories, 1822-1995* [database on-line]. Provo, UT, USA: Ancestry.com Operations, Inc., 2011.
Original data: *Rochester, New York, City Directory, 1927*.

562. *Democrat and Chronicle*, June 10, 1968, 5C (25). http://fultonhistory.com

563. "The Class History," *Highland Democrat* (Peekskill, NY), June 17, 1911.

564. Cornell University, *Official publications of Cornell University Catalogue Number 1911-1912* 3, no. 11 (June 1912): 93 (481). https://hdl.handle.net/1813/23450

565. *Hilton Record*, May 15 1913, 4.

566. *Democrat and Chronicle*, August 1, 1916, 15.

567. *Hilton Record*, July 16, 1942, 5.

568. *Hilton Record*, January 8, 1920, 4.

569. *Hilton Record*, October 3, 1940, 5.

570. *Hilton Record*, July 16, 1942, 4.

571. *Hilton Record*, July 10, 1930, 1.

572. *Hilton Record*, July 10, 1930, 1.

573. Ancestry.com. *Michigan, Marriage Records, 1867-1952* [database on-line]. Provo, UT, USA: Ancestry.com Operations, Inc., 2015.
Original data: Michigan, Marriage Records, 1867–1952. Michigan Department of Community Health, Division for Vital Records and Health Statistics, Lansing, MI, USA; *Michigan, Marriage Records, 1867-1952;* Film: *170;* Film Description: *1923 Monroe - 1923 St Clair*

574. *1930 United States Federal Census;* Census Place: Hamlin, Monroe, New York; Page: 9A; Enumeration District: 0217; Description: Hamlin Town (East Part), FHL microfilm: 2341182

575. *Hilton Record*, July 10, 1930, 1.

576. *Hilton Record*, July 3, 1930, 1.

577. Village of Hilton Historian, World War I Photograph Collection.

578. *State Population Census Schedules, 1925;* Election District: 03; Assembly District: 05; City: Parma; County: Monroe; Page: 6

579. *Democrat and Chronicle*, July 8, 1933, 11.

580. *World War II Draft Cards (Fourth Registration) for the State of New York;* Record Group Title: *Records of the Selective Service System, 1926-1975;* Record Group Number: 147; Box or Roll Number: 677.

581. *Democrat and Chronicle*, January 20, 1969, 2B (12).

582. *Democrat and Chronicle*, January 20, 1969, 2B (12).

583. *Hilton Record*, January 3, 1946, 1.

584. *Hilton Record*, January 26, 1950, 1.

585. *Democrat and Chronicle*, May 6, 1954, 47.

586. *Hilton Record*, September 9, 1965, 8.

587. *Democrat and Chronicle*, January 20, 1969, 2B (12).

588. *Democrat and Chronicle*, December 15, 1957, 15C (47).

589. United States Forestry Service-Pacific Northwest Region, *Rived Logs 4*, undated, historic photograph, WWI Spruce Production Division Siuslaw National Forest, flickr, uploaded October 8 2015, https://www.flickr.com/photos/forestservicenw/21852508608/in/faves-160033762@N07/

WITH OUR BOYS

[Under this heading we will give the news regarding the boys from Hilton and vicinity, who are fighting to "make the world a better place to live in." Bring in any news of interest regarding them.]

3

LETTERS HOME

The inspiration for the series name–*With Our Boys*–came from a column published in several issues of the *Hilton (NY) Record* during the World War. An explanation by Editor John E. Cooper below the column headline stated, "Under this heading we will give the news regarding the boys from Hilton and vicinity, who are fighting to 'make the world a better place to live in.' Bring in my news of interest regarding them."

Included in the news from "over there" were snippets of information on the journey or safe arrival of the military traveler; their training, meals, and living conditions; and, when not censored, their whereabouts. A rich source of information, the first-person narratives penned to paper detailed a soldier's experiences both at home and abroad during the United States' participation in World War I.

The letters were submitted to the *Hilton Record* by the recipients–family, friends, or Editor Cooper–providing the readers a glimpse of military life and an update on "their boys." These coveted connections to a loved-one are a historical reference of events from one hundred years ago–a connection to Parma's past.

Copies of the *Hilton Record* (published 1906-1968) were obtained through the online repository FultonHistory.com and microfilm provided the Village of Hilton Historian's Office. Transcriptions of letters published in the *Hilton Record* between 1917 and 1919 are presented in chronological order by publication date. When available, the date and location the letter was written from is included in the header of the transcription.

Unknown is whether the misspellings, incorrect punctuation, and grammatical errors found in the published newspaper were the result of the author or the newspaper's translation from letter to typeset. The transcribed letters on the following pages are verbatim from the printed newspaper, including those errors. In places where the newspaper was illegible, mangled, creased, damaged, or poorly imaged, a "[?]" is inserted to explain the inability to transcribe.

Thursday, May 24, 1917, Page 1

Down in Texas

Extracts From Letters Received from Corporal John H. Cooper of This Village

John Harlan Cooper of this village who is in the 3rd Aerio Squad of the Signal Corps at Fort Sam Houston, San Antonio, Tex., writes his father under date of May 15th from which we take the following extracts:

"Yesterday I was promoted to Corporal and given charge of a tent and ten men. Of course it is the lowest ranking officer but is better than private and a step on the way. I am going to try in every way to advance. Things are a lot better here in camp now. We have no shower baths here yet but we were taken down to a small stream yesterday for a bath and we enjoyed it. They will have bath houses here soon. We are getting better "eats" here now too. More of them and they are better than they were at first. We had a fine breakfast this morning: Post toasties, fried potatoes, beefsteak, bread and coffee. This noon we had boiled beef, cabbage, potatoes, bread, lemonade and rice. Didn't have any milk and sugar with rice but was able to eat it just the same. Tonight we had liver, mashed potatoes, gravy, corn, peas, bread, iced tea and pudding. We eat sitting on the ground as we have no mess hall as yet but will have one soon. Here is a list of bugle calls:

a.m.   1st Period

5:45—1st call—get up.

6:00—Reville-Everyone is dressed and out in front of the tent.

[?]—Assembly-I march my squad down to the end of the street to report.

6:30—Mess—[?].

7:15—General—The whole company forms [?] one end of the street and walks to the other end picking up all paper and other debris.

Unknown-First call for drill-squads fall in front of tent.

7:50—Assembly—We fall in, in company formation.

9:00—Recall—End of drill.

2nd Period

9:20—First call for drill/

9:30—Assembly.

10:30—Recall.

10:45—Sick call—All sick men must report at hospital tent.

11:00—First Sergeant's call—They report at headquarters.

11:30—Mess—Dinner.

p.m.

1:20—First call.

1:30—Assembly.

2:30—Recall.

3:00—Sick call.

4:00—1st Sergeant's call.

4:30—Mess_supper.

9:30—Tattoo—lights out.

10:00—Taps—no talking.

I have a good bunch of fellows in my squad, mostly Georgians, and I have had no trouble with them and don't think I will.

We have become so accustomed to aeroplanes that we hardly look up as they fly around over us, unless someone notices that one is doing some trick. It looks fine to see them floating around in the air. I am glad that I enlisted when I did. I think that the country needs every man who is able to go and has no one dependent upon him."

Kenneth Smith also of this village writes home that he belongs to Harlan's squad, so they are together in the same tent.

Thursday, May 31, 1917, Page 1

Hilton Boy with United States Army

Excerpts From Letter From Kenneth Smith Stationed at San Antonio, Texas.

This is the best day we have had since I left home, and Harlan and I took advantage of it.

We got up at 5:30 this morning and got all cleaned up–that is we washed our face and hands and cleaned our shoes. I wish I could find a place to take a bath. We had a good mess this morning and then we started for church at 7:45. We thought we were going to get a ride but we were mistaken. It is seven miles to town and we walked the whole distance. After we got there we walked about three more miles trying to find the First Baptist Church. We found it and heard the sermon. It was fine, and I decided that was the best place I had struck since I left home. It certainly was a treat even if we did have to walk. The minister of the church was away so they had Chaplain Fleming preach. He spoke about temptations. He said boys in the army are tempted not to go to church because there are so few that think of it, and those that do are made fun of and called mamma's boys. It was very good. Harlan Cooper and I were about the only soldiers there and there were about 400 citizens there. We were looked upon pretty strong. We are going next Sunday and go to the Sunday School because there is a good chance to get acquainted. They have Sunday School down here before church so we [?]we went up town and went to a restaurant where they give you the best dinner for 25 cents that I ever had for that price. We were told about the place by one of the men in our tent. We are going there to eat every time we go uptown because anywhere else it would cost 75 cents.

We were told to get back at [?] o'clock and it was 12:30 when we got through dinner and we were seven miles from camp and had to walk. We got back at 3:00 and reported. They said alright but we were a little scared. I am awful tired; I walked just 14 miles to church while at home it is only a step and you could hardly force me to go. It was a treat anyway because we haven't been allowed out of camp this week. I expect they will have transportation next week by automobile trucks; I hope so. Tomorrow we get drilling for the first time-that is by real officers. I hope I get a good nights sleep. We were told yesterday to clean up everything because General Pershing was coming and see this camp sometime today. It is 4 o'clock now and he hasn't yet arrived. I would like to see him. I am just beginning to like this a good deal better. I guess going to chuch made me feel good.

There are 1801 men in this camp alone and another camp about a mile away which has about 1200 and there has just arrived 300 more men, so it is some camp. They have ten cook tents feeding all these men-some cooking has to be done. A man in our tent was a cook on a steam ship and he has just been assigned head cook to a new cook tent. Maybe we can snatch a bit to eat from him seeing we know him. I have started a diary telling of my experience each day from the time I enlisted. I hope I can keep it up; it will be very interesting if I ever get through with this army life."

Thursday, September 20, 1917, Page 4
Advice to Members of the Next Draft Contingent

Homer Odell, who was among the first to go from this district, and who is now at Camp Dix, N. J., in writing to his parents, says: "Tell the boys to bring their kit, a good big suit case, old clothes that may be worn a month, good heavy comfortable shoes, a bath towel, two face towels, one dish towel, small wash cloth, tooth brush and toilet articles that they are used to—anything that the boys want. Kodaks will be O. K. and any sweater may be worn in barracks."

Thursday, September 27, 1917, Page 4
Good Advice

Editor The Hilton Record
Hilton, NY

Dear Sir:

Just a word to those who may be coming to camp soon. The U.S. government is doing wonders at equipping the soldiers, but much still remains to be done due to the immensity of the work. A list of the things needed are mentioned in the daily papers; be sure and bring those: old clothes are right even tho they don't seem proper to start with. A good pair of comfortable shoes is very necessary. We still are wearing the ones brought from home and they are worse for wear at present and yet no signs of new ones being issued. Eight hours of drill each day makes the feet a vital part to care for.

A small stiff shoe brush to brush mud from shoes. A scrubbing brush about 5x2 ½ inches to clean leggings and clothes. A small dish towel in addition to hand and bath towels, three or four bars of soap, both face and for washing clothes. I have tried for a week to buy soap for washing my clothes and have been unable to secure any.

A suit case is very proper and almost a necessity. The carpenter here will make a box for clothes and then the suitcase may be sent home with any clothes discarded after new ones are given out. An indelible pencil should be put in.

I may have forgotten some article but with the above a greater degree of comfort will be had than some of the boys are enjoying. (Send all mail to Camp Dix, [?] not to Wrightstown as it causes a delay.)

Yours truly,
Homer C Odell

Thursday, November 1, 1917, Page 4

Interesting Letter From Earl Burritt.

Camp Wadsworth, October 5, 1917.

Dear Mother;

Your long looked for and welcomed letter received today and was most pleased to hear from you.

Am still working hard every day at the usual duty of clearing land and making the camp as comfortable as possible. We have succeeded so well that we will start our severe training Monday morning. We had this afternoon off to wash our clothes and do some necessary work. This is the first time we have had off since we have been here and therefore it came in mighty handy.

This life surely is a great thing for me. We get up at a certain minute, meals at the exact time. Our daily routine of work is both healthful and strengthening. Am in bed at an early hour, meals are of wholesome material and of sufficient quantity. Do not indulge in any sweet stuff or tobacco and do not run around any at night. I was weight today and find that I am 148 pounds to the good. Am feeling fine and like it here fully as well as at Pelham Bay. It became rather an old story there at the last and was not sorry when we left.

An order was issued tonight that we will leave for France about the 8th of February. Our program of training is till that time. Major General O'Brien, the commander of my division, is in France now and they say we will follow him and that he is there now for the purpose of making arrangements for our coming "over there."

Lieutenant Sommers received a telegram Thursday morning stating that his mother in California was dead and left an hour afterwards for there. She surely was a fine woman having met her at the Basin while she was visiting there. Each one in the company gave 25 cents each for a floral piece.

When I read your letter telling of the fruit at home I cannot but wish I were there to help with it. If you will remember I had the second week in October last year from Eastmans to help you. I rather wish I could have that time now.

As you say it is a world of experience and education to go among the different parts of the country. Everyting is so much different here than home. One cannot believe things that are said till one actually sees the things for themselves. For instance, in the "north" the law is such that private property be fenced off. Here it is the opposite. I don't remember seeing a fence anywhere on our way from N. Carolina down. The law doesn't compel the use of fences. Another thing the whites are as poor as the blacks and in some cases the whites are employed by the blacks, but as a rule they are both a lazy, shiftless and poor population. Even under these circumstances the whites and blacks hold themselves apart from each other, such as divided railroad stations with waiting rooms on either side of the station. Trolley cars are divided and each enter at their respective part of the car. Numerous other things happen to make the South very much different than the North. Instead of seeing fields of waving grain and fruit orchards, great fields of cotton is the only thing in sight. I am getting rather tired of seeing cotton fields and [people] working in them like so many people in a berry field. Dixie is sure some odd place.

In the morning at 6 o'clock a bugle sounds which means "get up," fifteen minutes later a big cannon goes off. That means that we are to be on the street dressed and ready for the morning exercises. If we do not get out in that time we are out of luck and means a duty detail during our rest period. The same thing happens 6 o'clock at night after the cannon is fired that means "The end of a perfect day" for the most of us. I haven't been late yet and don't intend to if I can help it. At exactly 6 o'clock I am up, and dressed by 10 minutes afterwards.

Every morning we have one half hour of physical culture exercises, in our shirt sleeves regardless of the cold and in the forenoon a running exercise of another half hour, that is where my not using cigarettes is of benefit to my running endurance. Every night I have my cold water shower bath. Three times a day my teeth are cleaned and underwear changed three times a week. Every Wednesday and Saturday afternoons we have to wash clothes. I have 3 suits of underwear. Never before in my life have I felt so fine as I do now. Cold means nothing to me now, that is what training will do for a fellow. Everybody is telling me that folks will never know me when I return having changed in every way in the past few weeks.

We are to have a big clothing issue soon, being of new woolen uniforms, shoes, hats, overcoats and leggings. I think some cotton clothing will also be given out.

Good by and love to you all. I think of you every day and wonder if you are enjoying life as well as I.

Earl.

Thursday, November 15, 1917, Page 4
One of Our Boys

Camp Dix, N.J.

Dear Mother:-

How are you getting along, I am getting along pretty good. I got the box you sent me mother and was glad to get it. I felt just like crying mother when I got it for it did look so much like home.

I am very lonesome mother and I will never get over it until the day comes when I can come home mother. This is not much like home believe me, but I am trying to do the best I can.

I was guarding the high-way the other day and I liked it pretty well; I had a belt and a 30 shooter and 5 shells in it. I had on an overcoat and a band on the sleeve it said "M. P.," that means Military Police.

Everybody I told to move had to go even the ladies. One nice young lady in a car took hold of my hand and said "Oh you cop," and I said "Thank you," how she did laugh. She got away up the road and waved back at me.

Cars coming this way and that way, I tell you that you have to keep your eyes open. They are all autos and teams and have to stand in the middle of the road and tell them when to pass and when not to. I got along with it fine. They had to do as I told them. When they gave us any back talk all I had to do was to march them up to police headquarters and they took care of them.

Well, this is about all I can tell now mother. How are all the folks, tell them that I send my regards to them all and also to you, mother, above them all, because you are the only one I have to think of.

Dear mother, I never thought I would be very lonesome away from you but I have found it out now alright. If I ever get back home to you I will never leave you. When I go to bed nights you don't know how I feel. I feel good and all like that, but it is not like being home and saying good night mother. Oh dear, I don't know what to do. Well I will have to make the best of it that is all. Tell Jakie to come down and I will show him some guns and other things that he never saw. Mother I wish you could come down and see me. It would help me out a lot, I

tell you, if I only could see you.

Well I will have to close now mother because I want to go over to the Y. M. C. A. Some lawyers are going to speak and I want to hear them. It is now 15 to 7. I have a watch right on my wrist so all I have to do is look at it and see what time it is.

Lester Collins

Thursday, December 13, 1917, Page 1
My Experience of Plattsburg

Coming up to Plattsburg on the special from New York I remember having quite a case of nervousness because the men looked so keen and intelligent. They were mostly in their civilian clothes, and that metropolitan air of snap, of success was very much with them. I thought what fierce competition it would be, and it worried me a bit.

But when next day the change was made from civilian to military clothes and all individuality swallowed up in the misfit uniforms issued by the Government, you couldn't tell the Stock Exchange from the Fish Market, nor Fifth Ave. from the Bowery. The impressive business man whose figure had that well-fed, prosperously rounded appearance under the camouflage efforts of his civilian tailor, became merely a dumpy, somewhat ludicrous human cipher in the frankly revealing khaki. I learned once more the old, old lesson, that difficulties have a way of dissolving the closer you get to them.

The first day of camp we were lined up in the company street and arranged in assorted sizes, tall men on the right.

It was funny to see men manouvre about for little depressions or elevations in the road so that their height might correspond with some friend's height, and in that way get together in the same squad. I think now what a difference the matter of inches may make in a fellow's career.

For instance, if I had been an inch taller I would have been in the squad with Dave Goodrich of the Goodrich Rubber Co., or if I had been an inch shorter I would have been with Dick Waldo, the genius behind the New York Tribune, and one of the Country's biggest brains.

Being as intimately thrown together as squad members, one can never say where one's acquaintance with such men might lead one.

The first month at Plattsburg was made

rather uncomfortable by the three typhoid innoculations. It isn't the pleasantest sensation to stand in a long line with your arm bare, waiting your turn to get an inch of steel in the flesh. More than one man has toppled over in a faint before his turn [?]. It doesn't [?] entertaining an [?] bothers quite a lot. The injections come about ten days apart, and it seemed that just as one was getting back to normal again, and no longer sick from the serum, that it was time for another shot. When the medical orderly stamped the date on the third dose, it was one of the most agreeable ceremonies any of us witnessed at Plattsburg.

The first month of camp was devoted almost entirely to such routine work as close order drill, bayonet drill, physical exercise, signaling, etc.

About the fifth week we were introduced to something different. Shovels and picks were gently placed in our hands and we were led out into some wild country three miles away and put to digging trenches.

We spent two weeks digging, and in that time got some six miles of trench system dug. The system was complete as far as it went. There were the front line, or fire trench, the cover trench, and the support trench all running parallel to the supposed enemy, and then there were the connecting trenches leading to the rear, by means of which the troops moved into action and out of action. In addition we excavated huge places and made them into dugouts for various officers headquarters, and shelters for the men when off duty.

The trenches weren't dug merely to make us familiar with the shovel. We had to occupy them for 24 hours. One Friday morning at 8 o'clock we rolled our packs, slung packs and rifles across our shoulders and hiked out to our homemade trenches, the wind came up very hard and developed a violent sand storm, for the dirt we had thrown up loose in making the trenches was mostly sand. At noon we had to walk about a quarter of a mile down a trench for mess, and by the time we were ready to eat the stew, it was heavily flavored with sand. I didn't get enough enjoyment out of my meal to care about going after the next two meals. Promptly as night came it began to rain, one of the coldest and most disagreeable rains that ever happened. The dugouts began to leak very shortly, until there wasn't much choice between being on duty out in the open trenches, or off duty in a dugout. I remember curling myself up in in a fairly dry place, under a poncho hung to catch the water dripping through. I was having a pretty successful snooze when the poncho, having caught more water than it could hold, came down on me with its deluge of water. But even that didn't make me much more uncomfortable than I was.

During the night we had a chance to see a number of the night signaling devices used on the other wide. Of course there is the huge rocket that whizzes itself aloft and breaks on the way down. As it breaks it releases a little parachute to which is attached a ball of light. The parachute opens and holds the ball of light in the air a long time.

Then there is the rocket-bomb which goes [?]obbling straight up for three or four hundred feet, bursts and releases the parachute and light, and a second later gives another explosion to attract attention to the [?]. No man's land is literally as light as day when several star shells are set off.

Toward the end of camp we had a chance to watch an artillery bombardment of our trench. Nobody minded, I assure you, seeing those trenches blown to pieces. The battery of cannon were located about two miles from where we were observing, and aimed so that the shells would land about 200 yards from us. By watching closely I could see the burst of flame from the muzzle of the cannon, and then the [?] later, could hear the shell approach. The noise made is almost identical [?] a train, and you can follow the path [?] the noise so plainly that you actually [?] why you can't see the shell. [?] to follow that shell through [?] aerial train, so [?]. [?] your fingers at it through the air several hundred feet. The three-ince gun has a burst that you think of as being simply savage. It hits and everything goes before it.

Shrapnel is another interesting thing to watch. The shell case is packed with some 300 round bullets, and behind the bullets is a time fuse and a powder charge. The shell is shot from the cannon with the time fuse set so that it will explode the powder charge and scatter the bullets before the shell strikes the ground. So you can always tell shrapnel because the shell burns in the air, and the ground is spattered with bullets raining down.

We have been visited and lectured to by a number of British and French officers. The matter-of-fact way they tell about their experiences in first-hand killing is always a marvel to us who haven't had our baptism by fire. For instance, there is a trench raid. I'll quote the officer telling the story: "We come to the German first line trench, and apparently they are all killed or wounded. The artillery preparation has apparently been complete. But the Huns are tricky dogs. We don't trust'em. So as we clean up the trench we use our bayonets to make sure that every man is a dead one, and nobody playing dead. We move on up the trench and come to a dugout. We yell down the entrance to the Germans, "How many of you down there?" If Fritz answers "Five," we throw in one bomb. If he says, "Twenty," we toss in three. We always ask how many there are, to know how many bombs to throw.

Plattsburg has not made finished officers of the men in three short months, and nobody knows this better than the men themselves. It has only been able to outline what an officer must know and do. The men must themselves fill in the outline when they go with their troops, and really become officers through their experience.

When officers and men are so desperately needed, the Plattsburg method of developing leaders is about as good an emergency method as there is. The necessity of the situation, if nothing else, has justified the Officers Training Camp.

Written by—First Lieut. Allan Hovey

Thursday, December 27, 1917, Page 1

A Call To Duty

U. S. S. Iowa

Dear Friends:–

Not long ago it was my privilege to spend a few days at home and I was very much surprised to find such a feeling of uncertainly, almost doubt, in the minds of so many, as to the cause and outcome of the war. How can any one forget the awful need of Europe; Belgium broken, bruised and starting; Armena, Servia, Romania, crused, and we have only to look back to that great war counsel at Potsdam Palace when Emperor William told his generals of his dream of world empire, where even the name of Germania was suggested as the name which should be given to north America, after he had completed the defeat of Europe, for which service the soldiers were to return home with their pockets full of rings and jewels for their sweet hearts at home. Just stop and think where

these jewels were to come from. The hands of other men's wives, sweethearts, mothers and daughters, were robbed, other men's homes destroyed, all that one people might satisfy a selfish desire to rule; and this was not enough, just listen to the words of Wilhelm the second:

"After this war I shall stand no foolishness from America." Is this not enough? How dare America, latest called of the nations, most blest by freedom, falter. We shall not pass through the fire untouched, but we shall come out with the dross consumed and there shall rise a greater people, a people glorified, transfigured. It may be we shall know our Gethsemne, but the unnumbered generations shall glory in the freedom that we by suffering had secured for the earth. Let us remember: "He hath established their bounds that they shall not pass over." Let those at home remember that they are upholding the hands of those at the front. If they fail us the fight goes against us, but if they are true, then we shall be strong for the fight, wherever and whenever it will come. The greatest need of the hour is the calm earnest determination of our people, and a great belief in the cause for which we fight. I wish every one could read the article "What America Is Fighting" written by Newel Dwight Hillis in the Current Opinion.

Then there would come to them a real sense of conditions in Europe, which but for the Grace of God might be the case in America, had we been attacked first. Let every man and women be true to the cause American stands for and there will never be another such tragedy as today is darkening the world.

Yours Sincerely,
Lucius F. Bagley

Thursday, January 24, 1918, Page 1

I wish to thank my friends through this column for sending me so many nice Christmas presents. I never go so many at one time in all my life. Thanks a thousand times.

I received a pair of heavy winter socks from Mrs. Irving Smith, two nice cakes from Miss Baxter, a nice box of chocolate drop from Mrs. Ida Maxwell. From Evin Wood a nice pipe and tobacco, from John Waterstreet and James Snook, cigarettes, Henry Weitz and Charles Ducolon pipe and tobacco, Arthur and David Nundy a lot of cigars and 25 cents in change, also candy, nuts and gum; then of course mother sent me a Christmas box, very very packed with all the goodies I could think of. I tell you all this looked good to me and made me think of home. There were 45 of us in the hospital sick with the measles. They had a big Christmas tree and a nice Christmas dinner there for us but I was very sick and didn't feel much like eating. They were very good to us and we had the best of care. I got out the day before New Years and went back to the barracks where I had to stay for two weeks where it was nice and warm, but I caught more cold and thought I would have to go back to the hospital again but I got better. Now I think I will be right and will be out in a few days ready for drilling again. I like my officers. They are very good to us. Well I hope you had a merry Christmas, with my best wishes for a happy New Year to you all.

Corpal Lester Collins,
Camp Gordon,
Atlanta, Ga.

Thursday, February 7, 1918, Page 1
Private John Hundley

France, January 6, 1918

Dear Mother, Father and Brothers:

I received your letter and was glad to get it and will write this to let you know that we are back in our old places again and glad of it. We were cutting wood for three weeks and it was pretty cold, but we had all the wood we wanted to burn in the stoves. I had to purchase five Frank's worth of wood this morning in order to keep the room warm, but I will get some of this money back when the boys get paid as they were all broke. You wanted to know what we are doing and where we are. It is better mother that you do not know and you will feel better not knowing than as if I told you. I am hardening up now and can stand a lot of hard marches. We walked about twelve miles yesterday in two hours and a half and carried full packs, rested twice on the way. That was moving some, as the roads were all snow and therefore slippery. I carried two blankets, one hundred pounds of ammunition, rifle, etc., and they were quite heavy. How are the boys coming. Tell them that I am to have turkey to eat Monday and that I wish they were here for that day. I would show them more in that one day than they would see in the states in their lives. Have not received your box yet. Will close for this time, with love to all.

John Hundley

Thursday, February 21, 1918, Page 1
Up Above the Clouds

Kelly Field, Feb. 9, 1918.

Dear Dad.

Am not flying this afternoon and am all alone in my quarters so I can write letters. I received yours, this morning and mother's too.

You don't wish any more than I do that I could come home for a while and am going to make a big try for a leave of absence when I finish instructors' school, but I don't know whether it will be possible or not. You see after a fellow has had as much expensive training as I have had they dislike to let him go and lose the time and if they won't let me off I guess I'll have to grin and bear it as everyone has to do these days.

We had to fly in the rain this morning. None of us liked it very much. It was cold and the force of the rain driven back by the propeller stung our faces like hail. The wind was gusty too and we had to keep our mind on the job believe me. I had a good ship this morning though. It was a new one and flew fine.

The other day I was up above some fleecy white clouds for the first time. I've been up that high a good many times but there never happened to be clouds in the sky with patches of clear air so that I could get up through without being unable to see. It was one of the prettiest sights I ever hope to see. Just a sea of clouds with the sun shining on them and a place every now and then where I could get a peek at the earth to see where I was.

Yesterday I drove a machine from the front seat for the first time. It seemed rather queer and awkward at first but came out on it all right. Took another Lieutenant up as a passenger in the rear seat.

Lieut. John Harlan Cooper

Thursday, March 7, 1918, Page 1
"Ye Gods, What a Ride."

The following is an extract from a letter received here from Lieutenant J. A. Hovey, written Feb. 22 at San Antonio, Texas.

My able line assistant went down to the field early today. He reported back [?] I had risen from the blankets, that only one officer was needed for the whole section, the ret having permission to turn Washington's birthday into the holiday it is supposed to be. I relapsed to the prone position again, until I was most rudely around by an insistent tapping on my head, which turned out to be none other than J. Harlan Cooper. "Coop" pulled me out of bed and went over to his quarters for dinner. And now for the thrilling part. He had to fly today and he connived to slip me aboard. I climed into the rear seat and strapped myself in and took a last look around terra firma as I had known it all my life."

"Coop" opened up the throttle and we were off. Ye gods, what a ride and what a sensation. I loved every minute of it even if I did wonder whether we would come back to the ground en masse or in portions. We climbed I should say 600 or 700 feet when "Coop" shot the plane up and down in a series of waves. He would turn around and ask me if I liked it. As a matter of actual fact, I did like it, though it gives one a whole bunch of thrills when drops come. The straight away flying seems entirely safe, even to a novice. I found, and the distance down doesn't bother as I thought it did. I know that when we were flying straight and the plane was level, I felt perfectly like looking all around and admiring the scenery. The earth does look funny, laid all out in rectangles, squares and geometric patches of all sorts, with the roads like little ribbons and buildings like doll houses. I'll admit I was nervous on the turns when the machine was "banked." On some of these turns the machine was literally straight up and down so that the earth was at right angles to my vision, instead of parallel. And I always felt as if we were falling [?], only "Coop" would always straighten her out again. I had hard work to keep from yelling on the turns, but nobody could have heard me anyway. I couldn't hear my own voice. Landing was the best fun of all; with the engine shut off we went coasting almost straight down until we were going parallel again, and she[?]led slowly lower and lower until we began to bump the ground [?].

Thursday, March 28, 1918, Page 1
His Old Home Paper

San Diego, California
March 14, 1918

Dear Mr. Cooper:

It was rather a coincidence today that I should cut out of a Boston paper Edgar guest's poem on the "Home Town Paper" to send to you, and late the same day be reading in the Record of the same poet's stanzas on the Birdman.

I want to say, enough to get out paper and ink, that Edgar A. Guest knows whereof he speaks when he tells in his verses about the home town paper and how it feels to get it when a chap is a long way from home.

Being in the publishing business myself, when times are peaceful, I know that publishers don't get any too much praise for their work, and I am especially glad therefore to use this back-handed method of telling you how I feel about the Record. I should feel a real want if it failed to come, and I'm always concerned about losing an issue or two when I have to move to a new station. If the people who live right in the village don't often come and tell you that they like the paper, I can speak heartily for the boys who are away from home that they couldn't get along without it. I hope the cost of new-print paper doesn't rise so high that it stops the work.

Cordially yours
Allen Hovey

Thursday, April 18, 1918, Page 8

February 27th, 1918
Somewhere in France.

My Dear Mother, Father and Brothers.

I received your letter and two boxes and was very glad to receive them. I am in good health, the weather is fine, the sun shining most of the time. You asked what we had to eat; we have for breakfast: potatoes, bacon, bread, coffee and four times a week we either have syrup, rice or jam. For dinner: roast beef, mashed potatoes, bread, coffee. For supper: beef stew, bread and coffee. We have a good place to sleep, we have a stove and all the wood we want. I have three blankets. We are stoping in a small town in France and the French people think there is nothing like an American soldier and we have a good time with them. I can now speak a little of their language and can understand quite a lot of it. They still have the old way of doing things. I enjoyed the cake you sent me and it hit the right place.

With love to all
John A. Hunley

Supplement The Hilton Record
Thursday, April 4, 1918.

One of Our Boys

Very Entertaining Letter from Earl Burritt
of U.S. Army.

Dear Mother:

Sometime ago in one of my letters I told you
of being at the 27th Division rifle and pistol
range in the Blue Ridge Mountains, our period
of time there was from Feb. 8th to the 16th. In
that letter I told you of my trip back to the South
after my furlough home and of many pleasant
incidents up to that time, and now will tell you
of the trip we took to the top of Mt. Mitchell an
experience I would not like to have missed.

Sunday morning, the tenth, dawned with a
beauty and freshness beyond description. After
breakfast our Lieutenant who was in charge of
the first Machine Gun Platoon of my company
which comprised forty men, advised us to "beat
it" so as to escape any detail that might be
thrown upon us for the day, and I need not tell
you that we obeyed the order with all possible
speed. By eight o'clock a party of ten of us
started on a hike of the rocky side of Mt.
Mitchell. The crest is three thousand feet above
sea level, above the clouds when there are any
in that locality. This point we gained after a
tiresome two hours climb and from its dizzy
heights the beautiful country stretched around
us from every side. On the south miles of
beautiful S. Carolina could be seen. To the S.W.
the rugged northern extremity of Georgia could
be dimly distinguished against the distant
horizon, and again to the North and East N.
Carolina proved its wonder and beauty.

In this land "Above the Skies" as it is called,
strange and beautiful vegetation exists, such as
banana plants, some stunted specimens of
cactus, holly, mistletoe, pine and fir trees, and
countless numbers of strange foliage, that I had
never seen before.

Many small and picturesque streams and
waterfalls were found in some places, falling as
much as four hundred feet into a bed of banana
plants and blue grass.

It is beyond any comparison as far as beauty
is concerned, and beyond the power of my
vocabulary to clearly describe the wonders of
this Garden of Paradise in the mountains above
the clouds.

As we stood on the rocky peak hundreds of
feet above the sea, we gazed about us in
wonderment and marveled at its rare beauty. I
had heard many stories of these mountains but
never realized their true value until I had
witnessed for myself. Even then I could hardly
believe my eyes.

After spending some time in meditation we
continued our journey by starting northward
over an old time Indian trail which again led us
over hills and through valleys. We continued on
for about ten miles, passing a very few houses
but no villages. It was now past one o'clock p.m.
and we began to realize we had worked up quite
an appetite. We kept on going, hoping to find a
house where some "eats" could be had. After
about an hour we suddenly came upon a small
village, tucked snugly away at the base of a
mountain.

As we entered the village the inhabitants
hastened to the doors, and out in their yards to
get a look at us. It was evident that they had
never seen many soldiers. We hardly knew what
kind of a reception was in store for us, as we
were then in the heart of the "Moonshine"
country and a place as we found out later where
a civilian would never think of entering or if he
did would never leave alive.

After some time of convincing them, as to
what our purpose was in that section and who
we were, we finally made them believe we were
friends and in need of dinner. We split up in
twos and went to different places for dinner and
believe me we did eat.

The conditions under which these people
live are of the very roughest. The house, made
of hewn logs cemented together with some kind
of cement, consisted of one room. The logs
serve as shingles and floor alike. At one end of
the room was a gigantic fire place over which
was a shelf containing a few trinkets including
an old fashioned rifle and powder horn. At the
opposite side two old time home-made beds,
which to my estimation could not compare to
any comfortable little cot in our tent. Wall paper
and paint are unknown and no decoration of
any description adorn the walls. At the end was
a little "lean-to" which contained an odd
looking little stove and a home-made table
covered with well worn oil cloth and also home
made benches which served as chairs.

The entire "mess-gear" consisted of tin and
showed long and hard usage. Porcelain and
silver were unknown to them.

Our dinner consisted of red beans, cabbage,
coffee, cornbread, biscuits and molasses, also
fried pork and it was cooked to perfection and

we enjoyed the meal to the limit.

During the course of the meal a friendly talk ensued. We found to our surprise that the family of nine, the oldest being 97 had never been far away, some of them not over one hundred miles and had never seen a large city, lake, steam boat, steam or trolley car, any modern electrical contrivances, or a modern home with all its furnishings and modern conveniences and only a few automobiles.

They wondered and doubted as we told them of some of the wonders of New York state and some of its cities. And also of the different types of fighting craft of our navy; also of the great ocean liners we had seen and been aboard. We told them of the north and of our way of living also many other things.

These simple people, ignorant of the outside world, displayed a wonderful interest in the ways and doings of the north, and a desire to know more of the unknown.

They in turn told us of the moonshiners, their activities, and how it was carried on and the many attempts made by Revenue officers to wipe it out and their many failures; also of the terrible conclusion of some of these men's bright futures.

The oldest member of the family, a veteran of the civil war, told some of his experiences of his desertion for the Ku-Klux-Klan, which was just organized at that time.

The afternoon became well advanced before we were aware of it, and found that we would indeed have to hurry some to reach camp before dark. So bidding our newly made friends good bye, we left them at five o'clock, with a long hike ahead of us. We reached the top of Mt. Mitchell at seven and still had a perilous hike ahead of us over the treacherous peak of which we knew a very little. I had a flash light and radio-lite compass and with the help of these, reached camp in safety, save a few scratches and knocks due to the stumps and holds in the uneven ground.

Just as we were about to retire for the night fire was discovered in a part of the mountains over which we had passed but an hour before. A hundred volunteers were called from [?] Co. and Co. I. We started armed with waterpails, axes and shovels. The fire had gained considerable headway, due to the dry condition of the leaves and underbrush. We dug a wide circle around the fire, and cut down as many of the trees as we could safely reach. As no water

was handy we combined our efforts, by throwing loose earth upon the dry and burning wood, after a four hours fight had it subdued, but not until about three acres were totally destroyed. After we were satisfied everything was safe we returned to camp once more and made ready for bed. The time read "two bells" I slept fine that night; was awakened at six by the notes of the "revillie." As we had no calls to answer we did not exert ourselves until the forenoon as well advanced. We surely needed the rest, and therefore took it. You know it is a mighty poor soldier that cannot get what belongs to him.

The remainder of the time at the range up to the time we left was spent at ease, with no work to do. We were to shoot our automatic pistols, but no ammunition could be had until late Friday afternoon, when we shot about thirty rounds each.

Friday morning we packed our tents and extra equipment and that night made our beds in the woods. We collected balsams and pine boughs and upon these we spread our blankets.

After supper it started to rain and, with no tents up, we thought we were out of luck for the night. One of our party, while on the hike Sunday, discovered a log cabin a short distance from camp and made known his idea to us that we spend the night there. We gathered our equipment together and started for the place he had mentioned. We found a well built log cabin of two spacious rooms, with a fireplace in each one. We found some wood and soon had a fire, where we dried our clothes, and spread our blankets before the fire. Believe me we did "pound our ears" that night, in spite of the heavy rain and electrical storm that was general throughout the night.

Saturday morning broke bright and fair with the promise of a fine day in which to make our twenty mile hike back to Campobello, where we were to take the train back to Spartanburg.

We left the range at eight-thirty the morning with the conclusion of a week of experiences that will be of the pleasantest in my life up to then.

We are all anxious to go back again and think we will go some time this month to both pistol and machine gun practice.

Will close with the usual love and respect to all.

Your Son,
Earl Burritt.

Thursday, May 30, 1918, Page 1

Airplane Accident

Lieutenant John Harlan Cooper Injured at Kelly Field, Texas

Mr. and Mrs. J. E. Cooper of this village received the following telegram Wednesday morning:

Kelly Field, Texas, May 28th

"Your son Lieutenant John H. Cooper, in airplane accident here today. Suffered fracture of right clavicle, laceration over left eye and minor bruises. Hospital authorities think not serious."

Quackenbush

No further particularies have been received up to going to press although a dispatch is expected momentarily from Kenneth smith also from this village who is at Kelly Field and has been telegraphed to for further facts as to the nature of the accident and the condition of Lieutenant Cooper who has been at Kelly Field for over a year and has been on instructor-in flying for several months.

Thursday, June 6, 1918, Page 4

Getting Better

Saturday, June 1st

My Dear Mother:—

Received your letter after my accident and think I'll be able to secure a furlough for the period of two months. I was told I wouldn't have any trouble in getting [?] sometime before my arm gets back in shape.

Don't worry about me for I am getting along fine, my clavicle is broken and my eye is bruised and cut, but the pupil is not hurt. Besides a bruised body I am all right. It probably will be three or four weeks before I am discharged from the hospital, and then homeward bound for me.

They are very nice to me here, giving me the best care and treatment, making me as comfortable as possible.

Love to all

John Harlan Cooper.

Dictated by Harlan and written by Kenneth Smith.

Thursday, June 20, 1918, Page 12

From "Jack" Magee

Camp Crane, Allentown, Penna.

J. E. Cooper

Dear Boss:—

I have been going to write you for sometime but Uncle keeps me rather busy, and letter writing is not my specialty anyway, but the soldier sure has to write. The folks at home are good and write to us, but they all expect a letter in replay before we get another, so you can guess in order to receive, you must send.

The [?] question you will want to ask "Is how do we (Henry, Ross and myself) like it. Henry thinks it is fine, but shoveling [?] coal. They had him in the coal bin[?] but he says he didn't sweat any. He gets a little hair cutting in on the side, just enough to keep himself and me in cream. We all have to have an inch hair cut. Outside of Ross and myself, I believe [?]th is the happiest fellow in the army. Ross is pleased because he got into the Italian contingent with me and expects to sail anytime now for his native country. Sorry to say Henry got transferred to an ambulance company going to France. Suppose however they have someone there to stop the Kaiser when Ross and I get him running.

The camp here is in a beautiful place surrounded by hills, but, the hills when we [?] hiking. It seems to be up hill going and coming. Was on an all day hike last week when about 100 gave out and were brought in, in an ambulance. Rode about five minutes myself. They always put the tall fellow in front to set the pace and we keep up if we can.

Question No. 2, "Do you get good meals." No and yes. Sometimes I think the only things left in the country is ball{/}rs, weaners and beans. Breakfast is by far the best meal, we have plenty of sugar and wheat bread, but our butter never was acquainted with a cow.

Question No 3 "When do you expect to go across? Ross and I anytime, our things are packed and gone, but Uncle [?] kidding us so about going [?] given up hopes, but probably [?] some time next week. Henry will stay for at least a month. [?] patriotic citizens. Wish I could have been home to have helped. People are either for us or against us. Why spend money sending us over to fight just because they are thicker over there?

Yours as ever

Jack

Thursday, June 20, 1918, Page 5

A Letter from Henry Smith received here announced that John Magee and Rossario Disimone both of this village, had left Camp Crane and they will be shortly be heard from across seas.

Thursday, July 4, 1918, Page 1

A Morning Ride

Kelly Field, Texas, June 28th.

To Editor of Record:—

I had the supreme pleasure this morning of sailing through the clouds with Lieut. Dorrset, who is instructing on acrobatic flying.

This department is where the boys learn to do the different stunts, such as "loop the loop" "tail spins" and others.

We left the grounds at nine a.m., and ascended to about three thousand feet, and then he started looping the loop, then into a tail spin and nose dive and by the time we were through with that my "tummy" felt rather upside down. But I had that broad grin of mine and turning around in my [?] much to say, do it again [?] [?]yed at our distination.

[?] much satisfied with [?] and hope that I will have another chance soon.

"You take the best care of John while he is home so that he [?] come back in the best of condition for flying, for it sure is some [?]rt.

K. I. Smith

Thursday, July 18, 1918, Page 1

Washing in the Army

As Described by John Magee; Written Previous to Sailing for Italy.

Camp Crane, Allentown, Pa.

Dear Mr. Cooper:—

Since you asked me to write you a letter for publication, I have been rather busy getting ready for our little trip. They sure have kept me thumping the typewriter getting our passenger list, etc.; more red tape to this army than to Mayor Pratt's job.

It is Sunday morning and I have just finished washing. We claim "the better the day the better the deed." Our washing has to be done and Sunday is the only time we get to do it. After hikes and drills we are too tired and besides the crows carry away our washing at night.

Washing, anyway, is a thing that gets our goat. We would rather drill or hike any time than wash. The process is simple, so simple any housewife could go away and leave her husband to do it without fear of his getting the blueing too strong or the colored clothes in with the white.

The first operation is to collect our clothes and soap. This may seem simple, but when your clothespress is a bag about the size of a fifty-pound flour sack, it becomes more difficult. After overhauling two pairs of shoes, three

suits, five pairs of cotton and six pairs of woolen socks, five suits of underwear, toilet articles, Red Cross material, and other things we might be able to pack in, we finally capture our piece of soap at the bottom of the bag. Slippery stuff you know.

The two tubs and boards are surrounded as usual with an impatient bunch clamoring to get at them, so I took my brush and started for the showers. This is crowded but I finally secured a place or rather a stall, as it is in a horse stable. Mother says to wash in hot water, but I cheerfully used what I had, which for the most part was above freezing. The process, as I said before, was simple. Wet the piece and spread it out a little at a ti[?] on the partitions between the t[?]lls (a[?] board will do) soap with naptha and scrub. Every bit must be scrubbed on both sides, wringing is done by hand which saves the buttons.

After an hour and a half's work I had cloths tied on the line. I have often wondered what there was about a washing to make a woman proud of it, but I was proud of that washing. Why shouldn't I be; hadn't I spent an hour and a half hard work on it? But horrors how small it looked hanging there on the line. I thought a pair of socks, a suit of underwear, a shirt, and a couple of handkercheifs would make a bigger showing than that. It makes a fellow's heart sink to think of the big ones turned out at home.

The girls are becoming experts at factory work, street car running, street policing and voting while, while we are learning to cook, sew and wash, but we never will make them wives. No, when we come back they will have to do the sewing and washing.

Yours Truly
Jack.

Thursday, July 18, 1918, Page 5

Mr. and Mrs. Wi. I. Smith received word last week that their son, Kenneth, who has been at Kelly Field, Texas, since he enlisted in April 1917, has been transferred to an aviation field at Montgomery, Ala.

Thursday, July 18, 1918, Page 5

Word has been received that Base Hospital 19, organized in Rochester and of which Morley Hall, son of Mr. and Mrs. Robert Hall of this town is a member, is stationed at Vichy, a famous summer resort of France.

Thursday, August 1, 1918, Page 6

The following telegram was received Tuesday morning by J. E. Cooper from his son Lieutenant John Harlan cooper of Camp Kelly, San Antonia, Texas. I arrived here safely and on time. Reported flying Saturday morning. I am not instructing yet. Letter [?] follow.

Thursday, August 1, 1918, Page 1

Colonel Brown Writes Entertainingly of Camp Life in Georgia.

Camp Hancock, July 21, 1918

Dear Folks at Home:—

Another strenuous week of work and play, of successes and reverses (to myself) has passed. Another week nearer the coveted gold bars or back to the ranks as luck may have it. Another week nearer the carefree life at home or the bright lights of Paris as the Gods of War may will. Let the future take care of itself for it's enough to live in the present. Let us eat, drink and be merry to-day while there is yet time. Today I am camping on the hot sands of Georgia; tomorrow may be fraught with good and evil, but come what will, today I am happy and contented.

The prologue finished I will now proceed to write a letter or at least set down some words on paper that will convey to you the idea that I am still very much myself.

It is Suuday noon, but I have not received a letter from you this week. I'm not worrying because I know that you wouldn't have send that big box of candy and cookies if anything was wrong. The papers came last Tuesday, and as is often the case with mail here, had been delayed several days.

The past week has not been very hot so it has not been so hard on us as it might have been. In fact, all things concerned, we did our hardest work at Meade when we had full packs and rifles. We have had some real rainy weather but the old tent kept it off and our ditches carried it away. Besides we missed our British physical drill or "physical torture" as we call it. Everybody is happy when we miss a period with the "around me doubles" as we call the British Sergeant-Majors. The army is much like the farm though; they always have rainy-day jobs and sometimes they keep us busy.

Rumors and yet more rumors keep pouring and that's all there is to it. I think we're going to stay here a bit.

They have begun on [?] classed as advanced work in infantry, but still no machine guns. Later on we'll get that. In the meantime we have been learning the art of building barbed wire fences to keep the Germans in Germany, trench building, mapping, horseback riding and bomb or grenade throwing. This grenade throwing is very interesting, but I had a lame back for a couple of days after throwing them. There is a special way they must be thrown in order to get them up in the air to a sufficient height and it takes a lot of practice to get the trick. We practice with dummies of course. After we learn the mechanism and chemistry of the bomb, we'll have a few loaded ones. I think we will do some more of it this coming week, but I haven't seen this week's schedule as of yet.

One thing they are stiffening up on and that is our Saturday morning inspection. It wouldn't be a full week's work without an inspection, and by the way, let me inform you an army inspection is some occasion. A wedding or a funeral, an initiation into a secret society, or a murder trial are indeed very jovial parties, mere trivial occurrences compared with the austere solemnity of a Saturday morning inspection when, arrayed in spotless garments, you stand at attention and the Captain comes down the line to get your goat—and generally does. God help our brave sailors on the sea and our brave soldiers and marines in France and Italy but God help us, protect us and pity us every Saturday morning here in Camp Hancock. The captain confined 23 of our men to the company street over week-end for slight mistakes yesterday. A match stick in the street or a cup out of place on the bunk may lose week-end passes for a whole tent full. Luckily our crowd didn't get nailed for anything.

During the past week I had a chance to act as company commander for a day and got away with it all right. It is quite a sensation the first time you give a command and see 180 men move as one man. The day you are company commander everybody must do what you tell them. The very next day I waited on table, which only goes to show how democratic a company of candidates is.

Another thing I am rapidly learning is washing and sweeping and dusting. It's a cinch that I'll make somebody a good wife when the army musters me out. I did enough washing for a family of ten this morning and swept the whole blooming tent and the street in front of it. They certainly teach you a lot of things in the army. If the army decides that I should become a grand opera singer for the good of the country, then of course they would proceed to make me one and I would obey. They do things most as strange.

They are feeding us very well down here now. For dinner today we had sweet potatoes, baked ham, tomato salad, grape juice, white bread of excellent quality, apple butter, butter and asparagus. That isn't bad is it?

Well, I thank you ever so much for the candy and cookies and hope you write me. By the way, be sure and put anything you send in a good strong box, as the box was almost done for. I'll do my best to get a special edition out to the boys during the week. Hope that all is well on the farm.

[?] in the papers that the 28th Division, who trained here, are chasing the Huns over the Marne. That's the Pennsylvania National Guard; the N. Y. N. G. is the 27th Division.

With love,
Colonel

Thursday, August 15, 1918, Page 4
Willard E. Bush

Last Friday a telegram, was received by Clarence Bush of Rochester announceing the death of his brother, Willard E., at Paris Island, S. C., where he was stationed. No details were embodied other than that his death occurred Thursday evening, Aug. 8th at 6 p. m. the body arrived on the a. m. train Tuesday, and was taken to the home where the services were held the following day at 2 p. m. Six soldiers from Rochester acted as bearers, and the Military salute was fired at the grave.

At the time of this writing detailed explanations are still lacking.

Willard E. Bush was the son of Mr. and Mrs. Vincient Bush of the West town line. It was only on June 7th that he went into the service, having enlisted in the Marine Corps as a machinist.

He has a brother, Elmer J. Bush, who has been in the service over a year, in the department of Aviation, and is at present stationed at Fort Sill, Oklahoma.

Beside his father and mother, he is also survived by the Brother Clarence of Rochester, and a sister, who lives on the West Town Line.

The sympathy of all is extended to the bereaved family.

Thursday, August 22, 1918, Page 1

The following is an extract from a letter received Mon. by J. E. Cooper of this village, from his son Lieutenant John Harlan Cooper of Kelly Field, Texas.

"I am instructing instructors now and like it first rate. There are four of us who have that job and two of them live in the same quarters with me. Yesterday the other Lieutenant and I took two ships and flew to Austin and returned. Thirty miles of the way back was after dark. San Antonia surely looked pretty when it was all lit up. We got back and down all O. K. at 9:20 o'clock. I took an altitude test the other day and busted the record. They said I was in perfect condition and that I could as high as any plane could take me."

Thursday, August 29, 1918, Page 4

Mr. and Mrs. Frank McCulla of this village about two weeks ago received a letter from their son, Dr. Frank McCulla, who is now in France. Among other things he said that he had seen German prisoners being brought in who were only 14 years of age and that even German women were made to fight, being chained to the big guns so they could not get away, and so found when our troops advanced.

Thursday, September 26, 1918, Page 1

In a letter received by Mr. and Mrs. Fred McCulla from their son Lieut. Frank McCulla, who has recently been transferred to the 120th Ambulance Co., "Over There", he states that the dressing station where he is working is thirty feet underground, reminding him of the Subway. He sent a piece of a German Airplane recently brought down by the Americans.

Thursday, September 26, 1918, Page 1

One day last week two of the Rochester papers published a notice to the effect that John Hundley of this village had died in France from disease, while another Rochester paper gave out that he was seriously wounded. Both reports are undoubtly errors as Mrs. Geo. Hundley of this village, [?] mother, has received a letter from him this week, one dated the latter part of August and the other the 4th of this month, in which he says he is well and happy.

Thursday, October 3, 1918, Page 1

Extracts from a Letter from France

I am all right and have been, although the circumstances of surroundings are hardly condusive for much letter writing. Today I am writing on a small very much homemade table situated on the south side of a lovely dugout. The door of it opens into a trench that terminates about three rods away on the roadside. In the dugout we have sleepers, both uppers and lowers, two sets on the North side and one set on the South making room for six of us nicely. To the west of the table on the south side and near the door is a small "Fransay" stove. At present we have considerable kindling wood lying on the floor conveniently located for making a fire tonight. It gets rather cold here during the night but I rather enjoy the mornings because they are so bright and chilly.

There is a certain kind of flea that delights tn making bumps on us similar to mosquito bites, but itch much worse, often festering. Some of the boys are covered with blotches but so far only my wrists are affected.

I haven't heard a word from Harold or Lester but think we are fairly close together now.

Yellow jackets are as plentiful as flies and both more during a meal.

Just to think that today is my birthday and here I am. We are going to have a little blowout of our own tonight, just the "hungry six."

Sgt. Brower is getting along fine Sgt. Austin is near me. Everyone is a friend to Austin. He sure is a prince.

I have been thinking peaches all day today. By the time you receive this it will be all apples.

Labor Day was very appropriately celebrated and will long be remembered by this battery. I [?] souvenir of the day.

No do[?] you read of air battles. We [?]ad them and silently squeeze [?] our side.

Walter Klafehan is all O. K. He is a fine chap and well liked.

I feel fine and ready for anything that may come. Don't worry about me because I am all O. K.

Your loving son
Corporal Homer Odell

Thursday, October 3, 1918, Page 4

[The following letter was received by Wilfred Horex of this town from England, written by the sister of Jack Bridgeman relating to his being wounded in August. Mr. Bridgeman formerly lived in this town for a time coming here from England.]-Editor September 10, 1918.

"Jack was wounded on August 24th. Right knee fractured. He is in a hospital in Lancashire, England. It is no use to write him there as he may be moved at any time, but I will forward any letters. Let his friends know. I hope he will escape with only a stiff leg, but it is early yet to say just how it will go. You asked what you could send him. I should say candy. It is almost impossible to get sweets here now and he dearly loves them you know.

He was wounded before Mory. The Guards Division had got the Germans on the run when they suddenly came up against an old quarry full of machine guns. All of the officers were shot except a Second Lieutenant. He ordered the company to fix bayonets and charge, and they did so. Just as they got up the hill Jack was struck. He turned and crawled back to a shell hole and put on his first aid bandage and then crawled on to the dressing station. It took him from 10 a.m. to 3:30 p.m. to get there."

Thursday, October 3, 1918, Page 12

Under date of Aug. 23rd, Geo. Dean writes: "We get the best eats, I now tip the scales at one hundred and ninety-two. I shall be glad to be home in a peacable place but not until all of the peace disturbers are taken care of, and by the looks now it will not be long before we have them. I expect to land in Germany about next week. Have been there, but this time we expect to stay."

Thursday, October 3, 1918, Page 12

In a letter received by G. M. Madden last week from Fred C. Hall, one of our Hilton boys, written "Somewhere in France" he says: "Tell the boys everything is OK with me, I am feeling fine. Have been transferred to the 43rd Artillery C. A. C. Headquarters. Am now cooking for about 60 men instead of 240. Having fine warm weather and cool nights. Good sleeping except when some Boches come sailing over and drop few bombs. Then we get an attention call, we grab steel helmets and beat it for cover. Everything here is about 100 years behind the U.S.A.

Thursday, October 10, 1918, Page 1
In The Flying Service.

Under date of September 27th, Chester B. Williams Writes: "Was flying [?] 5 [?] morning as stand by [?] boat). Naturally I am about dead, however, I love it, and so far have had but one mishap. About a month ago we had notor trouble, and had to land, but it happened near shore and we managed to hobble along and land in S. Bay just south of Bay Shore. You would be surprised how much superstition there is in this work. The men know better and yet there is that feeling. Take for instance, Boat No. 1[?], it was flown from the L. W. F. Co. at College Point on Long Island, on Friday the 13th of the month. They had motor trouble on the way over and landed in N. Y. harbor. Narrowly missed a tug, and broke a wing tip pontoon. The next day it went on patrol, ran into a boat and smashed a wing. A little later it made a hard landing and the hull sprang aleak. The carpenters fixed that and the very first trip out, it ran into No 19 in the fog at about 1500 feet high, and it and the three men in it have never been seen since. Not even a piece of it has ever been found. After No 13 was gone, the next suspicious character was No 19, after the collision with No 13, nothing happened for a while, and we began to think our suspicions had no ground but all of a sudden it caught fire seventy miles at sea, and burned up. Just before it sank one of the gas tanks blew up, a steamer had been attracted by the smoke and picked the men up. Just now there is no suspicious boat, so every one feels quite easy***Wish I could give you an idea of one of the boats we are building here. It is so large it doesn't seem as though it could ever fly, but just wait. It weights about six tons and will lift about five tons including all stores and supplies and a crew of seven men: the pilots sit 19 feet above the water, it has three Liberty Motors, a six powder cannon and half a dozen machine guns. ***One and a half hours later. —Just back from an emergency call—one of our boats lost. We found it about 15 miles out being towed in by one of Uncle Sam's cruisers.

Thursday, October 10, Page 4
John Crook, who is stationed at Camp Jackson, S. C., in the Field Artillery Replacement Deta[?], is assistant to the Supply Sergeant. In a recent letter he stated that he issued fifty s{/} overalls in five minutes and [?] them at all that. He is [?] back at his old business

[?].

Thursday, October 17, 1918, Page 1
Another False Rumor

A false rumor was recently spread about that Corporal Lester Collins had been seriously wounded in France. The following communication to his mother shows the fallaciousness of the story:

The American Red Cross
Washington, D.C.
Oct. 9, 1918

My dear Mrs. Collins:

A report has just been received from Base Hospital No 33 stating that Corp. Lester D. Collins is being treated there for bronchitis.

As you may know, the War Department does not inform families when the men in the service are ill but they wish us to send out any information we may have in this connection.

We can assure you that your son is receiving excellent care and that we shall have another report on his case, which we will send to you as soon as it reaches this office.

The American Red Cross extends to you its sincere sympathy in your natural anxiety.

Very sincerely,
W. R. Castle, Jr., Director

Thursday, October 17, 1918, Page 8
Frank Sweeting received a telegram about midnight on Saturday last stating, his son Floyd was dead. He was serving his country as seaman 1st class on the Ohio, no information as to the cause of death has been received. Floyd enlisted early in the Summer and went to the Great Lakes Training Station and was recently transferred to Norfolk and to the above mentioned ship. He was 22 yrs. of age.

Published Date Unknown
With Our Boys

Kelly Field, Texas
Oct. 21, 1918

Dear Dad:-

I am in my glory now, as I have flown the scout twice. It is a fast machine, about 120 miles per hour.

Saturday I flew to Port Aransas, which is a small fishing town on an island in the gulf. There were four ships altogether. We left here about two o'clock and arrived there at five-forty-five. Had to land at Breeville which is about half way, to fill up with gasoline. We staid at a small hotel there that night and got up early in the morning to go fishing for tarpon. We went at the wrong time as the tide was going out and the fish weren't biting, but we had a good time and are going again. Some of the fellow had strikes but I keqt up my reputation as a fisherman and didn't get a bite. We hired a motor boat and some row boats and men to roe them as the tarpon are quite a distance out in the gulf. The tarpon measure up to six feet in length and put up some scrap. They will jump five or six feet out of water when they are hooked. We saw a big bunch of porpoises. They sure are big. I thought the first one I saw was a submarine cow. I also got my first sight of a pelican outside of a cage. There were hundreds of them there.

Anchored at the dock was a submarine chaser which we were lucky enough to look over. We got acquainted with the officer in charge who showed us over the whole ship and explained everything to us.

We started back about three p.m. and arrived in San Antonia at six. Altogether it was a very enjoyable trip as we didn't have any trouble with the ships and had a fine time there. Expect to fly to Dallas soon, which is about a three hundred mile trip. Will tell you all about it if it goes through.

With love to all
Luentenant John H. Cooper.

Thursday, October 24, 1918, Page 8
John Magee in Italy

Mantova, Italy, September, 15, 1918.
Dear Folks:—

Up to my last letter we were not allowed to tell where we were located, but now up to a certain point, we can tell. I hardly know where I am or what I belong to myself, as our section has been broken up and we have not organized as yet, so I will have to find out what to put on for a return address, but perhaps my old address will do, as in a couple of weeks we will be organized again.

This town is a small city; one you read about in books, with its most, high wall and city gates. One city we passed through they made a charge to enter through the gates, but here no charge is made. The most is much larger, than my idea of a moat, and of course, is not filled with water now, although there is a stream near the wall which is a sort of washing place for the women

of the city, and the bottom of the moat is a network or clotheslines. It sure looks ancient and beautiful as one crosses over the bridge, or rather, rides over the moat, and looks down and sees the women in their bright colored dresses washing their clothes.

The buildings of the city are all old, dating back six to nine hundred years, and one can almost see knights in armor riding out through these wide gates. Running through the center of the city is an open sewer (we thought it was a river) and the scene looks like the picture of Venice.

One old castle down town has its moat around it, and the top story projects out and has its loop holes to shoot down on those attacking them. Just above the level of the moat, are the windows of the dungeons. It surely is thrilling to stand there and think of some of those old "Knights in Armor Stories".

Our camp is right beside a castle nine hundred years old, with high wall, but for some reason, no moat. The side entrance is in itself a mansion. The park in which we are camped is like enough the field in which the knights held their sports.

In one of the small squares down town is a beautiful Cathedral. The exterior is old an plain but the interior is wonderful. There is a large dome in the center like our capitol at Washington only far more beautiful. I could never describe the beauty of the designs on the walls and ceilings, or the alters with their beautiful paintings and carving, set off by lighted candles. On one end is the tomb of Pope Clement VII, which is protected from air raids by bags of sand. It almost made one hate the Germans to think they would deliberately destroy such things.

Rev. Morrow surely was right when he said Italy had good roads but he forgot to say they were dusty. Of course, in the they are at times rather narrow with hair pin curves, but always well built and protected at dangerous places by stone walls. In the plateau where we are, they are straight and level. They don't dip into every little gulley as in the States, but are leveled right up. Another thing, there is never any detouring or repairing roads. Never yet have seen a road closed for repairs.

The scenery is great. Here and there farmers can be seen loading hay on their two wheeled carts which are drawn by oxen, or perhaps a farmer will be plowing either with a modern or an old fashioned plow, but always with oxen. It sure makes a beautiful sight with these scenes in the fore ground together with vineyards and snowcapped mountains in the distance. It is funny to see the old and the new contrasted together. In one lot I saw men mowing with the wide old fashioned seythe and in next a rather modern or an old fashioned plow, but always with oxen. In several farm yards we saw the whole family out thrashing with flails and throwing the grain into the air and "Letting the wind blow chaff away".

It certainly is funny to see the whole family go to town crowded into a small cart drawn by a donkey. It would be laughable but for the picturesque setting given it by their bright colored costumes. I remember one outfit of two beautifull oxen led by an old farmer and drawing an old two wheeled cart on which a peasant girl was sitting on some straw. She was a perfect picture of health with a fat rosy face and bright colored dress.

One cannot blame the artists for coming here to sketch these pictures, as besides these they get the contrast of the mountains with the plains. The mountains with the valleys and high peaks on which is often perched a villa or castle with its winding road leading up to it, and here and there nestled in the mountains is a quaint old farm house. The plains with the roads lined with well trimmed mulberry trees, on which the silk worm lives, the land far flatter than that around home, is separated by irrigating ditches instead of fences.

The weather here is much cooler on account of the altitude, but yet day times weren't enough to wear our cotton suits; nights cold enough to wear woolen socks and the other night on guard I wore my overcoat and Red Cross sweater for the first time. One wonders how things keep so green, as it never rains, but only one night in tent is enough to solve both the question and the temperature. You certainly must give Italy credit for its name "Sunny Italy" as the sun has shone every day since I have been here. Since being in Mantova I have eaten mess for the first time in the shade, as our kitchen is under the shade of some big trees.

A great contrast to the farming system is Italy's fast growing school system. One thing I would like to have the people in Hilton see is the beautiful country school builds. I camped beside one one night and where we would have standing a small packing box, so to speak they

had a large stone building with lavatories and other modern improvements. It was a building of perhaps four large rooms, and I understand there is always a play ground and in connection with each is a plot of ground. In every little hamlet that we passed, always standing out from other buildings would be a building with "Sohule Elementari" written or rather cut over the door. Most of the advancement in education has been made under this reign, and in the past few years a compulsory school law up to fifteen years has been passed.

For some reason I have not received any mail for two weeks and only two letters in four, so I should be getting some before long. The things Mother wants to know of how we live, eat and many other things, I cannot tell, but we are taken well care of so don't worry.

Yours with love,
John Magee

Thursday, November 7, 1918, Page 1

France, Oct. 10th.

Dear Mother—

I wish to let you know that I am quite well. Hope you are the same. We have fairly good weather here now, hope it stays that way for a while. I am at a hospital in France in the prettiest place I have ever seen since I came over. I was at a place two days which a rich old Frenchman, was rebuilding on a big mountain at the left of the city. You could see for miles around. He could speak good English and I and my [?] had a good time with him. He wanted to know what I did in the States. I told him I was a cook and he wanted me to come and cook for him and his people after the war. Wish you could be there to see all of the things. I am in one of the biggest hotels in the city. This is a summer resort where all of the rich people come and drink and bathe in the mineral water. I think I will be home by the first of April. What are the boys doing. Give them my best regards, also to Father.

John Hundley

Thursday, November 21, 1918, Page 8

Sunday, Oct. 13, 1918.

Dear Folks:—

This is the first chance I have had to write to you or anyone in two weeks, and the first day in weeks that I had had to myself. It surely does seem good to be quiet and have a very full stomach.

Last night, after we had reached our

destination, we made a raid on some German gardens which they had left behind. I thought I was tired but you should have seen me dig potatoes with a pick. I got enough for my "Bunkie," as we call our bunkmates, and myself and in the meantime he had been somewhere else and obtained some carrots, onions, and bread. We immediately proceeded to peel them for breakfast this morning. I got some bacon Greece and we had a regular feed; friend potatoes and onions and some fried bread, beside our regular breakfast. I did enjoy my own cooking for once. You should see the gardens they had just behind their line—string beans, potatoes, cabbage, onions, lettuce, strawberry plants and other things.

The dug-outs, too, are very good. They have, or rather had everything from barrooms to electric lights, if you can imagine what that could be. It looks as if they had expected to stay here a while, but had been disappointed

You asked me to tell you what I was doing, but that is impossible However, we have been at the front for some time and have had a few experiences. If everything goes well it may not be long before I can tell you.

Love to all
Lester Anderson.

Thursday, November 7, 1918, Page 5

Mrs. Frank McCulla of this village, has received a letter from her son, Lieutenant F. J. McCulla of the U. S. Medical Reserve Corp, now in France, in which he states that he is feeling fine and is near enough to the fighting line so that he can hear the big guns.

Thursday, November 21, 1918, Page 8

Kelly Field, Texas,
Nov. 2, 1918

Dear Mother:—

Thursday, Lieut. Lenihan, who has been officer in charge of the testing line left for his home in California. He is to have ten days leave and then is to report at Hoboken, N. Y., for overseas duty. I took him as far as DelRio, Texas, in a plane. DelRio is about one hundred and eighty miles from here and is on the border. I flew across the border a short distance in order to say that I had flown over foreign soil even if I don't get a chance to go over there. We arrived at DelRio at five-thirty, Thursday afternoon, and after Lenihan had taken train I went to the army camp there and stayed with some officers

over night. At ten o'clock the next morning, I left and after doing a few stunts for the people there, I came on back, arriving here about two o'clock. Had to stop half way to fill up with gas.

This morning O took a skip up with an Hispano Suiza motor in it and got up eleven thousand feet. The tank was only partly filled and I ran out there or would have gone higher. Am going to try it again with a full tank. That is the highest I have ever been up till now.

Perhaps you have read in the papers about the trip through the country that Prince Apel of Denmark is making, visiting different army posts and camps and aviation fields. The Colonel took him up for a ride while he was here and as they used one of the ships that I have charge of, I was right there to see him.

There has been a good deal of work for us lately and I have put in quite a lot of time in the air. This testing job is the best job on the field according to my notion.

Lieutenant John H. Cooper

Thursday, November 28, 1918, Page 1

Galveston, Texas, Saturday night
November 15, 1918

Dear Mother:-

Whew! I'm tired. We had some trip down here. I worked all this morning testing after going to a dance last night and started at Nonn for Galveston. There are four of us in the party with two planes. Our first stop was at Eagle Lake and believe me, that is a good name for it. I didn't find any eagle, but the whole country looked like a lake. Every field I could see was full of water as they had had a lot of rain. I had to land as I was out of gasoline or nearly so. After flying around low over a lot of fields, I finally found a small one that was comparatively dry and landed with about one quart of gasoline left. The next stop was at Houston, but as there is an aviation field there, we didn't have any trouble.

They told us there that we could land on the beach at Galveston if we happened to strike it at low tide, but didn't know where we could land if it were high tide. We took a chance and got here just before dark and at high tide. We saw a field that looked as though it might be good if there weren't so much water in it, but there was. I had a notion several times of landing on the seawall which is quite wide but there were too many people and automobiles on it. Finally Lt. Highley who was piloting the other ship found a little strip of beach and landed and I followed suit. Our troubles weren't over however as the people who gathered around told us that the tide would come up still higher and cover the beach, but told us that the field that we had seen was all right as the water was very shallow and the ground hard. It was dark by then, or rather moonlight, and I sure was glad to see that moon. I told Highley I'd take a chance and for him to come after me; so we piled the Lieutenants out that were riding with us and took off.

We couldn't see anything with our goggles on, so had to fly with them off. I got in the field fine except for splashing a lot of water all over me and sure was relieved. Highley flew around quite a while before he could make up his mind to land but finally did in the opposite direction to what I did and rolled right out to the road and stopped just three feet from a hydrant.

I hope our luck stays with us on our return trip tomorrow

Lieutenant John Harlan Cooper.

Thursday, November 28, 1918, Page 1

Columbus, S. C.
Monday, Nov. 18, 1918

Dear Mother:—

Monday night and all is well The wind is blowing a blue streak in the sunny south, and it is quite cold.

The main topic in camp these days is when we will receive our discharge. Some think we will be home by Xmas and others say we will be out in two weeks and then others think it will be about four months. But no one knows when we will receive the official papers. The training is still going on and will continue so until we are sent home.

There are a lot of strange happenings going on in camp. But we pay no attention to them. You folks at home are the only ones that really know peace has been declared. But we are still getting prepared for the Hun if he should try any dirty tricks on the U. S. But I don't think anything like this will happen.

There is too much commotion going on around me mother, to write any more. Jim, the Indian has the floor now. Hoping to walk in on you all.

I remain Your loving son,
John Crook.

Thursday, November 28, 1918, Page 1

Mr. and Mrs. C. A. Odell of Parma Center, have receive within two days three letters and two cards from their son Sargent Homer C. Odell. He was well and unharmed at the last date of writing. Oct. 28th.

Thursday, November 28, 1918, Page 1

Letter received by relatives and friends of Clarence Robinson of this place, who has been in France for several months, announces that he had been wounded, being struck in the leg by two pieces of shrapnel. He is in one of the base hospitals and is doing nicely.

Thursday, December 5, 1918, Page 8

Santo Benedeta, Italy,
Octocer 30, 1918.

Dear Folks:—

I believe I wrote you one other letter since I have been at this place, but don't believe I described the place. We are in an old castle and believe me when we hit the place about a week ago it was some dirty, but the U. S. never lets anything be dirty a minute, and now it is a clean as a whistle. The old place makes a fine barrack for us as everything is as comfortable as can be. Just at present we are eating mess in the court yard but later will move the dining room into a large room that was once used as a schoolroom. We can get warm water by going to the kitchen after it, and can take a bath in what was one of the bath houses of the castle. What was good enough for them ought to be good enough for us. We haven't all the electric lights in yet, but will have in a couple of weeks. There are only a few of us here, and we get good feeds as the cooks have time to put on extra dishes. We will hate to come down to living in an American house after spending the winter in a castle. In nearly every room there is a large fire place and we can buy wood, so I guess everything will be rosy.

I started to walk into Mantova last Sunday to see a chum of mine and also to see some sights that I had missed while there. God a ride part way in a two-wheeled cart. Met my friend hoofrng it out to meet me, so walked with him the rest of the way in. After seeing the sights, my chum and I rode bicycles back to where I am now stationed, and then returned to Mantova that night by train, and it took him just one hour longer to make the thirteen miles on the train than it did on the bicycle.

Besides being clerk for the bunch I have the mail, post exchange, library, nursing the sick, exchanging clothing, and keeping our three rooms clean. One room is where we keep our material and have our little hospital, one the office and the other, my bedroom. Have a fireplace in both office and bedroom. Baker, my office partner, and I have to arrange so that one of us is in the office all of the time. There is too much candy, cigarettes, clothing, etc., to trust alone. Just love to be busy as time sure does fly.

By today's news I guess I won't see much of the front, much to your glee and my disappointment I have not as yet had my hand on the wheel of an ambulance.

Get the Record all right, and Mr. Copper's articles about the boys at front certainly interest me. Wish I were with Homer, Lester and the other fellows in action.

John Magee.

Thursday, December 5, 1918, Page 8

Somewhere in Italy,
November 6, 1918.

Today I received 22 letters, which answers your questions of how and when I receive them: One was dated August 7th and the latest October 10th.

Doubtless you people have been wondering whether I have been in action or not, but so far have not heard the sound of a gun. We are stationed back of lines. The wounded are brought in from hospitals father toward the front to the Distribution Station where we are. Here they are classed according to a system and given to us to take to any a dozen hospitals. The Italian Sergent hands us a paper and says something, or at least, makes a noise for a long time, and we take the paper and say "Si" (yes) and the only thing we know is the number of the hospital and the number of wounded going to each one. Generally we know where the hospitals are located, but if not, we hunt for them.

The runs average about thirty miles round trip. We have good roads and can use lights at night, so what more can a man ask better. Since the surrender (Austrian) we have been carrying mostly Italians, who have been Austrian prisoners. The main trouble with them is that they are nearly starved to death. During the attack we carried both Austrians and Italians. Carried one girl about ten or twelve years old,

and another around twenty, victims of an air raid. The little girl was not badly hurt. Many of the prisoners can talk English, both the Italians anb Austrians.

Today I hear that Germany has signed up. Get some of the news from the Western front but very little. American is making a record that she will always be proud of. My only regret is that I am not behind a gun. The Italians celebrate every night. They sure have gone crazy over the victory.

Received a letter from Mr. Odell and also a card from Miss Barnes.

Love,
John Magee

Thursday, December 12, 1918, Page 4

108th Infantry, M.G.C.
27th Division

Dear Mother:-

Three letters just received from you making the total of [?} letters today. I am sure it is only necessary to describe the reception which they met with, being the news from home in 4 weeks. The 14th letter being the last to arrive before my going to the hospital.

I returned to my company week ago Sunday, making just [?] weeks away. I left the hospital week before then, and up to the time of meeting the Co., in one week I had visited every place from Paris, up to Cambria, for Cambria to Arras, from Arras to Amies, and from Amien some more. It was some experiense to see the Hindenburg line, many famous places such as above mentioned, including Albert, St. Quintine, Perussia, and not omitting "Big Bertha" the gun that shelled Paris (?). We had a 70 mile march in 5 days through area just mentioned. I was with the wagon train of the division. It consisted of wagons with from 1 to 2 teams of horses and mules attached, it was 7 to 8 miles long and was the longest train of its kind to travel together as one body for such a distance. We were up, had breakfast and started by 7:30 and by noon had reached our camping place for the night so we had the afternoon to ourselves.

Our beloved 1st Lieut. H.O. Sommers is dead, "Hy" Weber is also wounded, but not seriously. It was a heavy blow to us.

I didn't tell you the real cause of my trip to the hospital, but seeing I am all right now I will tell you, it was mustard gas which had caused not painful but rather irritating pains to come on my face, side, feet and hands, leaving me with red blotches on the parts affected, also another gas in the lungs which left me with a cough, that is causing me not a little trouble. I got out a lot of war by going when I did, as I might not have come back alive if it was not for the above mentioned.

Our foreign pay is increased 10 percent, $3.00 extra for 1st class gunners. My pay is $36.30. Money goes a long way here and have had plenty.

Yes, our ordeal at the front at Flanders was very nerve racking and haven't fully recovered. It wasn't so much the human destruction and noise but the condition under which we lived, the sleepless nights of nerve strain, on watch, the wet, the smell of decayed human flesh, and many other things which I do not care to discuss.

Eddie Ferris of Spencerport had a leg blown off recently, improving fine. Frank C. Owens was shot by accident in the knee just as we were going into action. The same bullet wounded another man, I helped carry Owens out.

Tim O'Ryan has just issued us each a letter (personal) congratulating us on our recent victory. I think we will be allowed to send them home.

My steel helmet is my best friend over here. I owe my life to mine; at the city of Ypries one night in search of adventure I saw the city, but it almost cost me my life.

Of course we met with hardships at times but when in a permanent place everything is comfortable. Two of us have a room about 12 feet long and 8 feet wide. We have filled our bed sacks with straw and with our 4 blankets, 2 rubber sheets, our shelter tent, 2 raincoats and 2 overcoats we have some bed. We have a table, 2 chairs, stove, bookracks, shelves, pictures, French newspapers, magazines, books and other fixtures which go to make this a real home. This sure is the life. So I repeat what I have said in other letters that your son is O.K. I have been in the service long enough to know how to look out for No 1 everytime. If I don't know one else will.

Will close now hoping you re all well and happy.

Your loving son
Prit. Earl W. Burritt

Thursday, December 12, 1918 Page 4

Camp Jackson, Sun. Dec 1, 1918
Boy Scouts of America
Troop 1 Hilton N.Y.

Dear Friends:-

A few lines to let you know I haven't forgotten you. First of all I want to thank you for the box of candy, you sent me on my birthday. It was great candy and I wasen't the only one in the Bty. that thought so.

Well Boys how is the organization going? I hope you are still keeping the good work up. Who have you got for Scout Master now?

The army is a great ga[?] and I like it very much. I have learned to put up with things I wouldn't stand for at home. But after a fellow gets hardened to such things he doesn't mind.

I would like to have gone cross and seen some real action. For it is hard to think you have done your bit by staying on this [?]e.

Again I say, stick by the U.S.A's., for they are the making of a great army if there is ever need for another. First you learn to read the compass, you learn signaling and knot tying. You get all that in the Heavy Artillery. You have your hikes, they also have those in the army.

We get up at 5:45 in the morning for revile, and then have mess; after mess the Barracks and area is polished up. From 8 o'clock until 11:30 we have drill and study periods. Then comes mess. At 1 o'clock more drilling until 4 o'clock. From 4 o'clock until 5:15 you have to clean up. Take a shave put on clean clothes and be sure your shoes are shined. 5:15 you fall out for retreat at 5:30 retreat is sounded. Then comes mess again. From then on the time is your own to do what ever you like. At 10 o'clock is taps, every one who is not on pass must be in bed [?] are out and no talking. Thus the routine we go through from day to day.

I had about three or four weeks of it, and was called to fill the position of assistant supply Serg. Although I have no stripes or warrant, I have the privilege of a Non Com. I don't stand reveille or retreat and dont have to drill. Some times I have to work day and night, and then for days I don't do a thing but lay around.

Well boys, I must close now. If things turn out the way I think, I will be with you soon.

But, be prepared, has been your mot and mine, so if I am kept here longer than I expect, I won't be disappointed.

Sincerely yours
Ex. Scout Master,
Priv. J. L. Crook

Thursday, December 19, 1918, Page 8

Mr. and Mrs. Fred McCulla of East Avenue, this village, last week received a letter from their son Dr. Frank McCulla from France, that he was all right. It was the first message they had received from him in several weeks.

Thursday, December 26, 1918, Page 1

Alabama, December 17, 1918

Dear Mother:-

Was glad to hear that you are all well yet. I am the same although there is a lot of sickness in our company just now, but none of the cases are serious. Received the copy of the Record and thank you for it. Got a nice box from aunt Anna the other day.

I am sorry that we did not get over anyway. Some days I get to wondering how I would have come out if they had accepted me when I tried to enlist.

Went to Annoston last Saturday after supper and stayed over night. That is my first visit to the place. It is about 7 miles from Camp and you have to take a buss or jitney. Another fellow and myself had a real bed in a hotel and did not have to get up for reveille in fact not until 10 bells. We had some good steaks off of real dishes but they sure do soak the price right to you. They have Woolworth 10 ct. store and a lot of theaters that you could put any two of them inside the Regent. The street cars are little four wheelers and run on a daily schedule.

We have about the same schedule as that John Crook gave in the paper, but it is changed frequently. We get up at 5:45 and breakfast at 6:10, dinner at 12 and retreat at 5 and then mess again and taps at 10:30. We are getting Wednesday afternoon off a lot having sports and football games and quite often a game on Saturday afternoon. I have been working today and yesterday helping put wiring and lights in the tents. They are going to wire up the Christmas tree before long.

So Chuck has got a new bear-killer. The Remingtons are as good as any rifle I think. Many of our army rifles are that make. I was shooting in a gallery at Annoston and a 22 feels like a pop gun after shooting the army rifle. Tell Chuck if he was in the army he would have to keep it clean as a whistle, not a bit of dust in a crack or screw head and the barrel shining. The regulations are very strict on the care of them. It is a court martial offense to clean the barrel from the muzzle always shove the rod in the breach. If six inches of the bore from the muzzle is perfect the rifle will shoot accurately, and don't leave the barrel more than 3 hours without cleaning and oiling after shooting. On the range we cleaned them after shooting.

Three of our company are home on 10 day furloughs. They are the first to get furloughs on application. It don't seem as though Christmas is coming next week. Those who bet we would be out of here by them are the losers. The weather is still warm and cold nights. The doctor has ordered the front of the tents to be left open nights. If you get a cold they say more ventilation.

You have had a lot of deaths around Hilton and it is too bad. Well bye bye for now.

Earl A. Ducolon

Thursday, December 26, 1918, Page 1

Verdun, France, Nov. 23, 1919 (1918)

Dear Folks at home:-

I have been sending mostly field service cards lately because they get them censorship very readily and I wished you to know that I remained well and uninjured "after the war was over."

I have seen several Rochester papers with articles relating to the work of the 309th, so I guess you know why I have been there. The Second Battalion acted as advance Battalion for the regiment and usually Battery "D" led that advance, so you may be well assured that "Bry D" had their share of the work. In the last Big Drive we were the first Battalion of "heaven" to go thru Grand Pre on the triumphant march toward Sedan. We were relieved while on the road and turned back after staying three days at Briquenery and within sight of Buzancy. The "Big News" came while we were at 82 [?] stopping for the night. We did not believe the news was official until late the next afternoon.

We passed through Apremont where I had met Lester Anderson sometime before and now we are at Verdun, the famous city of fighting France. "On ne passe pas" or "They shall not pass."

It is a great sight tho rather a sober one to

see the civilians returning, prisoners who have been liberated returning. They are happy but their happiness is sad. Many have only memories to live [?] from now on. I am living in a French cantenment camp and believe me it is good to know that we will not need to get under [?]. As for getting home we have but a vague idea when that happy moment will come

I am well and from now on hope I can write often until I need to write any more.

Serg. Homer C. Odell,
309 H. F. A. Batry D.,
U.S. Army, France

Thursday, January 2, 1919, Page 8
With Our Boys

Nov. 29, Occey, France.

Dear Uncle Elton:—

Well this is the end of another day of drill. We are at it the same as in camp. The weather is rainy but not so cold yet. We've got a god place to stay, that is dry. It is one of these French barns, we sleep in the loft which is above the living rooms of a French family.

Censorship has lifted considerably so we can mention more things of interest. This town is about forty Kilometers east of Dijon. You may be able to find it if you have a map of Europe. Distances are reckoned entirely by Kilometers. I haven't heard miles since being in France. Since coming over we have been at the front four different times. First the Toul sector which was quiet except an occasional shelling and the patrol encounters. Patrol duty between the lines is the most ticklish business in war, just ask an Inf. Man. We spent twelve days in the Toul front line, and somewhat longer time in reserve behind the line. The reserve lines are easily in range of shell fire,but were only frequently shelled. We took the line for our first time the night of the third of last July. Most dates I have forgotten but that is firmly fixed in my mind. I have acted as runner all through except during the last part of the time we spent beyond the Argonne on the Verdun front where I filled the place of gunner. The second front we held was called the Nancy front. The village of Pont-Mousson being just behind the front line. It can be found on the map because it is nearly as large as Toul. We had our machine gun positions raided twice by German patrols here. This sector was also quiet when we first went in. The second time our regiment drove in three or four Kilo's which was our share of the Saint-Mihiel

drive. From there we were sent to the Verdun front where we spent twenty five days in the line coming out just long enough once in a while to dry our feet and clothes. Our division drove about fifteen or sixteen Kilo's cleaning up their share of what was left of the Argonne and going the rest of the way in comparatively open country. This front was where we saw what war is. I'll tell you more when I get home. I haven't seen but very little hand to hand fighting; whenever I've seen the Fritz he has been coming in as prisoner or else going the other way as fast as possible; most of those taken prisoner were machine gunners which would sit at their gun and shoot until the Doughboy either put them out of action or granted them mercy in answer to their plea of Comrad. This would have been the fate of companies like mine if the Germans had been making the gain on us. As it has been though we have followed over with the second wave of In. usually and helped them hold the ground taken. The Inf. Are fellows that deserve a good deal of credit for they have made the biggest sacrifice in our operations over here;and say when you hear that word Barrage just imagine a hard thunder storm with the lighting striking close every second, then you have it. Well uncle I've told you some things about it. Guess I'll close for this time. I am writing by candle light and holding the paper on my knee, so excuse this writing. Best wishes to the rest of the family and friends.

From your nephew,
Harold Ingraham

Thursday, January 9, 1919, Page 1
With our Boys

Camp Upton, Jan. 1919

Dear Father, Sisters, Brother. Just a line to let you know I arrived safely back in the U.S.A. Am safe and sound feeling fine, can say I have done my bit. I spent from Sep 2nd up to the day the Armistice was signed, on the front and under fire, without any relief. We were supposed to be relieved by another outfit six weeks before, but on account of our good work and crack shooting they would not relieve us for a recruiting company would have to take our place. So it was up to us to stick it out and can say I am one lucky boy to get back alive to God's Country again. Had several close calls, but that is all in the game. I kind of miss the shells bursting around me now, after having go so used to them. They were always whistling through the air or around us somewhere. When you think of a shell weighing from 100 to 600 whizzing around over your head, you will sure duck some, most of all when you just 'go up to' the front [?] was through the Argonne Woods and the Bellean Woods which were the hardest fronts in France. These the Germans had held for four years. The best part of it was we won all battles and the Dough Boys deserve a lot of credit with our backing up. Will not say any more about war now, but will tell you all when I come out. I expect to get my discharge this week some time and will be out to see you all soon. Don't write, I will be gone before it gets here.

Your son and brother,
Fred C. Hall

Thursday, February 6, 1919, Page 1

Italy, Dec. 25, 1918

Dear Folks:

This is Christmas night and it is raining out like the dickens. It is the first Christmas that I know of that I have ever worn a rain coat. But nevertheless we spent a very good day.

Last night I was in charge of quarters, and had to stay in the office, but most of the fellows were in the office, as they expected the Y men over from the hospital to give out presents which we supposed were from home, but which the Y made up themselves. It surely was funny to see the fellows crowd in the office at half past seven. They were like a bunch of kids; could not wait until Santa came. At nine the Y man showed up as per schedule and gave u each a little box containing two packages of cigarettes, a box of tobacco, small bar of chocolate and a box of candies.

The Top Sergeant was away last night and I slept in the office in his place place to answer any calls that might come in. I was awakened by the hone ringing, but really I don't see why they phoned, because if a person wants to make time here the thing to do is to walk. There are men in the Central Office, and when we finally get it into their heads what we want, nine times out of ten they will say "occupate" (busy) and if they say anything else we generally hang up and call again when the operator feels better. Often when we do get a person they cut us off after a half hour. Just imagine the bawling out of the girls at home would get if they cut some of the women of Hilton off in an hour's talking?

After breakfast I stayed in the office all

morning and before I knew it someone shouted "Come and get it," so I went and got my mess kit, and believe me there wasn't a thing left out of that feed. Turkey, mashed potatoes, cauliflower, peas, coffee, bread and peach pie. Can you imagine a bunch of fellows leaving turkey, but that is just what we did—There was some left. In the afternoon the Sergeant and I went over to the hospital with some of the goodies to the boys over there. This is the first day that I have had a chance to walk around in a good long time, so I spent the afternoon around town in the rain.

I have been anxiously watching the Christmas boxes come in. Everytime that one is handed out to one of the fellows it makes us all sort of feel happy inwardly somehow. I never saw boxes so small that held so much. Some of the boys have received great big boxes. I guess the postal authorities were so pleased that the war is over that they let them come through. Of course, I am anxiously awaiting mine and hope to get it soon.

Venice is about two hours ride from here, and the other day a couple of us fellows spent the day there. They are taking the sand bags away from the principal buildings.

Yours as ever
JOHN H. MAGEE.

Thursday, March 6, 1919, Page 4

Newport News, VA., Feb. 18 1919

Dear Mother:-

Your boy luckily has arrived safely on this side of the big Blue. We were 14 days coming across and believe me it was some trip too, we were supposed to make it in 11 days but we got lost out on the middle of the ocean three days and did not know where we were. Just bouncing on the big waves. There came up a big storm and broke the wireless and they could not hear from others nor we from them. I expect to be home soon but I can't tell just when. We expect to be here 6 or 7 days yet, and then they ship us to the nearest camp to our homes, and then we get our discharge. But we don't just know what camp it will be. Oh how I do want to see you. I hope and pray the dear Lord will send me home right away. I'm feeling fine, weigh about 170 pounds. I get lots of good eats so don't worry. I'm in good shape so far. Hoping to hear from you soon.

Your Son
Corporal Lester Collins

(The Red Cross at Newport, VA. Writes Mrs. Flora Collins that her son Lester, who wrote the above letter, has just returned a wounded veteran of the great war.)

Thursday, March 20, 1919, Page 10

Vincenza, Italy, Feb. 4, 1919

Dear Mr. Cooper:

I remember promising to write you, but I have been pretty busy doing other things until now, so here is my chance to make good my promise at least once.

It is true that I have been running a machine nearly all the time I have been over, but it has been either a Corona or Underwood, and has not had much excitement onnected with it. This has not been of my own choosing I can assure you.

I believe I told you about our trip over except that the crew nearly starved ? and this the censor cut out. Funny thing censors will let one praise but not knock which I think has been a great thing for the morale of the people at home. However, I for one have no kick coming, as I have not missed a meal, getting three a day and have had a cot with a straw tick nearly every night. As a rule meals have been good, arthough we have had a little more gold fish and bully beal than mother would cook. Ambulance men are fortunate owing to the fact that they have cars enough to carry plenty of provisions.

We landed at Genoa where we had a wonderful reception by the natives, and each of us looked like a bed of roses when we finished our little parade. We established our camp about a quarter of a mile from the garage, which had already been started. Here we lived in tents all summer and it sure was some hot summer with only about two rain storms. We certainly had work to do as we had 480 G. M. C. ambulances, 45 G. M. C. tanks, 16 trouble shooters, 60 P. A. trucks, 10 P. A. tanks, 35 motorcycles, 40 Dodge trucks, 50 Dodge touring cars and 35 kitchen trailers besides 5 Cadalic touring cars to assemble before winter. The garage was mostly in the open but tents were erected as needed for various work. The body builder turned an old cow shed into a first class body building factory. Every ambulance body had to be completely put together and men who did this were especially trained for the work. Mechanics assembled the chassis while the body builders built the bodies, and we had a factory that would make Ford happy. Those of us who were not experienced

in this work did guard duty, as every inch of ground had to be guarded. When we were not guarding we were either unpacking the cars and hauling away the lumber, pitching tents to shelter those working, hawling food to feed the hungry workers, or doing something just as useful or as hard.

As fast as the cars were finished sections would leave for the front. Each section took twelve ambulances, one tank, one Dodge truck, one P. A. truck, one Dodge?

Be the next to go until finally orders came that fifteen sections were to report ? France at once. My section was among those chosen to go, but in France only 36 men were in each section while in Ialy there are 45, and being one of the last to join my section, of course, I was left behind much to my disappointment, and now my section is attached to the Army of Occupation in Germany.

Those of us left behind knew that we were "sort of out of luck" as they did not have enough extra ambulances to to make us into a section, so we were first one place and then another. They finally organized us into what they called the Repair Shop Detactment R. S. D., but why they ever named us this I do not know as the only thing we ever repaired were roads or perhaps a pick or shovel.

We are known in the Contingent as the R. D. D'S, the name taken from the branch of the Italian Army that is the first in the trenches after the artillery gets through with them. The reason for this is that we are always the first in every camp or castle to clean it after the officers get through picking out the dirtiest they can find.

We were ordered to Montova, the base, and here we were supposed to see some of the regular stuff, but again we were disappointed as we only had a castle to keep clean and a camp to guard. I was certainly kept busy with the clerical work as most clerks had just 45 miles while I had 95 and they were changing all the time along with the Sergeants. Finally they moved us to the Ducale Palace that we had been cleaning and fixing up. We just about got that one cleaned and in good shape when some one found another in a small town of Sanibetta Po, so we were sent out there to occupy that. Here the Quarter Master and myself established a very nice office and finally had everything wished off onto us. We ran the Y. M. C. A. with its books, stationary, canteen, etc., and I even expected that we would be asked to hold services other Sunday, but we were spared that, but several of the fellows were sick so we were nurses, took charge of the exchange of clothing, the post exchange and mess, besides our regular work, but we were happy when we were busy so did not mind. I was in this town three weeks and only got out of the court yard of the castle once.

During the offensive some of us were ordered to rush to the front to relieve the over worked sections there, and I was lucky enough to be among the ones to go. I was sent to Section 526 on the Piava near Venice. The fellows had been working 36 to 48 ours at a time and needed relief, but we were not much use to them as we did not know the roads. My time here was spent with the drivers, and we certainly had to know the roads and where the hospitals were located as no lights could be shown, and sometimes ? could only see ten feet ahead. The day before this section was ordered across the ? the Armistice was signed, although no cars had gone across before on a p?etoon bridge and could not get back for two days as the bridge was blown up. Work began to slack up so we were sent back to Vincenza where I stayed only a couple of days when I was ordered back to the same place but to another section. This section was short handed as several of its members were in the hospital with the flu (none died however,) and the pa?ets and the army were more than keeping the ambulances busy. The very first day I was sent out, as I knew the roads from my previous visit, and besides we could use lights now, and I was kept busy for sometime. We were sent from this section to section 387 at One (O-na) at the foot of Mt. Grappe, and here I nursed a boil on my figure and sort of helped and best I could around the barracks. Just got nicely acquainted with the fellows when back to Vicenza I was sent to be clerk at the Advance Base, and here I have been ever since. All of the business of the sections in the field is done through this office.

We are proud of our Contingent here in Italy, as we are one of the best equipped and one of the best organized of any organization that came across. We have been very fortunate not having lost a man by shell fire and only a very small number by sickness and only a small percentage wounded. Several of the sections have been citied for bravery and efficiency by the Italian Government. Only a few cars have been destroyed. We have the ? of being the first troops through the Mediterranean and the first

American ? Old Glory across the ? Trieste. Everywhere on ? one of our ambulances and the 332 Infantry from Ohio ? coming across when it was charging across. Since the armistice was signed the sections have been busy bringing patients back to the base hospitals but now work is slacking up and we are planning to get back into God's country again soon. When I get back I expect to sleep for one month.

Yours, Jack Magee.

Thursday, April 24, 1919, Page 1
Aviator to Land Owner
Lieutenant John Harlan Cooper Files on Land in Indian Wells Valley, California

Long Beach, California
April 15, 1919

Lieutenants Harwood, Turrill and myself last Saturday filed on three hundred and twenty acres of land each in Indian Wells Valley, California, which is one hundred and seventy miles north of Los Angeles. Harwood and I have adjoining property but Turrill is about nien miles from us. He is three fourths of a mile from a small town called Loyoken while we are two and one half miles from a little town called Brown. However the railroad and proposed Lincoln Highway go right through our property and there is a spur which may be used as a shipping point only one half mile from my land. The decided land in the valley is worth from twenty to forty dollars per acre without any improvements. Many settlers in the valley have wells and are irrigating and have very productive ranches. Water is bound to be brought here under a big irrigating project sooner or later which will then make the land worth at least $100 per acre. We are to move on the land in a few days.

Yesterday I met Doctor Knight, pastor of the Baptist Church here. He said he had been in Hilton visiting at Delos Tenny's. Was a classmate of Rev. Chas. Tenny. Was at Hilton when Mr. Traver was pastor of the Baptist Church.

This country surely is beautiful. We had to file our land in Bakersfield, which is across a range of mountains from our valley. It was the prettiest drive I believe I have ever taken. The road in many places was cut out of the side of mountains where you could see miles upon miles while down below about a thousand feet would be a little village and railroad tracks. From our land we can see Mt. Whitney, the highest peak in the United States, fourteen thousand six hundred and fifty eight feet. I wish you could all see the scenery here.

John Harlan Cooper

Thursday, April 10, 1919, Page 1
Died A Hero
Captain Herman Ulmer Writes of Lester Hiscock's Death.

March 21, 1919

Dear Mrs. Duane Hiscock:-

I have just received your letter asking for information concerning your son's death. It was quite a shock to hear that he had died for until your letter came, neither I nor anyone in the company knew of it. Lester was wounded October 14th, in the thigh, the wound being made by a machine gun bullet, and apparently was not dangerous. We were advancing very rapidly that day, and could not stop for anyone that fell. He was carried back to the First Aid Station and nothing further heard of him. We all took it for granted that he had recovered. [?] when he left us, he had only one leg wound. It is hard to believe he is dead, and the only way we can account for it is that after he left us, and was being carried back to the First Aid Station, it may be that he was again hit, in a vital spot. This often happened. This must have been the case with your son, for I am sure the wound he received while with us was not fatal.

We all miss him very, very much and the men of my company have asked me to extend to you their deepest sympathies.

Your son was very popular and his work at the front, in the fighting in the Argonne, was an inspiration to all of us. He was a crack shot, the best by far in the Battalion. When he was hit he was doing deadly execution among the enemy lines. You may be sure that the enemy paid very dearly for his life. We mourn his loss, but we are proud of his fearlessness, his skill and the wonderful work he has done for his country.

With all my heart, I sympathize with you.

Sincerely,
Herman Ulmer
Capt. 325 Inf.,
Comd'y Co. "A."

Thursday, June 5, 1919, Page1
Visits His Brother's Grave

A letter received by Mrs. Fishbaugh of Lake Ave. from here reads:

"I am back again with the [?] Guard Co., after having a nice vacation. We started on the night of the 12th and got [?] on the 28th day of April.

These are some of the places we visited: Paris, Amiens, Peronne, Cambria, lille, Ypres, P[?]hinge, Dijou, Tours and Borde[?].

We got off at Peronne and went right to Doingt and the Military Cemetery there and found Glenn's grave. Lt. Simms is also buried there as well as a lot of other boys of the 27th Division who died of wounds in the hospital. This little cemetery is situated by a French graveyard and is fenced off. All the graves are marked with a cross and they are all alike. I took some pictures of the graves. Over here they don't seem to know yet whether any of the bodies will be sent home or not. They say there is a bill before Congress now about it.

From there we walked over the battle grounds we fought over, for a couple of days. They have German prisoners filling up the trenches and shell holes and carrying off the artillery shells that did not explode. There are also lots of Chinese laborers winding up the barbed wire and cleaning up, but it's an awful mess—just ruins.

One thing we enjoyed while away was lots of good eats and nice beds to sleep on. We went to a few shows but spent most of our time walking around sight-seeing.

On getting back, I found thirteen letters and a lot of papers waiting for me.

The weather is rather cold here. I don't think the spring can be much earlier than in the states.

We have nearly 700 prisoners here now. Gen. Pershing came through here, but this is a large camp, so he didn't speak to one in a thousand, didn't even visit the prison.

I don't hear anything about going home, but don't worry about me for I am in no danger and you know I am well.

Son Ray,
Camp St. Sulpice
A. E. F.

LETTERS OF HOMER CHAUNCEY ODELL

At the end of the war and demobilization, two New York State historians, James Sullivan and Alexander C. Flick, were tasked with preparing a history of the state's role in the Great War. Through outreach to local historians, veterans groups, and local governments they attempted to gather stories, letters, photographs, and the like for use in their collection. While the history was never written, all the materials submitted were preserved by the New York State Archives. Ancestry.com obtained the microfilmed images of the collection and uploaded them to their online repository. Materials are indexed by county, then by the town or village that provided the materials. They are not indexed by individual names or subjects.

Mrs. Mary C. Stevens presented herself as the Town of Parma and Village of Hilton Historian to Mr. Sullivan and provided facts on the local contributions to the War Chest, the activities of the local Red Cross Committee, and a brief history of the community. The state created a questionnaire for war veterans to complete, listing their family members and chronicling their wartime service. Mrs. Stevens was not very successful in obtaining completed forms from Hilton's veterans, collecting only one from Justus Allan Hovey.[x] Mrs. Stevens exchanged several letters with Mr. Sullivan over a two-year period; her letters were included in the repository. All the following are sourced from the Town of Parma section in the archived collection.

In a letter dated December 21, 1921, she writes to Mr. Sullivan:

> I inclose what I can report, up to this date, but I am informed by the commander of Hiscock-Fishbaugh Post, that they have a meeting tonight. That all of the boys have the questionaires, now, and will hand them in then. I have told them, when the time would be up, long ago, but the dear, dilatory, procrastinating boys thought that was a long time ahead & just let it slide. So I send this now, and if you will keep the records open until I can get these exasperating soldier boys reports I will be glad. They do not know I am calling them names, but they <u>do</u> know they haven't done right. They are as dear as can be, and I am very proud of the most of them, and knew they <u>could</u> make a good showing. I wondered if perhaps you had written to the Commander, that made them do anything at all.

Mr. Sullivan promptly replied, "We can not but admire your sincerity, as well as your love for, and patience with the boys." Mrs. Stevens was not pleased with the response from the "boys" as she again eloquently opined to Mr. Sullivan on February 9, 1922:

> I am sending you with this, positively all the data I have received. I realize the importance of this work, but evidently our boys do not. This I think finishes up my work along this line, although if I get any more information I will surely send it to you.
> I am ashamed to send you the little I have, I feel it deeply, that the boys have not done the fair thing, but I don't seem to be able to help it. I send the list of their names anyway; with such data as I could get. I can do no more, yours truly Mrs. M. C. Stevens (over)

On the reverse of the note she wrote:

> John Crook, Hilton is still Commander of the Post. I would suggest that you drop a mild bomb on him, to help matters. He is a fine looking, & a fine character, & I do not understand his not helping us out. M.C.S.

In July 1923, Mrs. Stevens forwarded one more collection to Mr. Sullivan. She stated in her letter that "the son of a lifelong acquaintance sent me the war record that I am sending you." The "war record" was a collection of long and detailed letters written home by Homer

---

[x] Clarence Robinson's information was included when he filled out the form for the Town of Canisteo historian. It is filed under Steuben County, Town of Canisteo, in the repository. See page 219.

Chauncey Odell, to which Mr. Sullivan remarked, "The war record of Homer Odell is a splendid addition to the material you have already sent in and we thank you for it." The following transcriptions are Homer's letters home. They offer a unique and detailed perspective on military training, deployment, and life in France. The first two letters were typewritten, the remainder were sent on Y.M.C.A. stationery provided to frontline troops.

Same as the previous section, Homer's letters on the following pages are transcribed verbatim from the archive copies, including errors. In places where the documents were illegible or poorly imaged, a "[?]" is inserted to explain the inability to transcribe.

Montford, France.

Dec. 23, 1918

Scene 1; Act 1

Place—The Old Homestead

Time—Christmas Day.

Character—The Odell family seated around the fire in the sitting room

Father speaks--"Once more we are all together and we've heard what the older ones have had to say, now suppose you tell us, Homer, of your trip thru France as a soldier".

Homer--"If you wish a detailed description of my trip you must settle yourself for a long story. 'Willard fill up the apple dish with Baldwins and then I'll talk easier—thanks'. These apples are mighty good and to think that tho I was in France the apple crop was a complete failure.

Well, I left Camp Dix May 25, 1918. It was a Monday morning bright and early when the bugler blew first call. We all piled out easily for we had slept with most of our clothes on, expecting the call at any time. And Oh boy ! the night we spent. Never shall I forget Zeke Sanford as he threw a bucket of water in an open window directly on corporal Bray's bed; nor shall I forget beds that were pulled down spilling the sleepers broadcast over the floor. It was "a wild and stormy night" but we made harbor all right.

Our trip on the train began about 10 A. M. We headed thru Trenton toward New York City. At New York City we passed thru the Hudson River tubes. Train of freight cars and coal was passing thru at the same time. As we emerged from the tubes the New York City boys with us informed us that we were on the wrong track for Camp Upton or Hoboken. We knew then that we were headed for Boston or Halifax. We passed New Haven, Hartford, Springfield, Worcester, Fall River to Boston, landing at the docks about 11;30 P. M. About 12; 45 A. M. we made a final roll call and marched silently up the gang plank unto his Majesty's ship "Arawa". The ship was constructed and launched sometime before Columbus was a corporal in the Guines Army, but the bunk I got was soft and I soon went to sleep after learning that our crew was English. Oh yes ! I had some"Bloomin"bloody cheese and crackers for supper.

At 8 oclock the following morning the boat left dock and moved out into a dense fog. We didn't leave the harbor, however, until about 11 A. M. due to the fog. We were not allowed on deck and certainly a casual observer would never know there were troops on board.

We steamed away from harbor all alone and headed, as the crew said, for Halifax. About the middle of the afternoon the weather cleared, showing the deep blue sea and the faintly distant shore." Goodbye America". Hello ! What? Toward night we were issued life belts and ordered to put them on immediately as a "sub" had been seen "off the coast" somewhere. After that we slept with our life belts, ate with them. In fact they stuck to us like gas masks did later. Oh yes ! some of the boys got sea sick about this time. Why? I don't know because the sea was perfectly smooth with not even a weed in sight.

On the 29th about 11 A. M. we met a big transport on its way for more boys. At 8 P.M. we entered the Halifax harbor. We again were ordered out of sight and had to stay there until after dark. The next day was May 30th, Memorial Day. It was a day of memory all right. In the morning when we went on deck we found we were located very near the place where the big explosion took place early in the winter of '18. The Belgian Relief Ship'was still there with that sign printed on its side.

The commander of the troops aboard ship was from another outfit. He had his men on board too, and they had rather the worse of the bunks, being compelled to sleep in hammocks in the "hold". Well, this morning he ordered everyone on deck with entire packs and what did that old devil do but put all of his men in the good bunks and give us the poor ones. Very naturally there was a big storm and we offered to fight the other outfit out on deck for the rooms, but they being of the non-combatant forces of the army, thot it best to lay low. The privates of the Engineers had better bunks than did the sergeants of the Artillery. Can you beat it? Al that day the sun shone brightly, it was perhaps the only bright spot in the day. Small conflicts of tongues were every minute growing more numerous.

When the boys went to bed in their new but bad beds they began to 'cuss' the Engineers from the Commander down to the guard. They yelled and swore until an armed guard tried to stop the noise. Every time the guard would try to talk and tell them to shut up they would only yell the louder, calling them some appropriate but not altogether charming names. Finally they yelled themselves to sleep. I was fortunate enough to get a bunk with the sergeants, although I was only a corporal, so I escaped the worst place.

The next morning the Engineers had a guard place to make us go where and only where they thot best to let us. Needless to say that we went where we damned pleased guard or no guard. We tipped guard, gun and all out of our way. Oh, the atmosphere was tense and everyone expected a fight, but no one wished the responsibility of starting anything because everyone knew that an awful battle would follow should anyone start. There were several ships in the fleet now, as we could tell by the whistles. We couldn't see any of them (Oh yes ! I wrote a letter and sent it from Falifax so you know now how it happened) .

For two or three days we were in a thick fog. An ice berg was sighted. In fact the trip was something to tell about rather than to be wished for.

On June 3rd a few waves broke over the main deck very near where I was doing guard. The feed was the worst I ever hope to have in front of me. June 4th the fog lifted and our wandering ships fell into their formation again. Over the wireless we heard of the "President Lincoln" being sunk. We were glad to know that she was homeward bound because Camp Dix boys were her last load. June 5th the weather was fine and everyone felt great. Today's wireless brought news that the Annex held the Marne "Bridge Heat". Three "subs" were reported ahead and soon after we changed our course considerable. June 6th was great until about 8 P. M. when storm clouds began to gather. We heard of the sinking of 18 ships off the American coast (The sailors on board claim that the only thing that saved us from being attacked was the dense fog out of the harbor). You should have seen the boys get mad when they realized what the news meant. We were entering the danger zone - - everyone is anxious but no one (maybe a few are scared). June 7th cold and wet. I haven't been sea sick at all so far although I am quite sure I know about how a fellow feels when he is sick. We are supposed to be more than one half way across now. It seems ages since we left U. S. A.

June 8th at 8 P. M. the waves are rolling high. The sea remained rough all day. Many got homesick- - I mean seasick. I got homesick however. Why I don't know but I was.

June 9th. Today is Sunday and when I went on guard at 3;40 the sun was just rising. For dinner I had one half slice of bread, a small potato and a spoonful of soggy plum dupp. Oh for the thots of a regular Sunday dinner. One like I had May 12th for instance.

June 10th. As I was on guard this morning I could count 12 torpedo boat destroyers. We had one big battle cruiser with us all the way. Yes, all the ships were painted worse than Blanches Princes' face.

Some of the torpedo boat destroyers are English; some American. Give me the U. S. A. always. We were passed by a big transport today; one of the largest.

June 11th. As I came on deck this morning I noticed a change in the water and right away I thot of land. Some of the boys laughed at me, but at 9 A. M. a flock of sea gulls appeared and even they don't spend their time in mid ocean so I began to think I was right.

About 10 A. M. I went to bed and at 10:30 I was awakened by a terrific roar. It sounded to me as tho the ship had struck a rock. Everyone went running on deck but foolish I remained in bed to see what would happen next. A moment elapsed and then another roar came. Then I heard the boys outside my port hole laughing. I got up and stuck my head out in time to see the boys who slept in the "hold" come tearing up the hatchway on deck. The look in their eyes was what caused all the laughing. Four or five explosions occurred and by the time the last one came word came that it was depth bombs and that we had not been hit. The English sailors were real disgusted because the Americans laughed. One English guy said, "The Bloomin, bloody yanks, they laughed when the Lusiatania was sunk". The explosions were nearly three miles away. We claim that a sub was blown up or maybe two of them, but we never heard officially, Yes or No.

At 12 M. we passed the place where the Lusiatania was sunk. At 1 P. M. we sighed a light house on the English coast. Soon we could see the hills of Wales. At 3 oclock two "derigibles" came as an escort for us. They are wonderful things. At 8;20 we saw the hills or Ireland.

We landed at Liverpool on the afternoon of the 12th. It seemed wonderful to be land boys again, but I could hardly admire the city streets around the docks. We unloaded and marched up the dirty cobble stone streets to the railroad yards. Hundred of dirty kids asked us for pennies and tried to be nice to us.

We loaded into the train after eating a cheese sandwich for supper. At six oclock the train pulled out and as the sun didn't set until nearly 10 P. M. there we had four hours ride thru beautiful country of England. Every tree and shrub was neatly cared for, and Oh ! those lovely road ways and drives bordered on either side by wonderful low trimmed hedges. I hated to have darkness come but with darkness came rest. Not much of it either because we were in English carriages and not good old U. S. A. cars. Eight of us in one pigeon hole made it rather crowded. It was twelve oclock Wednesday night when someone said, "Everybody out for hot coffee". I thot a cup of coffee would go dood, but when I tasted the hot stuff they poured into my cup, I am sure the English got another cussing. I couldn't drink it at all and I really wanted some coffee too. Where we stopped it was called "Derby" so I named the coffee that. Early next morning I woke up and sat watching the scenery; the beautiful, lovely, thatched cottages with carefully trimmed hedges and winding roads were again the center of attraction for me. They looked as tho a person would just need to live and never worry in a place like that.

About 8 oclock we pulled into South Hampton. The boys asked the kids of the city the name of the place and they answered, "Sou' Ampton". I nearly laughed myself to death listening to the conversation. The boys couldn't understand So' Ampon at all.

The people here gave us a welcome but it was rather a retrained one. We marched to a rest camp where we went to three meals a day but had nothing to eat at any of them. All three meals might make a lunch for a well fed man. We love the English already. I slept most wonderfully that night after writing a letter to Mother and one to Mildred.

The next day at 1;15 P. M. we hauled on our packs and marched back to the station or dock(both). there we stayed until about 6 P. M. when we again took the gang plank. This time into the "Viper". She was a fast small boat. At 8 P. M. we left harbor on the last lap of water journey. The boat was small and fast and the channel was rough. Oh boy ! Everybody feed fishes most. I got wabbly but didn't get sick. I never did get real seasick or even enough to heave. The ship soon looked like a pig pen in distress. In the hold men lay on the floor asleep just like hogs in a puddle. Every nook and corner had someone in it. I was out of luck. I couldn't get to my overcoat nor I couldn't find a place to keep warm, so I walked around to keep warm.

As far as I know our ship was alone, but I do know that another boat came very near sending us to the bottom of the " deep blue". You see all boats running without lights give plenty of chances for collisions. Well, we didn't connect at all so why worry.

I was on deck when the boat pulled into harbor at La Havre. At was a grand sight, also feeling, to know that France was at hand; that the ocean was crossed without accident. We docked at 4 A. M. We landed and marched quietly (singing taboo) thru our first French town, typical of most of the others I've been thru since, the pavement or large stones, 8" x 5" x 5", I should judge; narrow side walks, yes for most part narrow streets.

We marched about 3 miles to another rest camp (No. 1, Section B). The street peddlers tried to sell us or-an-gees, but they only wanted .25 for 3 oranges. We landed at camp at 11 A. M. and right away the cooks were detailed to get dinner. It was a real feed too and tasted like Camp Dix again. We had small white tents only room enough for 6 but 8 of us slept there on soft, pine boards for beds.

I took two vapour baths here. Gee ! they are great too. You go in a hot room where water is boiling so that the steam and your sweat does the washing, then go to another room and get under a cold shower.

(June 17th)

Monday we pulled out for somewhere with the day's rations. After leaving LaHavre the train passed tunnel after tunnel. We went thru Rouen about dark. We passed just to the west of Paris thence westward towards Vannes. That night from 11 P. M. 'til 4 A. M. I slept in the rack in the upper part of the car. I came near being jarred off when the train made a quick stop. We met several trains of wounded English soldiers going to England and also saw a few train loads going to the Front.

We landed at Vannes only being on the train about 24 hours. We took a narrow gauge railroad to Camp DeMeucon. The camp was 8 kilometers from Vannes. It was raining hard when we landed at Camp. We hiked to our new home, which was one story barracks, a door at each end. Mess halls were separate buildings. French system of sewerage (no good). The French are slow to take advantage of good systems. For about a month here we received drill nearly all day long every day and then we got our 6 inch guns (4 of them) and a few over 200 horses, mostly stallions, and believe me, we had some time teaching them how to draw the guns because most of the men had never handled horses before at all. I could write a book on our stay at DeMeucon, but will cut that short to get to the front soon.

We took three practice hikes at Meucon and did good work enough to get a compliment from the French instructor. I mean the 2nd battalian (some soldier that can't spell). I do remember sleeping standing up all night in the rain. Oh boy ! I was tired.

On August 22nd we entrained for somewhere on the Front, taking our horses, wagons, guns and everything with us. We passed thru Rennes, Orleans, Nantes, Tours, Dijon and thence to Toul. On the morning of the 26th we landed and lined up about day break for our hike thru to Gongerville about 3 kilos toward Nancy from Toul. There we put up that day and night and the next day at 5 P. M. we pulled out for the Front. We hiked all night - - dark and rainy - - Oh boy 1 that was a memorable night. What we were going to land in we didn't know. Early the next morning we found ourselves relieving the famous 1st Division. They told us they had fired 17 shots since being there. In a few days we had fired several hundred.

The first shot fo the regiment was fired by our battery on the night of August 30th, but on September 2nd we did our first real firing when we had a German Anti aircraft battery for a target and an airplane to do observing for us. We got direct hits and blew the "huns to Hell". They never fired again. We were very near Jezanville (Harold Ingraham was on our right). The 82nd was on our right.

I must get as far as the big drive and then quit. On September 10th wemoved to a position farther forward and got things ready. It rained every minute from the 9 til the 12th, the best weather possible for us as airplanes could not see us work. The night of the 12th was the darkest dark I ever saw(I couldn't see). Honestly the only way I could get around was to feel the way. Walking on the road I had to keep where I could hear the mud splash or I would have been lost more than once. The boys worked 72 hours with only 3 hours sleep, getting ready for the drive. Then they had to go and heave shells all night. I had most of my work down before dark that night, so at 1 oclock, the appointed hour, I was ready to watch the others and the effects. As the time drew near everyone was tense, because we didn't know if the Germans knew our game and would start shelling as soon as we did. Oh ! the feeling when the first gun roared, then another and another, until the woods was one continuous roar and the flashes lit up the sky almost like day. We didn't get any shells in return because the Huns were too busy seeing which could run the fastest. We moved ahead twice in a couple of days and then held a position very near Pont-a-Mousson, just west of the Marselle River. Later we moved north of Verdun behind Grand Pre."

Most close for now or I'll be sued for waste of paper.

Lovingly, Homer.
Sgt. H. C. Odell,
309 H. F. A.
Battery D,
U. S. Army

Montfort, France.
February 10th, 1919

Dear Folks:

It has been about a week since I last wrote you a letter. It hasn't been that long since I wrote a letter, however.

My letter telling about the big trip across the "waves", England and France must be around the chain by now, therefore, I submit for your approval the remaining history of Homer, as far as Montfort. This will necessarily be mostly in diary form due to my suing another fellow's notes to make me remember what happened to me.

September 12th will probably be remembered the longest, it being the first time I ever heard so many big guns. "Coughing iron" at one time the night was terribly dark before the Artillery preparation begun at 1 A. M. and then the sky was so illumed by flashes that it was much easier to find the way around the position. (Just to try to explain how dark it was. Before 1 A. M. if you tie a blindfold over your eyes on a dark night and place yourself in the middle of our woods at home, trying to imagine trenches running hitcher and yon around you, also barbed wire entanglements, to feel your way thru or by. If after you have completed this you don't get the sensation, just try to imagine that the Boche may at any minute turn loose some big shells near you. It will be easy then).

At 5:30 the Infantry went "over the top". We fired a barrage. Oh ! boy, what a noise those guns turned loose make. At 8:00 some of the boys met German prisoners being taken to the rear.

September 13. Second platoon moved out on road near the stone quarry. When into position for counter attach, Doud woke me up calling "Gas", but didn't wake up himself until after he had his as mask on. Took up one telephone line that ran to Batt. Hdg.

September 14th. Entire Battery moved to hill west of Montanville (or K 3). Danny Monroe's team, wagon, shells and all went over a ten foot embankment due to me giving him incorrect orders (nobody but you every found that out, however) No one, or nothing was injured in the spill although there were 25 O. A. (or High Explosive) shells on the wagon. The wagon tipped bottom side up.

At K 3 we moved into old French positions so no gun pits had to be made. These pits hadn't been used since the first year of the war. From this position we could look at Joan de Arc monument, which stands towering above Pont-a-Mousson. Also we could see the ridges of hills in Germany (I mean in Alsace, maybe its Lorraine, I don't know).

Most of the boys had dugouts in this place but I got there late so had to sleep in my tent. Doud, Gordon, Loney, Allen, Duff and I occupied these two tents. Two men tents with three each in them. Ballon shot down by Boche just back of us.

The next few days were calm. Fired on Pagney. Got several direct hits on a Hdg. Building there. We had very poor eats and not nearly enough to satisfy. Our "picket line" was in the valley just below us. On the 26th a raid on Pagney was staged by the doughboys. Our guns were firing "double zero" charges. The guns went "out of order" one after the other until only one remained firing. This one the boys fired four times per minute until it got so hot that they fired one shot in four minutes. The doughboys raid was very successful owing to the fact that the Boche were wise to it.

On the night of the 27th I moved with the 1st platoon to what is commonly known as the "forward position". It was just to the right of Vilcey-sur-tri, on the forward slop of the hill and just above the German dugout village, where dugouts were as common as trees. The guns were in an open position concealed only by second growth trees and artificial camouflage.

I was in charge of the telephone communication there. George Stapleton and Joe Coleman were with me. Harry Marshall and George Cheeseman came the first night to help string the wires. The horses were still hitched to the guns when a shell burst not over twenty feet from where I stood. Gun No. 1 went into position with a bang, although before the shell landed everyone was grunting and heaving to push it into place.

We unloaded a big reel of wire, all two men could lift, let alone trying to carry it and unreel it. I was at a loss to know how to string the wire. A whiz bang followed closely by another came singing to its resting place near us. No longer did I have to worry how the wire was to be strung. Ehresman and Marshall grabbed it and away they went at a run and I followed and laid the wire. One would almost think that the Boche could see us by the way they fired. Those whiz bangs kept dropping just back of us no matter how fast we went. It didn't take long to string most of the wire. It got so hot that we quit work and went into a dugout to sleep leaving word with guard to call us early Before daylight Stapleton and I were out and at 11 A. M. we had things working. As yet no breakfast. Imaging putting in a telephone line two miles long in less than half a day, all in working order too. We connected with "C 95's". Communications poor due to German wire. German telephone wire "par bon".

Stapleton and I spent the night in a dugout all alone both slept until late next morning with no gas guard. The others were gassed and wore their gas masks for nearly two hours. "lucky boys again." Telephone wire shot all to pieces during the night. George and I worked all morning to mend the breaks and splicing in American wire in place of the German wire. Communications fine at 11;30 A. M. (Late dinner again).

Firing by direct observation from "out post" (O.P.) began at about 12 M. Firing for adjustment only, then changed to a moving target. At a little after one I arrived at the gun position after taking plenty of time to eat. God there just in time to see the first Boche shell land about 20 feet from the working gun squad and about 15 feet from me. Both guns were ordered to fire 6 rounds as fast as possible, but before the third round was on its way Lt. Hopkins' of Syracuse order came to abandon guns and seek shelter. Just as the first gun squad was leaving Sisco got hit in the posterior extremity of his anatomy while Whitbeck was hit(slightly) in the chin.

Shells landed thick and fast for a half hour. All telephone lines out during the first, five minutes(as usual). When the shelling became less severe I went to fix the wires. I made twelve splices in one place while standing in a shell hole that had been made not over twenty minutes before. In fact smoke still issued from the torn ground. The camouflage net over No.1 gun was burned off. Several H. E. shells were ruined. A powder box was on fire. Oh ! things were in a fine mess around there. A hole about 1 ½ inches in diameter had been blown in the gun's shield. We fired no more from that position.

As we started for supper that night shelling began again. Hugh Abbott said, "Ship 'em over Fritzie, if we don't get you someone else will".

September 29th. Austin and Goodridge were wounded while returning from supper. Austin was hit on the arm and Goodie was hit eleven times, or at least he had eleven wounds. Most of the boys had to sleep in the kitchen that night.

September 30th. Next day the guns were moved back to another position about a kilometer to about even with the third line of infantry. We got shelled no more in this position, but land ! how the shells turned loose on our old position. We had left our second camouflage net as a ruse to have them keep firing there.

Stapleton, Ehresman and I now occupied a little machine gunner's dugout that served very well as a home. I hadn't written home since September 20th. No one wrote because the mail didn't go out.

October 4th we had orders to move. We left about 4 P. M. for the position of the second platoon. When we got there they were moving, in fact, most of them were gone. That night was long and dreary. We marched all night but didn't get far owing to the fact that the entire regiment was moving. Part of our outfit was left behind due to a gun getting stalled. The kitchen was there too. Horrors of war, that is the one of them leaving a kitchen behind plus all rations.

October 5th we pulled into Nonsard about 10:30 A. M. after going thru Fliary, Limey and Pannes. We had dinner(no breakfast nor supper) at 12M and supper about 4:30 P. M. Immediately after supper we packed our circus and pulled out. Hardly had we left the town when big German shells began to drop where we just left. (Lucky again)

We hiked on and on for what seemed like ages, always pulling into camps in the dark and nearly always it was raining hard. On the night of the 5th we passed thru Hendencourt to Lavingneville.

October 6th. Moved out across the Meuse thru Trogan and Lammerville

October 7th. Days rest, time to shave.

October 8th. Moved out at 8 A. M. thru Flury, St. Andri (near Brinzeax)

October 9th. Stone and I lay on the ground (no tent). Used one shelter half under us and one over. Dew was so heavy that all the blankets were wet thru by morning. Salt in the coffee instead of sugar. Willis Winter had his foot run over by a big gun Wheel. Thanks to the mud that he didn't lose his foot. Joe Loney had boils so badly that he would hardly walk but an old grey horse kicked him just the same.

October 10th. Pulled into camp in daylight (What a wonderful sensation). Near Futeau saw some armored Lord cars. Better yet I took a bath, the first for over a month.

October 11th packed and moved into Arrogonne forest thru Les Isletts and La Calon, camping near La Chalade. (Entire brigade here)

October 12th. Moved to a River flat near Aprimont, passing near Varrenes.

October 13th. Prepared to moved but didn't, pitched tents again. Saw Lester Anderson today while he was working at Aprimont. He was a Corporal then and still attached to Co. E 303 Engineers.

October 14th. Firing supposed to stop at 12 oclock. We were shelled out at 12:05 A. M. Packed again but didn't move. We are a regular Ringing Brothers now.

October 15th. Big shell hit near tents, close to Battery F's picket line. Ed Ryan ducked under his shelter half for protection. Big laugh from the boys. Moved to a position on a hill across the road. Sent Christmas coupon home.

October 16th. Pulled out at 2 P. M. to a camp near Autry, going thru Apprimont and Chatel. Had to double up teams to make the Chatel Hill.

October 17th. Ate breakfast at 8.00. dinner at 10.00, then went out with Capt. Herr to Grandham near Senuc where we took our position to relieve the 306 H. F. A (or 77th Division Artillery). Guns arrived about 4 P. M. the position was nicely camouflaged. Looked good to me except for gas. At about 12 P. M. we were gas shelled out of our position (10 horses killed) and the entire Battery, yes, 2nd Battalion went trailing off thru the woods. It was a bright moonlight night but rather cold for standing around.

October 18th. Raided the kitchen after returning from the First Battalion, Battery B. Entire Battery ate gassed food and suffered from the effects afterwards for a couple of weeks or more. Moved to a hill near Senuc for better protection. Two Frenchmen and twenty five horses killed on next hill.

October 19th. Adjusted guns on Belle Joeuse farm. I was at the O. P. watching the shells land.

October 20th. Bridge to Grandham shelled out.

October 21st. Rubber boots issued today. Lt. Willis shot in the leg. Joe Loney was with him at the O. P. Mail came today.

October 22nd. Most of the boys sick with gassed stomachs causing extreme weakness. Guns fired alternately all night. 850 shells.

October 23rd and 24th. German Airplane dropped"funny" propaganda, such as, "Come over and board with us this winter. Why are you fighting for England. Why should you die in the shell holes of France when you might be safe over here". Big Airplane fight. German pursued planes, chasing our "Bombers".

October 25th. Big day today. We're paid."What are you going to do with it now that you have it?"

October 26th. The French, 155 min. rifles below us were shelled prettily We laughed at the frogs as they dodged shells.

October 27th. We fired one shot in Belle Joeuse Farm. I was to blame for the shel being fired. Gave incorrect orders.

October 29th and 30th. Light Artillery fired gas shells for 36 hours, 300 rounds per Battery per hour (Bois des Loages). We fired on La Chenarey Farm and accidently hit an ammunition dump causing a series of explosions. Fire burned all afternoon.

October 31st. Order No. 18, 506 shells fired about 3:30 A. M.

November 1st. 15 rounds or 60 shots fired on German Infantry hidden back of Bois des Losges). Moved in afternoon thru Senuc and Thermes toward Grand Pri, turned to the left just before getting to Grand Pri and took up a position near Thelma. Bill Doud of Rochester instantly killed by shell not more than twenty feet from where I stood. We had parted but a moment before; he went one side of a little shack and I the other (Lucky for me again). A "Dud" landed in the midst of a gang of the boys. My heart went pitty-pat until I realized it was a "dud". Fme. De Talma will long be remembered by the 2nd battalion, as the place where shells fell like hail stones. That night I slept with Loney in a little hole hardly big enough for me. Our outfit of 155's had gone "over the top", so to speak. We were only 500 meters from the German front line that night, an unheard of event for Heavy Artillery to perform.

November 2nd. Moved back to Termes where I spent a terrible night in a small hole in the ground. Ed Ryan was with me.

November 3rd. Moved forward thru Grand Pri. We were the first Artillery Battalion thru Grand Pri, two 75's were ahead of us, but they were with the Infantry. We passed La Mort Homme (or Dead man's Hills), saw several dead Boche killed from shell fire---Briquenay, and Therorquis. Saw Lester

Anderson again. His outfit passed us while we were held up due to traffic being almost unbelievable heavy. Hdg. Were at Fme De Resille.

November 4th. Received chocolate from Y. M. C. A. the first we ever had given us by that organization. Morrison and Korwan were on telephone. They took telephone into the tent but didn't attach the wires so I received a bawling out the next morning by Lt. Berkey (common occurrence, however). Moved back to Camp near Briquenay, too. Enemy plane dropped bombs on Briquenay about 7 P. M. A Major and several men of the 6th Division were injured due to smoking cigarettes while fritzie was looking at 'em from above. The 6th Division hiked and hiked. They tell wonderful tales how they fought but records show they never were in the front lines at any time. (Also a common occurrance).

November 5th. Prepared to move but pitched tents again. Orders were to take position 3 kilos beyond Authe. At the time we received the order the German still held Antha. (Theirs not to reason why, theirs but to do and die.) Many there were who wondered but only one had blundered. A bridge was shot up so we didn't move. Captain. Kerr, Corp. O'Donnell and Howell, Private Duff returned from scouting trip to explain how they had been shelled. They also told of conditions in the towns they passed thru. How the Germans had taken all the young boys down to the age of about 12 years, and how they had taken all the girls and young women with them during the retreat.

November 6th. Still in camp. Pete Bubel and I rode to Themorguies to see if a Y. M. had yet come to town. We found a Salvation Army joint. You don't have to pay in a Salvation Army Canteen unless you want to. You pay the U. M. whether you want to or not. Pete and I did see truck loads of women and children who had been left without food when the Boche retreated. I saw a girl of about sixteen who held a little boy by the hand, a baby on her lap and her condition showed that the third child would soon be with the two. Every woman looked old and worn, far from the healthy appearance of most of the French. The kids talked better German than they did French. I saw one little boy with his fingers all cut off. "Boche did it" his mother said.

November 7th. Took a bath today. It lacked two days from being a month after my last one. Autos had head lights on tonight. Many Infantry boys coming to field hospital tired out and with sore feet due to chasing the Huns so fast and far. Peace talk very strong. We argue that with Austria out plus the big drive that Germany would be fighting with her back to the Rhine inside of two weeks. We had broken the line in to at Sedan. Sedan was the eventful place during the war of 1870.

November 10th. Sunday. Will always move on Sunday and we never move unless it is cold or raining hard. Heavy frost, ground frozen, some shelter half frozen stiff. Head to thaw it out before I could roll my pack. Moved out early. 7:30 we were on the way. If you've ever seen a circus pull stakes you will have a little idea just what we looked like. It always meant business for me because I had to see to telephone lines being taken up, wagons packed and all the valuable instruments on board. We moved out thru Briqunay, Champigneyville to St. Juvin getting there about noon. I stood in line two hours for a couple of bars of chocolate that a Canteen was selling. Hurrah I the Y. M. gave me some hot cocoa (two marks for the Y. M. now) Grand celebration tonight from a rumor that the war was over. A bunch of [guys] nearly went wild. They began shooting their pistols, colored rockets were sent up, but Homer lay tight in his bed waiting for the noise to stop so that sleep would be easy. Loney and I slept in a horse box stall that night.

November 11th. Up bright and early today for good start back thru the Argonne forest. I ate dinner sitting close beside several dead horses, appetizing to a great extent. I ate canned horse meat (which was worse, I don't know). Climbed a terrible hill; very bad roads. Along toward dusk I picked out places I had seen before and soon we passed thru Chatel and Aprimont across the Aire river up a big hill or hills to Epionville near Monfaucon. I slept with Lt. Willis in a dugout. Here we found mud knee deep. We walked in mud nearly all day and all night. We would not believe that the war was over until Lt. Willis asked a French Captain about it. He merely said "Fini La Guerre". Maybe the war was over but our hike wasn't and after you've hiked from 7:30 A. M. until about 1 A. M. next morning thru long, deep slushy mud holes, you don't give a ———if the war is finished or not.

November 12th. We pulled out about 8 A. M and passed thru Montfaucon, Cusieg to Bethencourt. There was one wall left standing at Bethencourt. The ruins were grass rown. Ed Ryan, Danny O'Donnell. Loney, Spitz and Maurice Shea and I slept in a elephant iron shack that night. Most of the boys nearly froze but we kept very warm. We were headed for "Esnes", but during the night new orders came and we started for Verdun thru (this was Forges). A sign we found telling the name of the ruins that were. Up over the hill into the Meuse a little suburb of Verdun, across the River. We passed thru the old gates and around the noted Verdun Circle. Our sleeping quarters were now in an old cantonment used by the French before the war, very much shot up at present, although their structure is strong, built entirely of stone and iron. A cellar had been dug under the building to protect under heavy shelling. Verdun was fired on from almost four sides, being nearly surrounded during 1915. Tis stated that the Germans lost 300,000 men trying to capture the town. The French say that they lost at least as many in defending it. Nearly every French Regiment passed sometime in Verdun, thousands of their best troops were killed there. We drilled some two hours per day. All wagons, guns, harness and horses were cleaned up ready as we were told to "turn in". I lost my "Jack" horse. He slipped his halter and never came so was reported missing in action. He was a fine horse gentle but lively. He didn't like some of the boys but I always found him ready to go or do what I wished. Pete Bubel took care of him except on the march when I did the dirty work myself. Only a few of us (six besides the officers) had single mounts. The cannoneers walked behind their guns. My horse was one of the best, non excepted, so I had plenty to be thankful for.

17 of us left Verdun on a seven day leave, plus travel, for Mont Dore, Pye de Donne the 1st of December.

December 8th. The rest of the outfit left Verdun and after a hard ride and a long walk they landed at Montfort, near Montford, Cote de Pre. The lucky 17 joined the outfit again at Montfort about the 20th of December.

Our seven day leave had taken nearly 21 days. What a glorious time I had at Mont Dore. Regular Hotel accommodations, fine French beds, room for two but single beds, two in a room, three meals at a sure-"nuf" table with silver tools and china plates. We could beg all the eats we wanted. In fact I made myself sick the first day by eating too much chocolate. The Y. M. there was a dandy. In fact it was nearly the whole team or town. The hot spring baths made our dirty hides clean once more although it took several of them before we ever got to the real hide.

On the way from Mont Dore to Montfort some champagne was stolen by the boys on our train. The entire train was searched by a French Policeman or Gendarme including our car. Of course, none was found but that is not saying there was none around the car, however.

We landed at Montfort about 8 P. M. Oh yes, it was dark and muddy too then. I was shown to a bed in the hay, as they said "for tonight". Well, I'm still there every night.

Montfort has an old castle in ruins, plenty of stone houses, mostly in ruins and lots and lots of rain, although today and for the last five days the sky has been cloudless and the sun warm, making an al-most livable place out of a terrible hole. Our kitchen is out doors; we eat out doors and sleep in a barn. Perry VanArden died the night of February 10th. He comes from around Brockport somewhere. He died from pneumonia. Lots of the boys are sick, the lack of medical attention and too much exposure.

We drill about three hours a day, got out on foolish problems once or twice a week. Today some outfit is firing big guns—more foolishness. Personally I am feeling fine. Weight about 180 pounds, eat and sleep very regularly. I have only drilled one day sine being here, because I am working on the Regimental History. I am Also Captaiin of the in door baseball team. We have only been beaten twice so far. We have only played two games.

The latest rumors would have us leaving France about April 1st. I only hope that such is the case for then we would be home at least by May 10th.

My history from Montfort to U. S. A. will have to be written at a later date and it will complete the major experience of one boy in the army.

Will close now with the fondest regards and love for all. Please keep this letter as it is the only record I have of the events that happened to me during that time. This coupled with its former pal of like character as the result of lots of thinking and some help from others notes.

Lovingly yours,
Homer.

Sgt. H. C. Odell,
309 Heavy Field A.,
Battery D,
1st U. S. Army,
1st Army Corps.

It is reported at the Battery that Willis Winters is very low condition at the hospital in Senuc due to pneumonia. Its another fine day today and I feel fine. February 13th.

Montfort, France 1919
April 18th

Dear Mother and all

Its Friday night and I am again at Grandmais with Stonie and Joe. It has been a beautiful day and I never felt better in my life. I leave Montfort Monday for Bordeaux. It is rumored that we sail from France about the 20th of May, but I don't know any more than is usually the case in the Army.

For the last twelve days the rain has been the main feature until today when really we had a perfect day

I've written a whole lot of short letters lately because I haven't any thing to tell in particular. I can say tho with all honesty that I am Captain of the best Base Ball team that I ever played in. We have only been beaten once and then it was stolen from us 6-5. We won from "A" Battery 25-2 and from 2nd Bn officers 26-7 so you see we are hitting the ball home.

Letters are coming regularly from Home and from Lima as you may suppose. Mail comes lots quicker than it did during the war.

I understand that Winters is home. I hope so anyway. He sure had his share of sickness this winter. [No other pages were included from this letter, so there wasn't a closing.]

Postmarked April 23, 1919

The Bundles of paper have come and I surely have appreciated reading them. Letters from Winnie Newton and Lina as well as the three in one from Home.

Mildred writes that her folk are changing houses this spring due to so many houses being purchased in Hilton.

Well honestly I am longing each day to be back but am sleeping 9 or 10 hours per day plus. No work except baseball. Why should I worry. I had rather work on the 8 hours system than lay around with nothing to do.

I am sure now that I will be home long before I promised last fall that I would be. I expect to be in the house at Parma Center on June 10th. What do we think of that!

I've got a headache tonight from laughing so much at the game this afternoon.

I must close now but don't worry if my letters are short and infrequent from now on because in a couple of days I'll be on the first lap toward home.

Your loving son and brother and uncle
Yours Homer
Sgt H.C. Odell
309 H.F.A.
Battery D

4
A BLUE STAR WITH MY BROTHER

A BLUE STAR

Patriotism and duty were met with honor and distinction when men and women answered the call to take up arms against German aggression in Europe. Starting in World War I, it was a symbolic gesture to hang a banner in the window of a home or business in which a five-pointed blue star could be seen. The all-fabric banner, designed with a white background and bordered in red, displayed a blue star for each person who was serving in the armed forces from that home or business.

The banner's creator, Robert Louis Queisser, was born on August 9, 1866, in Indianapolis, Indiana, to German-born parents Ernst Julius and Henriette Jennette Caroline (Schliebitz) Queisser. Robert attended public schools in Indiana.[1] At the age of sixteen he enlisted in the Indiana National Guard as a Private and was assigned to Co. I, 1st Infantry, in Indianapolis. Robert promoted twice in 1883, first to Corporal, then Sergeant. He was commissioned a Second Lieutenant in January of 1884 and discharged the following year in April of 1885. Moving to Zanesville, Ohio, he joined the Ohio National Guard as a First Lieutenant and Regimental Adjutant, moving through various positions and units until 1908.[2]

By 1887, Robert met his future wife, Jessie L. Fried, of Springfield, Ohio; they had two sons, Charles and Robert, both of whom served during World War I. In their honor, Robert designed a banner with two blue stars—one for each of his sons. Robert L. Queisser's design gained popularity, not only in his adopted town of Cleveland, Ohio, but also in the United States Congress. During Congressional discussions on September 24, 1917, Ohio Republican Congressman Henry Ivory Emerson took the floor to make an announcement. The following is a transcription from the September 24th *Congressional Record*:[3]

> Mr. EMERSON. Mr. Speaker, I ask unanimous consent to address the House for two minutes.
> The SPEAKER. The gentleman from Ohio asks unanimous consent to address the House for two minutes. Is there objection? [There was no objection.]

Mr. EMERSON. Mr. Speaker and gentlemen of the House, on my house in Cleveland hangs a service flag given me by Capt. R. L. Queisser, the designer of this flag.

The flag may be of any size, with a red border and a white center, with stars in the center to indicate the number from that household or place of business that are in the service of the United States during this war.

This service flag has been adopted by Hon. Harry L. Davis, mayor of Cleveland, the Cleveland Chamber of Commerce, East Cleveland City Council, and by the governor of Ohio. The flag is displayed in many homes and factories in Cleveland and all over the United States.

The Cleveland Trust Co. and the Guardian Trust Co., two of the largest banks in Cleveland, have this service flag displayed. There is nothing to do but to have Congress ratify what has been accepted by the people of this country as a proper service flag.

I am certainly proud of the fact that my only son is now in the service of the United States, not as an officer but as a private. I know that every family in Cleveland and all over the United States that have a member of the family in the service would be proud to display this flag. The Government should give one to every family that have sons or daughters in the service.

In these closing days of this extra session let us pass this resolution and give the fathers and mothers of this country who give their sons and daughters freely to this great cause, some recognition, so that the world may know as it passes those families who gave to this great cause of liberty. We give a button to those who buy a liberty bond. Why not give a flag to those who are willing to give their own flesh and blood; the dearest thing in all the world to a father and mother–their children?

Robert submitted two patents to the United States Patent and Trademark Office on October 1, 1917. Both his watch fob and banner designs received patent approval on November 6th of the same year. Robert Louis Queisser passed away in Cleveland, Ohio, on April 22, 1939, and is buried in Knollwood Cemetery in Mayfield Heights, Ohio.

The banner started as a symbol for a loved one serving in the military and is a tradition that remains to this day. For those who give their lives in service to their country, the blue star becomes a border for a smaller gold star placed on top of the blue star, signifying a life lost. Nine families would replace a blue star on their service flag with gold overlay.

UNITED STATES PATENT OFFICE.

ROBERT L. QUEISSER, OF EAST CLEVELAND, OHIO.

DESIGN FOR A WATCH-FOB OR SIMILAR ARTICLE.

51,463.   Specification for Design.   **Patented Nov. 6, 1917.**

Application filed October 1, 1917. Serial No. 194,160. Term of patent 7 years.

To all whom it may concern:

Be it known that I, ROBERT L. QUEISSER, a citizen of the United States, residing at East Cleveland, in the county of Cuyahoga, State of Ohio, have invented a new, original, and ornamental Design for a Watch-Fob or Similar Article, of which the following is a specification, reference being had to the accompanying drawing, forming part thereof.

The figure represents an elevation of a watch fob showing my new design. The same design may be used for other articles of adornment, as stick pins, buttons, or brooches.

I claim:

The ornamental design for a watch fob, or similar article, as shown.

Signed by me, this 26th day of September, 1917.

ROBERT L. QUEISSER.

Copies of this patent may be obtained for five cents each, by addressing the "Commissioner of Patents, Washington, D. C."

DESIGN.

R. L. QUEISSER.

WATCH FOB OR SIMILAR ARTICLE.

APPLICATION FILED OCT. 1, 1917.

51,463.

Patented Nov. 6, 1917.

Robert L. Queisser

Inventor

by Merkel and Saywell

his attorneys

UNITED STATES PATENT OFFICE.

ROBERT L. QUEISSER, OF EAST CLEVELAND, OHIO.

DESIGN FOR A FLAG, PENNANT, SIGN, EMBLEM, OR ARTICLES OF A SIMILAR NATURE.

51,464.　　　Specification for Design.　　　**Patented Nov. 6, 1917.**

Application filed October 1, 1917.　Serial No. 194,161.　Term of patent 7 years.

To all whom it may concern:

Be it known that I, ROBERT L. QUEISSER, a citizen of the United States, residing at East Cleveland, in the county of Cuyahoga, State of Ohio, have invented a new, original, and ornamental Design for Flags, Pennants, Signs, Emblems, or Articles of a Similar Nature, of which the following is a specification, reference being had to the accompanying drawing, forming part thereof.

The figure is an elevation of a flag, showing my new design.

Said design is of a service flag and consists of a center field of white upon which are placed two blue stars, said field being surrounded by a red border.

I claim:

The ornamental design for a flag, pennant, sign, emblem, or articles of a similar nature, as shown.

Signed by me, this 26″ day of September, 1917.

ROBERT L. QUEISSER.

Copies of this patent may be obtained for five cents each, by addressing the "Commissioner of Patents, Washington, D. C."

DESIGN.

R. L. QUEISSER.

FLAG, PENNANT, SIGN, EMBLEM, OR ARTICLES OF A SIMILAR NATURE.

APPLICATION FILED OCT. 1, 1917.

51,464.

Patented Nov. 6, 1917.

MY BROTHER

Brothers Glenn (left) and Ray Fishbaugh, ca. 1916-1917

Unlike today, where the Military Selective Service Act does have a provision for surviving sons, to include deferment from a draft or service, such policies were not in effect or provisions in place for draft and service exemptions during World War I.

It is interesting to note that of the ninety-nine World War I veterans from Parma, New York, whose names are embossed on the *Honor Roll*, thirty of them were brothers. Some *Honor Roll* brothers served together in the same branch, even the same unit. Other brothers entered the military at different times and places, destined for different services, locations, and experiences. Of the thirty siblings, three would lose their brother.

Andrew J. Bennett
US Army

Louie Bennett
US Army

★ Glenn W. Fishbaugh
US Army

Raymond A. Fishbaugh
US Army

Foster F. Hiscock
US Army

★ Lester P. Hiscock
US Army

George S. Kirk
Unknown

William E.G. Kirk
US Army

Harry W. Markel
US Army

Raymond F. Markel
US Army

Edwin W. Oviatt
US Navy

Seldon H. Oviatt
US Navy

Frank L. Flemming
US Navy

John H. Flemming
US Army

Samuel W. Flemming
US Army

Elmer J. Bush
US Army

★ Willard E. Bush
US Marine Corps

Fred C. Hall
US Army

Lynn J. Hall
US Army

Justus A. Hovey
US Army

Walton H. Hovey
US Army

Gerald C. Lee
US Navy

Willard J. Lee
US Navy

Carlyle B. Newcomb
US Navy

Douglas A. Newcomb
US Navy

Alton V. Sleight
US Army

Vernon A. Sleight
US Army

Frank H. Turgon
US Marine Corps

Frederick H. Turgon
US Army

William V. Turgon
US Army

NOTES
Chapter 4

1. Ancestry.com. *The Book of Clevelanders : a biographical dictionary of living men of the city of Cleveland.* [database on-line]. Provo, UT: Ancestry.com Operations Inc, 2005.
Original data: *The Book of Clevelanders : a biographical dictionary of living men of the city of Cleveland.*. Cleveland: Burrows Bros. Co., 1914.

2. Ancestry.com. *U.S., Adjutant General Military Records, 1631-1976* [database on-line]. Provo, UT, USA: Ancestry.com Operations, Inc., 2011.
Original data: *Roster of Troops of the Ohio National Guard.*

3. 55 Cong. Rec. H7385-7386 (September 24, 1917). https://www.govinfo.gov/content/pkg/GPO-CRECB-1917-pt7-v55/pdf/GPO-CRECB-1917-pt7-v55-22-2.pdf

ABOUT THE ARTIST

The details surrounding the *Honor Roll* and its commission are lost with time. Fortunately, for posterity, ninety-nine names of those called to serve during World War I from Parma, New York, are recognized by the painting. Unveiled in 1919, the painting first hung in the State Bank of Hilton before the American Legion Hiscock-Fishbaugh Post 788 became its keeper, where it was displayed in the Post Home on East Avenue in the village of Hilton for many years. When the Post Home and property were sold around 1970, the *Honor Roll* became part of the permanent collection of the Town of Parma Historian's artifacts and records. It moved to its current home in the Parma Museum–a joint collection of the Town Historian and the Parma Hilton Historical Society–in the early 1990s.

The artist of the *Honor Roll*, Bowen Aylesworth Haines, also known as B. Aylesworth Haines and Aylesworth B. Haines, was born in Ernestown, Ontario, Canada, to parents Ira Elijah and Sarah Ann (Aylsworth) Haines on December 21, 1858. Ira, born April 20, 1820, in Canada, supported his family as a wagonmaker and book agent but changed occupations and worked as a shoemaker for over forty years. Immigrating to the United States in 1865, with his wife and children, they settled in the town of Henrietta, south of the city of Rochester, New York.

The youngest of six siblings, Bowen and his family moved to Kansas in 1873, his father finding work as a shoemaker while his mother took care of the family. Learning all things cowboy–riding horses and mastering "shoot on the draw"[2]–Bowen took these experiences from his teenage years in the wild west, to include being known as a champion rifle shot, and applied those skills as "overseer" on a horse ranch near Kansas City, Kansas.

Meandering east, Bowen spent time in Pennsylvania working in oil fields and lumber camps and, by 1880, was employed as a painter while living in Portage Township of Cameron County, Pennsylvania. Moving north and returning to New York state, Bowen worked as a carriage painter in Honeoye Falls,[3] eventually settling near Hilton. In 1881 he met Eliza Jane Hunt of Parma Center, New York, and the two were married on December 24th. They would call the village of Hilton and town of Parma home for the next sixty years, raising three girls along the way.

Failing health forced Bowen to change occupations. With Eliza supporting the family as a dressmaker, Bowen returned to school in 1893. For three years he studied art, pursuing his life-long dream to one day become an artist.[4]

Haines realized his dream, finding employment as a commercial pen artist in Rochester's first print-engraving plant, creating hand-drawn pictures for local newspapers such as the *Post Express* (1882-1923), the *Union and Advertiser* (1886-1918), and the *Democrat and Chronicle* (1870-present). It was at the latter where his first assignment was a pen drawing of Republican nominee, and future United States President, William McKinley. The drawing (at right) appeared on the front page of the June 19, 1896, issue of the *Democrat and Chronicle*.

Working for thirty years in the engraving industry, Bowen created hundreds of illustrations for newspapers in Rochester as the technology to transfer printed photographs to daily print newspapers had yet to be developed. Some illustrators left an obvious signature on their work. For Bowen, his signature was more of an elegant

WILLIAM McKINLEY.

script than block letters and was part of his drawing, most of the time not obvious to the reader. A flourish for "B," the letter not closed but was to be interpreted as such. With the thin long lines narrowly placed side-by-side for his "H," inside would be found the "A," his initials discreetly hidden within the details. In the image below, his signature is the flourish below the two women. (Follow a line down from the tip of the nose of the woman on the right.)

Retiring in 1930 due to his health, he focused his time on painting landscapes, writing short stories, and assisting in community events where his artistic abilities would be of such use as lettering and sign work. Starting in 1932 Bowen advertised his business in the *Hilton (NY) Record*, which he conducted from his home on East Avenue in the village of Hilton. He offered his services to paint signs, pictures, and illustrations, in addition to personalized art instruction.

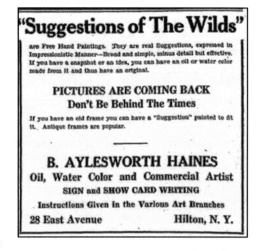

A life-sized thermometer painted by Bowen in 1942 was on display in the State Bank of Hilton.[5] Its purpose was to mark the progress of fundraising efforts by the local chapter of the American Red Cross, part of a national campaign during World War II. His high-visibility art piece kept the community informed by updating bank visitors of the fund-raising progress, prompting them to raise the mercury and beat the goal.

Bowen was a member of the Rochester Art Club and participated in fourteen exhibitions between 1902 and 1920.[6] He was also a member of the Rochester Memorial Art Gallery and the Painters and Illustrators Society of Philadelphia. He received recognition during exhibitions– his name mentioned in local newspapers describing the event and work submitted, to include an edition of the *Buffalo (NY) Courier* from 1919.

Bowen's name was also in the newspaper for another artistic accomplishment, though this one did not involve a pen. One evening in 1935, while walking on the beach at Bogus Point–a promontory on the south shore of Lake Ontario in the town of Parma, an object in the sand grabbed his attention. Picking it up and cleaning it, he realized he was holding a button. He would eventually learn the significance of the Forget-Me-Not symbol engraved inside the pewter circle–the button belonged to a British soldier who had once been encamped on the same shoreline during the British campaign against the French in 1759.

RED CROSS MERCURY RISES

This thermometer in front of Hilton State Bank records progress of Red Cross drive in that village. The mercury now stands at nearly $1,300, two workers in the drive, Doris Diver, left, and Mrs. Evelie Campbell, note with elation.

The button became an inspiration for Haines' new home, already under construction just a "short way down the shoreline from where he found the pin." Regional historian Arch Merrill, in a December 13, 1953, article in the *Democrat and Chronicle*, wrote about the fad of octagonal style houses in the latter part of the 19th century. Merrill supposes in the article that Haines' home was perhaps "the last octagonal structure built in the state." Octagonal-style homes were not new in design and could be found dotted around Western New York. Haines is quoted in a 1937 interview, saying "all art work to be really art is composed of round, radiating, and curved lines. That is why I chose the octagon with its curving corners and straight lines. The forget-me-not runs through all the conventional work."[7] Bowen started building the foundation for his home in 1919, finishing it in 1935 at seventy-seven-years-old.

Author Elizabeth Keller opined in the *Democrat and Chronicle*, "The house is Haines' own work from the first nail to the last. Every pail of concrete was mixed and poured by him alone. Every nail was driven and every board measured, cut and fitted into place with his own hands. All the interior decorating was done by his artist's brush. He has had some assistance in wiring the building and with the tinsmithing work, but otherwise it is the result of the labor of one man."[8] He would name his cottage the Forget-Me-Not.

For the next ten years, Bowen and his bride, Eliza, would enjoy summers in the octagon house where "walls, ceilings and even windows are decorated throughout with pictures painted by his own brush;" where "in the center of the main room he constructed an eight-side concrete chimney that rests on eight octagon posts. Thus was formed a fireplace with eight openings in the center."[9]

On November 27, 1945, Eliza passed away at the age of eighty-four and less than a year later, on September 21, 1946, Bowen would follow—together they are buried in Parma Union Cemetery in Parma, New York.

Perhaps Bowen Aylesworth Haines left behind a legacy of paintings and illustrations, of support for his communities of Parma and Hilton, and his hand-crafted home on the shore of Lake Ontario as his way of saying, Forget-Me-Not.

Another example of B. Aylesworth Haines newspaper artwork.[10]

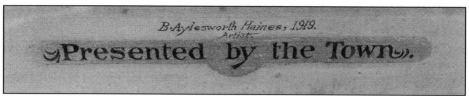

B. Aylesworth Haines signature on the bottom of the *Honor Roll.*

NOTES
About the Artist

1. Bowen Alyesworth Haines, photo provided by grandson Thomas Logan, September 21, 2018.

2. Elizabeth Keller, "Octagonal Cottage Nearing Completion," *Hilton Record*, October 29, 1936, 6.

3. Keller.

4. Keller.

5. "'Mercury' Climbs in Parma as Red Cross Nears Quota," *Democrat and Chronicle*, January 26, 1942, 12.

6. Art Librarian, Memorial Art Gallery of the University of Rochester, e-mail correspondence with the author, September 2018.

7. Arch Merrill, "Have You Ever Been in an Eight-Sided House," *Democrat and Chronicle*, December 13, 1953, 10E.

8. Elizabeth Keller, "This is the House History Built," *Democrat and Chronicle*, February 7, 1937, 2E.

9. Keller, *Democrat and Chronicle*.

10. *Democrat and Chronicle*, January 31, 1897, 4.

BIBLIOGRAPHY

Ancestry.com. *1910 United States Federal Census* [database on-line]. Lehi, UT, USA: Ancestry.com Operations Inc, 2006.
Original data: Thirteenth Census of the United States, 1910 (NARA microfilm publication T624, 1,178 rolls). Records of the Bureau of the Census, Record Group 29. National Archives, Washington, DC.

Ancestry.com. *1911 England Census* [database on-line]. Provo, UT, USA: Ancestry.com Operations, Inc., 2011. Original data: *Census Returns of England and Wales, 1911*. Kew, Surrey, England: The National Archives of the UK (TNA), 1911. Data imaged from the National Archives, London, England.

Ancestry.com. *1920 United States Federal Census* [database on-line]. Provo, UT, USA: Ancestry.com Operations, Inc., 2010. Images reproduced by FamilySearch.
Original data: Fourteenth Census of the United States, 1920. (NARA microfilm publication T625, 2076 rolls). Records of the Bureau of the Census, Record Group 29. National Archives, Washington, DC.

Ancestry.com. *1930 United States Federal Census* [database on-line]. Provo, UT, USA: Ancestry.com Operations Inc, 2002.
Original data: United States of America, Bureau of the Census. *Fifteenth Census of the United States, 1930*. Washington, DC: National Archives and Records Administration, 1930. T626, 2,667 rolls.

Ancestry.com. *1940 United States Federal Census* [database on-line]. Provo, UT, USA: Ancestry.com Operations, Inc., 2012.
Original data: United States of America, Bureau of the Census. *Sixteenth Census of the United States, 1940*. Washington, DC: National Archives and Records Administration, 1940. T627, 4,643 rolls.

Ancestry.com. *British Army WWI Pension Records 1914-1920* [database on-line]. Provo, UT, USA: Ancestry.com Operations Inc, 2010. Original data: The National Archives of the UK (TNA). War Office: Soldiers' Documents from Pension Claims, First World War (Microfilm Copies); (The National Archives Microfilm Publication WO364); Records created or inherited by the War Office, Armed Forces, Judge Advocate General, and related bodies; The National Archives of the UK (TNA), Kew, Surrey, England.Ancestry.com. *New York, Abstracts of World War I Military Service, 1917-1919* [database on-line]. Provo, UT, USA: Ancestry.com Operations, Inc., 2013.

Ancestry.com. *New York, Abstracts of National Guard Service in WWI, 1917-1919* [database on-line]. Provo, UT, USA: Ancestry.com Operations, Inc., 2014.
Original data: *Abstracts of National Guard Service in World War I, 1917–1919*. New York State Adjutant General's Office. New York State Archives, Albany, New York.

Ancestry.com. *New York, Abstracts of World War I Military Service, 1917-1919* [database on-line]. Provo, UT, USA: Ancestry.com Operations, Inc., 2013.
Original data: *New York State Abstracts of World War I Military Service, 1917–1919*. Adjutant General's Office. Series B0808. New York State Archives, Albany, New York.

Ancestry.com. *New York, County Marriage Records, 1847-1849, 1907-1936* [database on-line]. Lehi, UT, USA: Ancestry.com Operations, Inc., 2016.
Original data: *Marriage Records. New York Marriages*. Various New York County Clerk offices.

Ancestry.com. *New York, Mexican Punitive Campaign Muster Rolls for National Guard, 1916-1917* [database on-line]. Provo, UT, USA: Ancestry.com Operations, Inc., 2013.
Original data: *Abstracts of Muster Rolls For National Guard Units Mustered Into Federal Service During the 1916 Mexican Punitive Campaign, 1916-1917*. Series B0802 (38 volumes). New York (State). Adjutant General's Office. New York State Archives, Albany, New York.

Ancestry.com. *New York, Passenger and Crew Lists (including Castle Garden and Ellis Island), 1820-1957* [database on-line]. Provo, UT, USA: Ancestry.com Operations, Inc., 2010.
Original data: *Passenger Lists of Vessels Arriving at New York, New York, 1820-1897*. Microfilm Publication M237, 675 rolls. NAI: 6256867. Records of the U.S. Customs Service, Record Group 36. National Archives at Washington, DC; *Passenger and Crew Lists of Vessels Arriving at New York, New York, 1897-1957*. Microfilm Publication T715, 8892 rolls. NAI: 300346. Records of the Immigration and Naturalization Service; National Archives at Washington, DC; *Supplemental Manifests of Alien Passengers and Crew Members Who Arrived on Vessels at New York, New York, Who Were Inspected for Admission, and Related Index, compiled 1887-1952*, Microfilm Publication A3461, 21 rolls. NAI: 3887372. RG 85, Records of the Immigration and Naturalization Service, 1787-2004; Records of the Immigration and Naturalization Service; National Archives, Washington, DC; *Index to Alien Crewmen Who Were Discharged or Who Deserted at New York, New York, May 1917-Nov. 1957*. Microfilm Publication A3417. NAI: 4497925. National Archives at Washington, DC; *Passenger Lists, 1962-1972, and Crew Lists, 1943-1972, of Vessels Arriving at Oswego, New York*. Microfilm Publication A3426. NAI: 4441521. National Archives at Washington, DC.

Ancestry.com. *New York, State Census, 1905* [database on-line]. Provo, UT, USA: Ancestry.com Operations, Inc., 2014.
Original data: *New York, State Census, 1905*. Population Schedules. Various County Clerk Offices, New York.

Ancestry.com. *New York, State Census, 1915* [database on-line]. Provo, UT, USA: Ancestry.com Operations, Inc., 2012.
Original data: *State population census schedules, 1915*. New York State Archives, Albany, New York.

Ancestry.com. *New York, State Census, 1925* [database on-line]. Provo, UT, USA: Ancestry.com Operations, Inc., 2012.
Original data: *State population census schedules, 1925*. Albany, New York: New York State Archives.

Ancestry.com. *New York, World War I Veterans' Service Data, 1913-1919* [database on-line]. Provo, UT, USA: Ancestry.com Operations, Inc., 2011.
Original data: *World War I Veterans' Service Data and Photographs*. Series A0412. New York State Education Dept. Division of Archives and History. New York State Archives, Albany, New York.

Ancestry.com. *Pennsylvania, Federal Naturalization Records, 1795-1931* [database on-line]. Provo, UT, USA: Ancestry.com Operations, Inc., 2011.
Original data: *Naturalization Records*. National Archives at Philadelphia, Philadelphia, Pennsylvania.

Ancestry.com. *U.S., Army Transport Service, Passenger Lists, 1910-1939* [database on-line]. Lehi, UT, USA: Ancestry.com Operations, Inc., 2016.
Original data: *Lists of Incoming Passengers, 1917-1938*. Textual records. 360 Boxes. NAI: 6234465. Records of the Office of the Quartermaster General, 1774-1985, Record Group 92. The National Archives at College Park, Maryland.
Original data: *Lists of Outgoing Passengers, 1917-1938*. Textual records. 255 Boxes. NAI: 6234477. Records of the Office of the Quartermaster General, 1774-1985, Record Group 92. The National Archives at College Park, Maryland.

Ancestry.com. *U.S., Department of Veterans Affairs BIRLS Death File, 1850-2010* [database on-line]. Provo, UT, USA: Ancestry.com Operations, Inc., 2011.
Original data: *Beneficiary Identification Records Locator Subsystem (BIRLS) Death File*. Washington, DC: U.S. Department of Veterans Affairs.

Ancestry.com. *U.S., Headstone Applications for Military Veterans, 1925-1963* [database on-line]. Provo, UT, USA: Ancestry.com Operations, Inc., 2012.
Original data: *Applications for Headstones for U.S. Military Veterans, 1925-1941*. Microfilm publication M1916, 134 rolls. ARC ID: 596118. Records of the Office of the Quartermaster General, Record Group 92. National Archives at Washington, DC; *Applications for Headstones, compiled 01/01/1925 - 06/30/1970, documenting the period ca. 1776 - 1970* ARC: 596118. Records of the Office of the

Quartermaster General, 1774–1985, Record Group 92. National Archives and Records Administration, Washington, DC.

Ancestry.com. *U.S. Marine Corps Muster Rolls, 1798-1958* [database on-line]. Provo, UT, USA: Ancestry.com Operations Inc, 2007.
Original data: *U.S. Marine Corps Muster Rolls, 1893-1958.* Microfilm Publication T977, 460 rolls. ARC ID: 922159. Records of the U.S. Marine Corps, Record Group 127; National Archives in Washington, DC.

Ancestry.com. *U.S. National Homes for Disabled Volunteer Soldiers, 1866-1938* [database on-line]. Provo, UT, USA: Ancestry.com Operations Inc, 2007.
Original data: *Historical Register of National Homes for Disabled Volunteer Soldiers, 1866-1938*; (National Archives Microfilm Publication M1749, 282 rolls); Records of the Department of Veterans Affairs, Record Group 15; National Archives, Washington, DC.

Ancestry.com. *U.S., Social Security Applications and Claims Index, 1936-2007* [database on-line]. Provo, UT, USA: Ancestry.com Operations, Inc., 2015.
Original data: Social Security Applications and Claims, 1936-2007.

Ancestry.com. *U.S., World War I Draft Registration Cards, 1917-1918* [database on-line]. Provo, UT, USA: Ancestry.com Operations Inc, 2005.
Original data: United States, Selective Service System. *World War I Selective Service System Draft Registration Cards, 1917-1918.* Washington, DC: National Archives and Records Administration. M1509, 4,582 rolls. Imaged from Family History Library microfilm.

Ancestry.com. *U.S., World War II Draft Registration Cards, 1942* [database on-line]. Lehi, UT, USA: Ancestry.com Operations, Inc., 2010.
Original data: United States, Selective Service System. *Selective Service Registration Cards, World War II: Fourth Registration.* Records of the Selective Service System, Record Group Number 147. National Archives and Records Administration.

Blazich Jr., Frank A. "United States Navy and World War 1: 1914-1922." Naval History and Heritage Command. Published August 23, 2017. https://www.history.navy.mil/research/library /online-reading-room/title-list-alphabetically/u/us-navy-world-war-i-redirect.html

Braun, Vice Admiral Robin, US Navy. "A Century of Service" *Proceedings*, March 2015. https://www.usni.org/magazines/proceedings/2015-03

Cochrane, Rexmond C. *Gas Warfare At Belleau Wood 1918.* Washington, DC: United States Army Chemical Corps Historical Office, 1957. http://cdm16635.contentdm.oclc.org/cdm/search /searchterm/10565686

Crosman, Kathleen. "The Army in The Woods." *Prologue*, Summer 2014. https://www.archives.gov/files/publications/prologue/2014/summer/woods.pdf

Democrat and Chronicle (Rochester, NY). Published 1871-, multiple dates. Available: https://www.newspapers.com/title_3749/democrat_and_chronicle/ and Rochester Public Library, Rochester, NY, on microfilm.

Garamone, Jim. "World War I: Building the American military." *DoD News*, April 3, 2017. https://www.army.mil/article/185229/world_war_i_building_the_american_military

Greece Press (Greece, NY). Published 1934-1958, multiple dates. Available http://fultonhistory.com, http://nyshistoricnewspapers.org/, and Rochester Public Library, Rochester, NY on microfilm

Hilton Central School District. *The Hiltonian.* Vol. 1, No. 1. Hilton, NY: Hilton Central School District, 1911. http://dns.hilton.k12.ny.us/yearbooks/YearBook_1911/YearBook_1911.htm

Hilton Record (Hilton, NY). Published 1897-1974, multiple dates. Available http://fultonhistory.com and Village of Hilton, NY, Historian on microfilm (partial)

Husted, Shirley Cox. *Pioneer Days of Hilton, Parma, and Ogden.* Self-published. Albany, NY: Registered as a Research Project With the State Department of Education, 1959.

Lerwill, Lieutenant Colonel Leonard L. *The Personnel Replacement System in the United States Army.* Department of the Army Pamphlet 20-211. Washington, DC: August 30, 1954. https://history.army.mil/html/books/104/104-9/CMH_Pub_104-9.pdf

Miles, L. Wardlaw. *History of the 308th Infantry, 1917-1919.* New York: G.P. Putnam's sons, 1927. http://www.longwood.k12.ny.us/cms/One.aspx?portalId=2549374&pageId=7511397

Records of 20th Century Military Burial Case Files from 1915-1939, All Branches, Record Group 92, ARC Identifier 595318, Records of the National Archives and Records Administration; National Archives and Records Administration - National Archives at St. Louis

Rochester (N.Y.) City Historian. *World War Service Record of Rochester and Monroe County, New York.* 3 vols. Rochester, N.Y.: Du Bois Press, 1924-30. http://www.libraryweb.org/~digitized/books/World_War_service_record_vol_1.pdf http://www.libraryweb.org/~digitized/books/World_War_service_record_vol_2.pdf http://www.libraryweb.org/~digitized/books/World_War_service_record_vol_3.pdf

Smucker, John R. Jr. *The History of the United States Ambulance Service with the French and Italian Armies 1917-1918-1919.* Allentown, PA: United States Army Ambulance Service Association, 1967. http://www.ourstory.info/library/2-ww1/Smucker/usaacTC.html#fore

Suburban News (Spencerport, NY). Published 1961-Present, multiple dates. Available http://fultonhistory.com and Rochester Public Library, Rochester, NY, on microfilm.

Times-Union (Rochester, NY). Published 1918-1997, multiple dates. Available http://fultonhistory.com and Rochester Public Library, Rochester, NY, on microfilm.

United States Army. *A short history and illustrated roster of the 108th Infantry.* Philadelphia: Edward Stern & Co., Inc., 1918. https://archive.org/details/shorthistoryillu00philrich

United States Army. *American Armies and Battlefields in Europe.* Washington DC: 1938. Reprint, Washington DC: United States Army Center of Military History, 1992. Also referred to as CMH Publication 23-24; available at: https://history.army.mil/news/2018/180416_battlefieldOfEurope.html

United States Army. *Order of Battle of the United States Land Forces in the World War.* 5 vols. Washington DC: 1937. Reprint, Washington DC: United States Army Center of Military History, 1988. Also referred to as CMH Publications 23-1 through 23-5; available at: https://history.army.mil/html/bookshelves/collect/oob_us_lf_wwi.html

United States Army. *United States Army in the World War 1917-1919.* 17 vols. Washington DC: 1948. Reprint, Washington DC: United States Army Center of Military History, 1988. Also referred to as CMH Publications 23-6 through 23-23; available at: https://history.army.mil/html/bookshelves/collect/oob_us_lf_wwi_1917-1919.html

Surgeon General of the Army. *The Medical Department Of The United States Army In The World War.* Col Frank W. Weed, editor-in-chief. 15 vols. Washington, DC: Government Printing Office, 1923-1925. http://resource.nlm.nih.gov/14120390R

Village of Hilton Historian Office. Photographic collection. Village Offices, Village of Hilton, NY. Accessed July 2018.

Wilson, John B. *Maneuver and Firepower: The Evolution of Divisions and Separate Brigades.* Army Lineage Series, Jeffrey J. Clarke, general editor. Washington DC: United States Army Center of Military History, 1998. https://history.army.mil/html/books/060/60-14-1/cmhPub_60-14-1.pdf

BIBLIOGRAPHY

Wright, Leith L. *Hilton-U.S.A., An Illustrated History of the Settlement, Growth and Development of the Village of Hilton 1805-1981*. Rochester, NY: Genesee Printers, 1984.

Yockelson, Mitchell. "They Answered the Call." *Prologue*, Fall 1998, https://www.archives.gov/publications/prologue/1998/fall/military-service-in-world-war-one.html

Please reference this updated
Index of Veterans
for the correct page number

INDEX OF VETERANS

H – Died in service

INDEX OF VETERANS

★ – Died in service